VISUAL INSIGHTS

VISUAL INSIGHTS

A Practical Guide to Making Sense of Data

KATY BÖRNER & DAVID E. POLLEY

The MIT Press
Cambridge, Massachussetts
London, England

MIT Press books may be purchased at special quantity discounts for business or sales promotional use. For information, please email special_sales@mitpress.mit.edu

This book was set in Open Sans by Samuel T. Mills (graphic design and layout), Cyberinfrastructure for Network Science Center, School of Informatics and Computing, Indiana University. Printed and bound in the United States of America.

Library of Congress Cataloging-in-Publication Data is available.

ISBN: 978-0-262-52619-7

10 9 8 7 6 5 4 3 2 1

This book was written for all visual insight creators and consumers.

Table of Contents

Note from the Authors

This book will be used as a companion resource for students taking the Information Visualization MOOC in January 2014 (http://ivmooc.cns.iu.edu). As such, we prioritized the timely availability of the text. While the text has been proof-read many times by several experts and two copy editors, and the workflows have been tested by many novice and power users on different operating platforms, we do appreciate error and bug reports sent to cns-sci2-help-l@iulist.indiana.edu so that remaining issues can be corrected in future editions.

There were many concepts we wished to cover in the book but were unable to, due to lack of space. Visual perception, cognitive processing, or how to perform human subject experiments are just a few facets out of many.

Finally, we acknowledge that the large size and interactive nature of some visuals contained in this book does not lend itself well to exploration via print format. Therefore, we have added a page to our website that contains links to high-resolution figures, conveniently organized by chapter and figure number (http://cns.iu.edu/ivmoocbook14). The green magnifying glass seen throughout the book indicates which figures are available online, and the associated links can be found in the figure titles.

Preface

In September 2012, I received a phone call from the deans of both iSchools at Indiana University (IU). Dean Robert B. Schnabel, School of Informatics and Computing, and Dean Debora "Ralf" Shaw, School of Library and Information Science, were interested in having me teach a massive online open course, or MOOC, in Spring 2013. I was immediately interested to explore this unique opportunity as the idea of "open education" fits extremely well with the "open data" and "open code" that the Cyberinfrastructure for Network Science Center (CNS), under my direction, is creating and promoting. I had been teaching open data and code workshops in many countries over the last ten years, and more than 100,000 users had downloaded our plug-and-play macroscope tools.[1] David E. Polley had recently joined our team, testing and documenting software, and teaching tool workshops at IU and international conferences. My PhD student Scott B. Weingart turned out not only to be a remarkable researcher and juggler but also an inspiring teacher. A January deadline seemed feasible—particularly with extensive support by IU—and I said yes to teach an Information Visualization MOOC (called IVMOOC) in the Spring 2013 semester.

We soon learned that Indiana University had decided to use the open source Google Course Builder (GCB)[2] platform for all MOOC development and teaching. At that moment in time, GCB had been used once—to teach *Power Searching with Google*[3] to more than 100,000 students. GCB had no support for sending out emails or grading work; setting up the course or assessments involved low-level coding and scripting. Interested to have IVMOOC students interact with me, others at CNS, each other, and external clients, we hired Mike Widner and Scott B. Weingart to implement a Drupal forum for GCB. To fill the need to grade work, Robert P. Light designed the IVMOOC database that captured not only students' scores in assessments but also who collaborated with whom, who watched what video for how long, etc. Ultimately, MOOC users need new techniques and tools to be most effective—teachers need to make sense of the activities of thousands of students, and students need to navigate learning materials and develop successful learning collaborations across disciplines and time zones—for example, to conduct client project work (see Chapter 9 on MOOC Visual Analytics).

In parallel to developing and recording materials for the IVMOOC, I was working on the *Atlas of Knowledge*, which has the subtitle "Anyone Can Map," inspired by Auguste Gusteau's catchphrase "Anyone Can Cook." The *Atlas* aims to feature timeless knowledge (Edward Tufte called it "forever knowledge"), or, principles that are indifferent to culture, gender, nationality, or history. In contrast, the IVMOOC features "timely knowledge," or, the most current data formats, tools, and workflows used to convert data into insights.

---

1 Börner, Katy. 2011. "Plug-and-Play Macroscopes." *Communications of the ACM* 54, 3: 60–69.

2 http://code.google.com/p/course-builder

3 http://www.google.com/insidesearch/landing/powersearching.html

Specifically, IVMOOC materials are structured into seven units to be taught over seven weeks (see Chapters 1–7 in this book). Each weekly unit features a theoretical component by me and a hands-on component by David E. Polley. The first theory unit introduces a theoretical visualization framework intended to help non-experts to assemble advanced analysis workflows and to design different visualization layers. The framework can also be applied to "dissect visualizations" for optimization or interpretation. The subsequent five units introduce workflows and visualizations that answer when, where, what, and with whom questions using temporal, geospatial, topical, and network analysis techniques. The final unit covers visualizations of dynamically changing data and the optimization of visualizations for different output media. The hands-on components feature in-depth instruction on how to navigate and operate several software programs used to visualize information. Furthermore, students learn the skills needed to visualize their very own data, allowing them to create unique visualizations. Pointers to the extensive Sci2 Online Tutorial[4] are provided where relevant. The theory component and the hands-on component are standalone. Participants can watch whichever section they are more interested in first, and then review the other section. After the theory videos there are self-assessments, and after the hands-on videos are short homework assignments.

Before, during, and after the course, students are encouraged to create and use Twitter and Flickr accounts and the tag "ivmooc" to share images as well as links to insightful visualizations, conferences and events, or relevant job openings to create a unique, real-time data stream of the best visualizations, experts, and companies that apply data mining and visualization techniques to answer real-world questions.

This graduate-level course is free and open to participants from around the world, and anyone who registers gains free access to the Scholarly Database[5] with 26 million paper, patent, and grant records and the Sci2 Tool[6] with 100+ algorithms and tools. Students also have the opportunity to work with actual clients on real-world visualization projects.

The IVMOOC final grade is based on results from the midterm exam (30%), final exam (40%), and projects/homework (30%). All participants that receive more than 80% of all available points will receive both a letter of accomplishment and badge.

Feel free to register for IVMOOC at http://ivmooc.cns.iu.edu and enjoy.

Katy Börner
Cyberinfrastructure for Network Science Center
School of Informatics and Computing
Indiana University
August 18, 2013

---

4 http://sci2.wiki.cns.iu.edu

5 http://sdb.cns.iu.edu

6 http://sci2.cns.iu.edu

Acknowledgments

I would like to thank Robert Schnabel, Dean of the School of Informatics and Computing, and Debora Shaw, then Dean of the School of Library and Information Science, Indiana University for inspiring the development of the IVMOOC.

This MOOC would not have been possible without the institutional support of Lauren K. Robel, Munirpallam A. Venkataramanan, Jennifer W. Adams, Barbara Anne Bichelmeyer, and Ilona M. Hajdu as diverse copyright, terms of service, and legal issues had to be resolved before any student could register.

We would like to thank Miguel Lara for extensive instructional design support throughout the development and teaching of the IVMOOC; Samuel T. Mills for designing the IVMOOC web pages; Robert P. Light and Thomas Smith for extending the GCB platform; Mike Widner, Scott B. Weingart, and Mike T. Gallant for adding a Drupal forum to GCB; Ralph A. Zuzolo and his team for recording the teaser video; and Rhonda Spencer, James P. Shea, and Tracey Theriault for marketing.

Many visualizations used in the IVMOOC and in this book come from the *Places & Spaces: Mapping Science* exhibit, online at http://scimaps.org, and from the *Atlas of Science: Visualizing What We Know* (MIT Press 2010). The Sci2 Tool and the Scholarly Database were developed by more than forty programmers and designers at CNS.

We would like to thank Samuel T. Mills for designing the book cover, redesigning many figures and tables featured here, and performing the complete book layout, Joseph J. Shankweiler for gathering the screenshots for the book, Tassie Gniady and Arul K. Jeyaseelan for testing the Sci2 workflows in the book, Scott R. Emmons and Simone L. Allen for providing feedback to a draft of the book, and Todd N. Theriault and Lisel G. Record for editing the book.

Marguerite B. Avery, Senior Acquisitions Editor, and Karie Kirkpatrick, Senior Publishing Technology Specialist, both at The MIT Press were instrumental in having the book edited, proofread, and published in time for the 2014 IVMOOC.

Last but not least, we thank all 2013 IVMOOC students for their feedback and comments, enthusiasm, and support.

Support for the IVMOOC development comes from the Cyberinfrastructure for Network Science Center, the Center for Innovative Teaching and Learning, the School of Informatics and Computing (SoIC), the former School of Library and Information Science—now the Department of Information and Library Science at SoIC, the Trustees of Indiana University, and Google. Open data and open code development work is supported in part by the National Science Foundation under Grants No. SBE-0738111, DRL-1223698, and IIS-0513650, the U.S. Department of Agriculture, the National Institutes of Health under Grant No. U01 GM098959, and the James S. McDonnell Foundation.

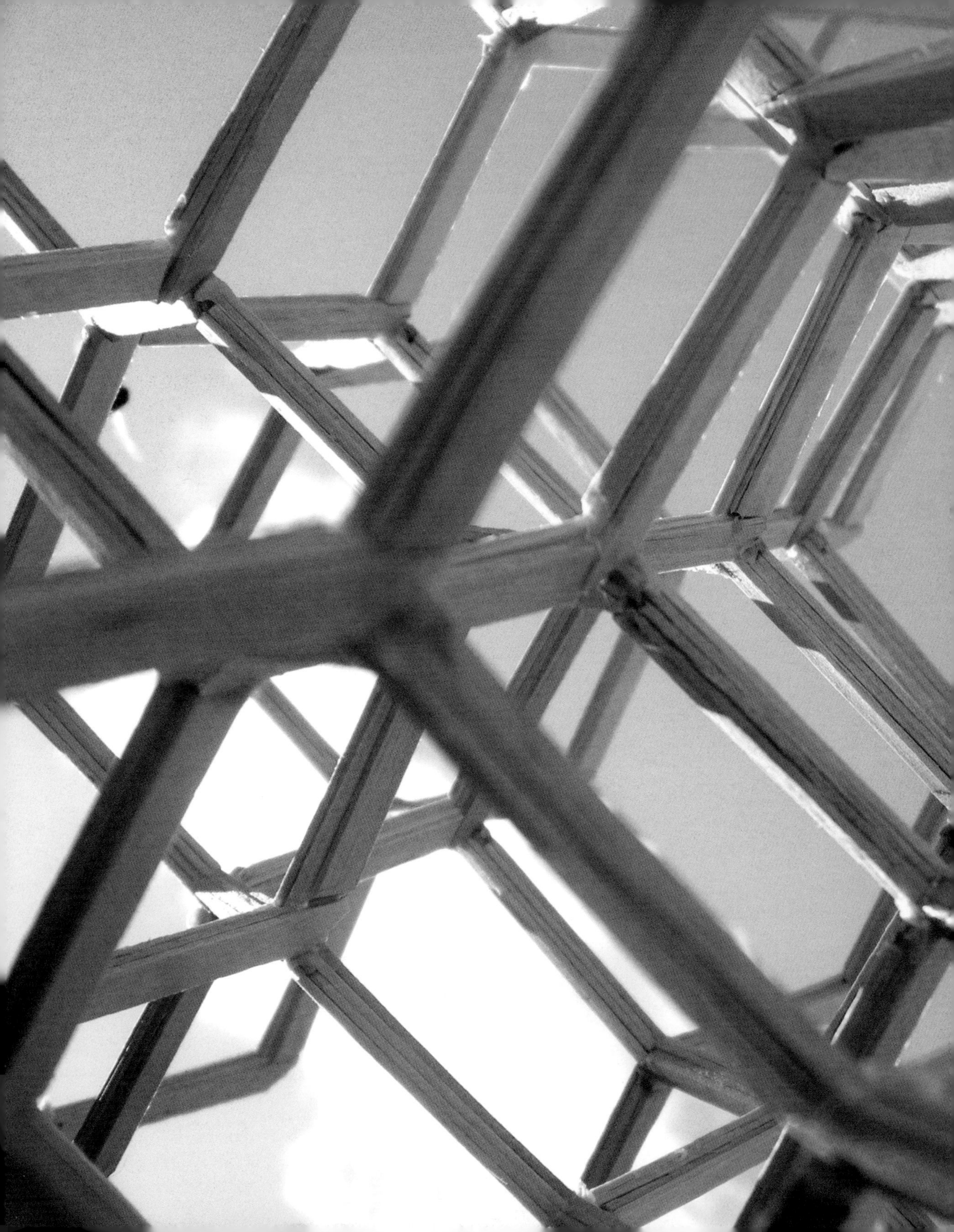

Chapter One

Visualization Framework and Workflow Design

Chapter 1: Theory Section

Welcome to the Information Age, where each one of us receives more information via tweets, emails, news, and other data streams each day than can humanly be processed in 24 hours; and anyone with an Internet connection has access to a majority of humankind's knowledge. Our offices are filling up and our email inboxes are overflowing (see Figure 1.1, left). We urgently need more effective ways to make sense of this massive amount of data—to navigate and manage information, to identify collaborators and friends, or to notice patterns and trends (see Figure 1.1, right).

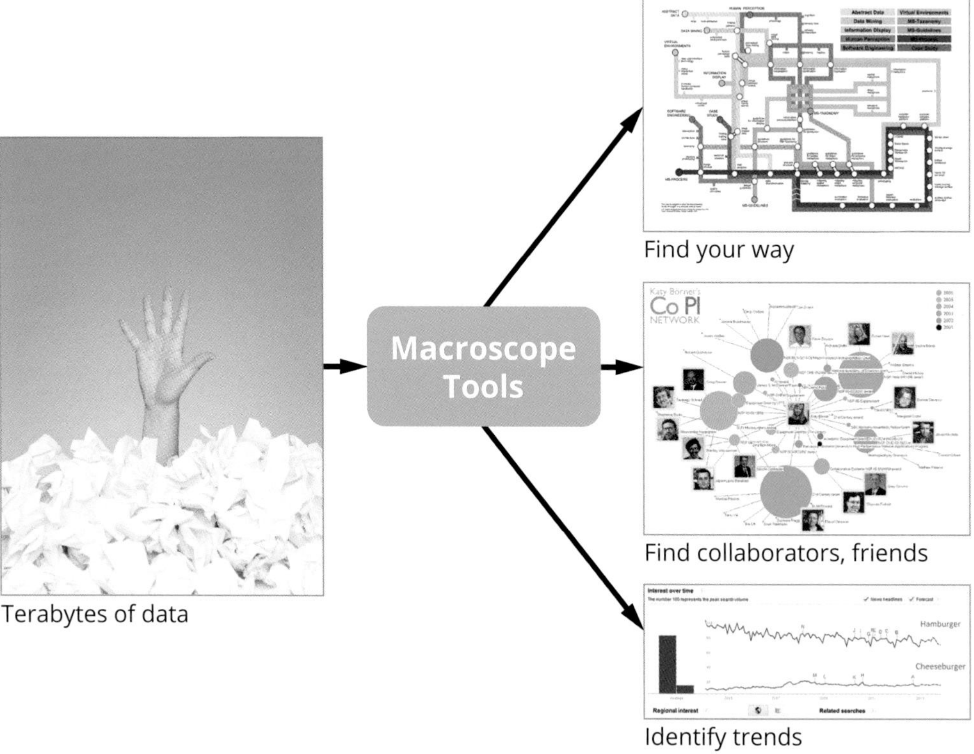

Figure 1.1 Converting data into actionable insights

This book teaches you how to use advanced data mining and visualization techniques to convert data into insights. Each chapter has a theory part on white background paper and a hands-on section on gold. The theory part comes with self-assessments while the hands-on part contains homework assignments.

This first chapter presents a theoretical visualization framework that helps to select the most appropriate algorithms and to assemble them into effective workflows. Its hands-on section introduces so-called macroscope tools[1] that empower anyone to read, process, analyze, and visualize data.

1.1 VISUALIZATION FRAMEWORK

This section introduces a framework that helps organize and group visualizations and supports the identification of what type and what level of analysis is best to address specific user needs.

The use of grouping to develop organizational frameworks has a long history outside of information visualization. In fact, science often begins by grouping or classifying things. For example, zoologists classify animals so that tigers and lions and jaguars end up in the family Felidae (big cats). Dmitri Mendeleev grouped chemical elements in the periodic table according to chemical properties and atomic weights, leaving "holes" in the table for elements yet to be discovered. Similarly, the systematic analysis and grouping of information visualizations helps in the design of new visualizations, and also in interpreting visualizations encountered in journals, newspapers, books, and other publications.

There are various ways to group visualizations, such as those shown in Figure 1.2. Visualizations can be grouped by user insight needs, by user task types, or by the data to be visualized. They can also be grouped based on what data mining techniques are used, what interactivity is supported, or by the type of deployment (e.g., whether the visualizations are printed on paper, animated, or presented on interactive displays). Details and references to existing taxonomies and frameworks can be found in the *Atlas of Knowledge.*[2]

Here, a pragmatic approach is applied to teach anyone how to design meaningful visualizations. Starting with the types of questions users have, the framework supports the selection of data mining and visualization workflows as well as deployment options that answer these user questions.

Levels of Analysis and Types of Analysis

The visualization framework distinguishes three levels of analysis: micro, meso, and macro. The **micro** level, or the individual level, consists of small datasets, typically between 1 and 100 records—for example, one person and all of his/her friends. The next level is the **meso**, or the group level, about 101 to 10,000 records. An example might include information about researchers working at a single university or on a certain research topic. Finally, the broadest level of analysis is the **macro**, sometimes referred to as the global or population level. Datasets for projects at this level of analysis typically exceed 10,000 records, such as data pertaining to an entire country or all of science.

---

1 Börner, Katy. 2011. "Plug-and-Play Macroscopes." *Communications of the ACM* 54, 3: 60–69.

2 Börner, Katy. 2014. *Atlas of Knowledge: Anyone Can Map*. Cambridge, MA: The MIT Press.

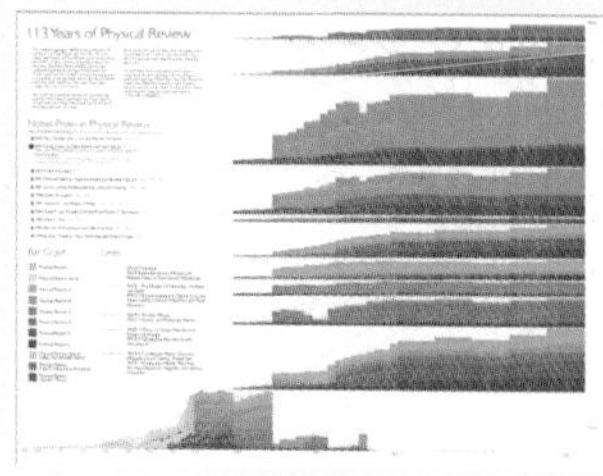
113 Years of Physical Review

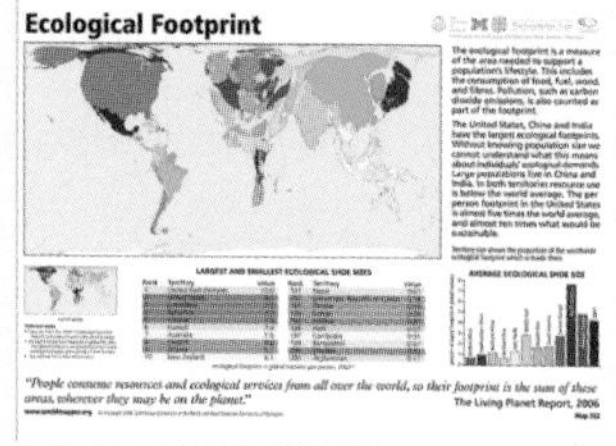
Ecological Footprint
"People consume resources and ecological services from all over the world, so their footprint is the sum of these areas, wherever they may be on the planet."
The Living Planet Report, 2006

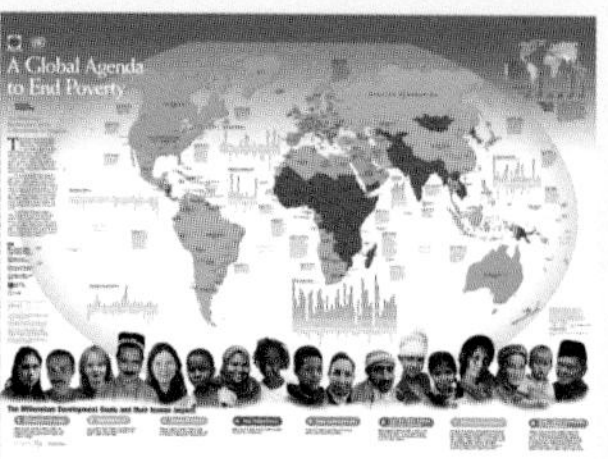
A Global Agenda
to End Poverty

Language Communities
of Twitter

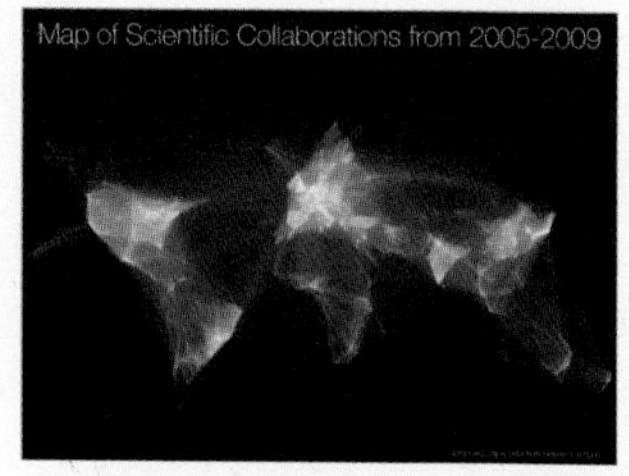
Map of Scientific Collaborations from 2005-2009

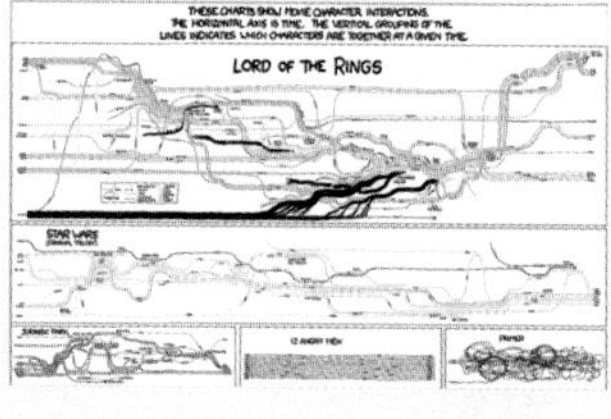
LORD OF THE RINGS
STAR WARS

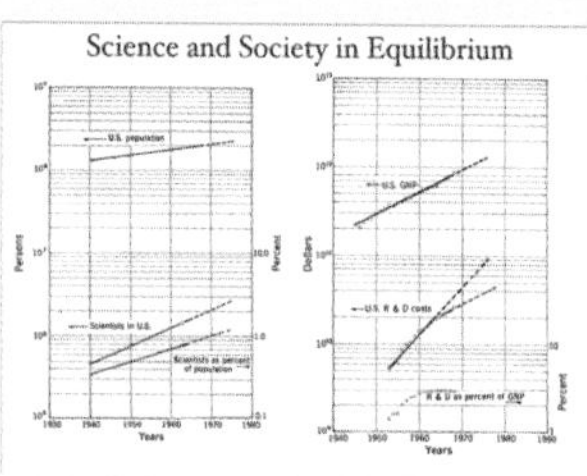
Science and Society in Equilibrium
U.S. population
Scientists in U.S.
U.S. GNP
U.S. R & D costs
Years

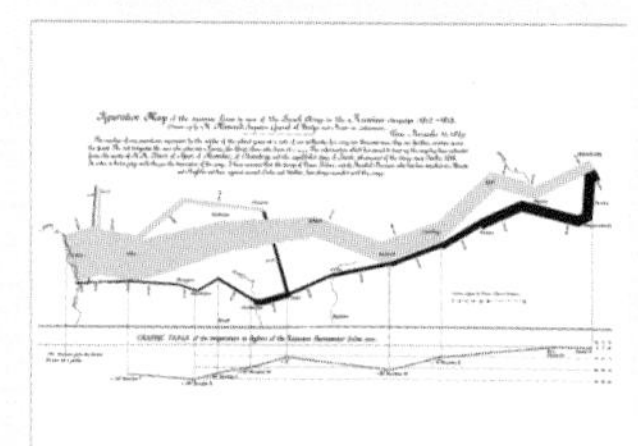

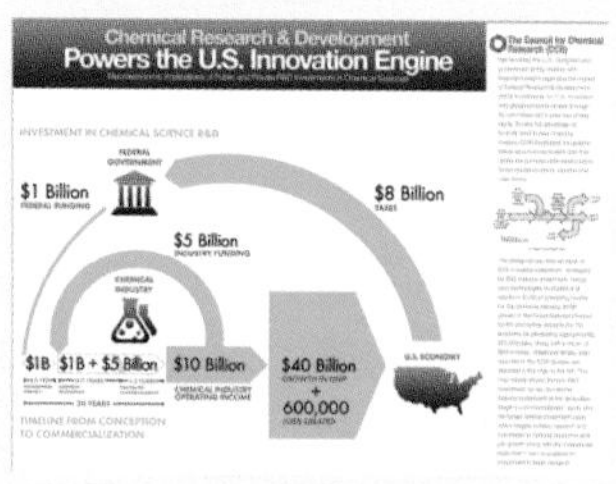
Chemical Research & Development
Powers the U.S. Innovation Engine
$1 Billion
$8 Billion
$5 Billion
$1B
$1B + $5 Billion
$10 Billion
$40 Billion
600,000

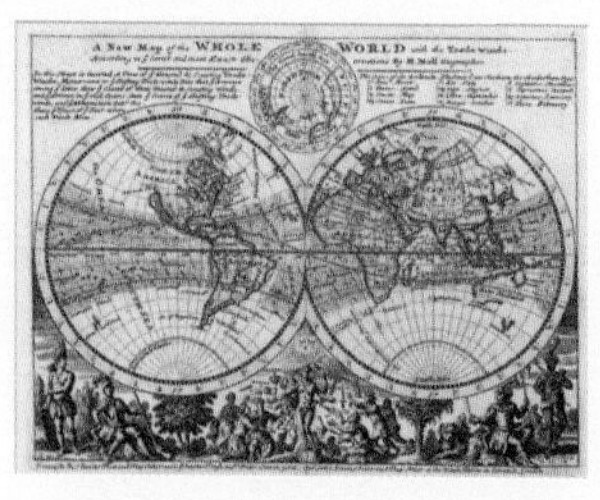

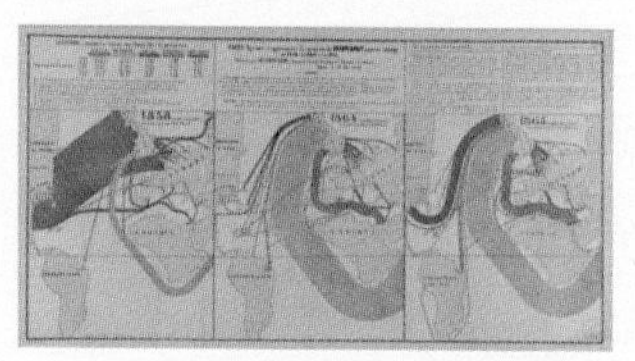

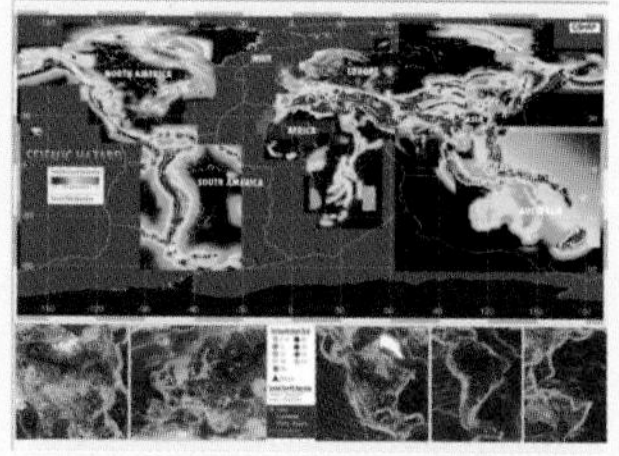

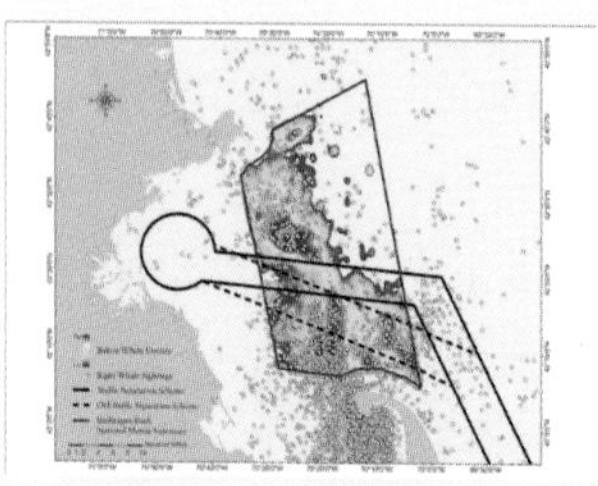

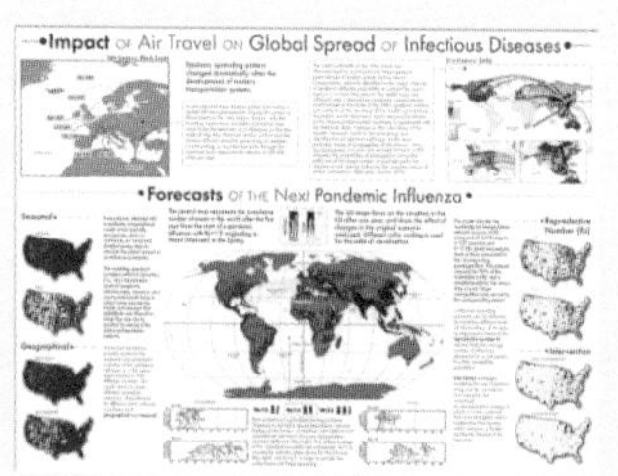
Impact of Air Travel on Global Spread of Infectious Diseases
Forecasts of the Next Pandemic Influenza

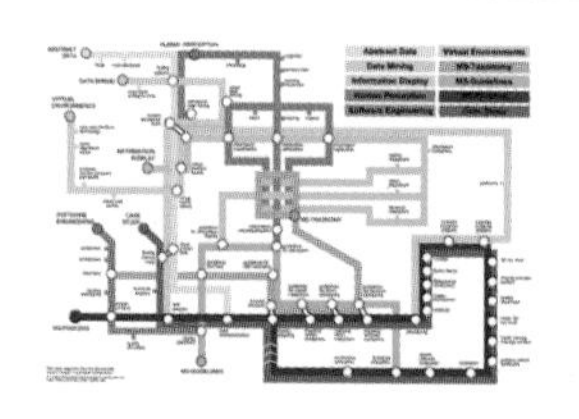

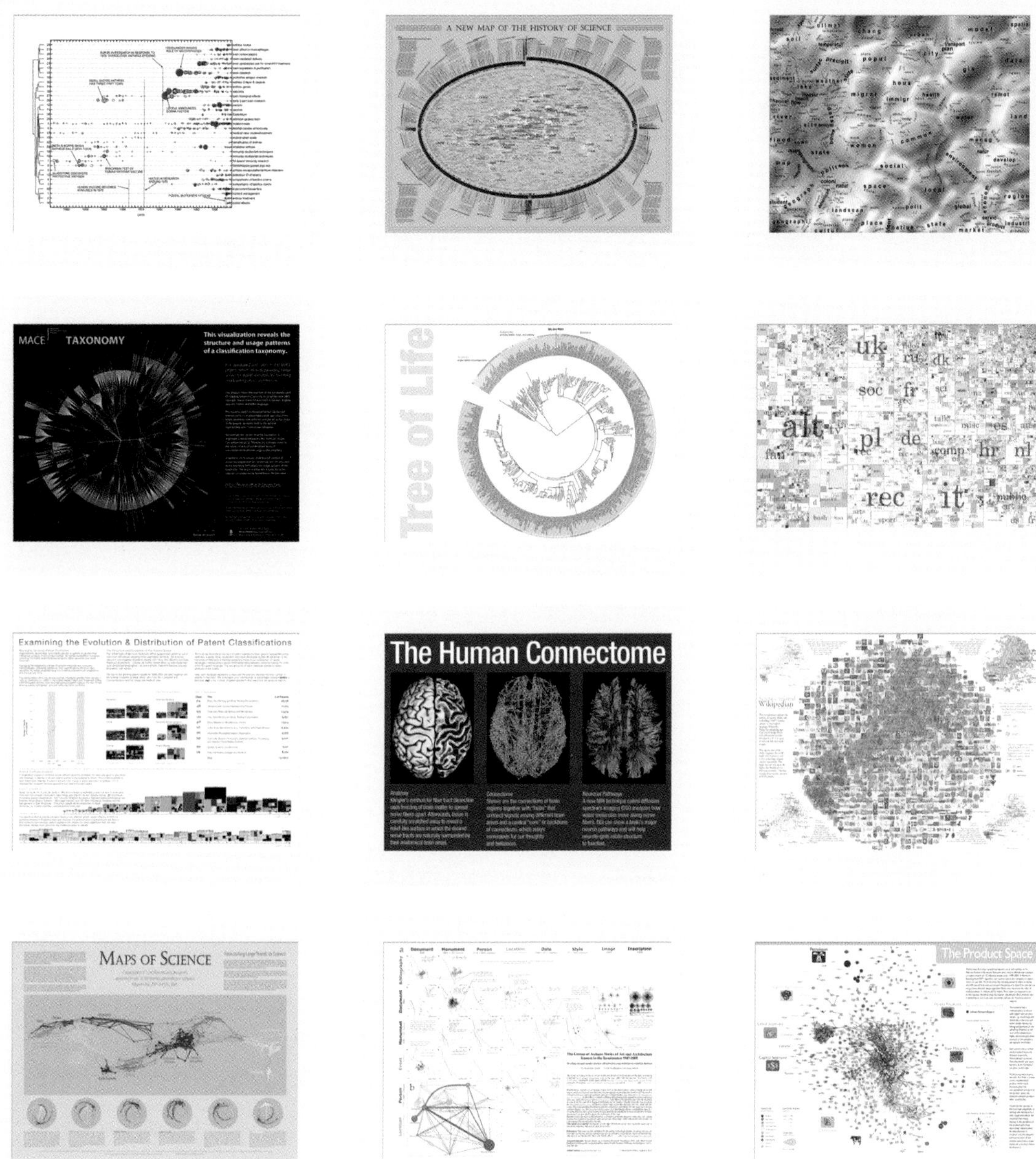

Figure 1.2 A collection of maps from the *Places and Spaces: Mapping Science* exhibit

At each level of analysis, there are five possible types of analysis: statistical analysis/profiling, temporal analysis, geospatial analysis, topical analysis, and network analysis . Each of these types of analysis seeks to answer a specific type of question. For example, temporal analyses help answer WHEN questions, while geospatial analyses answer WHERE questions. The types and levels of analysis can be organized into a table with the types of analysis displayed on the left and the level of analysis displayed across the top (see Table 1.1).

Micro/individual-level projects can occasionally be done by hand. For example, a network of five friends could be drawn with a pen and paper. However, projects at the meso/local level cannot realistically be done by hand but require the use of a computer. Furthermore, projects at the macro/global-level often require supercomputers to perform the necessary computations.

Some projects aim to answer more than one question. For example, when visualizing the topical evolution of physical research over 113 years, temporal and topical questions are addressed. Several of the visualizations in Table 1.1 appear twice. Subsequently, all the visualizations featured in Table 1.1 are discussed. For each, the temporal, geospatial, topical, and network data types and coverage plus the respective type and level of analysis are given below the figure.

Exemplification

The first visualization is shown in Figure 1.3. We created it to show pockets of innovation in the U.S. state of Indiana and the pathways that ideas take to make it into products. The visualization exemplifies both geospatial and network analysis at the meso level.

For this visualization we used a dataset of funded projects, but also project proposals that were not funded. Each of these projects had to have industry and academic partners to encourage the translation of research results into profitable products. We created the visualization by geocoding industry and academic institutions and overlaying their positions and collaboration network on a map of Indiana. That is, nodes represent academic institutions (colored in red) and industry collaborators (in yellow). Nodes are size-coded by the total dollar amount of all awards. Links denote collaboration; academic-to-academic collaborations are given in red, industry-to-industry in yellow, and academic-to-industry in orange.

As the dataset covers mostly biomedical research, Purdue University in Lafayette and IUPUI in Indianapolis, with a variety of academic and industry activity in this research area, are the largest nodes. The strongest collaboration linkages exist between Lafayette and Indianapolis, and between Lafayette and South Bend (home of the University of Notre Dame).

The interactive online interface supports search (e.g., for finding names and topics, for filtering by years and institutions, and for the retrieval of details for specific projects and

Table 1.1 Types of Analysis vs. Levels of Analysis

	• **Micro/Individual (1-100 records)**	● **Meso/Local (101-10,000 records)**	⬤ **Macro/Global (10,000+ records)**
Statistical Analysis/Profiling	Individual person and the number of publications, patents, grants	Expertise profiles of larger labs, centers, universities, research domains, or states	All of NSF, all of USA, all of science statistics 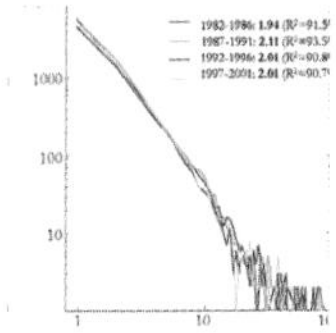
Temporal Analysis (When)	Evolving funding portfolio of one individual	Mapping topic bursts in 20 years of *PNAS* 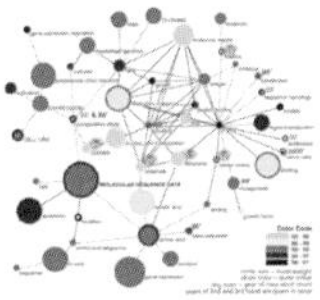	113 years of physics research 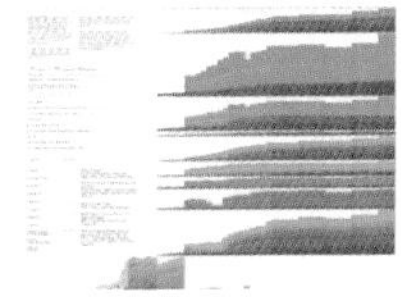
Geospatial Analysis (Where)	Career trajectory of one individual	Mapping a state's intellectual landscape 	International collaboration and citation networks 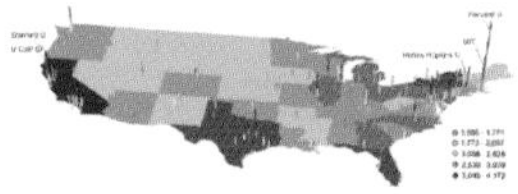 
Topical Analysis (What)	Base knowledge from which one publication draws	Mapping topic bursts in 20 years of *PNAS* 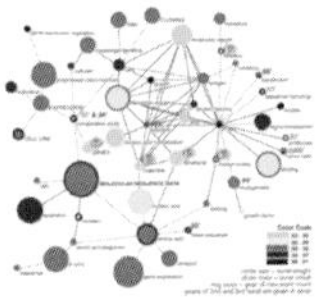	113 years of physics research 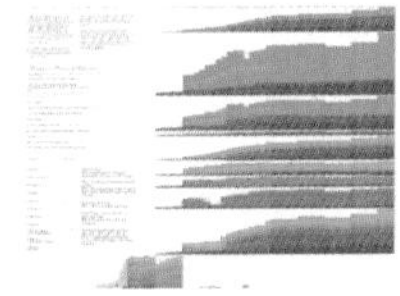
Network Analysis (With Whom)	NSF Co-PI network of one individual 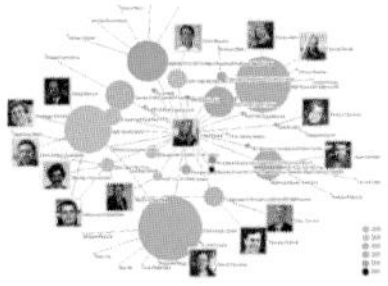	Co-author networks 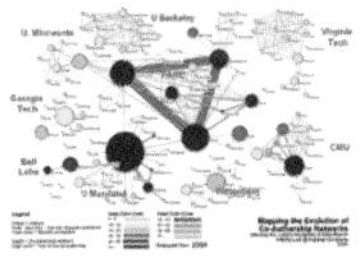 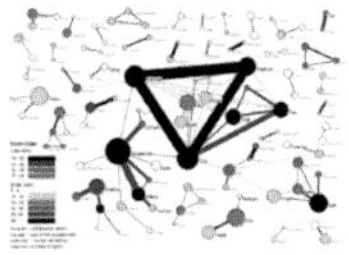 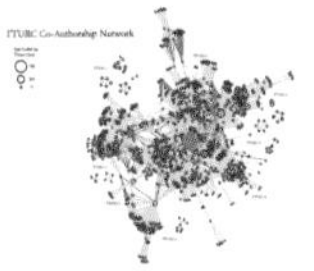	World-wide collaborations by the Chinese Academy of Sciences 

proposals). It can be explored to help answer the following questions: What are the major pathways that ideas take to make it into products? What ideas are born where? How do these ideas become products that generate revenue?

The second visualization (Figure 1.4) aims to communicate bursts of activity in a dataset that captures 20 years of publications from the *Proceedings of the National Academy of Sciences (PNAS)* in the United States. First, we selected the top 10% of the most highly cited publications. Then we identified the top 50 most frequent and "bursty"[3] words using a burst detection algorithm explained in Section 2.4. We laid out the 50 words and their co-occurrence relations as a network, simplified the network, and then visually encoded it (see Section 2.6 for a complete step-by-step workflow). The circles, each representing one of the 50 words, are size-coded according to the burst weight (i.e., how suddenly an increase in frequency occurs). Node color represents the burst onset coded by years. To determine the bursting year of a particular node, use the key in the lower right-hand corner of the visualization. The node border color corresponds to the year of the maximum word count, and the years of the second and third bursts are provided. Notice that the interior color is typically brighter than the exterior color, which means that words burst first and then experience wider usage.

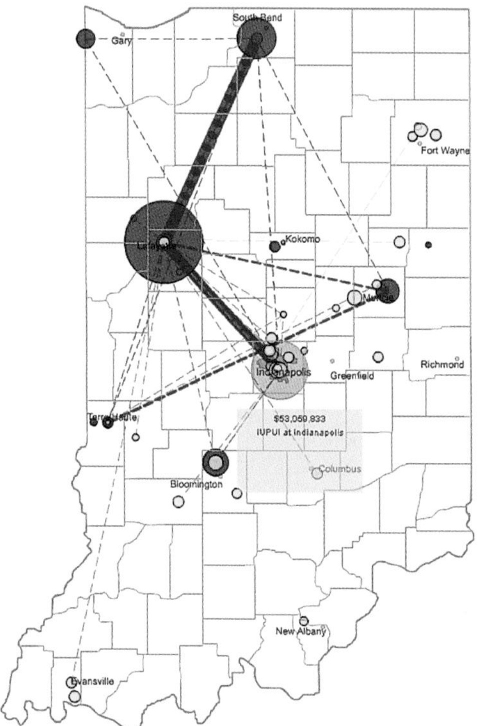

Data Types & Coverage	
Time Frame:	2001-2006
Region:	Indiana
Topical Area:	Biomedical Research
Network Type:	Academic-Industry Collab.

Analysis Types/Levels	•	●	⬤
Temporal		X	
Geospatial		X	
Topical			
Network		X	

Figure 1.3 Mapping Indiana's intellectual space

3 Kleinberg, Jon. 2002. "Bursty and Hierarchical Structure in Streams." In *Proceedings of the 8th ACM/SIGKDD International Conference on Knowledge Discovery and Data Mining*, 91–101. New York: ACM.

It would be interesting to compare this dataset with the same data collected for the years 2001–2012 to see if the subsequent ten years really show that protein, for instance, experienced widespread usage. Currently, the visualization is restricted to publications in one journal; adding more data to capture all publications of a researcher team or all publications in one area of science would be valuable.

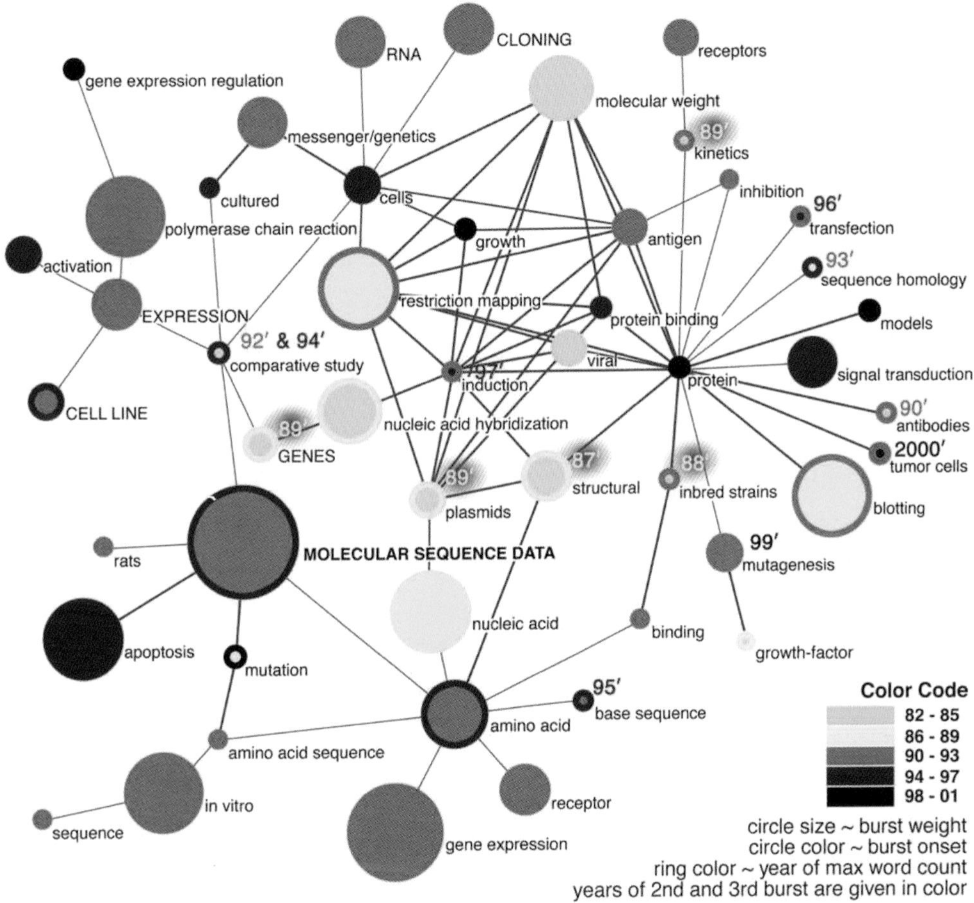

Data Types & Coverage	
Time Frame:	1982-2001
Region:	World
Topical Area:	Mostly Biomedical
Network Type:	Word Co-Occurence

Analysis Types/Levels	● (small)	● (medium)	● (large)
Temporal		X	
Geospatial			
Topical		X	
Network		X	

Figure 1.4 Mapping topic bursts in *PNAS* publications

The third visualization (Figure 1.5) uses the very same 20-year *PNAS* datasets to find out if the physical location of scholars still matters in the Internet age. Does one still have to study and work at a major institution to be highly successful in research (e.g., as measured by the number of citations)? As the dataset captures the introduction and widespread use of the Internet, we might expect to see that, over time, as the Internet came into existence, the number of institutions citing each other would increase irrespective to the geographic distance (see log-log plot in Figure 1.5, right). In other words, the curve would get flatter as scholars' online access to publications improves and they cite over longer and longer distances. However, the curve becomes steeper as time progresses—as the Internet comes into existence, researchers are citing more locally.

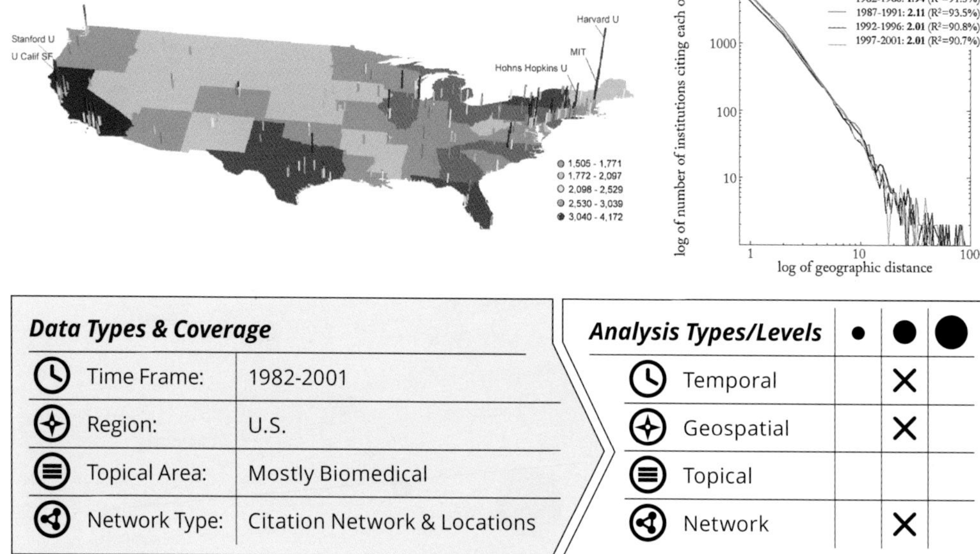

Figure 1.5 Spatio-temporal information production and consumption of major U.S. research institutions

One of the most compelling arguments for this counterintuitive result is by Barry Wellman, Howard White, and Nancy Nazer, who obtained a similar result using different data.[4] They argued that as we are flooded with more and more information, the importance of social networks increases. Social networks are much easier to create and maintain locally and hence people tend to cite papers by close-by colleagues.

The fourth example (Figure 1.6) demonstrates a micro-level analysis of project collaborations for one scholar—Katy Börner. Using data on all her projects funded by the National

4 White, Howard D., Barry Wellman, and Nancy Nazer. 2004. "Does Citation Reflect Social Structure? Longitudinal Evidence From the 'Globenet' Interdisciplinary Research Group." *Journal of The American Society for Information Science and Technology* 55, 2: 111–126.

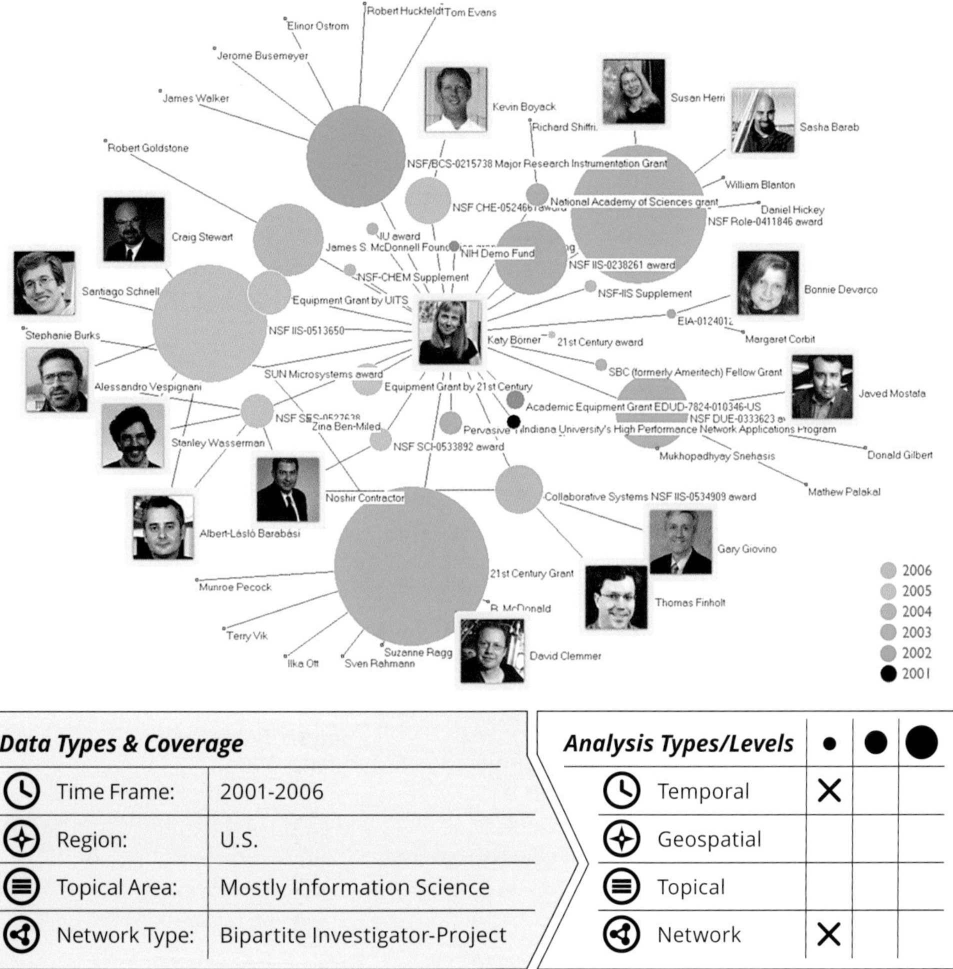

Data Types & Coverage	
Time Frame:	2001-2006
Region:	U.S.
Topical Area:	Mostly Information Science
Network Type:	Bipartite Investigator-Project

Analysis Types/Levels	•	●	⬤
Temporal	X		
Geospatial			
Topical			
Network	X		

Figure 1.6 Börner's bipartite investigator-to-project network for NSF awards

Science Foundation (NSF) for the years 2001 through 2006, we extracted a co-investigator network. This bipartite network has two types of nodes: the projects (colored in green) and the investigators (represented by small white nodes or their picture, when available). The project nodes are color-coded based on the year the project came into existence, ranging from the dark nodes (2001), to the light green nodes (2006). Node area size corresponds to total award amount. By design, the dataset contains all projects by Börner for the given time frame (i.e., her node is large and central to the network). Only partial data is available for collaborators. Still, it is easy to see who is collaborating on what project. For example, Noshir Contractor was involved in three projects during this time frame. One of them, the left-most node labeled NSF IIS-0513650,[5] financed the development of the Network Workbench, the first OSGi/CIShell-based macroscope tool.[6]

The fifth visualization (Figure 1.7) shows a co-author network of authors that published in the IEEE Information Visualization Conference between 1974 and 2004.[7] Each author node is labeled by its family name, area size-coded by number of publications, and colored based on the number of citations the author received. Links denote collaborations; they are size-coded by the number of times two authors appear on a paper together and color-coded by the year of the first collaboration—collaborations that started between 1986 and 1990 are orange.

Overall, Ben Shneiderman at the University of Maryland has the largest node, which means he has published the most papers in this dataset. Furthermore, his node is very dark in color, meaning he has been cited extensively. Other nodes, John Stasko for example, are very large yet light. In other words, these researchers have published a lot of papers, but are not highly cited. In Stasko's case, most of his papers have been published recently and have not been cited yet. With a few more years of data, this visualization could look completely different.

The overall network consists of many densely connected subnetworks of researchers working at the same institution. Only a few of the institutionally (and hence geospatially) constrained networks are interlinked (e.g., the CMU network is connected via Stephen Eick to the PARC network). Ben Shneiderman has close collaborations with Jock Mackinlay and Stuart Card, and his student Ben Bederson collaborates with Bell Labs, further increasing the interconnections and reach of the University of Maryland team.

Note that Shneiderman's collaboration network at a university is rather different from the collaboration "triangle" that Jock Mackinlay, Stuart Card, and George Robertson have at PARC. While most universities have one (or no) information visualization researcher who works and publishes with his/her students, many national labs have teams of visualization researchers that closely collaborate for decades.

The sixth visualization (Figure 1.8) uses the very same dataset to try to understand if science today is driven by prolific individual experts or by high-impact co-authorship teams.[8] This collaboration network size-codes edges by citation credit (i.e., thick edges represent

---

5 National Science Foundation. 2005. "NetWorkBench: A Large-Scale Network Analysis, Modeling, and Visualization Toolkit for Biomedical, Social Science, and Physics Research," Award no. 0513650. http://www.nsf.gov/awardsearch/showAward?AWD_ID=0513650 (accessed September 4, 2013).

6 Börner, Katy. 2011. "Plug-and-Play Macroscopes." *Communications of the ACM* 54, 3: 60–69.

7 Ke, Weimao, Katy Börner, and Lalitha Viswanath. 2004. "Major Information Visualization Authors, Papers and Topics in the ACM Library." Analysis and Visualization of the IV 2004 Contest Dataset. Presented at IEEE Information Visualization Conference, Houston, Texas, October 10–12, 2004. This entry won first prize.

8 Börner, Katy, Luca Dall'Asta, Weimao Ke, and Alessandro Vespignani. 2005. "Studying the Emerging Global Brain: Analyzing and Visualizing the Impact of Co-Authorship Teams." In "Understanding Complex Systems," special issue, *Complexity* 10, 4: 57–67.

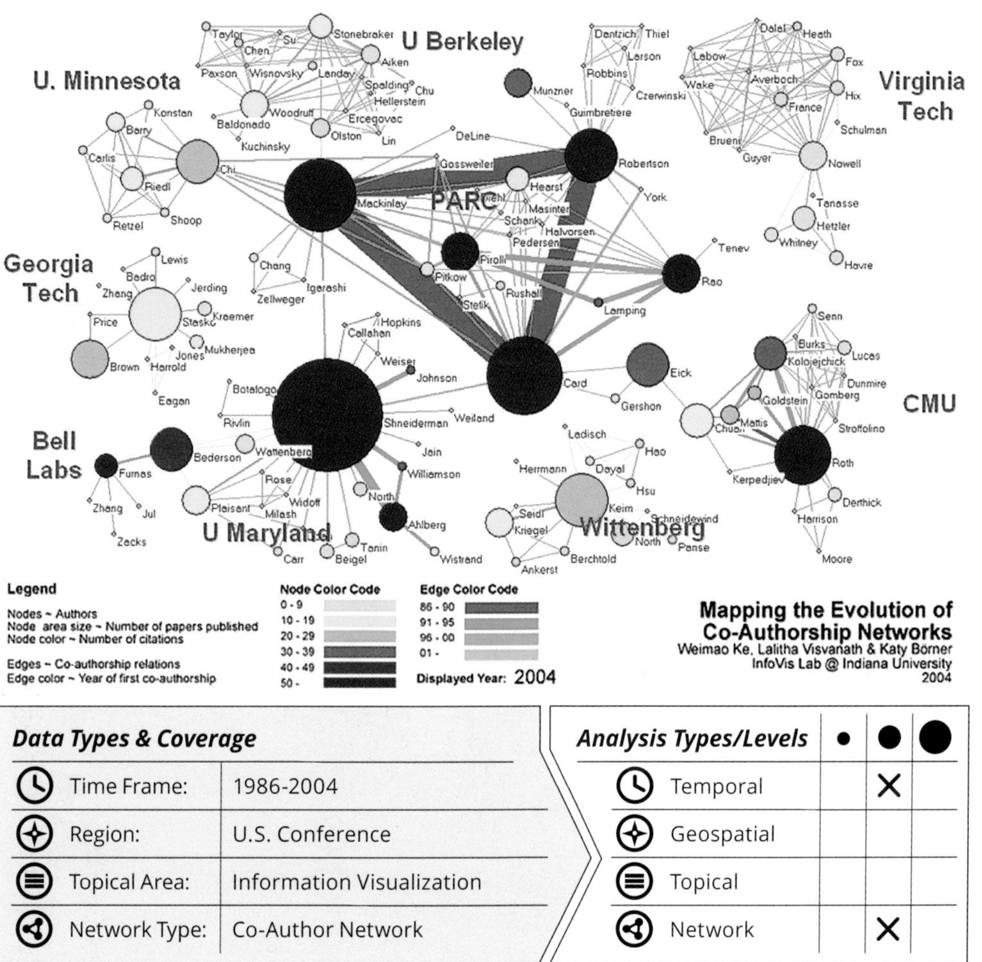

Data Types & Coverage	
Time Frame:	1986-2004
Region:	U.S. Conference
Topical Area:	Information Visualization
Network Type:	Co-Author Network

Analysis Types/Levels	● (micro)	● (meso)	● (macro)
Temporal		X	
Geospatial			
Topical			
Network		X	

Figure 1.7 Mapping the evolution of co-authorship networks, 1986–2004 (http://cns.iu.edu/ivmoocbook14/1.7.html)

successful collaborations that attracted many citations). This new approach to allocate citation credit—not to authors, but to co-authorship relations—makes it possible to examine the citation success that a collaboration between researchers had on scholarship in the field. The original paper also presents a novel author-centered entropy to identify truly prolific research teams. Results show that researchers who collaborate effectively are able to gain more citation counts than those who work on their own.

The seventh visualization (Figure 1.9) shows 113 years of publications in *Physical Review*.[9] This demonstrates topical analysis and citation analysis at the macro level, worldwide in

---

9 Herr II, Bruce W., Russell J. Duhon, Katy Börner, Elisha F. Hardy, and Shashikant Penumarthy. 2008. "113 Years of *Physical Review*: Using Flow Maps to Show Temporal and Topical Citation Patterns." In *Proceedings of the 12th International Conference on Information Visualization, London, UK, July 9–11*, 421–426. Los Alamitos, CA: IEEE Computer Society Press.

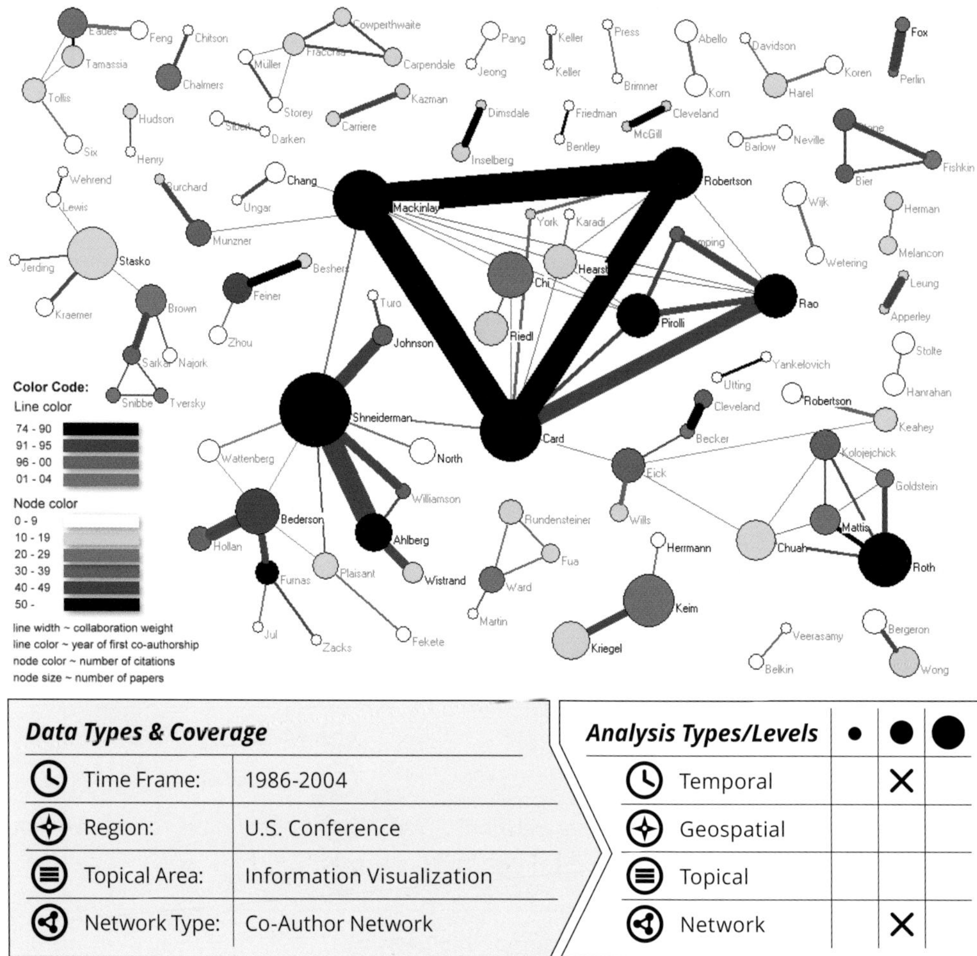

Data Types & Coverage	
Time Frame:	1986-2004
Region:	U.S. Conference
Topical Area:	Information Visualization
Network Type:	Co-Author Network

Analysis Types/Levels	•	●	⬤
Temporal		X	
Geospatial			
Topical			
Network		X	

Figure 1.8 Studying the emerging global brain: Analyzing and visualizing the impact of co-authorship teams, 1986–2004

its scope. The 389,899 publications are plotted left to right on a timeline spanning 1893 to 2005. Publications published from 1893 to 1976 take up the left third of the map. The 217,503 publications from 1977 to 2000, for which partial citation and Physics and Astronomy Classification Scheme (PACS)[10] data is available, occupy the middle third on the map. The 80,634 publications from 2001 to 2005, for which complete citation and PACS data is available, fill the last third of the map. The PACS code number runs up the right side of the map. For each of the different PACS codes (e.g., *PACS 0: General*) we can see how many publications were published in what journal (see color code legend on right). Publications without a PACS code are given in the lower part of the map. On top of this base map, all

[10] PACS was introduced in 1977.

citations from the publications published in 2005 are overlaid. It is interesting to note that physicists cite extensively backwards in time—all the way to the 1800s.

Each year, Thomson Reuters predicts three Nobel Prize awardees in physics based on citation counts, high-impact papers, and discoveries or themes worthy of special recognition. The small Nobel Prize medals indicate all Nobel prize-winning papers, and correct predictions by Thomson Reuters are highlighted.

The eighth visualization (Figure 1.10) aims to communicate the impact of different types of funding by the National Institutes of Health. Investigator-initiated funding on tobacco use is compared in terms of the number of publications and evolving co-author networks with Transdisciplinary Tobacco Use Research Center (TTURC) Center awards made for the same time span and research topics. Shown at the top of Figure 1.10 are co-author networks extracted from publications that acknowledge R01 funding. The figure below depicts the considerably denser co-author network resulting from TTURC funding. Nodes in each of the two networks are color-coded by the different projects. For example, all authors that acknowledged LR01–5 (in the upper left corner) are shown in blue. Some of them collaborated with authors that acknowledged R01–13, denoted by yellow nodes.

Investigator-initiated funding and TTURC funding are both advancing tobacco research. While investigator-initiated funding appears to have a higher return on investment, this visualization shows that number of citations per dollar spent[11] and TTURC funding result in denser, more transdisciplinary networks that support faster information diffusion across disciplinary boundaries.

The final sample visualization shows the global collaboration network of researchers at the Chinese Academy of Sciences (CAS) in Beijing (Figure 1.11).[12] The academy's collaboration links are aggregated at the country level (i.e., collaborations between China and the United States are represented by a link from Beijing to the mass point of the United States). Countries are colored on a logarithmic scale by the number of collaborations from red to yellow. The CAS in Beijing has the darkest red representing 3,395 collaborations of CAS researchers with others around the globe. A flow map layout was applied to bundle edges, improving legibility. The width of each flow line is linearly proportional to the number of collaborations with researchers in locations to which they link. As the visualization shows, the CAS has the largest number of collaborations with the United States.

Taken together, data analyses and visualizations can be performed at different levels—from micro to macro. Co-authorship networks (see Figures 1.6 and 1.11) can be rendered

---

[11] Note that TTURC funding is also used for infrastructure development, education, training, or workshops.

[12] Duhon, Russell Jackson. 2009. "Understanding Outside Collaborations of the Chinese Academy of Sciences Using Jensen-Shannon Divergence." In *Proceedings of the SPIE Conference on Visualization and Data Analysis 2009, San Jose, CA, January 19*, edited by Katy Börner and Jinah Park. Bellingham, WA: SPIE Press.

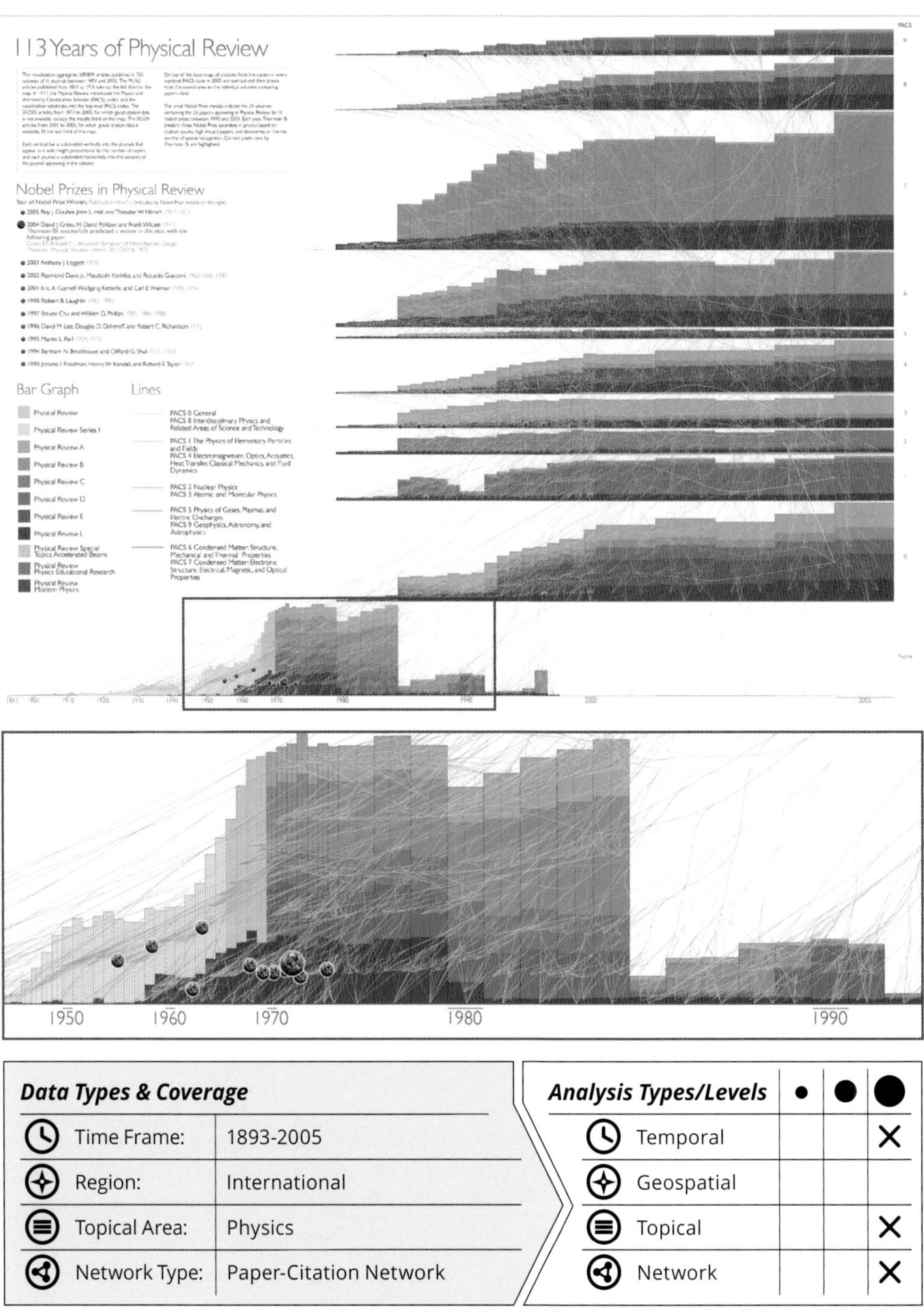

Figure 1.9 *113 Years of Physical Review* (2006) by Bruce W. Herr II, Russell J. Duhon, Elisha F. Hardy, Shashikant Penumarthy, and Katy Börner (http://scimaps.org/III.6)

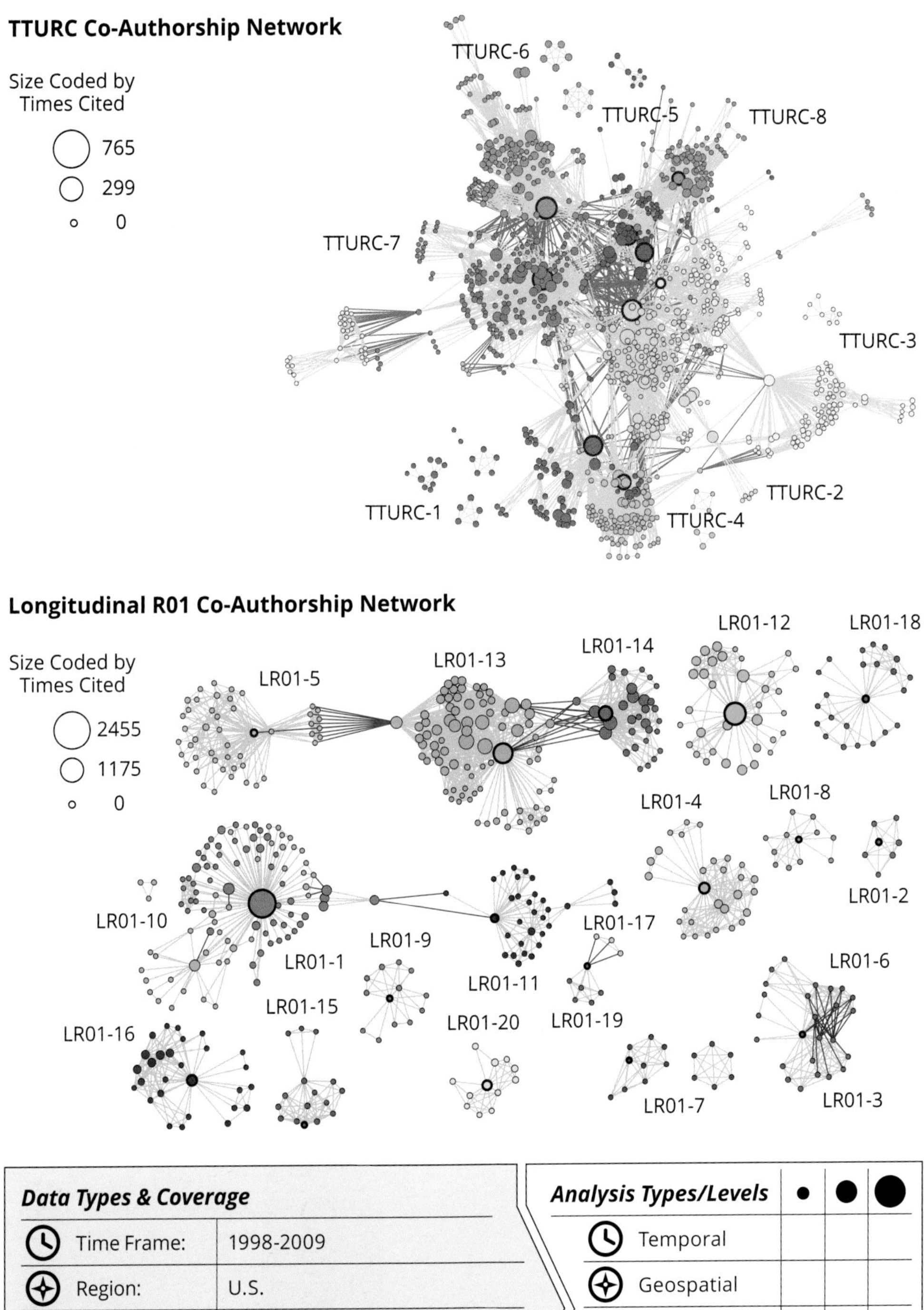

Figure 1.10 Mapping transdisciplinary tobacco use research publications

using network layout or geospatial base maps. Before creating a visualization, identify what question(s) it aims to answer and at what level of analysis. Determine its temporal, geospatial, topical, and network scope as it will help interpret the visualization and ultimately put the information conveyed to use in decision-making processes.

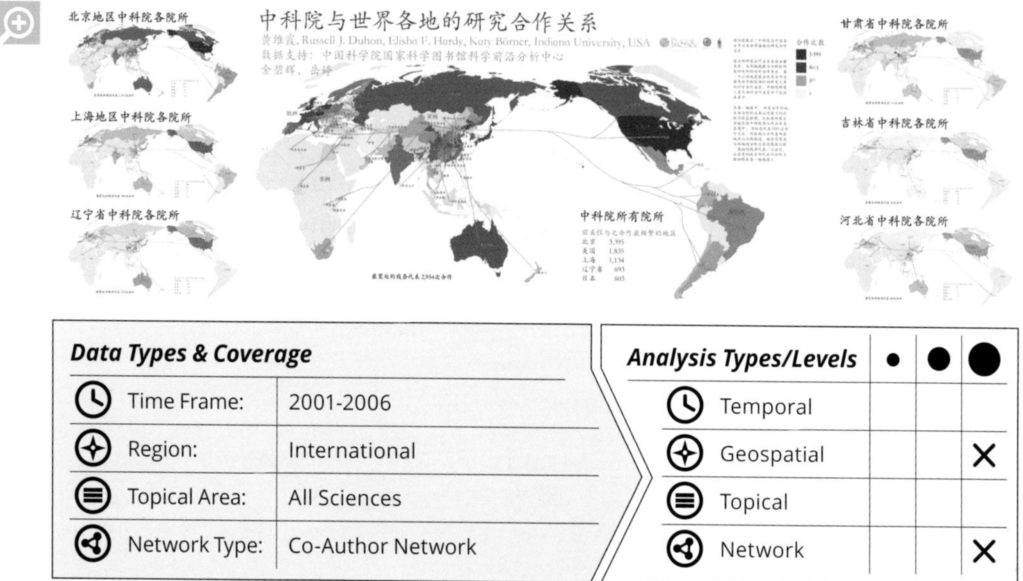

Figure 1.11 Worldwide research collaborations by the Chinese Academy of Sciences (http://cns.iu.edu/ivmoocbook14/1.11.jpg)

1.2 WORKFLOW DESIGN

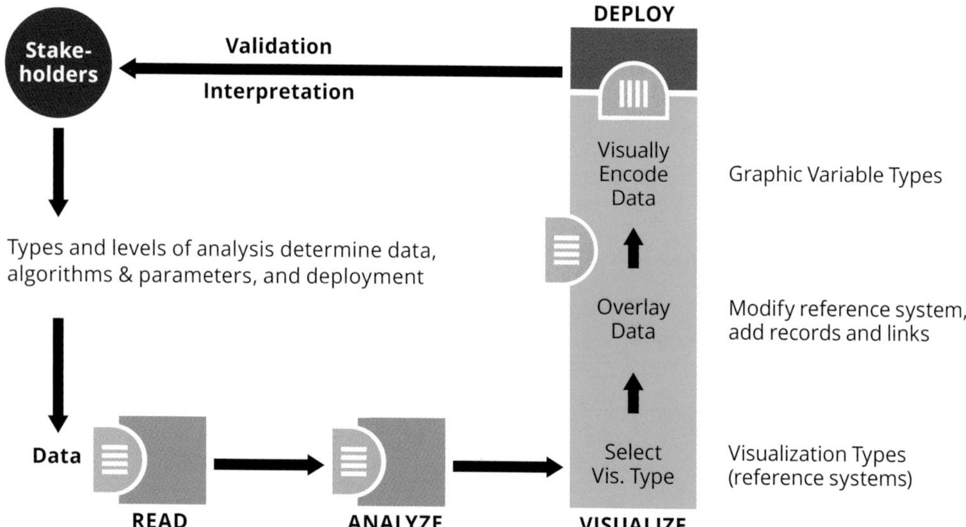

Figure 1.12 Needs-driven workflow design

In this section we introduce how to design workflows that meet the needs of users. The visualization types we examine include tables, graphs, networks, and geospatial maps. Data overlays, such as dots or linkages, can be overlaid in different base maps. Data overlays can be used to encode additional information using graphic variable types, such as color and shape coding and size coding. A deep understanding of visualization types, data overlays, and graphic variable types is needed not only to design visualizations but also to interpret them.

The iterative process of needs-driven workflow design is schematically depicted in Figure 1.12. The very first step is to find out what stakeholders want and need in their lives and how data mining and visualization techniques might improve their decision making. Equipped with knowledge about the questions users have, the type and level of analysis can be determined. The next step is to obtain the highest quality and highest coverage data—time and budget constraints might demand compromises. Data are frequently supplied by stakeholders, purchased from major data providers, or retrieved from open sources. It needs to be parsed and read **(READ)**. Extensive cleaning and preprocessing might be needed. Temporal, topical, or other analyses might be performed to identify trends and patterns **(ANALYZE)**. The visualization phase **(VISUALIZE)** comprises three major steps. First, the appropriate reference system must be identified. This reference system becomes the stable base map onto which data are layered. Second, the reference system might be modified (e.g., a map of the United States might be distorted to display election results; see Figure 3.9 in Section 3.2 for an example). Third, additional data variables are visually encoded using diverse graphic variable types. Ultimately, the visualization must be deployed **(DEPLOY)** (i.e., printed, published online, etc.) Last but not least, the visualization is presented to stakeholders for validation and interpretation.

It is important to remember that information visualization is an iterative process. During the validation and interpretation phase, stakeholders may identify missing data or propose new requirements. As user needs change, the design process repeats: acquiring new data, reading the data, conducting analysis, redesigning the visualization, deploying it again, and then re-sharing the new visualization with the stakeholders.

Visualization Types

In this book we discuss five major visualization types: **charts**, **tables**, **graphs**, **geospatial maps**, and **network graphs**. We show examples of each in Figure 1.13.

The term **chart** refers to visualizations that have no inherent reference system. Examples include pie charts or word clouds (see Figure 4.5).

The next visualization type is **tables**, a simple but very effective way to convey data (see Figure 1.9 in this chapter). Table cells can be color-coded or sorted, and they can contain graphic symbols or miniature icons (see Figure 4.6). There are tables that support browsing through a hierarchy of data using categorical axes, or hieraxes (again, see Figure 4.6).

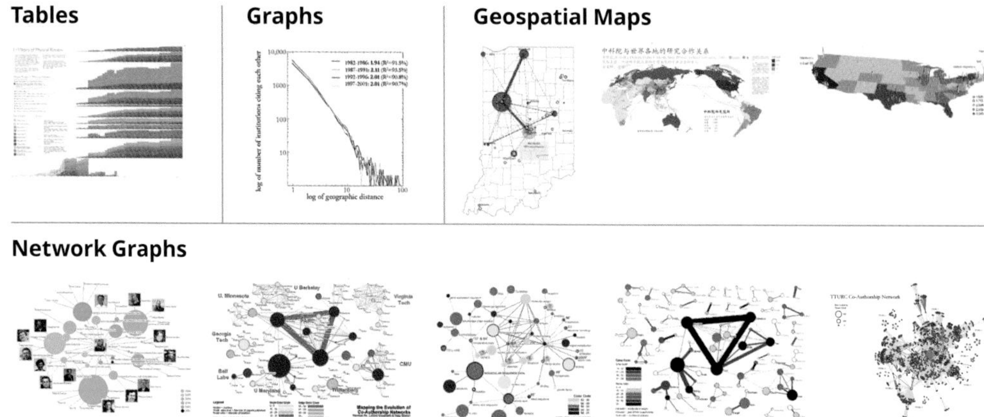

Figure 1.13 Various visualizations organized by visualization type

The next visualization type is **graphs**, which are the most commonly used visualization. Graphs can display quantitative or qualitative data. Examples are timelines, bar graphs, or scatter plots. We provide many examples of graphs throughout this book.

Then there are **geospatial maps**, which use a latitude and longitude reference system. Examples are world maps, city maps, or topographic maps, among others.

The fifth type covered here are **network graphs**. Examples are trees, such as hierarchies or taxonomies, or network graphs, such as social networks or migration flows.

Each visualization type defines its own reference system or base map and a mapping of data onto it. For example, latitude and longitude information must be available for an institution in order to place it on a geospatial map.

Once the appropriate visualization type and reference system has been determined (see the **Select Vis. Type** step in Figure 1.12), data can be overlaid. There are three ways to visually encode data attributes: use them to (1) distort the base map, (2) place records, or (3) encode them via visual variable types. In the workflow design illustrated in Figure 1.12, types 1 and 2 are called **Overlay Data** whereas type 3 is called **Visually Encode Data.**

In addition, title, labels, legends, and explanatory text are frequently added to provide the necessary context for the visualization. Proper attribution of map authors allows people to get back with their comments and suggestions, or with a commission to do work for them.

The following are examples that come from the *Places and Spaces: Mapping Science* exhibit (http://scimaps.org). The first example (Figure 1.14)[13] shows a distortion of geographic area sizes, or, a **cartogram**. Cartogram visualizations assume a familiarity of the actual shape and size of geographic areas in the world. Here, the large maps distort the size of countries to represent their ecological footprint—how much area they actually need to support their population's lifestyle. When comparing the distorted map with the original map in the lower left corner, the United States, for example, has a rather large footprint while many of the countries in Africa have a very small footprint.

Alternatively, you can take a map of the world and visually encode the map areas to create a so-called **choropleth map**. For example, *The Millennium Development Goals Map* (Figure 1.15)[14] by the World Bank Data Group, National Geographic, and the United Nations uses color-coding to display relative levels of income, per capita gross national income (GNI) in U.S. dollars for 2004. The colors range from red, representing low-income ($825 or less) to dark green, representing high-income ($10,066 or more).

In the next example (Figure 1.16), Twitter data was geolocated and overlaid on a map of Europe. Dots are color-coded by language. There are many Dutch tweets (in light blue), and most are posted in the Netherlands. Similarly, Italian tweets (in darker blue) are mostly seen in Italy. Furthermore, Paris and other capital cities are very dominant in these maps. Obviously, many more people live and tweet in urban areas than in rural areas.

The next example[15] shows worldwide scientific collaborations between 2005 and 2009 overlaid as linkages on a map of the world (Figure 1.17). Elsevier Scopus data was used to identify who was collaborating with whom. A few patterns are immediately identifiable. For example, researchers in the United States collaborate quite a bit with each other. The same is true for Europe and Asia. Despite the amount of collaboration that exists within continents, there is also much collaboration going on between the different continents, particularly among those that speak the same language.

All the examples discussed so far use a well-defined reference system—chart, table, graph, geospatial map, and network graph—and data overlays that use data to either (1) modify the base map (e.g., cartograms), (2) place records and linkages, or (3) visually encode geometric symbols (point, line, area, surface) using graphic variable types.

---

13 Dorling, Daniel, Mark E.J. Newman, and Anna Barford. 2010. *The Atlas of the Real World: Mapping the Way We Live.* Revised and expanded. London: Thames & Hudson.

14 Department of Public Information, United Nations. 2010. *We Can End Poverty 2015: Millennium Development Goals*. http://www.un.org/millenniumgoals (accessed August 2, 2013).

15 Beauchesne, Olivier H. 2011. *Map of Scientific Collaborations from 2005 to 2009.* http://collabo.olihb.com/ (accessed August 2, 2013).

Ecological Footprint

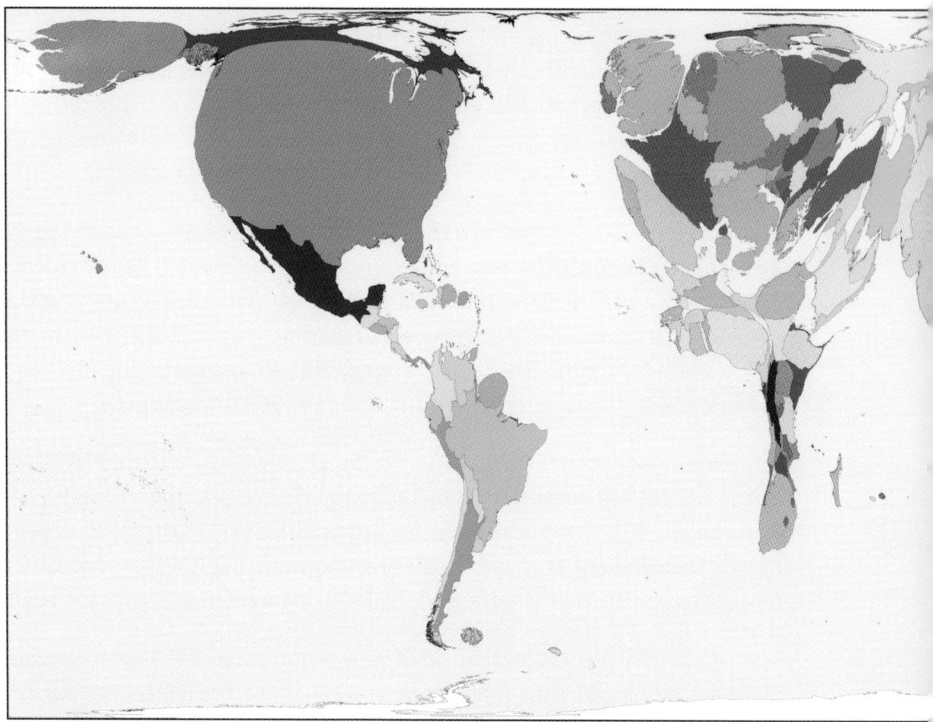

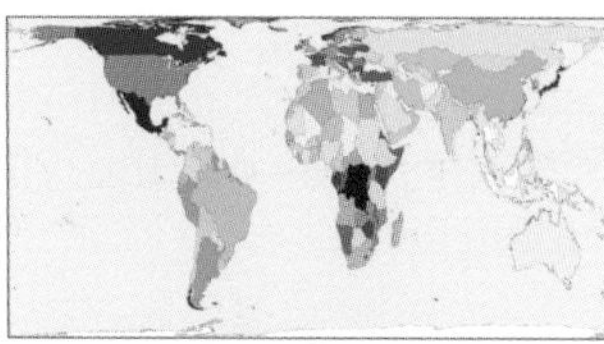

Land area

Technical notes

- Data are from the WWF (Worldwide Fund for Nature) International and Institute of Zoology.
- Ecological footprint is measured in global hectares. One global hectare is an area that has the world average biological productivity of one hectare.
- See website for further information.

LARGEST AND SMALLEST ECOL

Rank	Territory	Value	Rank
1	United Arab Emirates	10.6	191
2	United States	9.7	192
3	Greenland	7.7	193
3	Bahamas	7.7	194
5	Canada	7.5	195
6	Kuwait	7.4	196
7	Australia	7.0	197
8	Finland	6.8	198
9	Estonia	6.1	199
10	New Zealand	6.1	200

ecological footprint in global hectar

"People consume resources and ecological services fro areas, wherever they may be on the planet."

www.worldmapper.org

Figure 1.14 *Ecological Footprint* (2006) by Danny Dorling, Mark E.J. Newman, Graham Allsopp, Anna Barford, Ben Wheeler, John Pritchard, and David Dorling (http://scimaps.org/IV.6)

Produced by the SASI group (Sheffield) and Mark Newman (Michigan)

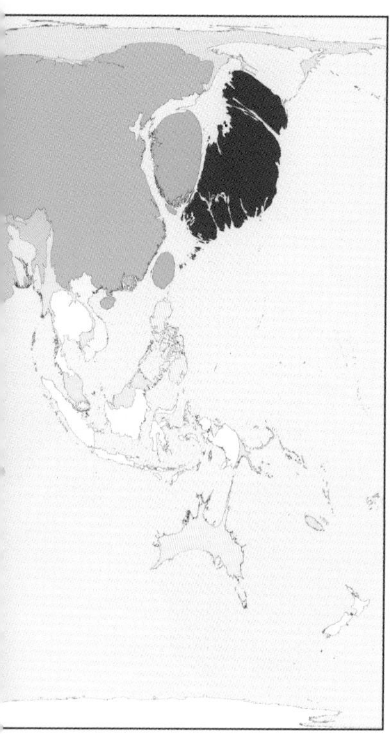

The ecological footprint is a measure of the area needed to support a population's lifestyle. This includes the consumption of food, fuel, wood, and fibres. Pollution, such as carbon dioxide emissions, is also counted as part of the footprint.

The United States, China and India have the largest ecological footprints. Without knowing population size we cannot understand what this means about individuals' ecological demands. Large populations live in China and India. In both territories resource use is below the world average. The per person footprint in the United States is almost five times the world average, and almost ten times what would be sustainable.

Territory size shows the proportion of the worldwide ecological footprint which is made there.

L SHOE SIZES

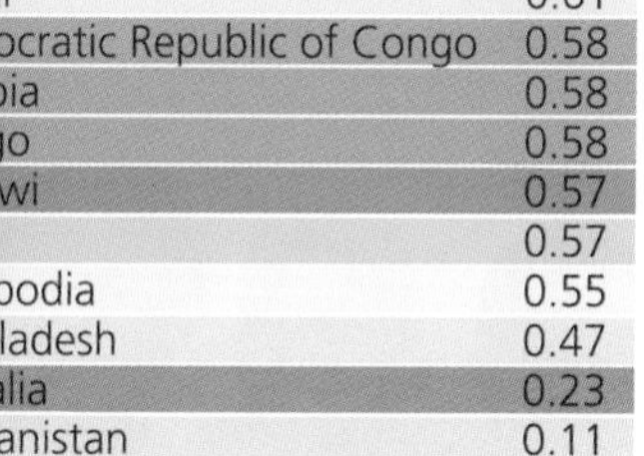

itory	Value
al	0.61
ocratic Republic of Congo	0.58
bia	0.58
go	0.58
wi	0.57
	0.57
bodia	0.55
gladesh	0.47
alia	0.23
anistan	0.11

*son, 2002**

AVERAGE ECOLOGICAL SHOE SIZE

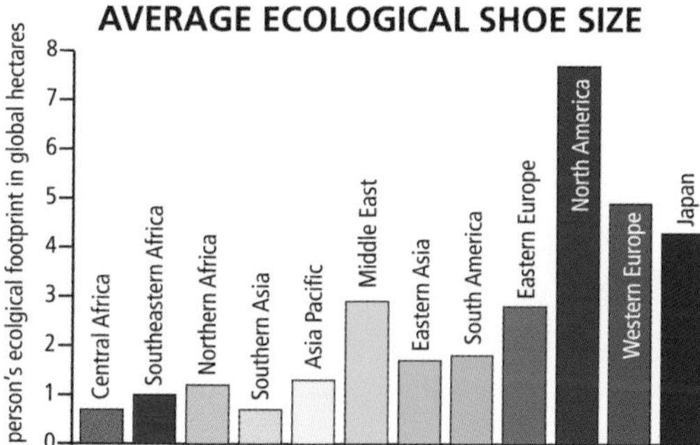

l over the world, so their footprint is the sum of these

The Living Planet Report, 2006

Map 322

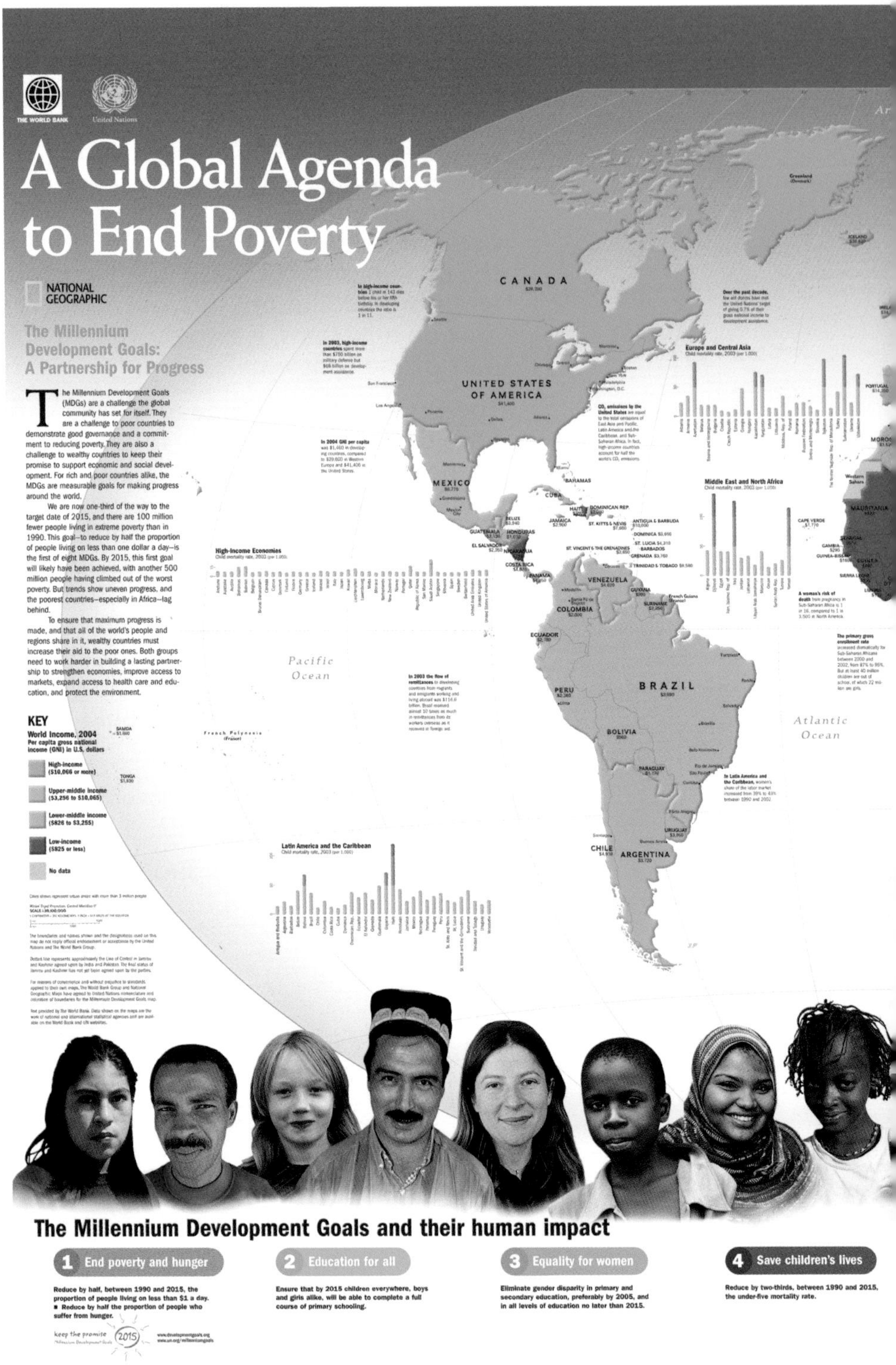

Figure 1.15 *The Millennium Development Goals Map* (2006) by the World Bank and National Geographic (http://scimaps.org/V.10)

5 Make motherhood safe

…duce the maternal mortality ratio by three-…arters between 1990 and 2015.

6 Stop HIV/AIDS, malaria and other diseases

Have halted by 2015 and begun to reverse the spread of HIV/AIDS. ■ Have halted by 2015 and begun to reverse the incidence of malaria and other major diseases.

7 Protect the environment

Integrate the principles of sustainable development into country policies and programs, and reverse the loss of environmental resources. ■ Reduce by half the proportion of people without sustainable access to safe drinking water and basic sanitation. ■ Achieve significant improvement in the lives of at least 100 million slum dwellers by 2020.

8 Build a global partnership for development

Address needs of the least developed countries. ■ Further develop an open trading and financial system. ■ Deal comprehensively with developing countries' debt. ■ Develop job strategies for youth. ■ Provide access to affordable essential drugs in developing countries. ■ Make available new technologies, especially information and communications.

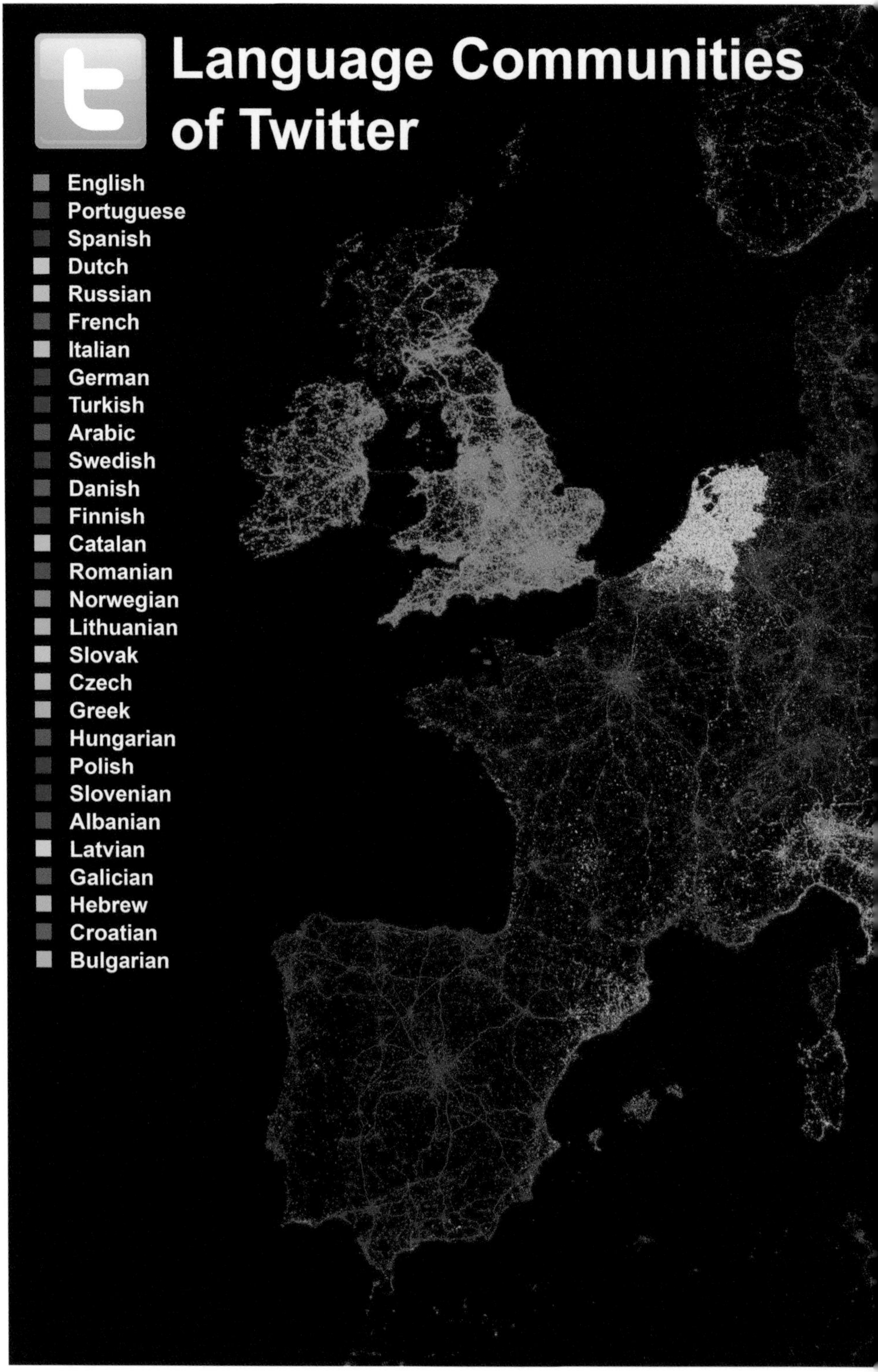

Figure 1.16 *Language Communities of Twitter* (2012) by Eric Fischer (http://scimaps.org/VIII.9)

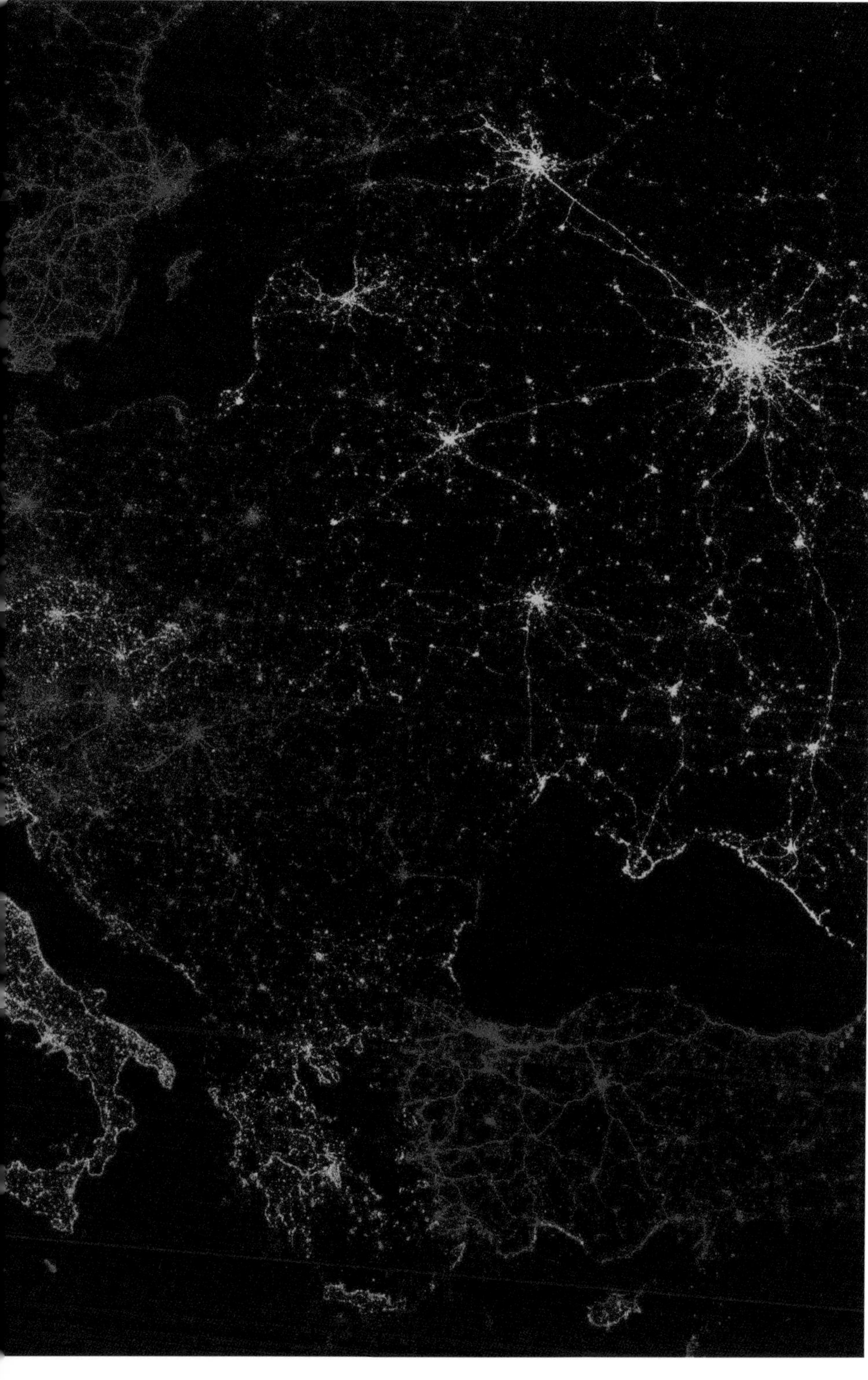

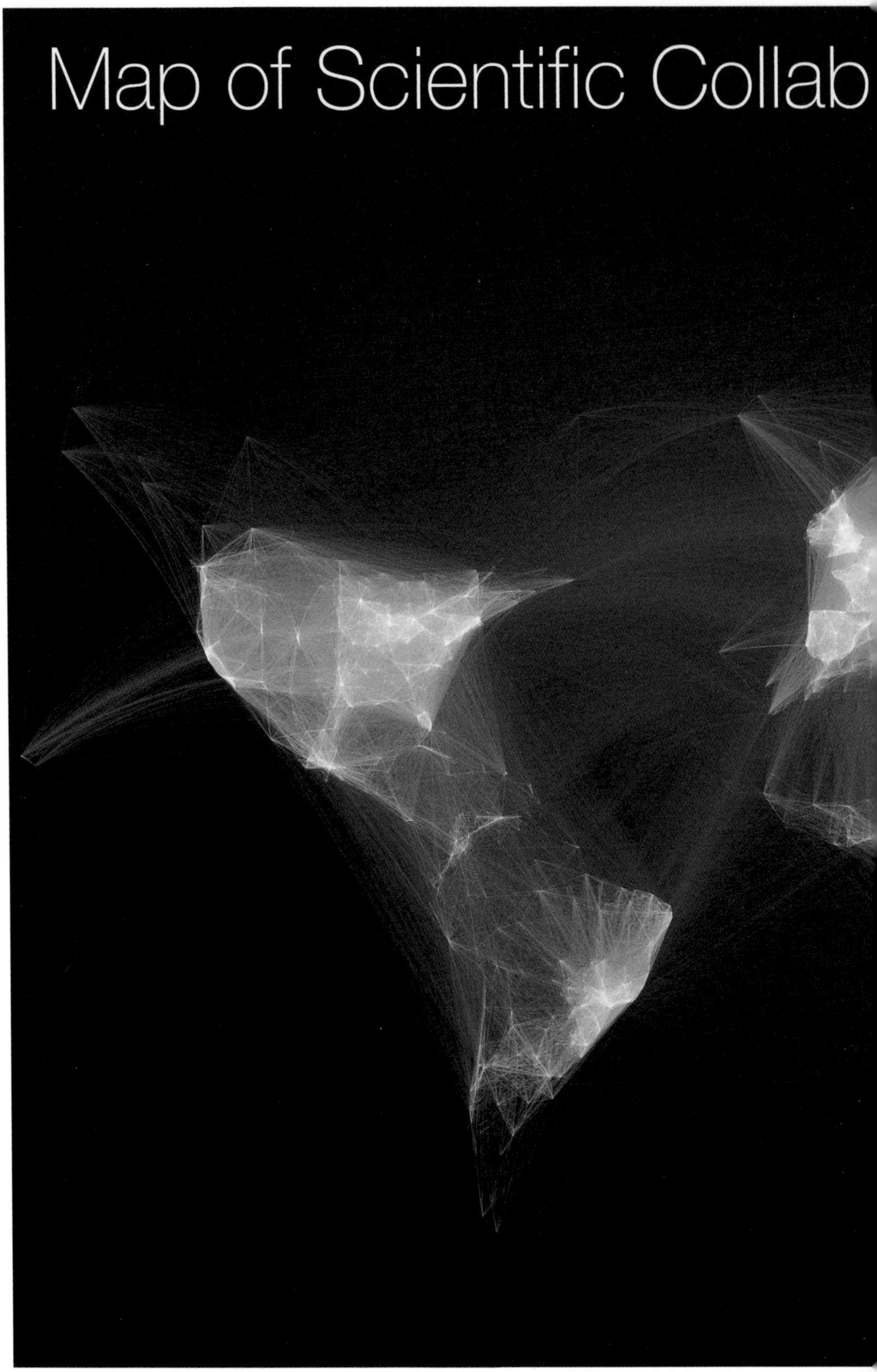

Map of Scientific Collab

Figure 1.17 *Scientific Collaborations between World Cities* (2012) by Olivier H. Beauchesne (http://scimaps.org/VII.6)

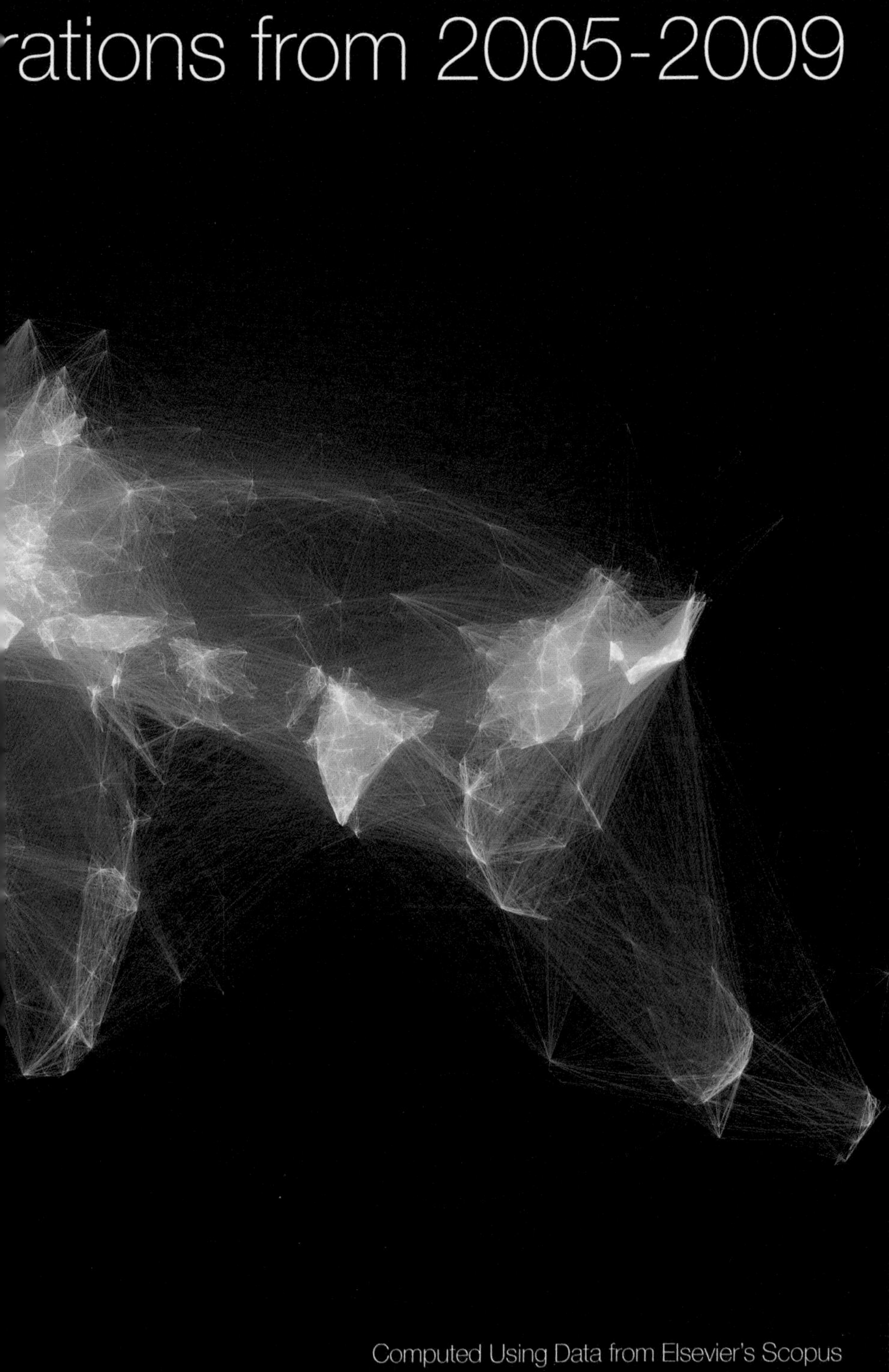
rations from 2005-2009
Computed Using Data from Elsevier's Scopus

Graphic Variable Types

Many different visual encodings have been proposed and used to encode data visually. Please see the *Atlas of Knowledge*[16] for a detailed review and comparison of different approaches. Generally, graphic variable types include **position**, **form**, and **color**. Less frequently used graphic variable types include **texture** and **optics**. See Figure 1.18 for an overview.

Position typically involves *x*, *y*, and sometimes *z* coordinates, if the visualization is three-dimensional. Keep in mind that three-dimensional visualizations are harder to read because data points can occlude each other more easily, perspective drawing renders close-by objects larger than remote ones, and colors of nearby objects are brighter than those of far-away objects. If objects are rendered three-dimensional then true colors are even harder to identify due to spotlights and shadows.

Form comprises size and shape—two very commonly used forms of visual encoding. In addition, the orientation of visual encodings can carry meaning. For example, a tree icon might be shown upright if the tree is alive, or laying horizontally if it was cut down.

Color has three attribute values: value, hue, and saturation (see example in Figure 1.18).

Texture attributes such as pattern, rotation, coarseness, size, or density gradient can be used to encode data attributes.

Optics includes crispness, transparency, and shading, among others.

Data Scale Types

There are four data scale types: **categorical**, **ordinal**, **interval**, **and ratio** (see Figure 1.19).

A **categorical** scale, which is also called a nominal or category scale, is qualitative. Categories are assumed to be non-overlapping, such as words or numbers constituting the names and descriptions of people, places, things, or events.

Ordinal scale is qualitative. Data appears in a sequence or rank-ordered scale. Examples are days of the week or rankings. A Likert scale, from *very poor* to *very good,* is an ordinal type as well.

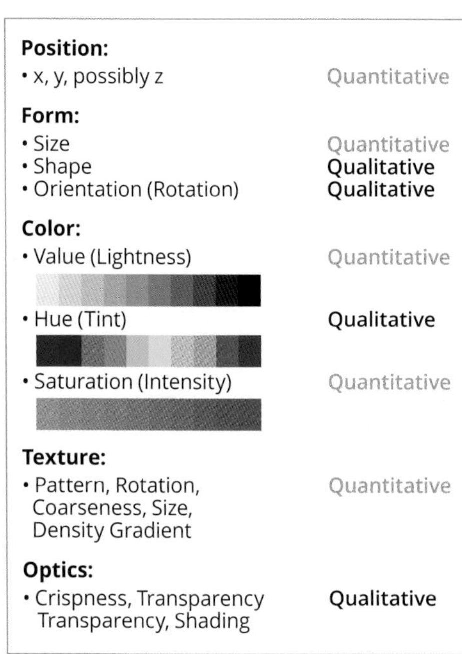

Figure 1.18 Visual encoding using colors

16 Börner, Katy. 2014. *Atlas of Knowledge: Anyone Can Map*. Cambridge, MA: The MIT Press.

Interval scale, also called value data, is a quantitative scale of measurement, where the distance between any two adjacent values or intervals is equal but the zero point is arbitrary. Examples are degrees of temperature in Celsius or time in hours.

The **ratio**, also called proportion scale, is quantitative. It represents values organized as an ordered sequence, such as weight or height. On the ratio scale there is a meaningful zero point.

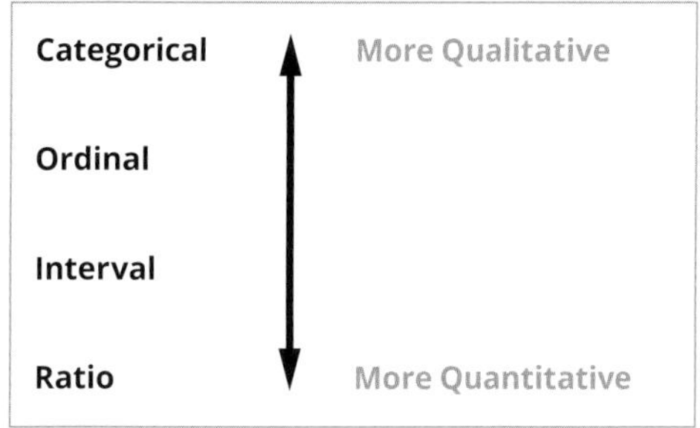

Figure 1.19 Data scale types on the qualitative to quantitative scale

In order to encode data visually using graphic variable types, the data scale type of data variables has to be taken into account. For example, a categorical variable, say occupation, can be encoded using color hue, which is categorical and qualitative. Gender should not be encoded using quantitative color variables such as value or saturation (see Figure 1.18). More examples will be discussed in Section 1.3.

SELF-ASSESSMENT

1. What 'Level of Analysis' is required to study the career trajectory of a scholar?
   a. Micro
   b. Meso
   c. Macro

2. What 'Type of Analysis' is best for studying and visualizing the number of researchers in the top-100 research universities?
   a. Temporal
   b. Geospatial
   c. Topical
   d. Network

3. Which visualization type(s) have quantitative or qualitative axes?
   a. Charts
   b. Tables
   c. Graphs
   d. Geospatial maps
   e. Network graphs

Chapter 1: Hands-On Section

1.3 EXAMPLES

In order to effectively apply graphic variable types (see Section 1.2), we must know the data scale types of the diverse data variables. Certain graphic variable types work better for encoding qualitative data, and we should use others only for encoding quantitative data.

Color hue and orientation are qualitative graphic variable types, and we should use them to encode categorical or ordinal data. Note that there are a few shapes people cannot name, and people are not good at estimating what degree of rotation a shape has.

Size and color value are both quantitative and are commonly used to size- and value-code geometric symbols based on interval or ratio data.

As a concrete example, Table 1.2 lists different data attributes—name, age, zip code, and profession—and identifies whether or not they are quantitative or qualitative. Some of these are fairly obvious, such as age being quantitative or profession being qualitative. Zip code is interesting as it is represented by a number, making it look quantitative. However, U.S. zip code numbers are not continuous—instead they are qualitative reference numbers. They can be converted into latitude and longitude values, which are quantitative.

Table 1.2 Data Scale Type Examples

Name	Age	US ZIP	Profession
Eva	30	47401	Teacher
Bruce	46	47405	Engineer
Qualitative	Quantitative	Qualitative	Qualitative

Table 1.3 shows these different data attributes along with different ways they could be visually encoded using different graphic variable types. These mappings are performed during VISUALIZE (see the workflow design in Figure 1.20). That is, original or computed data variables are mapped onto the graphic variable types. The data scale type of the different data variables impact what visual encodings are possible.

Table 1.3 Graphic Variables vs. Data Scale Types

	Name	Age	US ZIP	Profession
Position		×	×	
Size		×	×	
Color Hue	×			×
Shape	×			×
	Qualitative	Quantitative	Quantitative	Qualitative

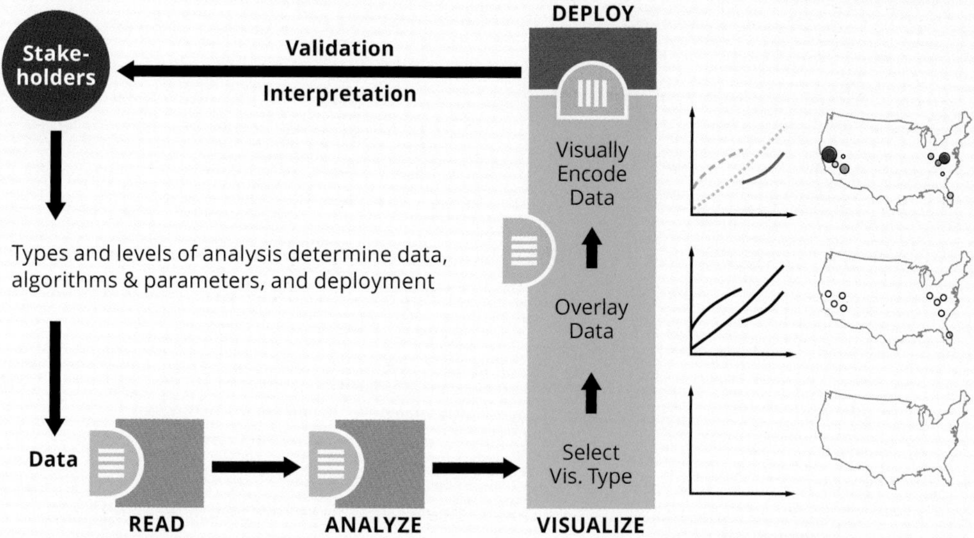

Figure 1.20 The visual encoding process exemplified on a graph and a geospatial map

Figure 1.20 exemplifies the (1) selection of a visualization reference system, (2) data overlay, and (3) visual encoding of data variables using line style, color, and size-coding for a simple graph and a geospatial map. Following these 1-2-3 steps eases the design of meaningful visualizations.

1.4 DOWNLOAD AND INSTALL SCI2

We will use the Sci2 Tool version 1.1 to run temporal (Chapter 2), geospatial (Chapter 3), topical (Chapter 4), and network analyses (Chapters 5 and 6) and to render results visually. The Sci2 Tool is a so-called plug-and-play macroscope[17] tool that can be easily extended and customized to meet diverse needs; see Appendix on how to add additional plugins. Sci2 is a stand-alone desktop application that installs and runs on all common operating systems. It requires Java SE 5 32-bit version 1.5.0 or later to be pre-installed.[18]

To download the Sci2 Tool, go to the main Sci2 web page,[19] and click on the "Download Sci2 Tool" button. Registration is free, only takes a few minutes, and is required to download the tool. After clicking the "Register Now" button, check for the email confirmation with instructions, create a password, and download the tool by selecting the operating system of your

17 Börner, Katy. 2011. "Plug-and-Play Macroscopes." *Communications of the ACM* 54, 3: 60–69.

18 You can run a check on the Java site: http://www.java.com/en/download/installed.jsp

19 http://sci2.cns.iu.edu

choice. The Sci2 Tool and its associated files will be zipped up in a file. Save this zipped file, unzip it, and double-click the Sci2 icon (sci2.exe) to run the program (Figure 1.21). Make sure to save and run the program in a file directory, where the tool has permission to create new files (e.g., log files). Your Desktop will work; the Programs file directory can sometimes cause errors.

Sci2 installation and usage is the same across all operating systems. The Hands-On sections in this book demonstrate using a PC, but the processes for each workflow will be the same for Mac and Linux.

After running Sci2, a splash screen and shortly thereafter the Sci2 interface will appear. The interface is divided into four parts: menu on top, 'Console' below, 'Scheduler' in lower left, and 'Data Manager' on right (Figure 1.22).

configuration	12/4/2012 9:26 AM	File folder	
features	11/27/2012 3:13 PM	File folder	
licenses	11/27/2012 3:13 PM	File folder	
logs	12/4/2012 9:36 AM	File folder	
plugins	12/4/2012 9:26 AM	File folder	
sampledata	11/27/2012 3:14 PM	File folder	
scripts	11/27/2012 3:14 PM	File folder	
workspace	11/27/2012 3:20 PM	File folder	
artifacts.xml	11/27/2012 3:13 PM	XML Document	41 KB
eclipsec.exe	11/27/2012 3:13 PM	Application	24 KB
sci2.exe	11/27/2012 3:13 PM	Application	52 KB
sci2.ini	11/27/2012 3:20 PM	Configuration sett...	1 KB

Figure 1.21 Sci2 download directory showing the Sci2 (sci2.exe) icon being selected

The menu provides easy access to 'File' load, 'Data Preparation', 'Preprocessing', 'Analysis', 'Modeling', and 'Visualization' algorithms. The main menu is organized from left to right by the common sequence of steps in a normal workflow. Within each menu, algorithms are organized by type of analysis (e.g., Temporal, Geospatial, Topical, Networks).

The '**Data Manager**' keeps track of all the files loaded into Sci2 and any subsequent files generated during analysis. All operations performed on a file are nested below the original file in a tree structure. The type of loaded file is indicated by its icon:

Text – text file

Table – tabular data (CSV file)

Matrix-data (Pajek.mat)

Plot – plain text file that can be plotted using Gnuplot

Network – Network data (in-memory graph/network object or network files saved as Graph/ML, XGMML, NWB, Pajek.net or Edge list format)

Tree – Tree data (TreeML)

You can view and save files easily from the 'Data Manager' by right-clicking on a file and selecting 'Save' or 'View'. To remove files from the 'Data Manager', simply right-click and select 'Discard'. If you discard a file that has other files nested beneath it, all of these files will also be discarded.

The '**Console**' logs all the operations that are performed during a session; it also displays error messages and warnings; acknowledgment information on the original authors of the algorithm, developers, and integrators; paper references; and links to online

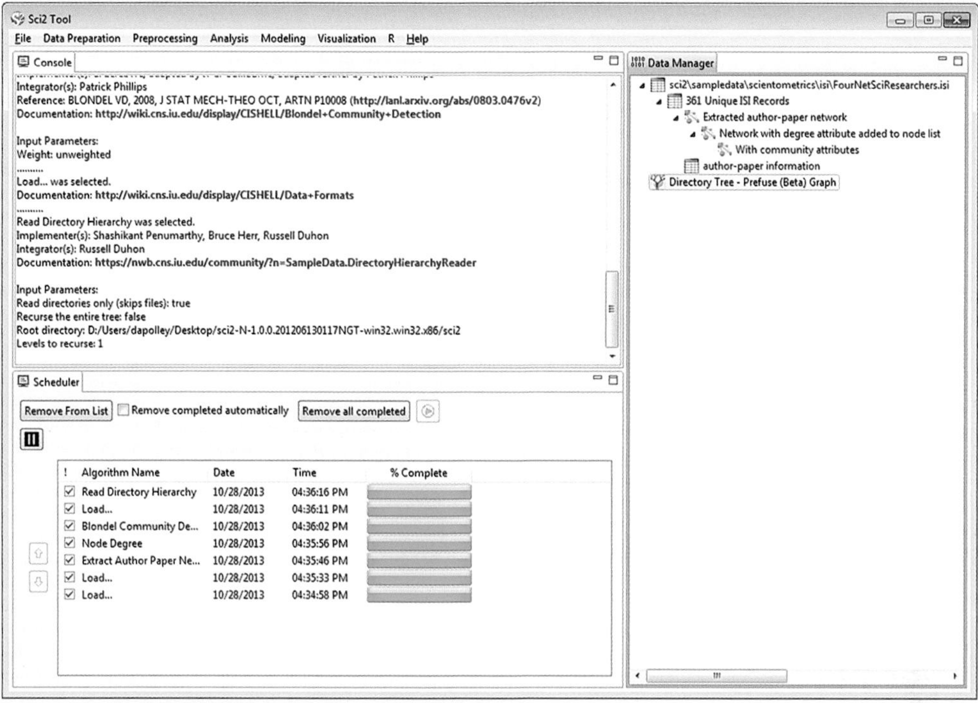

Figure 1.22 Sci2 user interface

documentation in the Sci2 Wiki.[20] The same information is also stored in log files in the *yoursci2directory*/logs directory.

Finally, the **'Scheduler'** shows the progress of operations being performed in the tool.

To uninstall the Sci2 Tool, simply delete *yoursci2directory*. This will delete all sub-directories as well, so make sure to backup all files you want to save.

Homework

Register at (http://sci2.cns.iu.edu) and download the Sci2 Tool. Install it and run it. Load a CSV file (e.g., *KatyBorner.nsf*[21]) using *File > Load*. Right-click the file in the 'Data Manager' and select 'View' to open it in MS Excel or 'View With...' to open it in another spreadsheet program. Sort the 'Awarded Amount to Date' column to answer: What is the project with the highest funding amount? Then, right-click the file in the 'Data Manager', 'Rename' it, and then 'Discard' it.

20 http://sci2.wiki.cns.iu.edu

21 *yoursci2directory*/sampledata/scientometrics/nsf

Chapter Two

“WHEN”: Temporal Data

Chapter 2: Theory Section

Chapters 2–6 introduce different types of analysis and resulting visualizations that answer a specific type of question. This chapter aims to answer "WHEN" questions using temporal data, analyses, and visualizations. The main goal is to understand the temporal distribution of datasets; to identify growth rates, latency to peak times, or decay rates; to see patterns in time-series data, such as trends, seasonality, or bursts.

Each theory part of the subsequent five chapters starts with a discussion of exemplary visualizations followed by an overview and definition of key terminology, and introduction of general workflows. This chapter also introduces burst detection, which is widely used to identify sudden bursts of activity or surges of interest.

2.1 EXEMPLARY VISUALIZATIONS

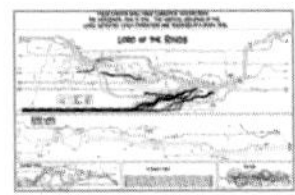

The first visualization (Figure 2.1)[1] shows different movie narratives that plot character trajectories in several popular films, for example, *Lord of the Rings* or *Star Wars*. Time is arranged from left to right and horizontal lines track events in time. The vertical arrangement of lines signifies character groupings and partings while aiming to minimize line overlaps and crossings.

The largest of the five charts, the *Lord of the Rings* map, at the top, has characters color-coded according to the major races of Middle Earth. There are hobbits, elves, dwarfs, men, wizards, and ents. The smaller charts at the bottom use a similar approach to make witty commentary on their films' plots.

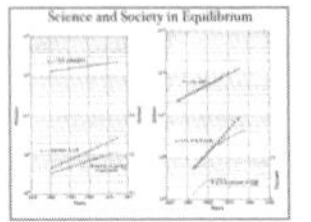

The next visualization, *Science and Society in Equilibrium*,[2] (Figure 2.2) consists of two graphs. The graph on the left plots the total U.S. population and the number of scientists in the United States. The right graph plots total U.S. gross national product (GNP) and the amount of money spent on research and development (R&D) costs. (R&D costs as percent of GNP is also shown.) The two graphs invite comparison between the number of scientists relative to the total population, and the amount spent on research and development relative to the GNP, from 1940 to 1975.

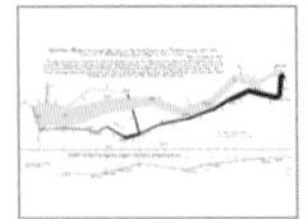

The third visualization (Figure 2.3) is frequently used as an example of excellence in statistical graphics. It was created by Charles Joseph Minard in 1869[3] and shows Napoleon's retreat in the Russian campaign during the winter of 1812. Shown on the left are 422,000 soldiers who started off at the Polish border. The brown band on the top shows the long

1 Munroe, Randall. 2013. *xkcd*. http://www.xkcd.com (accessed September 3).

2 Martino, Joseph P. 1969. "Science and Society in Equilibrium." *Science* 165, 3895: 769–772.

3 Tufte, Edward R. 1983. *The Visual Display of Quantitative Information*. Cheshire, CT: Graphics Press.

march to Moscow. Its thickness represents the number of soldiers, which decreased when 60,000 stayed behind. The crossing of the Moskva River caused a loss of 27,100 men, as many fell through the ice and drowned or froze to death. Only about 100,000 soldiers arrived in Moscow, 322,000 fewer than at the beginning of the campaign. Finally, there was a very long, disastrous retreat as the temperatures were dropping. Many of the soldiers who made it back home had frozen fingers and toes, and the memories of the retreat would stay with them forever. The soldiers rejoined the 60,000, which were left behind, and a total of 10,000 men, about 4% of those who started, made it back home.

Edward Tufte argues that this chart is one of the best statistical graphics ever drawn. There are six variables plotted in one map. First, the line width continuously marks the size of the army. Second and third, the line itself shows the latitude and longitude of the army as it moves from Poland to Moscow. Fourth, the lines show the direction that the army is traveling, both in advance and during retreat. Fifth, the location of the army with respect to certain dates is marked. Finally, the temperature is shown below the chart, making it clear how bitter cold the retreat was.

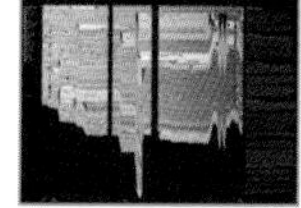

The next visualization (Figure 2.4) by Martin Wattenberg and Fernanda Viégas shows author contributions to the Wikipedia article on abortion.[4] Vertical bands in this **flow map** indicate changes in text. They can be positioned in equal distances, independent of when the changes were made. Or, as in this example, they can be plotted in a way that the distance between them represents the time that has passed. Each contributing author is color-coded. Whenever text pieces get inserted, the Wikipedia page becomes longer. When text is deleted, they become shorter. Black areas indicate deletions.

When exploring the overall map, in the beginning there is one green user who is editing the entire page. Later on, other authors start to make changes. There are also mass deletions, that is, one author deletes the entire page. This happened twice—as indicated by the two black vertical stripes. While the mass deletion was counteracted rather quickly, given that time is equally spaced, the deletions are visually very dominant. Notice also that the Wikipedia entry was very long at some point in time, but then got shortened and compressed again by the editing of many authors. On the right-hand side of the map, the actual Wikipedia page is shown with each text piece color-coded by its respective author.

This final visualization (Figure 2.5) was created by the Council for Chemical Research.[5] It shows the different feedback cycles involved in chemistry research and development

[4] Viégas, Fernanda B., Martin Wattenberg, and Kushal Dave. 2004. "Studying Cooperation and Conflict between Authors with History Flow Visualizations." In *Proceedings of SIGCHI, Vienna, Austria, April 24–29*, 575–582. Vienna: ACM Press.

[5] Council for Chemical Research in cooperation with the Chemical Heritage Foundation. 2001. *Measuring Up: Research and Development Counts for the Chemical Industry.* Phase I. Washington, DC: Council for Chemical Research. http://www.ccrhq.org/innovate/publications/phase-i-study (accessed August 28, 2013).

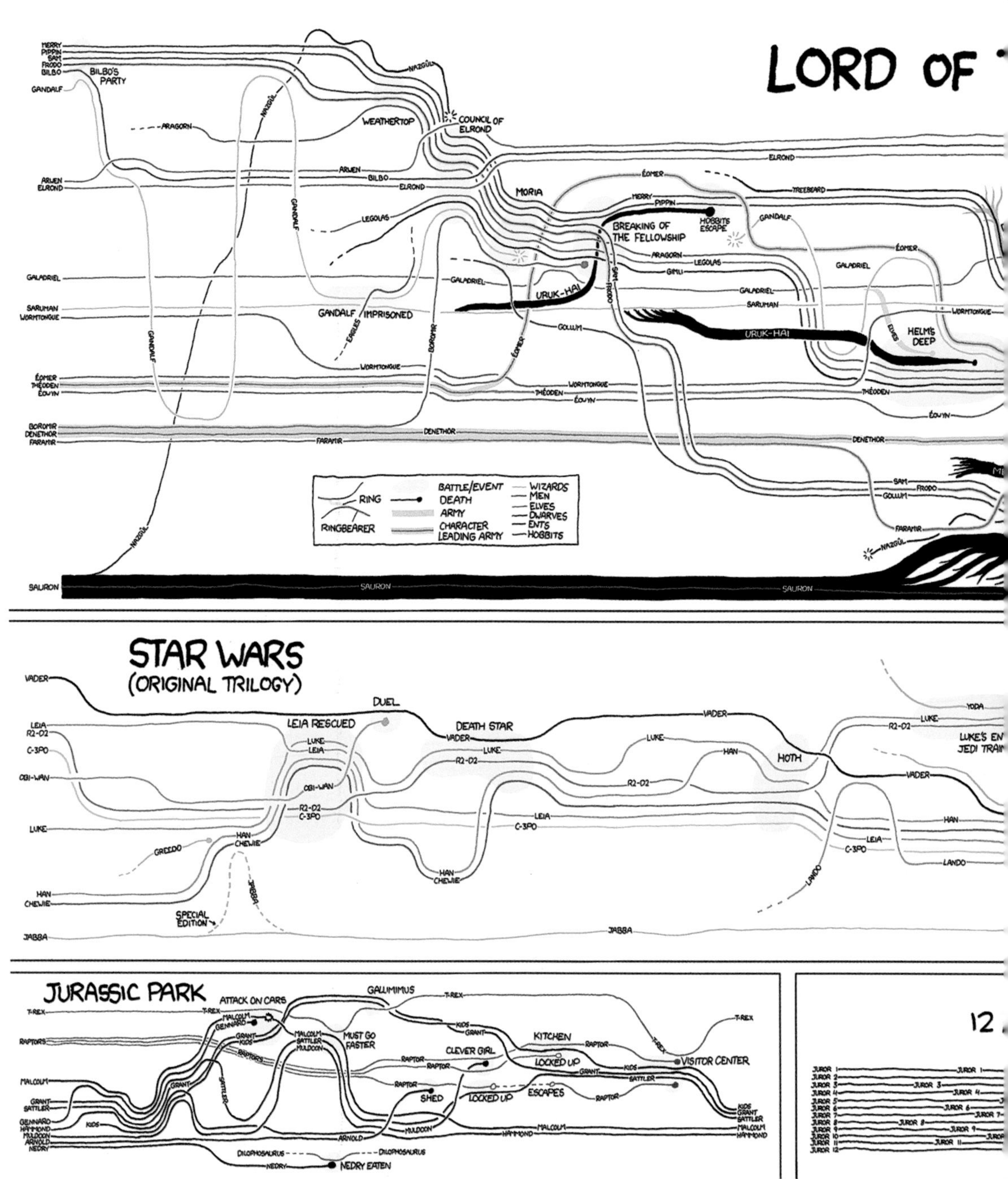

Figure 2.1 *Movie Narrative Charts (Comic #657)* (2009) by Randall Munroe (http://scimaps.org/VIII.2)

CHARACTER INTERACTIONS.
HE VERTICAL GROUPING OF THE
S ARE TOGETHER AT A GIVEN TIME.

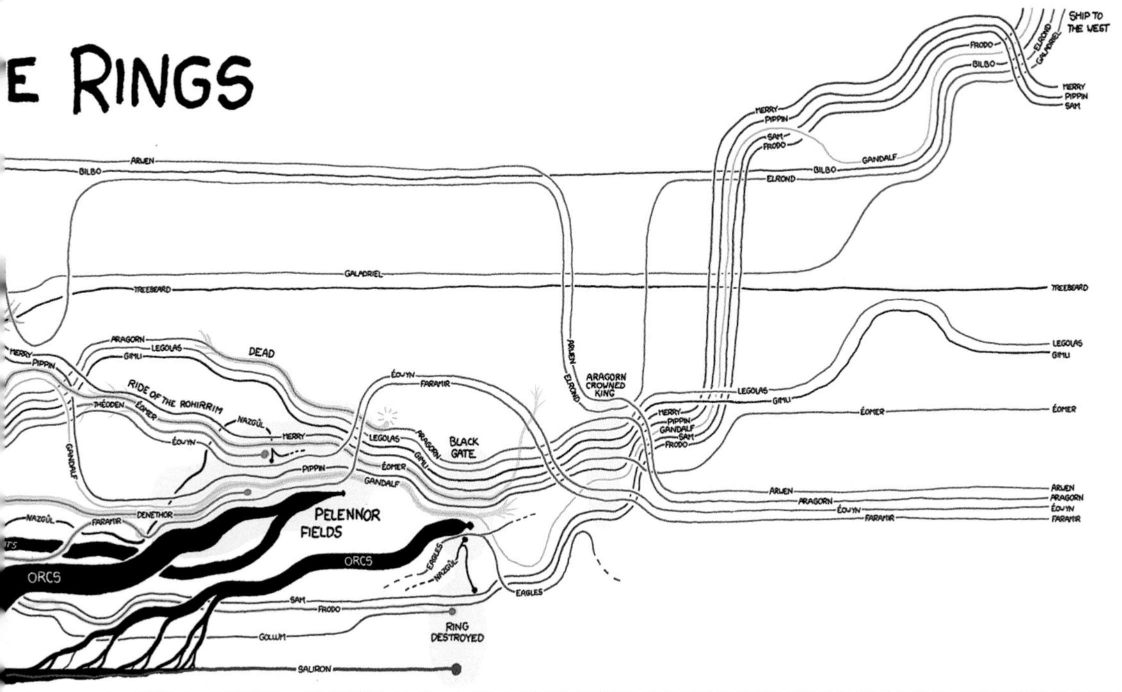

E RINGS

SHIP TO THE WEST
FRODO
BILBO
ELROND
GALADRIEL
MERRY
PIPPIN
SAM
GANDALF
ARWEN
TREEBEARD
ARAGORN
LEGOLAS
GIMLI
DEAD
RIDE OF THE ROHIRRIM
THÉODEN
ÉOMER
NAZGÛL
ÉOWYN
FARAMIR
DENETHOR
BLACK GATE
ARAGORN CROWNED KING
PELENNOR FIELDS
ORCS
EAGLES
GOLLUM
RING DESTROYED
SAURON

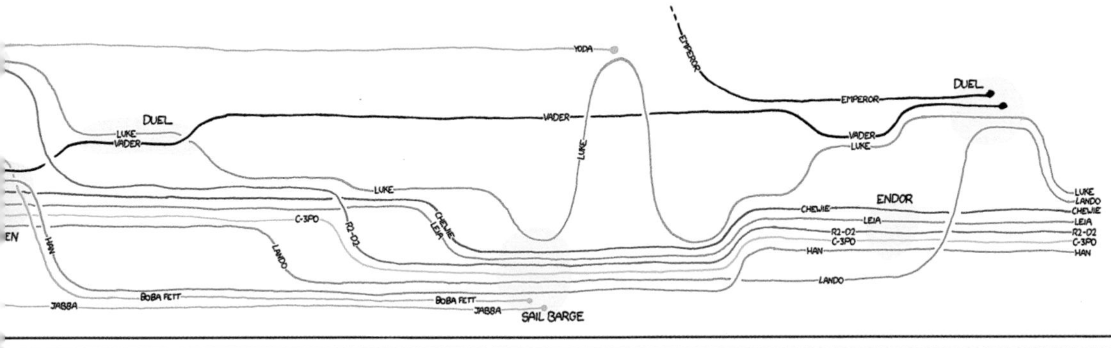

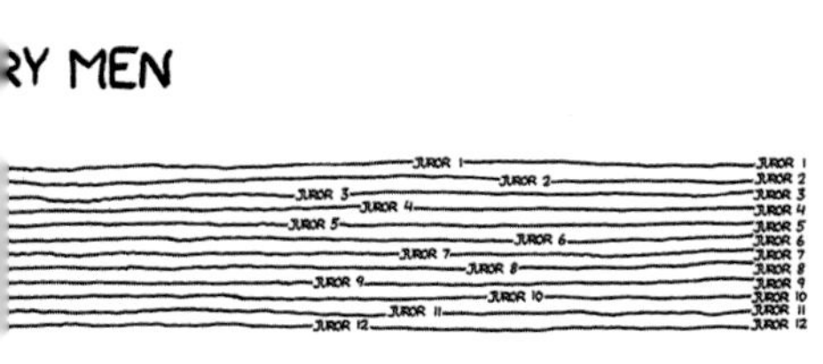

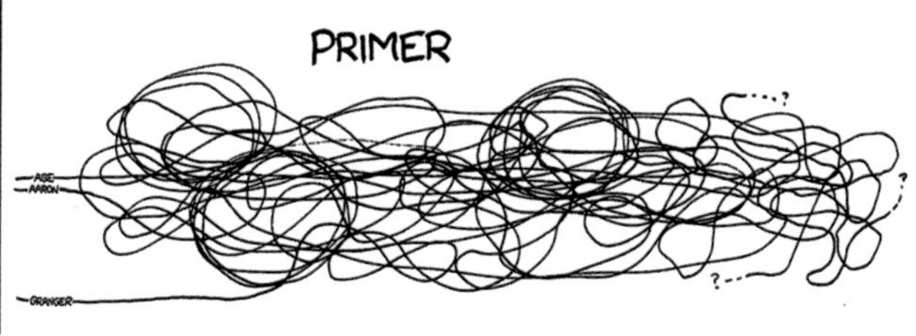

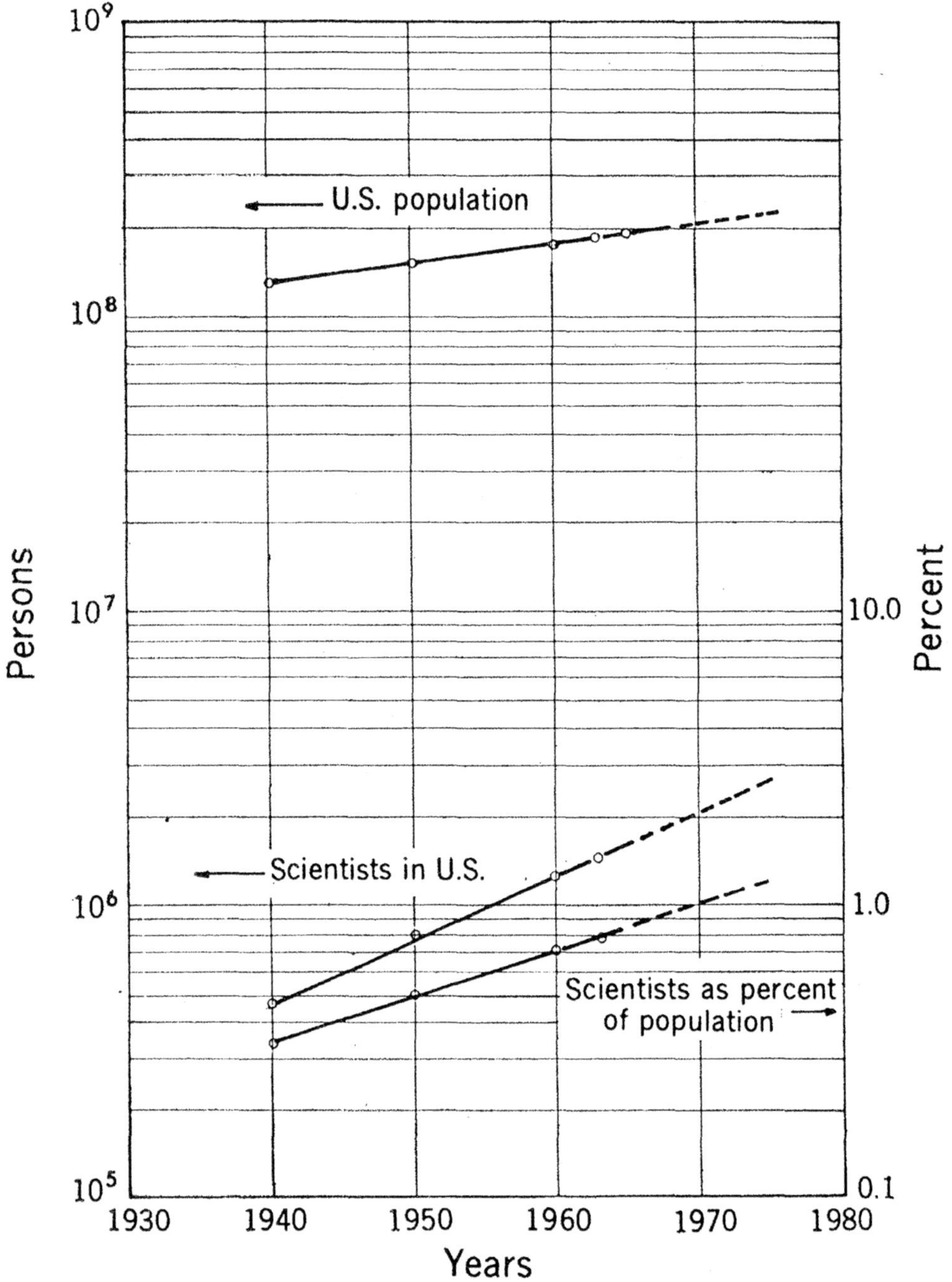

Figure 2.2 *Science and Society in Equilibrium* (1969) by Joseph P. Martino (http://scimaps.org/V.1)

ty in Equilibrium

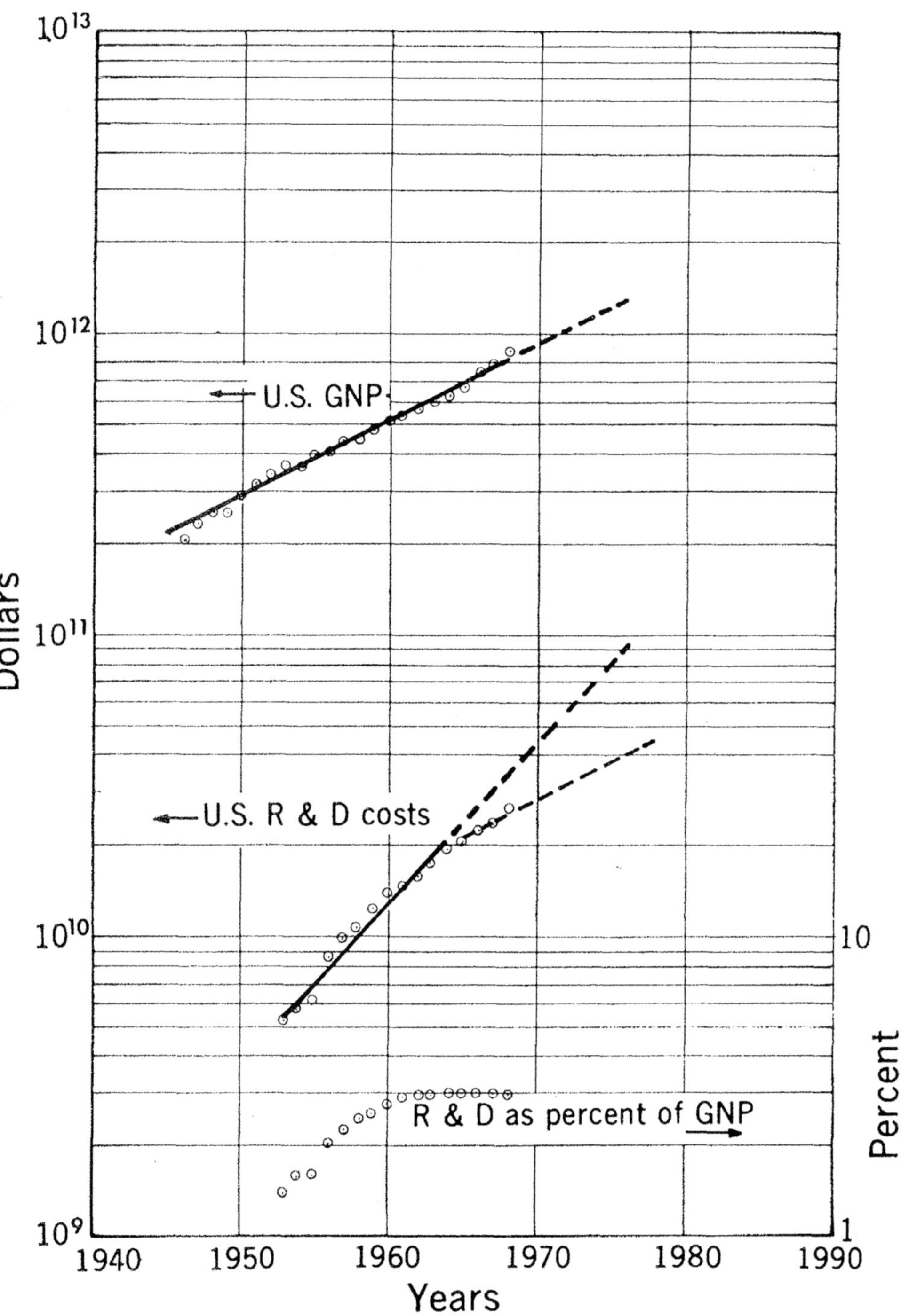

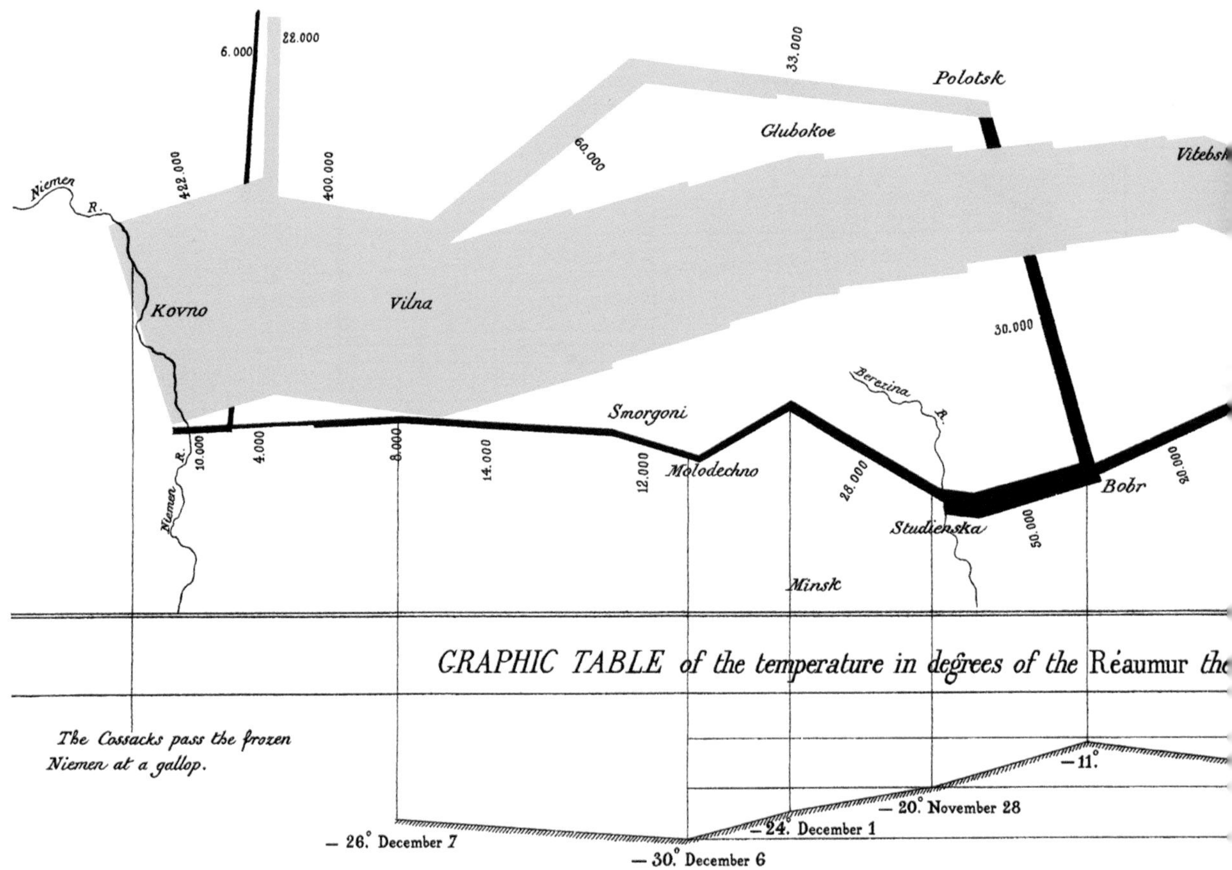

Figure 2.3 *Napoleon's March to Moscow* (1869) by Charles Joseph Minard (http://scimaps.org/I.4)

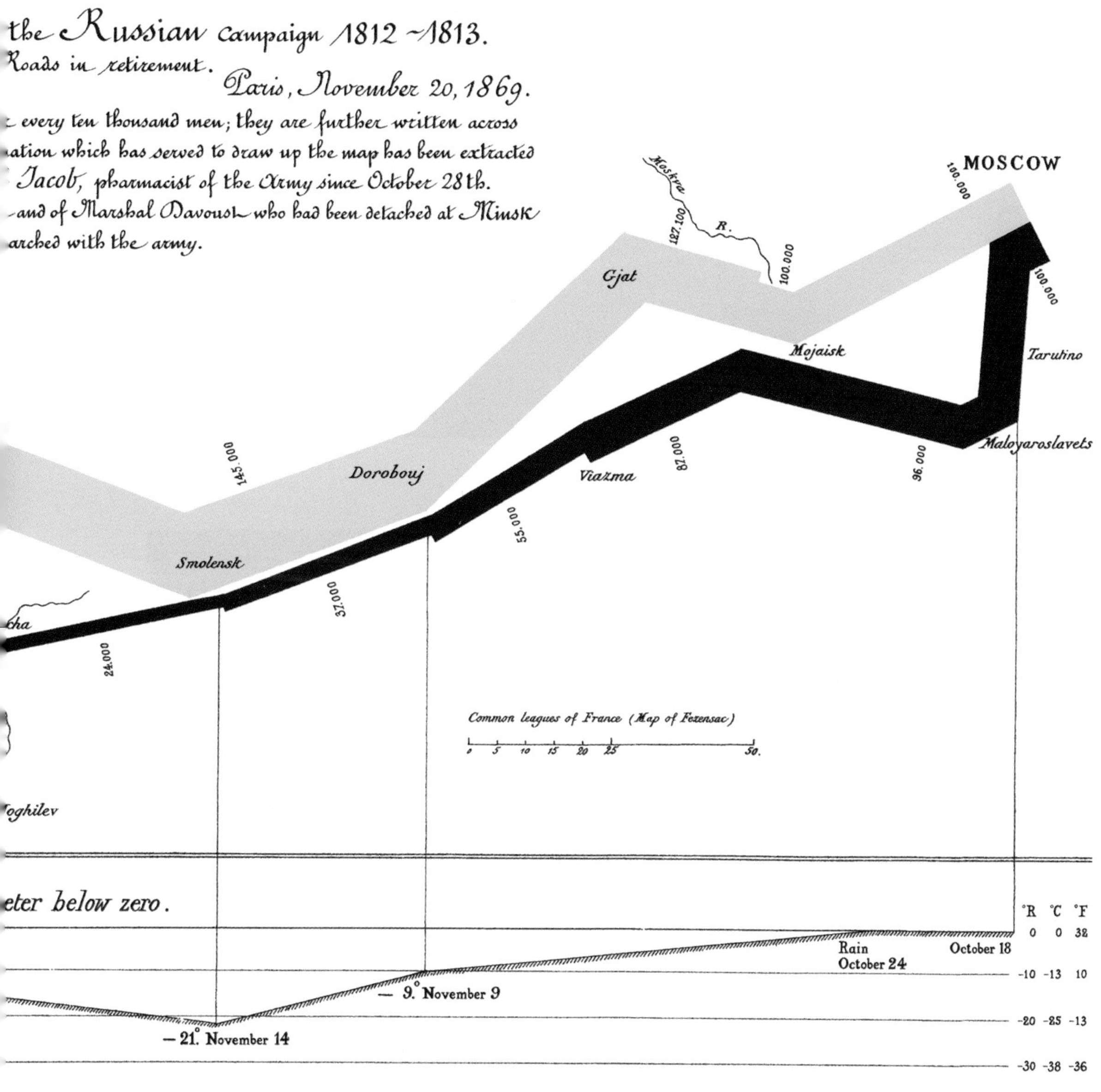

the Russian campaign 1812–1813.
Roads in retirement.
Paris, November 20, 1869.
every ten thousand men; they are further written across
ation which has served to draw up the map has been extracted
Jacob, pharmacist of the Army since October 28th.
and of Marshal Davoust who had been detached at Minsk
arched with the army.
MOSCOW
100.000
Moskva R.
127.100
100.000
100.000
Gjat
Mojaisk
Tarutino
Maloyaroslavets
87.000
96.000
Viazma
145.000
Dorobouj
55.000
Smolensk
37.000
tha
24.000
Common leagues of France (Map of Fezensac)
0 5 10 15 20 25 50.
oghilev
eter below zero.
°R °C °F
0 0 32
Rain October 24
October 18
-10 -13 10
— 9.° November 9
-20 -25 -13
— 21.° November 14
-30 -38 -36

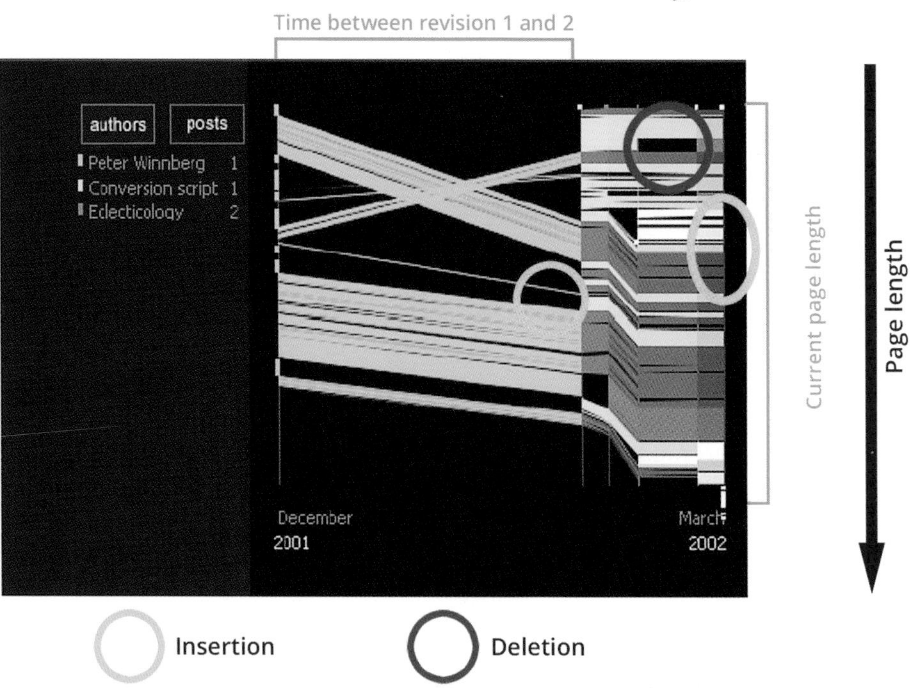

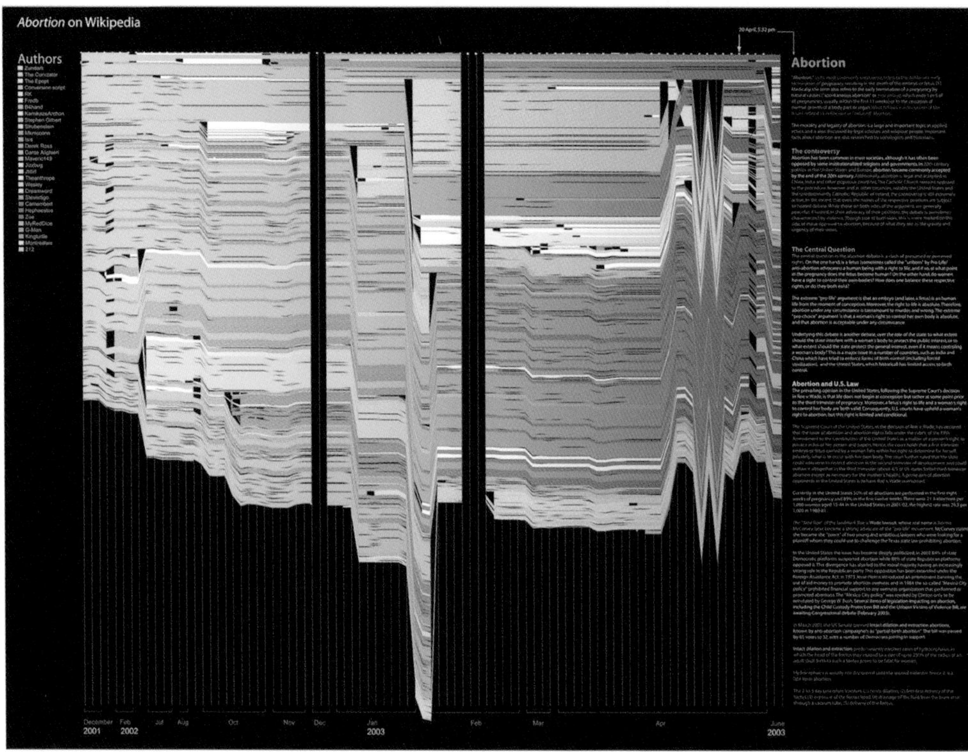

Figure 2.4 *History Flow Visualization of the Wikipedia Entry on "Abortion"* (2006) by Martin Wattenberg and Fernanda B. Viégas, with a demonstration of how to read the map (http://scimaps.org/II.6)

funding by governmental and industry. Also shown are delays in the science system. To understand the visualization, let's start at the point in time at which the federal government decides to spend $1 billion in federal funding for chemistry research. The funding is mostly used for foundational research that is expected to take four to five years. It is matched by chemical industry funding at about $5 billion. The $1 billion federal funding plus $5 billion industry funding help support invention and development expected to take about nine to eleven years. The final stage, technology commercialization, typically takes about five years or longer.

The resulting chemical industry operating income is about $10 billion, which stimulates growth in GNP, creates jobs in the U.S. economy, and provides about $8 billion in taxes. The federal government spends about $1 billion of these taxes to fuel the positive feedback cycle. This timeline from conception to commercialization is important to understand. It takes about 20 years in chemistry to get from an idea to a product that generates revenue. A similar time frame is likely valid in many other areas of science and technology development.

This visualization started out as the yellow arrow graph shown on the right-hand side. It was used in Congress for making an argument for the U.S. innovation engine and the importance of the chemical industry. Data details and supplemental information are provided in three reports.[6,7,8]

2.2 OVERVIEW AND TERMINOLOGY

In this section we provide an overview of the key terminology used in temporal data visualizations. A **time-series** is defined as a sequence of events and observations that are ordered in one dimension: time. Time-series data can be **discrete** (i.e., there are only a finite number of values possible or there is a space on the number line between each two possible values). **Continuous** data makes up the rest of numerical data and is usually associated with some sort of physical measurement.

---

6 Council for Chemical Research in cooperation with the Chemical Heritage Foundation. 2001. *Measuring Up: Research and Development Counts for the Chemical Industry*. Phase I. Washington, DC: Council for Chemical Research. http://www.ccrhq.org/innovate/publications/phase-i-study (accessed August 28, 2013).

7 Council for Chemical Research. 2005. *Measure for Measure: Chemical R&D Powers the US Innovation Engine*. Phase II. Washington, DC: Council for Chemical Research. http://www.ccrhq.org/innovate/publications/phase-ii-study (accessed August 28, 2013).

8 Link, Albert N., and the Council for Chemical Research. 2010. *Assessing and Enhancing the Impact of Science R&D in the United States: Chemical Sciences*. Phase III. http://www.ccrhq.org/innovate/publications/phase-iii-study (accessed August 28, 2013).

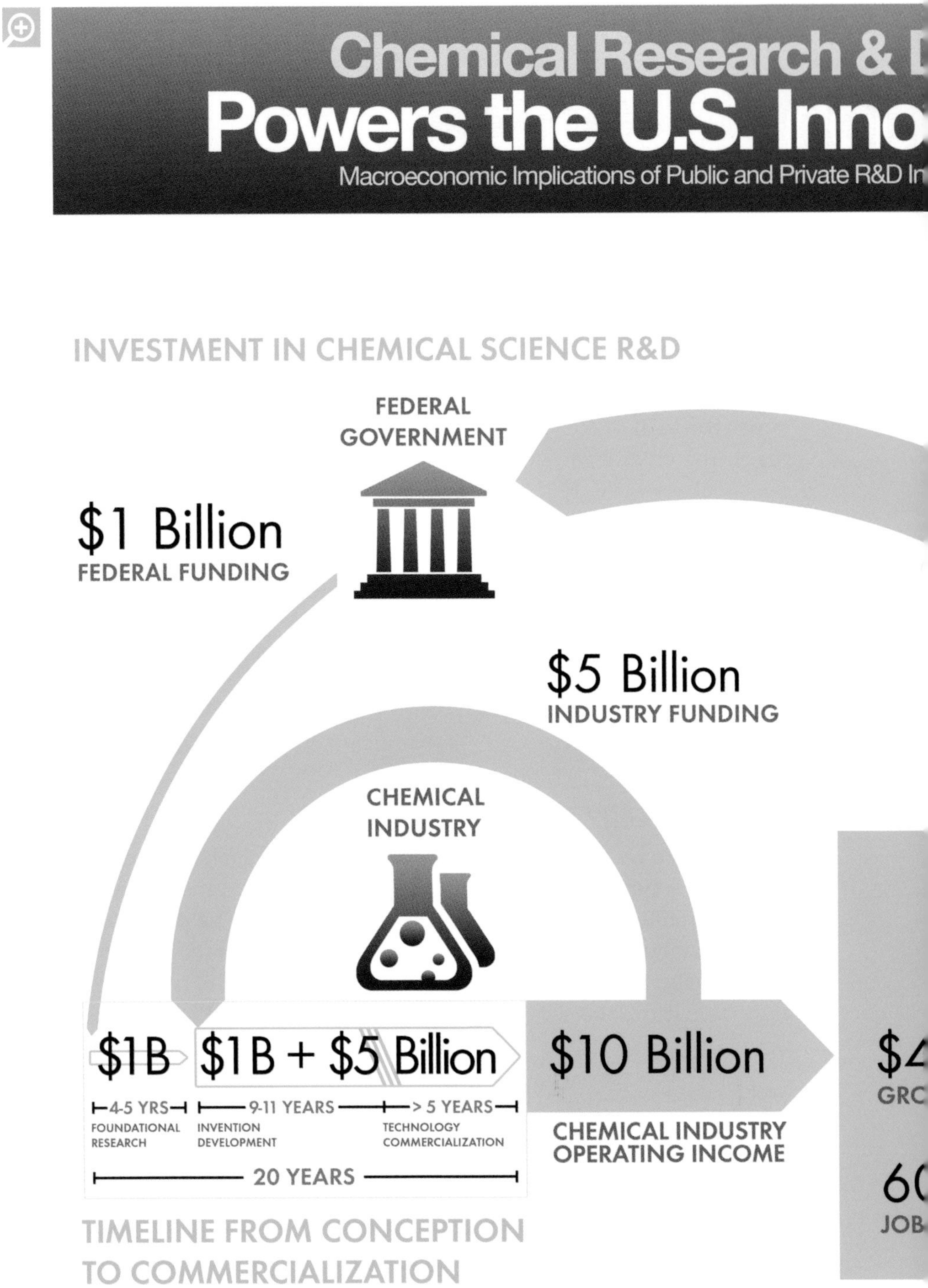

Figure 2.5 *Chemical R&D Powers the U.S. Innovation Engine* (2009) by the Council for Chemical Research (http://scimaps.org/V.6)

velopment
tion Engine
ents in Chemical Sciences

The Council for Chemical Research (CCR)

has provided the U.S. Congress and government policy makers with important results regarding the impact of Federal Research & Development (R&D) investments on U.S. innovation and global competitiveness through its commissioned 5-year two phase study. To take full advantage of typically brief access to policy makers, CCR developed the graphic below as a communication tool that distills the complex data produced by these studies in direct, concise and clear terms.

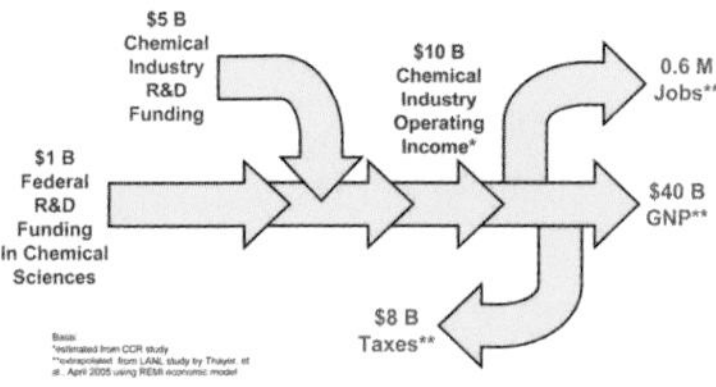

The design shows that an input of $1B in federal investment, leveraged by $5B industry investment, brings new technologies to market and results in $10B of operating income for the chemical industry, $40B growth in the Gross National Product (GNP) and further impacts the US economy by generating approximately 600,000 jobs, along with a return of $8B in taxes. Additional details, also reported in the CCR studies, are depicted in the map to the left. This map clearly shows the two R&D investment cycles; the shorter industry investment at the innovation stage to commercialization cycle; and the longer federal investment cycle which begins in basic research and culminates in national economic and job growth along with the increase tax base that in turn is available for investment in basic research.

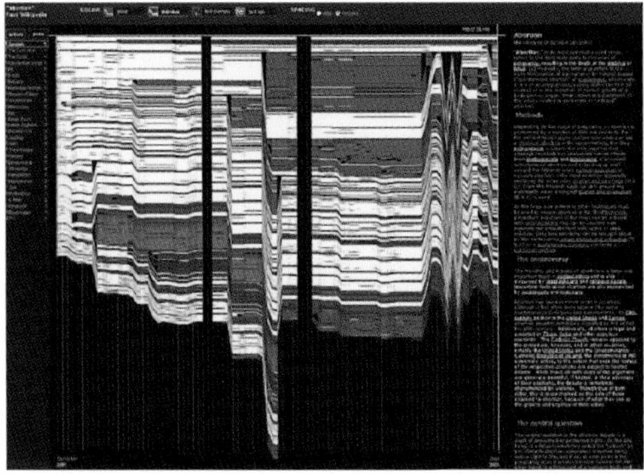
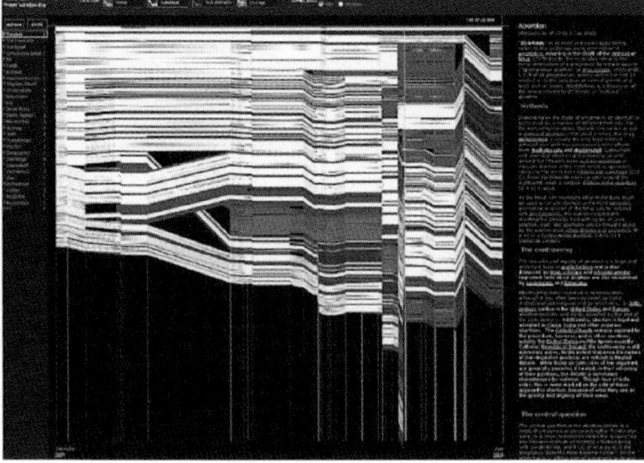

Figure 2.6 Activity on the Wikipedia page for abortion shown in equal distance spacing (left) and date spacing (right)

Wikipedia editing activity can be captured as time-series data. Figure 2.6 (left) shows the history flow visualization from Figure 2.4—edits to Wikipedia pages are equally spaced. The figure on the right shows edits spaced by dates, providing a rather different view of the data.

Another important element of temporal analysis and visualizations is **trends**. As for trends, there are general tendencies (Figure 2.7). There could be an **increasing** tendency or a **decreasing** tendency. It could be **stable**, just the same value all the time. Or there could be seasonal **cycles**, ups and downs, such as in annual temperature changes.

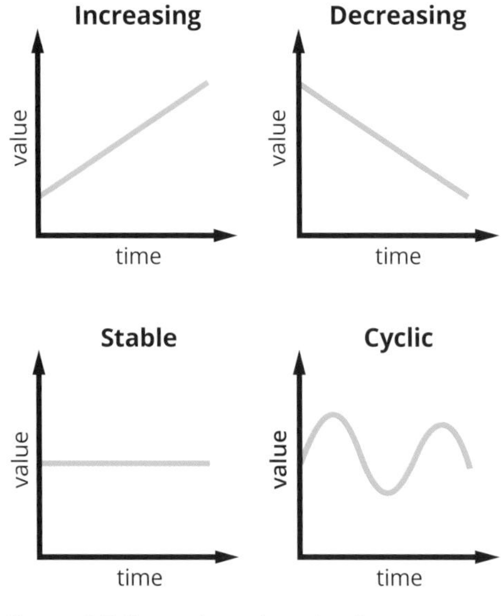

Figure 2.7 General trend tendencies

An example is the online interactive display of names from census data provided in the Baby Name Wizard.[9] Search for "Alice" to see a **stacked graph** depicting how many people were named Alice between 1880s and 2011 (Figure 2.8). Enter your own name to see if you have a very popular name or when your name was most popular. Note that only the top 1,000 most used names are displayed—rarely used names are not covered in the dataset.

Another example is Google Trends.[10] Simply enter different terms to see the number of Google searches that use those terms. Figure 2.9 exemplarily shows the result for the terms "hamburger" and "cheeseburger." A **histogram** in the top

9 http://www.babynamewizard.com/voyager#

10 http://google.com/trends

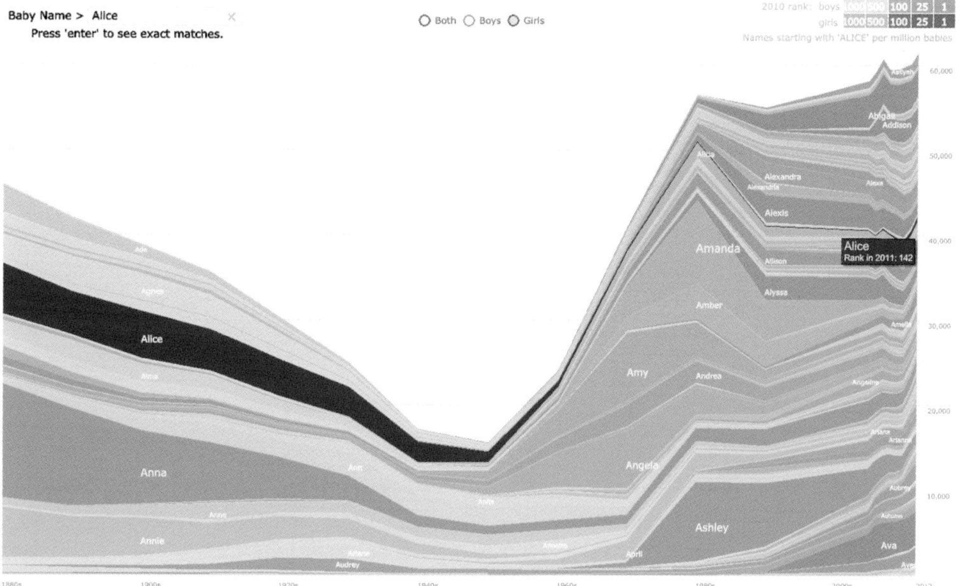

Figure 2.8 Baby name frequencies over time for "Alice"

left shows the average number of times each search was run. The graph on the top right shows the search frequency of both terms over time. Interestingly, or perhaps not, many more people actually query for hamburger than for cheeseburger.

Google Trends also reveals regional interest—the darker the color the higher the number of searches. Germany seems to have a particularly keen interest in "hamburger". However, closer examination of the terms that are actually googled for (see listing in lower right with temporal bar graphs plotting the number of searches) reveals much activity for *Hamburger Abendblatt* and *Hamburger Mogenpost,* two newspapers in Hamburg, a city in the northern part of Germany. Germans also google for *Hamburger Hafen*, which is a very important harbor in Germany, and *Hamburger Dom*, a church in Hamburg. We need to carefully examine the results to draw correct conclusions.

We can also use Google Trends to understand search activity for the pop singers "Madonna" versus "Adele" (Figure 2.10). The graph on the top shows that the world has been googling "Madonna" for a long time while the term "Adele" only recently became very popular. Markers on the trend lines help understand why there is such an increased activity. For example, C indicates that Adele won six Grammys, whereas B, for Madonna, indicates that she dazzled Super Bowl attendees. There's another peak in June 2012, labeled A, when Adele was pregnant with her first child. As can be seen, major events impact the number of Google searches and thus the trends for these two people.

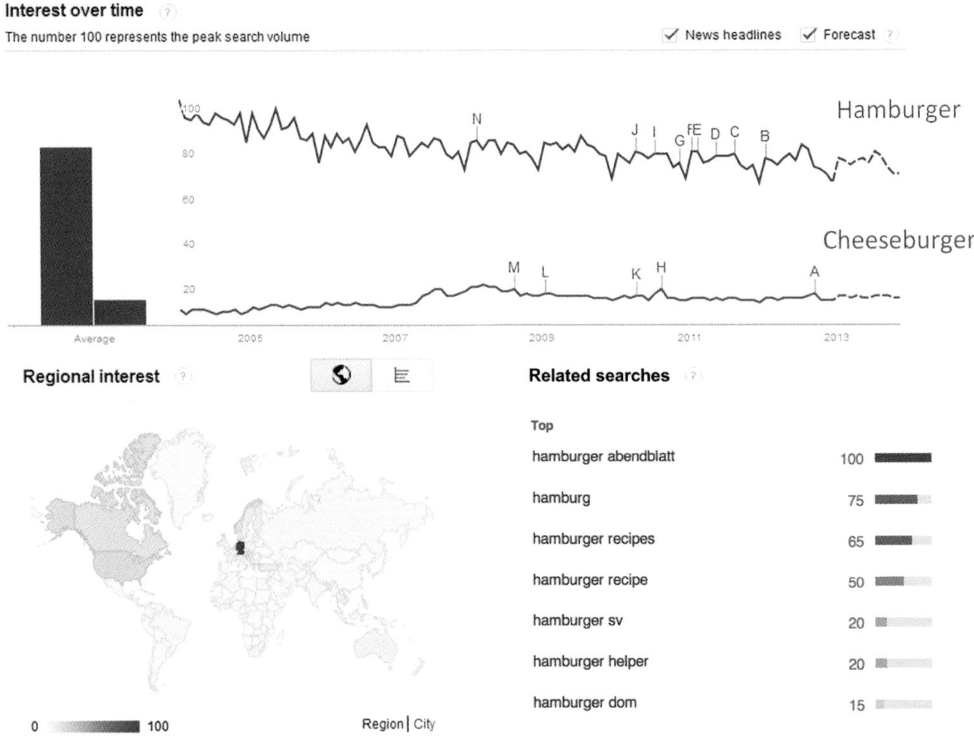

Figure 2.9 Google Trend analysis results for the terms hamburger (blue line) and cheeseburger (red line)

Below the graph are two world maps, color-coded by regional interest for Madonna (lower left) and Adele (lower right). Italy in dark blue has the highest number of searches for Madonna, which means *My Lady* in Italian. By searching for "Madonna", we might also have meant to search for the religious figure Madonna, an appellation of Mary the mother of Jesus.

Another, rather different online service that can be used for trend analysis is DataMarket,[11] which provides easy access to a treasure trove of high-quality, freely available data. Figure 2.11 shows the fertility rate in total births per woman from the 1960s to 2011. Data for Algeria, Chile, Japan, Kazakhstan, the United Arab Emirates, United Kingdom, and United States were selected via checkboxes and can be explored interactively. The graph shows the enormous change over only 50 years: until the 1980s, Algeria (blue) had an average birth per woman of 7.4; since then it has decreased to a little bit above two. Japan (yellow) was at about two children per woman in 1960 and now is about 1.4. In Chile (orange) the

11 http://datamarket.com

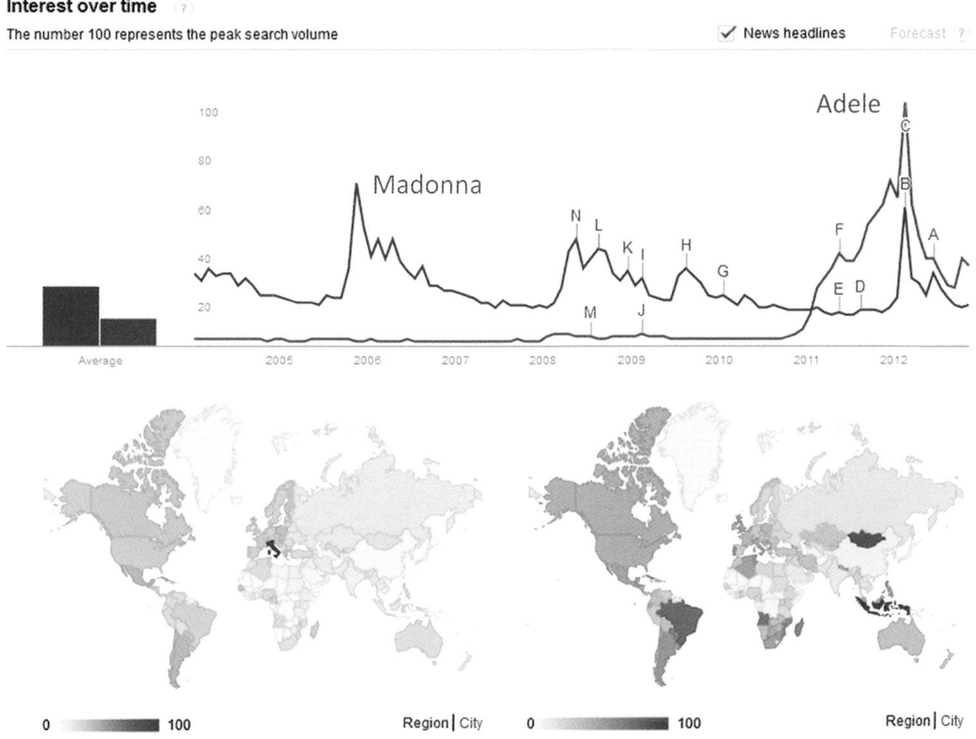

Figure 2.10 Google Trend analysis for Adele and Madonna

decrease in the number of children happened much earlier than in Algeria. Hovering over the lines brings up text boxes with data details.

It is not only interesting to understand changes in fertility rates, but also changes in population pyramids over time. Figure 2.12 shows population pyramids for 1956, 2006, and 2050 (projected) as published by Christensen et al.[12] Each depicts the number of male (blue) and female (red) persons per age. In 1956, many children were born but many of them died young. Very few people reached a high age. The impact of the two world wars (1914–1918 and 1939–1945) can be seen as well as the large number of baby boomers—people born between the years 1946 and 1964. The 2006 population pyramid shows the data 50 years later in time—baby boomers are now 40 to 50 years of age. Fewer children are born but they live to be much older. The projection for 2050 shows much more of a continuum—even fewer people are born but many reach higher ages. Note that the projection assumes a world without major world wars.

12 Christensen, Kaare, Gabriele Doblhammer, Roland Rau, and James W. Vaupel. 2009. "Ageing Populations: The Challenges Ahead." *The Lancet* 374, 9696: 1196–1208.

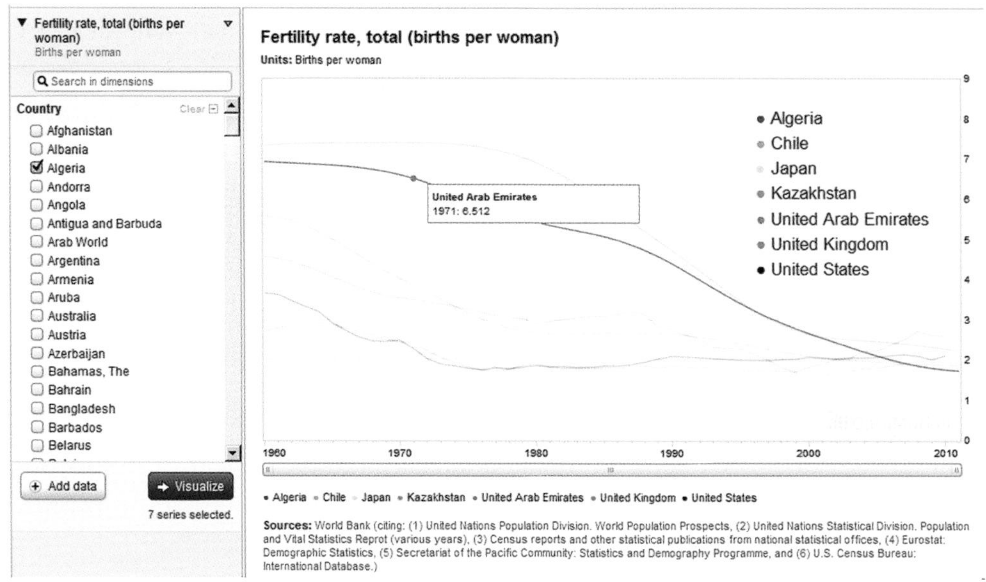

Figure 2.11 Fertility rate (births per woman) from 1960 to 2011 for different countries

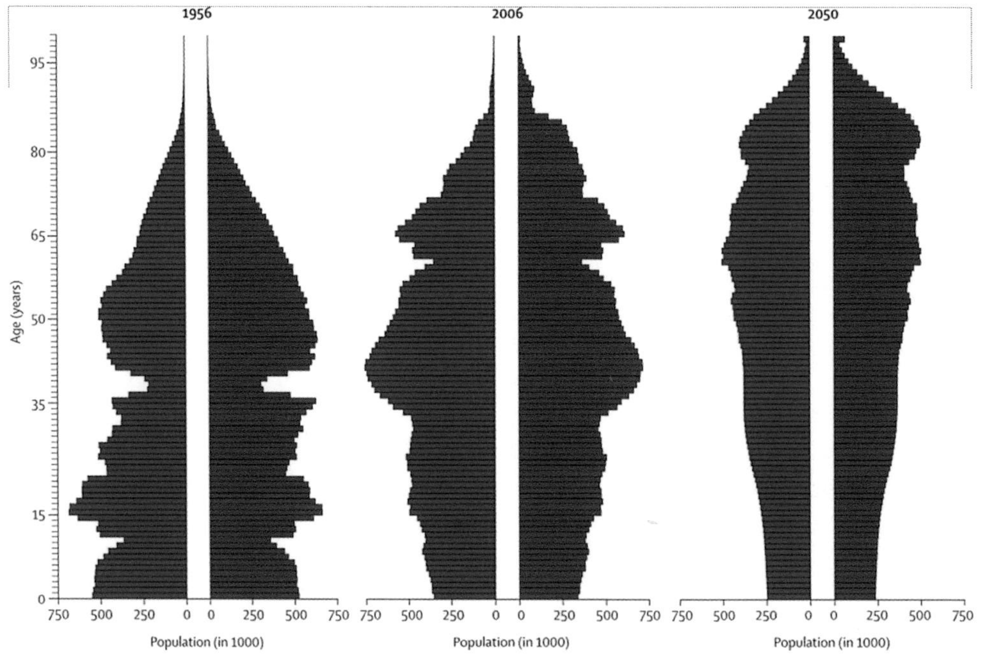

Figure 2.12 Ageing pyramids for 1956, 2006, and projected for 2050

Research by Oeppen and Vaupel from the same research team examines world life expectancy rates.[13] A key result from the paper is reproduced in Figure 2.13. The graph shows all the numbers for the record female life expectancy from 1840 to present. Horizontal black lines indicate asserted ceilings on life expectancy published by different organizations. Short vertical lines indicate the year of publication. For example, the World Bank projected that life expectancy is going to average at 82 or 83 years of age. In a later projection, they named 90 as the maximum age. Running a linear regression on all data points results in the black line that has a slope of 0.243. Extrapolations are shown as dashed lines. Limits to life expectancy seem, in fact, to be broken: Whenever a leveling-off appears likely, new advances in hygiene, medicine, or lifestyles expand life expectancy. For the last 160 years, the best female life expectancy has steadily increased by about a quarter of a year each year. That is, every 40 years later you're born, you have about 10 more years to live!

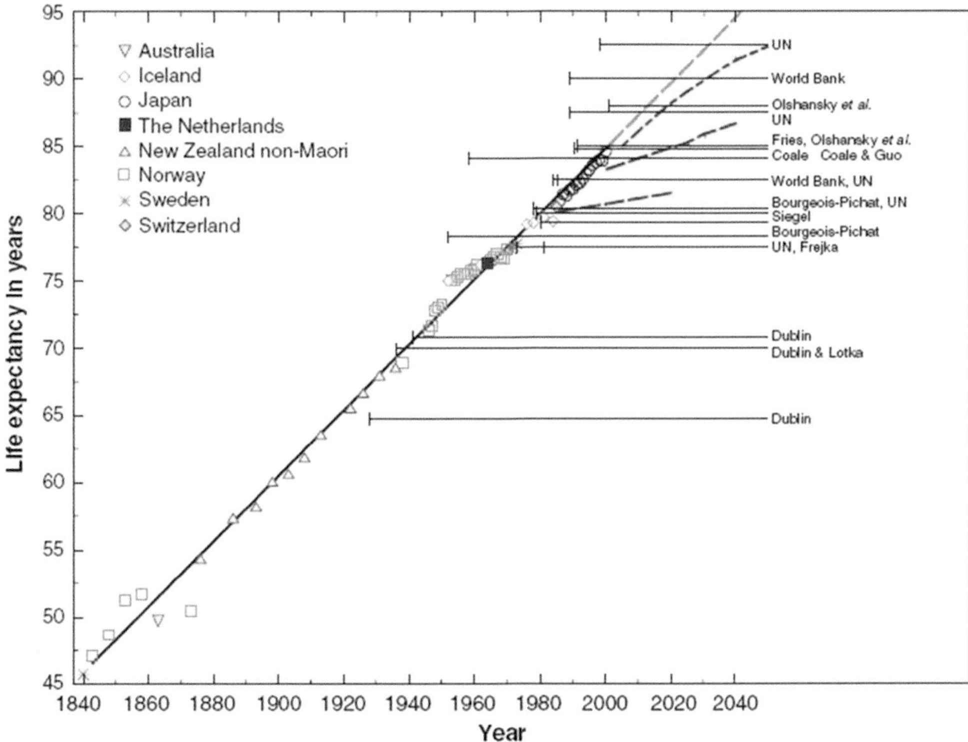

Figure 2.13 Broken limits to life expectancy

---

13 Oeppen, Jim, and James W. Vaupel. 2002. "Broken Limits to Life Expectancy." *Science* 296 (5570): 1029-31.

Taken together, temporal data can be represented in many different formats. **Line graphs** show trends over time as in the cheeseburger/hamburger and Madonna/Adele examples. **Stacked graphs** are used in the Baby Name Explorer. **Temporal bar graphs** show the beginning, end, and properties of events—they are discussed in the Hands-On section (Section 2.5). **Scatter plots**, which show relationships, will be discussed in the next section. **Histograms** are great for showing how many observations of a certain value have been made; see, for example, the number of times people are searching for Madonna or Adele (Figure 2.10, top left). Plus, time-stamped data can be overlaid over a geospatial map or topic map; see Napoleon's retreat (Figure 2.3) and evolving co-author networks (Figure 1.6).

2.3 WORKFLOW DESIGN

The design of workflows for temporal visualizations starts with a deep understanding of what stakeholders need and want (Figure 2.14; see also Section 1.2). User needs guide the identification of the types of analysis (here temporal) and levels of analysis (micro, meso, or macro). Next, data is read, analyzed, and visualized, and the visualization is deployed for validation and interpretation. We discuss each step subsequently.

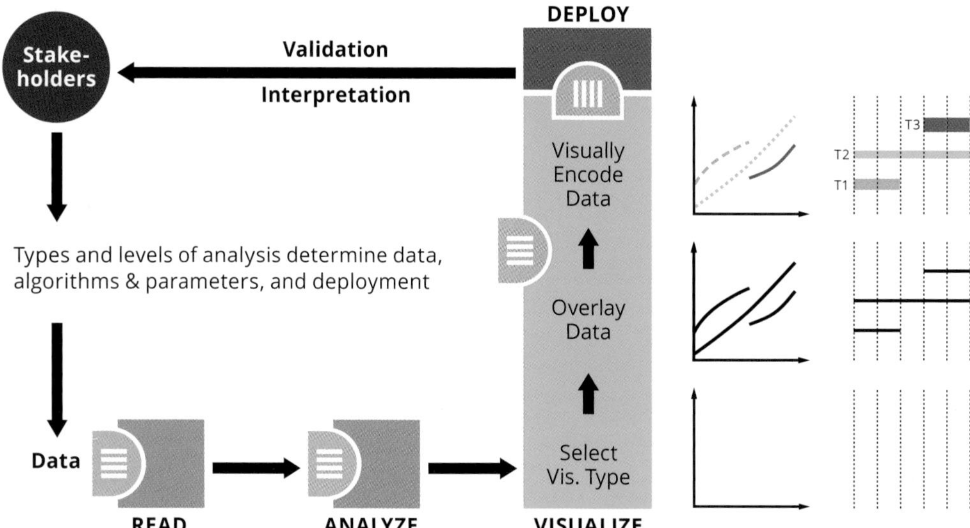

Figure 2.14 Needs-driven workflow design for temporal data

Read & Preprocess Data

There are a growing number of data repositories that provide easy access to high-quality data. For example, data.gov[14] features almost 100,000 U.S. federal datasets provided by 170 agencies. The Eurostat DataMarket,[15] discussed in Section 2.2, features European data and supports the upload and sharing of data. IBM Many Eyes[16] has more than 350,000 datasets. Gapminder Data[17] provides high-quality data on life expectancy as well as economic datasets for different countries. The Scholarly Database[18] at Indiana University supports bulk downloads for 26 million paper, patent, grant, and clinical trial records; we will use this database in the Hands-On section of this chapter. There is no shortage of places to obtain data for temporal visualizations, but data selection strongly depends on user needs.

Typically, data comes in text format, tabular format, or as a database. An example is comprehensive email data where each email has a subject header, a date, and a time stamp. It might be compiled as a text file, a spreadsheet table, or as a database. Another example is gathered Amazon book rankings over time for each book.

Much of the data preprocessing aims at normalizing data formats (e.g., making sure dates are in a consistent format). In addition, we might filter data based on attribute values (e.g., all emails received in the year 2012 or only papers that have been cited at least once). We also need to identify and remove anomalies such as large spikes in the data (e.g., caused by a major spamming of your email account). Next, we need to normalize the data. For example, if emails were harvested from different email accounts, we need to de-duplicate them and unify the data formats.

If we use data from different sources, we might need to convert units. For example, European data typically uses the metric system, and number and date formats are different from those used in the United States. Additionally, we might need to adjust currencies for inflation, if, for example, we are analyzing housing market data. We might also need to adjust different time zones if our data spans a large geographic region.

Preprocessing might also require us to integrate and interlink different data sources. For example, it might make sense for us to interlink email data and family photos taken based on their time stamps. Aggregations (e.g., by hour, day, or year, etc.) help us deal with large datasets.

---

14 http://data.gov

15 http://datamarket.com

16 http://www-958.ibm.com/software/data/cognos/manyeyes/datasets

17 http://www.gapminder.org/data

18 http://sdb.cns.iu.edu

Time Slicing

Time slicing the data is an important pre-processing step for us to show progression over time. Three different options exist (Figure 2.15). In **disjointed** time frames every single row in the original table is in exactly one time slice. An example is shown in Figure 3.2. In **overlapping** time slices some selected rows appear in multiple time slices. In **cumulative** time slices every row in a time slice appears in all later time slices. This last option is especially useful if growth is animated over time. See Figure 1.7 and its animation[19] over time for an example.

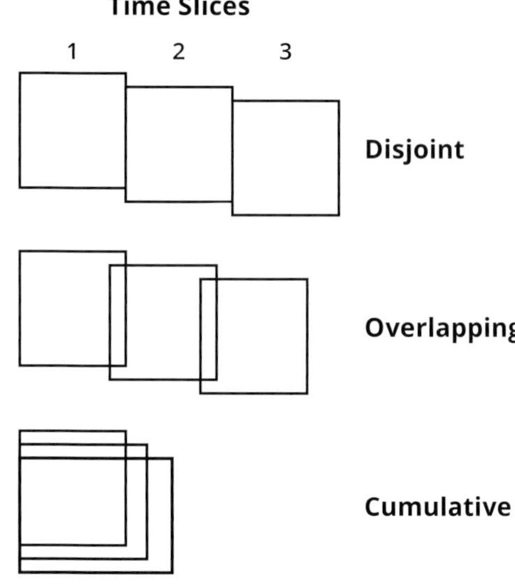

Figure 2.15 Three types of time slicing.

In some applications, time slices might be aligned with the calendar. For example, if the first event is on June 7, 2006, and yearly time slices are chosen, then the first time slice will be from June 7 to June 6 in the next year, if they are not aligned. If they are aligned, then it would be January 1 to December 31. The first time slice would be shorter because the time slice starts in June and ends in December. Depending on the purpose of the analysis, time slices might also be aligned with fiscal cycles.

Analyze & Visualize

A key concept in temporal analysis and visualization is **seasonality**. For example, Figure 2.16 shows the seasonality in chicken pox cases in New York City for the years 1931 to 1872. Every spring the number of cases goes up and in fall it goes down. There are noticeable differences in the number of chicken pox cases, and it could be interesting for us to correlate this data (e.g., with temperature data for New York during the same years).

Another more general but key concept is **correlation**. Correlation is how closely two variables are related. If one changes over time, how likely is it that the other changed over that same time period? If it's very likely, then the two are said to be highly correlated. Let's look at an example. Figure 2.17 shows the annual rate of change in gas prices from January 1997 to October 2012 for Germany, Estonia, and the other 27 countries of the European Union (EU).

---

[19] http://iv.cns.iu.edu/ref/iv04contest/Ke-Borner-Viswanath.gif

If we look closely, the yellow line for Germany seems to follow along with the orange line for the other 27 EU countries, while the blue line for Estonia bounces up and down largely independent of what the other two are doing. Just at a glance, it seems that German gas prices are highly correlated with the rest of the EU, while there's low correlation between the EU and Estonia.

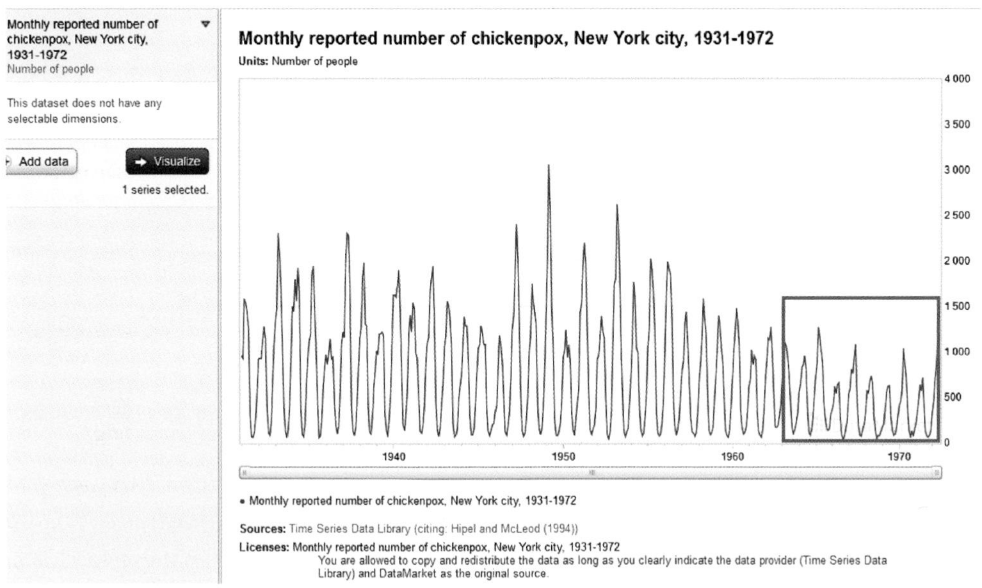

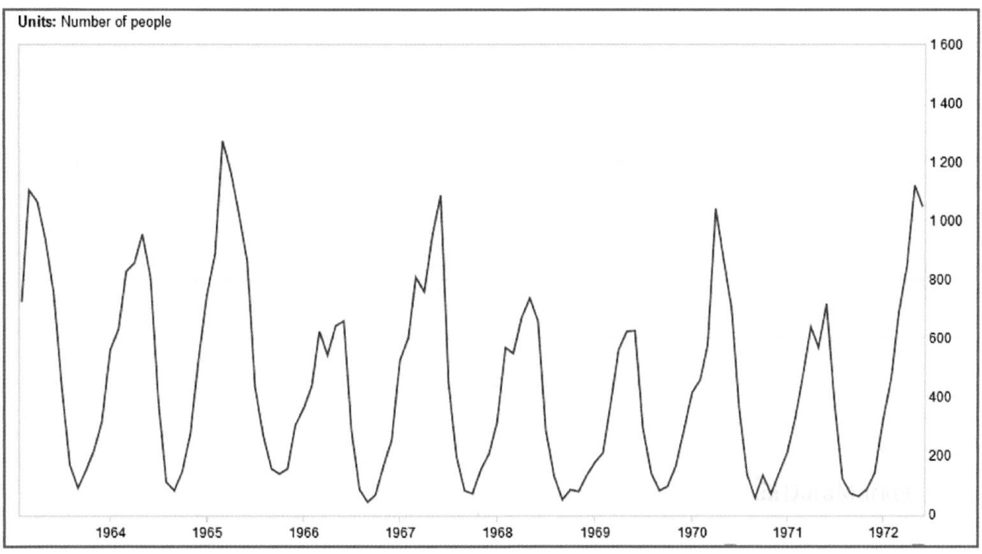

Figure 2.16 Monthly reported cases of chicken pox in New York City, 1931–1972

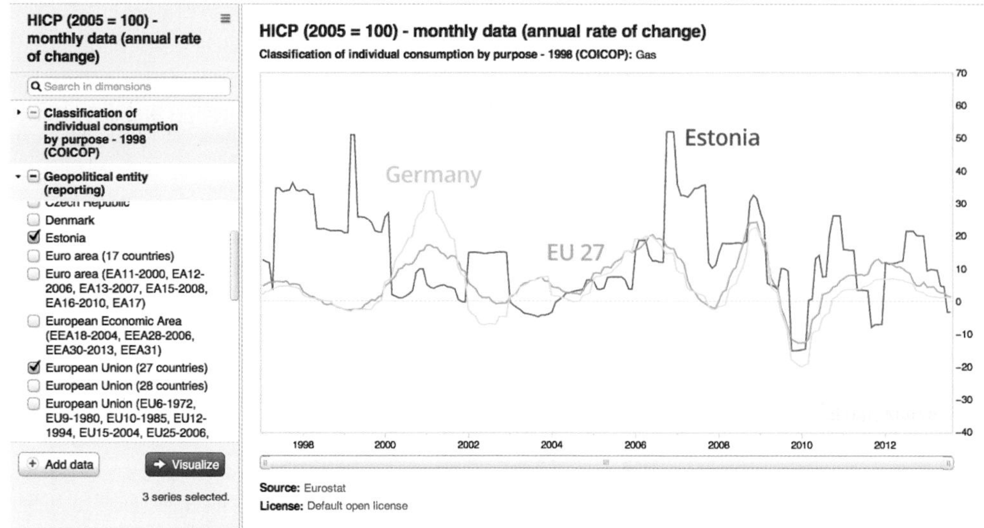

Figure 2.17 Correlation in gas prices between Germany (yellow), Estonia (blue), and the European Union (orange)[20]

Using this data downloaded from the DataMarket[21] and opened in a spreadsheet (Figure 2.18), we can calculate exactly how strong of a correlation exists between these variables. The equation used to calculate the sample correlation coefficient is:

$$\mathit{Correl}\,(X,Y) = \frac{\sum (x - \bar{x})(y - \bar{y})}{\sqrt{\sum (x - \bar{x})^2 \sum (y - \bar{y})^2}}$$

where $\bar{x}$ and $\bar{y}$ are the means of their respective time series and $\sum$ indicates to take the sum over the entire set. While we can do this manually, this is rarely calculated by hand anymore, as most spreadsheets and other data tools include functions to do this for you. In Microsoft Excel this can be done using the *CORREL* function (Figure 2.19). Notice that the temporal sequence of data pairs does not impact the results. That is, if the data rows aren't written in time order, the same correlation results.

A correlation of 1 denotes 100% direct correlation, with a change in one variable always being matched by a change in the other in the same direction, while a correlation of -1

---

20 Explore interactive chart at http://datamarket.com/en/data/set/1a6e/#!ds=1a6e!qvc=4b:qvd=10.m.e&display=line

21 DataMarket, Inc. 2013. "Gas Prices from Jan. 1997 to Oct. 2012." http://datamarket.com/en/data/set/1a6e/#!ds=1a6e!qvc=4b:qvd=10.m.e&display=line (accessed September 19)

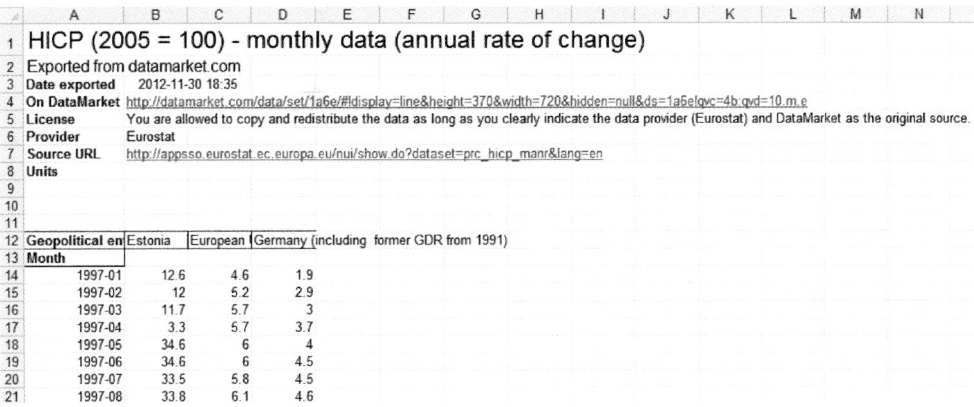

	A	B	C	D
1	HICP (2005 = 100) - monthly data (annual rate of change)			
2	Exported from datamarket.com			
3	**Date exported**	2012-11-30 18:35		
4	**On DataMarket**	http://datamarket.com/data/set/1a6e/#!display=line&height=370&width=720&hidden=null&ds=1a6elqvc=4b:qvd=10.m.e		
5	**License**	You are allowed to copy and redistribute the data as long as you clearly indicate the data provider (Eurostat) and DataMarket as the original source.		
6	**Provider**	Eurostat		
7	**Source URL**	http://appsso.eurostat.ec.europa.eu/nui/show.do?dataset=prc_hicp_manr&lang=en		
8	**Units**			
9				
10				
11				
12	**Geopolitical en**	Estonia	European	Germany (including former GDR from 1991)
13	**Month**			
14	1997-01	12.6	4.6	1.9
15	1997-02	12	5.2	2.9
16	1997-03	11.7	5.7	3
17	1997-04	3.3	5.7	3.7
18	1997-05	34.6	6	4
19	1997-06	34.6	6	4.5
20	1997-07	33.5	5.8	4.5
21	1997-08	33.8	6.1	4.6

Figure 2.18 Data on gas prices for Germany, Estonia, and the European Union downloaded from DataMarket

E15 =CORREL(C14:C203,D14:D203)

	A	B	C	D	E	F	G
11							
12	**Geopolitical en**	Estonia	European	Germany (including former GDR from 1991)			
13	**Month**						
14	1997-01	12.6	4.6	1.9			
15	1997-02	12	5.2	2.9	0.905826		
16	1997-03	11.7	5.7	3	0.049288		
17	1997-04	3.3	5.7	3.7			

Figure 2.19 Calculating the correlation between German gas prices and EU gas prices, and Estonian gas prices and EU gas prices in MS Excel

denotes a perfect inverse correlation, that is, as one goes up, the other always goes down. A correlation coefficient of 0 indicates that the two variables act independently of one another and knowing about how one is changing tells us nothing about what might be happening to the other. We illustrate this with the simple example in Figure 2.20. Assume there are three times series: A, B, and C. A and B are identical and they have a correlation factor of 1. As for B and C, there exists a negative correlation because, basically, whenever B is high, C is low, and the other way around. This negative association has a correlation of -1.

When comparing changes in fuel prices for the 27 European countries and Germany, the result is 0.9—the very high correlation we predicted earlier. For the EU and Estonia, the correlation is only 0.05, indicating that the two are largely independent of one another. A look at Figure 2.21 shows a clear trend when data are plotted between Germany and the 27 EU countries, while the same plot between Estonia and the EU countries produces a featureless cloud.

We could also use correlation analyses to show a relationship of Twitter activity to stock market behavior or publication download counts to citation counts—but be aware that

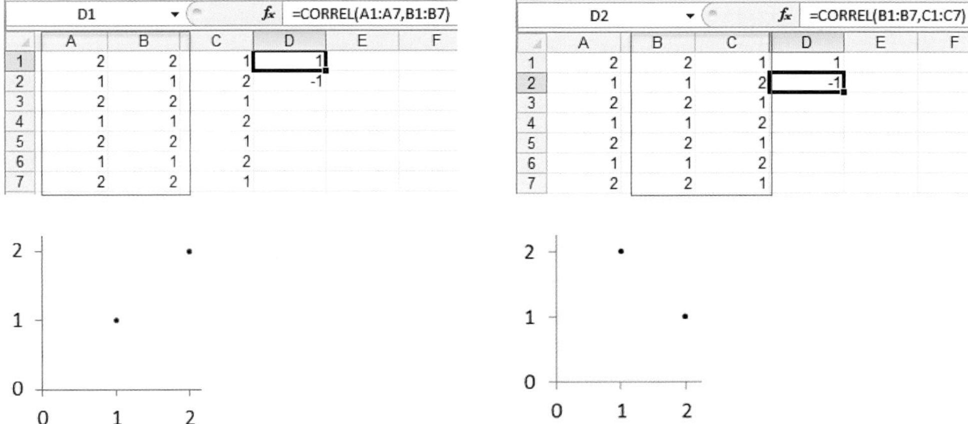

Figure 2.20 Positive (left) and negative (right) correlations

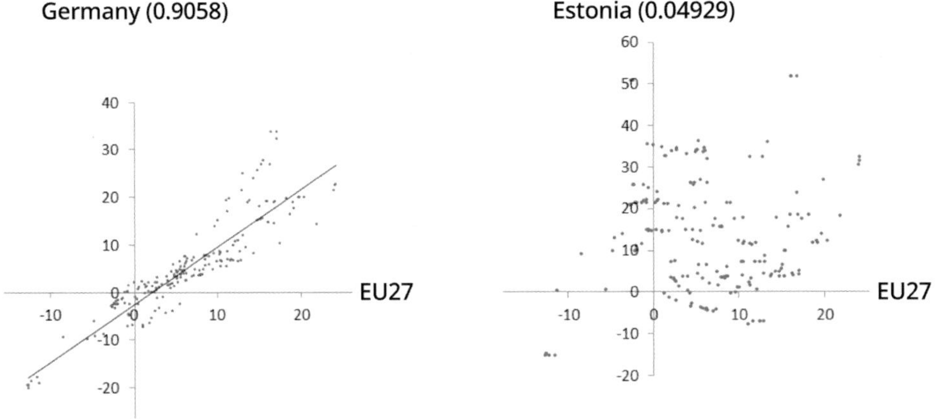

Figure 2.21 German and EU gas prices are correlated. No correlation exists between Estonian gas prices and EU gas prices

correlation does not imply causation. Whenever we have two columns of data that we think may be linked in some way, correlation analysis should come to mind as a valuable tool.

In order to visualize temporal data, we can use spreadsheet programs such as Microsoft Excel or the free Apache OpenOffice[22] to render diverse charts and graphs. We will also explore temporal bar graphs in the Hands-On part of this chapter. Try out TimeSearcher from the HCI Lab at the University of Maryland[23] as it has many features to interactively explore time series data. Another option is Tableau, which is freely available for students and supports the design of interactive online visualizations.[24]

22 http://www.openoffice.org

23 http://www.cs.umd.edu/hcil/timesearcher

24 http://www.tableausoftware.com

2.4 BURST DETECTION

In this section we introduce Kleinberg's burst detection algorithm, which helps to identify sudden increases in the usage frequency of keywords in temporal data streams.[25] The input to Kleinberg's algorithm is time-stamped text. Figure 2.22 shows a table in which the A column has a year, and the B column shows characters representing different words. The words might represent the title of a publication, they could be the subject headers of your emails, they could be book titles, or the entire text of a book written in this particular year. With time-stamped text, we can use the algorithm to identify bursts. In this particular very simple example, the word A is present in all years, so it does not burst (see green horizontal line in the graph of Figure 2.22). However, B occurs in the beginning, then again—and actually stronger—between 1985 and 1988, and then never seen again. C only appears between 1997 and 2002. The graph also shows the bursts over time as dashed lines. B has two bursts—one smaller one and then a larger one. C is basically zero until it bursts in the very end of the dataset.

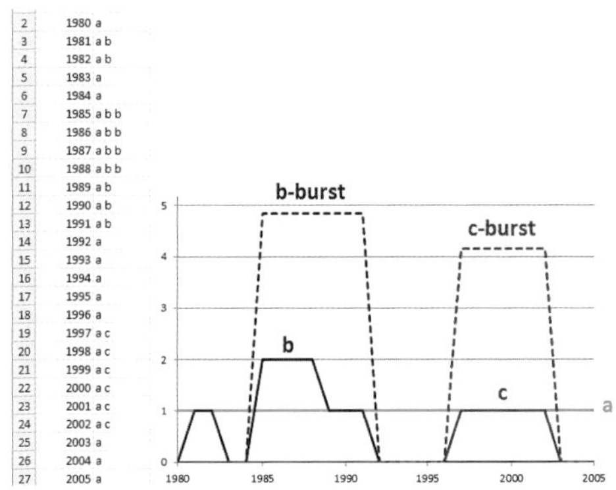

2	1980 a
3	1981 a b
4	1982 a b
5	1983 a
6	1984 a
7	1985 a b b
8	1986 a b b
9	1987 a b b
10	1988 a b b
11	1989 a b
12	1990 a b
13	1991 a b
14	1992 a
15	1993 a
16	1994 a
17	1995 a
18	1996 a
19	1997 a c
20	1998 a c
21	1999 a c
22	2000 a c
23	2001 a c
24	2002 a c
25	2003 a
26	2004 a
27	2005 a

Figure 2.22 Usage frequency and bursts

If we run burst detection using the Sci2 Tool, then the output is a table with burst begin and end dates and a burst weight indicating the level of "burstiness." We can use burst weight to threshold; for example, we might use only those words that have a burst higher than three. Please see the Hands-On Section 2.6 of this chapter for detailed examples and workflows. Next, we discuss the inner workings of the burst detection algorithm.

The algorithm reads a stream of events (e.g., a set of keywords and a time stamp). Assuming there is an imaginary finite automaton that generates this event stream, a hidden Markov model is used to find the optimal sequence of states that best fits the data. The bursts are then the states of this imaginary automaton, and as soon as the sequence is known, all bursts are known. Figure 2.23 shows a sample state diagram with three states, and it takes a finite sequence of zeroes and ones as input. For each state, we have a transition arrow leading to the next state for both zero and one. Here, upon reading a symbol, this automaton would jump deterministically from one state to another by following the transition arrows. For example, when starting at S_0, if the next event in our sequence is 0, we transition to S_2. If the next event is a 1, we transition to state 1. At S_1, two options exist—a 0 event transitions us to S_2, a 1 keeps us at S_1.

[25] Kleinberg, Jon M. 1999. "Authoritative Sources in a Hyperlinked Environment." *Journal of the ACM* 46, 5: 604–632.

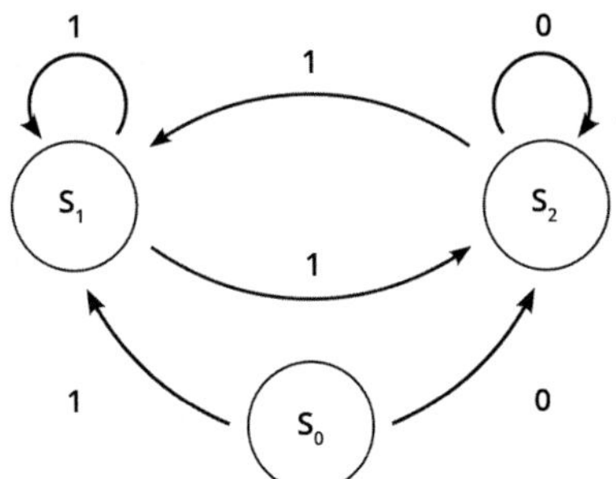

Figure 2.23 Sample state diagram with three states

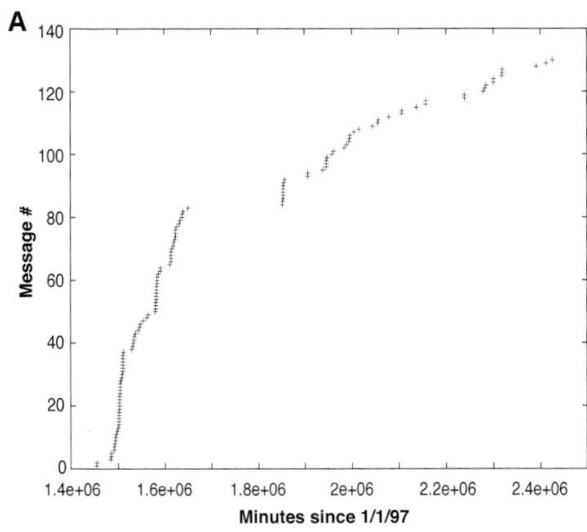

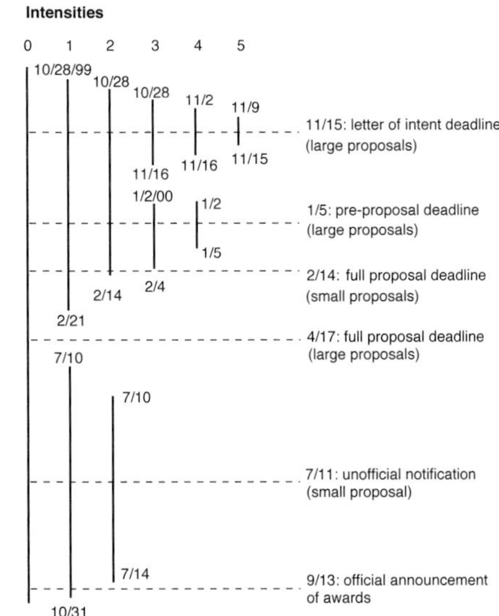

Figure 2.24 Cumulative number of received email messages (A), burst intensities and external events (B)

Kleinberg[26] exemplifies burst detection using a set of emails. The dataset covers a time frame during which he needed to make a number of deadlines—particularly for two grant proposals, one small and one large—submitted to the U.S. National Science Foundation. Figure 2.24 (top) shows the cumulative number of messages he received. The image below shows the intensities of bursts happening together with external events, such as the letter of intent deadline, the pre-proposal deadline, and the full proposal deadline. There is a burst around the time when he is telling his collaborators that they potentially got the award. And then there's the final, official announcement.

We can use burst detection in many applications. We can apply it to identify spikes of activity in Twitter activity, Flickr data, or news data streams. We can use it to identify surges of interest in the number of citations to a specific publication, the amount of funding awarded to an institution, or the number of your new friends/collaborators participating in a MOOC. Furthermore, we can **correlate** burst analysis results with external events such as deadlines to gain a richer understanding of the data in its real-world context.

26 Kleinberg, Jon. 2002. "Bursty and Hierarchical Structure in Streams." In *Proceedings of the 8th ACM/SIGKDD International Conference on Knowledge Discovery and Data Mining*, 91–101. New York: ACM Press.

Kleinberg's algorithm has also been used to map and possibly predict future topic bursts in publications. As mentioned when discussing Figure 1.3 in the previous chapter, bursts often precede high word usage. It would be interesting to re-run this very analysis on more recent data to understand if the word *protein* is truly used widely from 2002 onwards. Feel free to use the workflow detailed in Section 4.9 to replicate this analysis or to run your very own studies.

Be aware that burst detection might pick up on trends in language use or the construction of text. For example, patents are written in a very different style than publications, so the algorithm will pick up on this.

Self-Assessment

1. What visualization should be used to show trends over time?
   a. Line graph
   b. Temporal bar graph
   c. Scatter plot
   d. Histogram
2. What visualization should be used to show how many observations of a certain value have been made?
   a. Line graph
   b. Temporal bar graph
   c. Scatter plot
   d. Histogram
3. When using disjoint time slices,
   a. Every row in the original table is in exactly one time slice.
   b. Selected rows are in multiple time slices.
   c. Every row in a time slice is in all later time slices.
4. In Kleinberg's burst detection algorithm, how are bursts defined?
   a. As states of an imaginary finite automaton.
   b. A mode of operation where events occur in rapid succession.
   c. Sudden increases in the frequency of state transitions.

Chapter 2: Hands-On Section

2.5 TEMPORAL BAR GRAPH: NSF FUNDING PROFILES

Data Types & Coverage	
Time Frame:	1978-2010
Region:	Indiana University
Topical Area:	Informatics, Miscellaneous
Network Type:	Not Applicable

Analysis Types/Levels	● (small)	● (medium)	● (large)
Temporal	X		
Geospatial			
Topical			
Network			

In this section we show how to read National Science Foundation (NSF) funding data for an individual researcher to visualize the number, duration, dollar amount, and type of funded projects over time. The workflow can be run for multiple researchers in support of comparison; it can also be run for entire departments, schools, geospatial locations, or countries.

As an example, we will use the extensive NSF funding record of Geoffrey Fox, School of Informatics and Computing, Indiana University. Load the file *GeoffreyFox.csv*[27] into Sci2 using *File* > *Load*. Alternative files are provided for other researchers at Indiana University: *MichaelMcRobbie.nsf* and *BethPlale.nsf* in the same directory. You can load these as well, but we will not use them for this specific workflow.

Select *GeoffreyFox.csv* in the 'Data Manager'. Run *Visualization* > *Temporal* > *Temporal Bar Graph* using the parameters shown in Figure 2.25. Notice that the European date format (Day-Month-Year) has been selected to align with the NSF date format.

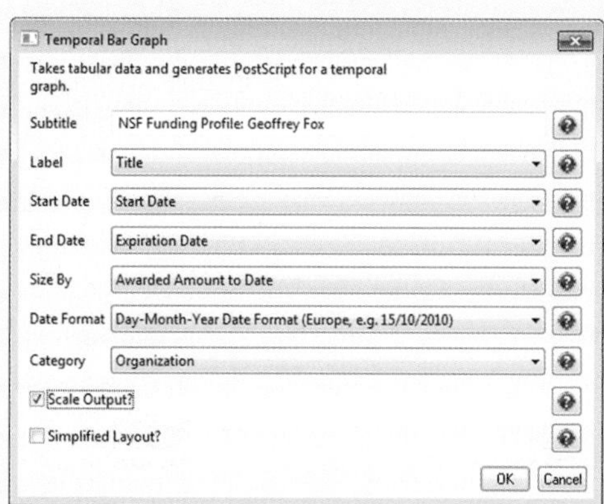

Figure 2.25 Generating a temporal bar graph of Fox's NSF funded projects

The visualization is rendered into a PostScript file in the 'Data Manager'. To view this file, save it by right-clicking on the file and selecting 'Save'. Convert the PostScript file to a PDF for viewing; see p. 286 in the Appendix for further instructions. All 26 project records are shown; each is represented by a horizontal bar

27 *yoursci2directory*/sampledata/scientometrics/nsf

that starts at the 'Start Date' and ends at the 'Expiration Date', with time running from left to right (Figure 2.26). Each project bar is color-coded by the 'Organization' at which Fox worked or collaborated with (see color legend in lower left corner). Each bar is labeled on the left with the 'Title' of the project. The area size of each bar represents the awarded dollar amount. We can see number of large grants; the top two are Extensible Terascale Facility (ETF): Indiana-Purdue Grid (IP-grid) at $1,517,430 and MRI: Acquisition of PolarGrid: Cyberinfrastructure for Polar Science at $1,964,049.

Temporal bar graphs are useful for visualizing an individual researcher's funding profile, comparing the funding profile of multiple researchers, or visualizing the funding profile of an entire institution.

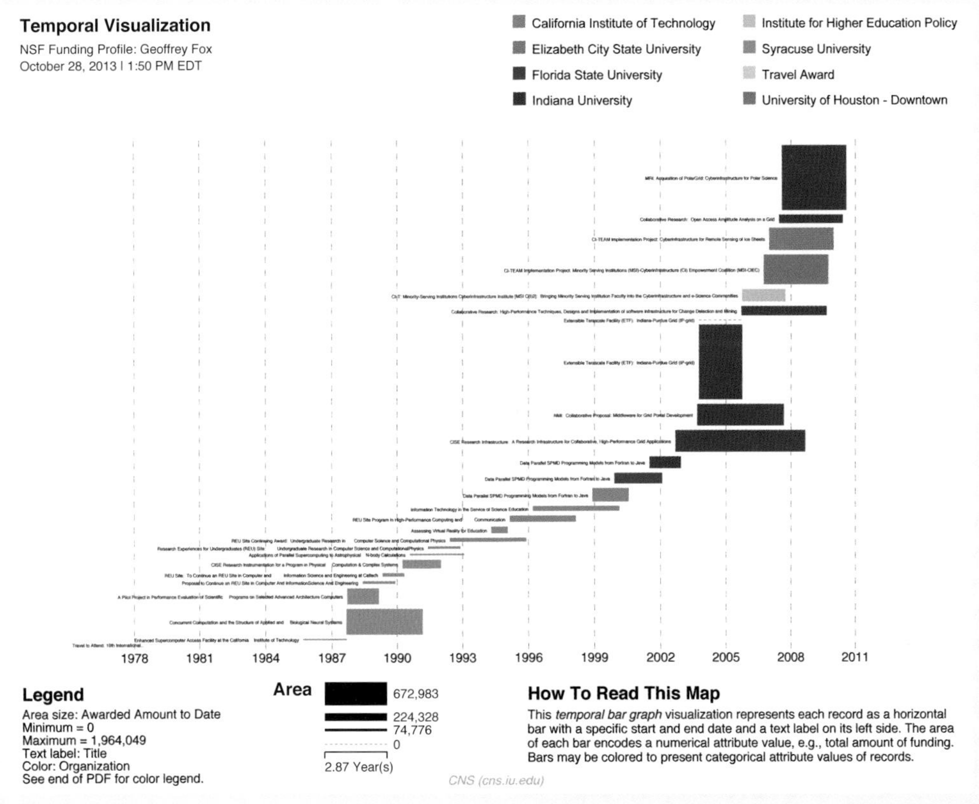

Figure 2.26 Temporal bar graph of Geoffrey Fox's NSF profile (http://cns.iu.edu/ivmoocbook14/2.26.pdf)

2.6 BURST DETECTION IN PUBLICATION TITLES

Data Types & Coverage	
Time Frame:	1990-2006
Region:	Multiple Universities
Topical Area:	Multiple
Network Type:	Not Applicable

Analysis Types/Levels	• (small)	● (medium)	⬤ (large)
Temporal	X		
Geospatial			
Topical			
Network			

We can understand a publication dataset as a discrete time series—a sequence of events/observations that are ordered in time. Observations exist for regularly spaced intervals (e.g., each publication year). The burst detection algorithm (see Section 2.4) identifies sudden increases or "bursts" in the frequency-of-use of entities over time. This algorithm identifies topics, terms, or concepts that increased in usage quickly, were more active for a period of time, and then faded away. These "bursting" entities can generally be considered important within the dataset.

We will use a dataset containing publications authored or co-authored by Alessandro Vespignani from 1990 to 2006 to identify "bursts" in data. In 2006, the last year in this dataset, Vespignani was a physicist and Professor of Informatics and Cognitive Science at Indiana University. Over his career he has also worked at the University of Rome, Yale University, Leiden University, the International Center for Theoretical Physics, and the University of Paris-Sud. His work covers many topical areas such as informatics, complex network science and system research, physics, statistics, and epidemics.

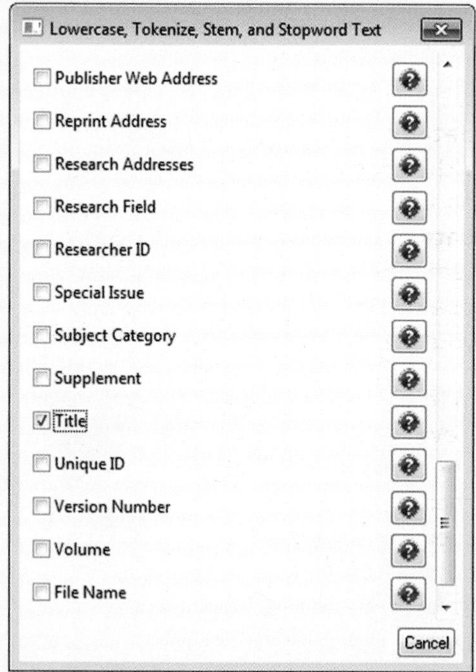

Figure 2.27 Normalizing the 'Title' field prior to burst detection

Load Alessandro Vespignani's ISI publication history into the Sci2 Tool using *File > Load*. The file is located under IVMOOC Sample Data in Section 2.5 of the Sci2 wiki.[28] We will use the title of publications to identify "bursty" terms. Since the burst

[28] http://wiki.cns.iu.edu/display/SCI2TUTORIAL/2.5+Sample+Datasets

detection algorithm is case-sensitive, it is necessary to normalize the 'Title' field before running the algorithm. Once you have loaded the *AlessandroVespignani.isi* file into the 'Data Manager', select the '101 Unique ISI Records' file and run *Preprocessing > Topical > Lowercase, Tokenize, Stem, and Stopword Text*. Scroll down the list and check the 'Title' box to indicate that you want to normalize this field (Figure 2.27).

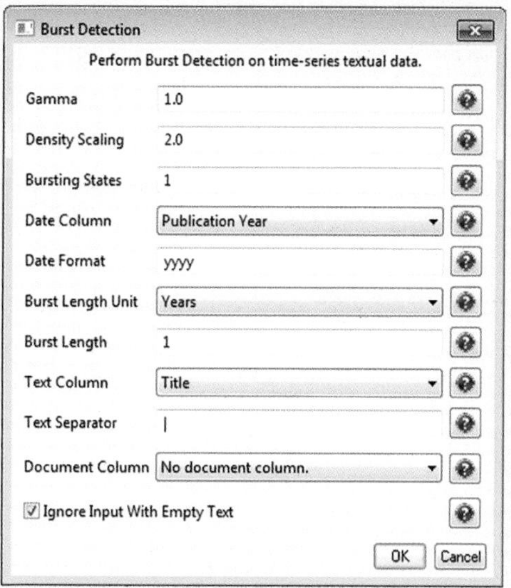

Figure 2.28 Burst detection for the 'Title' field

Select the resulting 'with normalized Title' table in the 'Data Manager' and run *Analysis > Topical > Burst Detection* and set the parameters to those shown in Figure 2.28. For more information on the parameters and how the burst detection algorithm works, see the online algorithm documentation.[29]

	A	B	C	D	E	F
1	Word	Level	Weight	Length	Start	End
2	free	1	3.232962	3	2002	2004
3	critic	1	4.31613	6	1993	1998
4	complex	1	3.538345	6	2001	
5	transform	1	4.492169	6	1990	1995
6	sandpil	1	4.650639	3	1998	2000
7	approach	1	3.381684	4	1994	1997
8	self	1	3.764748	6	1993	1998
9	fractal	1	3.767573	8	1990	1997
10	network	1	12.33559	5	2002	
11	renorm	1	3.560887	5	1994	1998
12	fix	1	3.840594	6	1990	1995
13	absorb	1	3.049794	3	1998	2000

Figure 2.29 Burst detection analysis result table

A table will be created called 'Burst detection analysis (Publication Year, Title): maximum burst level 1'. Right-click on this table and select 'View' to see the data in Excel. On a Mac or a Linux system, right-click and 'Save' the file, then open using the spreadsheet program of your choice (Figure 2.29).

In this table, there are six columns: 'Word', 'Level', 'Weight', 'Length', 'Start', and 'End'. The 'Word' column identifies the specific character string that was detected as a "burst". 'Length' indicates how long the burst lasted over the selected time parameter—in this case, years. The higher burst 'Level', the more pronounced the change in word/event frequency. 'Weight' is the magnitude of this burst over its 'Length'. A higher weight could be the result of a longer 'Length', a higher 'Level', or both. 'Length' is the duration of the burst. 'Start' identifies when the burst began, according to the specified time parameter. 'End' indicates when the burst stopped. An empty value in the 'End' field indicates that the burst lasted until the last date present in the dataset. If needed for

29 http://wiki.cns.iu.edu/display/CISHELL/Burst+Detection

visualization, manually add the last year present in the dataset; in this case, 2006 was added for the words *complex* and *network* (Figure 2.30).

	A	B	C	D	E	F
1	Word	Level	Weight	Length	Start	End
2	free	1	3.232962	3	2002	2004
3	critic	1	4.31613	6	1993	1998
4	complex	1	3.538345	6	2001	2006
5	transform	1	4.492169	6	1990	1995
6	sandpil	1	4.650639	3	1998	2000
7	approach	1	3.381684	4	1994	1997
8	self	1	3.764748	6	1993	1998
9	fractal	1	3.767573	8	1990	1997
10	network	1	12.33559	5	2002	2006
11	renorm	1	3.560887	5	1994	1998
12	fix	1	3.840594	6	1990	1995
13	absorb	1	3.049794	3	1998	2000

Figure 2.30 Burst detection analysis table with 'End' data added for complex and network

Reload the file into Sci2 using *File* > *Load* selecting 'Standard csv format' in the pop-up window. Select the loaded table in the 'Data Manager' and run *Visualization* > *Temporal* > *Temporal Bar Graph* with the parameters shown in Figure 2.31.

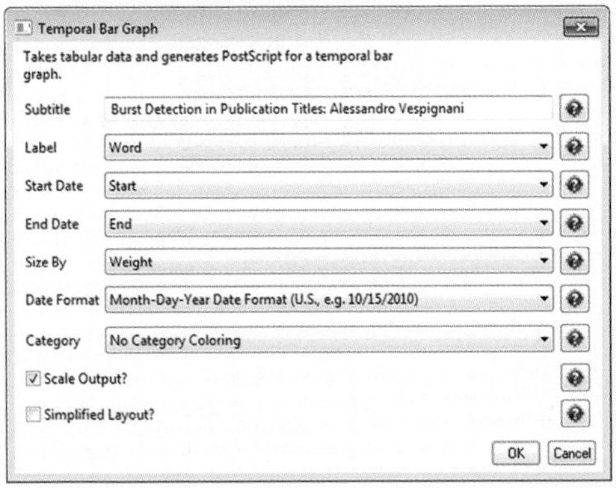

Temporal Bar Graph
Takes tabular data and generates PostScript for a temporal bar graph.
Subtitle: Burst Detection in Publication Titles: Alessandro Vespignani
Label: Word
Start Date: Start
End Date: End
Size By: Weight
Date Format: Month-Day-Year Date Format (U.S., e.g. 10/15/2010)
Category: No Category Coloring
Scale Output?
Simplified Layout?
OK Cancel

Figure 2.31 Parameters for visualizing burst using a temporal bar graph

The Temporal Bar Graph visualization will be rendered as a PostScript file in the 'Data Manager'. Right-click on the file in the 'Data Manager' and select 'Save.' Convert the file to a PDF for viewing; see p. 286 in the Appendix for further instructions.

The visualization shows a change in the research focus of Alessandro Vespignani for publications beginning in 2001 (Figure 2.32). For example, the bursting terms *fractal*, *growth*, *transform*, and *fix* starting in 1990 are related to Vespignani's PhD dissertation in physics entitled "Fractal Growth and Self-Organized Criticality." Other bursts also related to physics follow these, such as *sandpil*. After 2001, bursting terms such as *complex*, *network*, and *free* appear, signifying a change in Vespignani's research area from physics to complex networks, with a larger number of publications on topics such as weighted networks and scale-free networks.

To see the impact of different parameter values, run the burst algorithm again for the same dataset but with a different 'Gamma' value, which controls the ease with which the automaton can change states. With a smaller gamma value, more bursts will be generated. Select the table 'with normalized Title' in the 'Data Manager' and run *Analysis* > *Topical* > *Burst Detection* with the parameters shown in Figure 2.33.

Running the algorithm with these parameters will generate a new table named 'Burst detection analysis (Publication Year, Title): maximum burst level 1.2' in the 'Data Manager'. Right-click on the table and select 'View' (Figure 2.34).

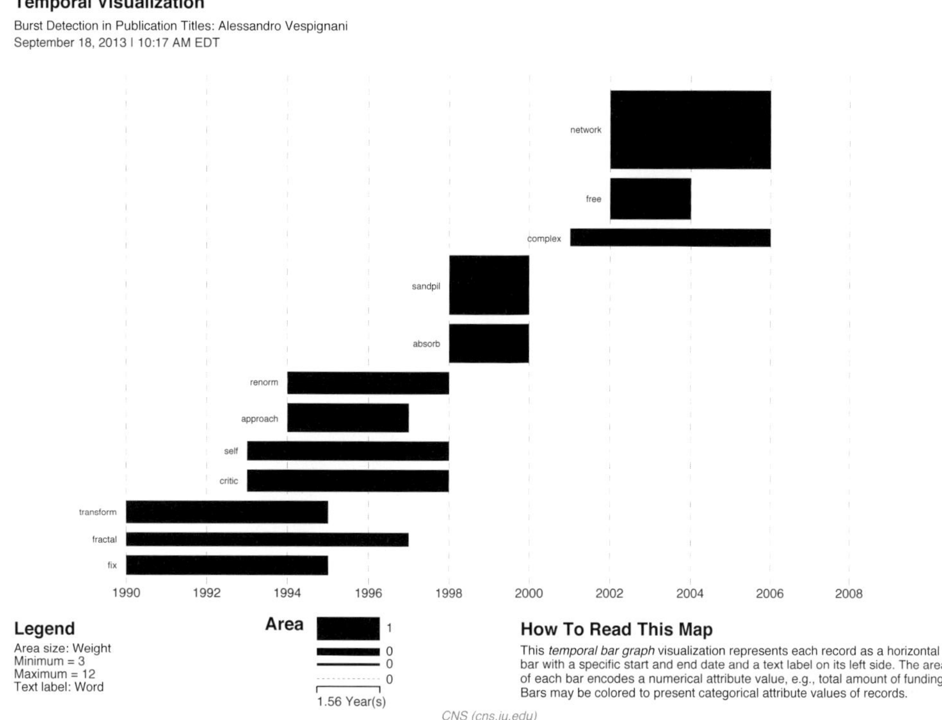

Figure 2.32 Temporal bar graph visualization of bursts in titles of papers from Alessandro Vespignani (http://cns.iu.edu/ivmoocbook14/2.32.pdf)

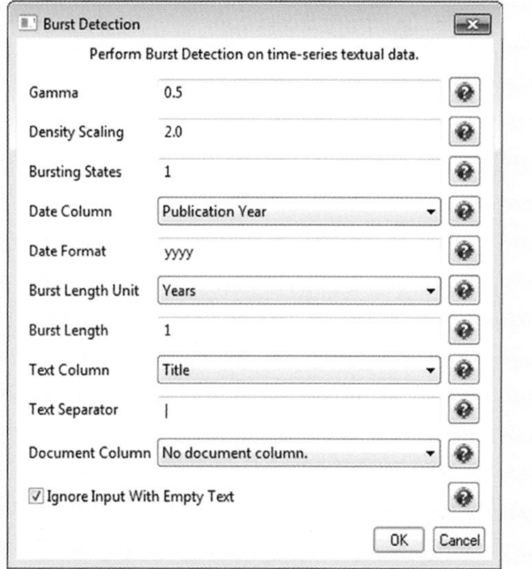

Figure 2.33 Burst detection for the 'Title' field with 'Gamma' value set to 0.5

	A	B	C	D	E	F
1	Word	Level	Weight	Length	Start	End
2	free	1	3.232962	3	2002	2004
3	epidem	1	2.532198	6	2001	
4	disloc	1	2.267251	2	2001	2002
5	system	1	1.45763	4	1996	1999
6	critic	1	4.31613	6	1993	1998
7	complex	1	3.538345	6	2001	
8	transform	1	4.492169	6	1990	1995
9	conserv	1	1.972471	3	1998	2000
10	field	1	1.834723	4	1997	2000
11	fractur	1	1.593632	6	1994	1999
12	dynam	1	2.404396	2	2001	2002
13	forest	1	1.809792	3	1995	1997
14	phase	1	2.446386	1	2000	2000
15	weight	1	2.716894	3	2004	
16	aggreg	1	2.50294	5	1991	1995
17	sandpil	1	4.650639	3	1998	2000
18	approach	1	3.381684	4	1994	1997
19	growth	1	2.839977	8	1990	1997
20	limit	1	1.45763	5	1991	1995
21	self	1	3.764748	6	1993	1998
22	similar	1	1.45763	5	1991	1995

Figure 2.34 Burst detection analysis table for 'Gamma' value set to 0.5

Again, where the 'End' field is empty, manually add the last year present in the dataset—in this case, 2006 (Figure 2.35).

Save the modified CSV file and load it into Sci2 using *File > Load*. Select 'Standard csv format' in the pop-up window. A new table will appear in the 'Data Manager'; select it and run *Visualization > Temporal > Temporal Bar Graph*, using the same parameters shown in Figure 2.31. A new PostScript file containing the temporal bar graph will appear in the 'Data Manager'. 'Save' it as a PostScript file and then convert it to a PDF for viewing (Figure 2.36).

As expected, a larger number of bursts appear, and the new bursts have a smaller

	A	B	C	D	E	F
1	Word	Level	Weight	Length	Start	End
2	free	1	3.232962	3	2002	2004
3	epidem	1	2.532198	6	2001	2006
4	disloc	1	2.267251	2	2001	2002
5	system	1	1.45763	4	1996	1999
6	critic	1	4.31613	6	1993	1998
7	complex	1	3.538345	6	2001	2006
8	transform	1	4.492169	6	1990	1995
9	conserv	1	1.972471	3	1998	2000
10	field	1	1.834723	4	1997	2000
11	fractur	1	1.593632	6	1994	1999
12	dynam	1	2.404396	2	2001	2002
13	forest	1	1.809792	3	1995	1997
14	phase	1	2.446386	1	2000	2000
15	weight	1	2.716894	3	2004	2006
16	aggreg	1	2.50294	5	1991	1995
17	sandpil	1	4.650639	3	1998	2000
18	approach	1	3.381684	4	1994	1997
19	growth	1	2.839977	8	1990	1997

Figure 2.35 Burst detection analysis table with End data added for *epidem*, *complex*, *weight*, *global*, and *network*.

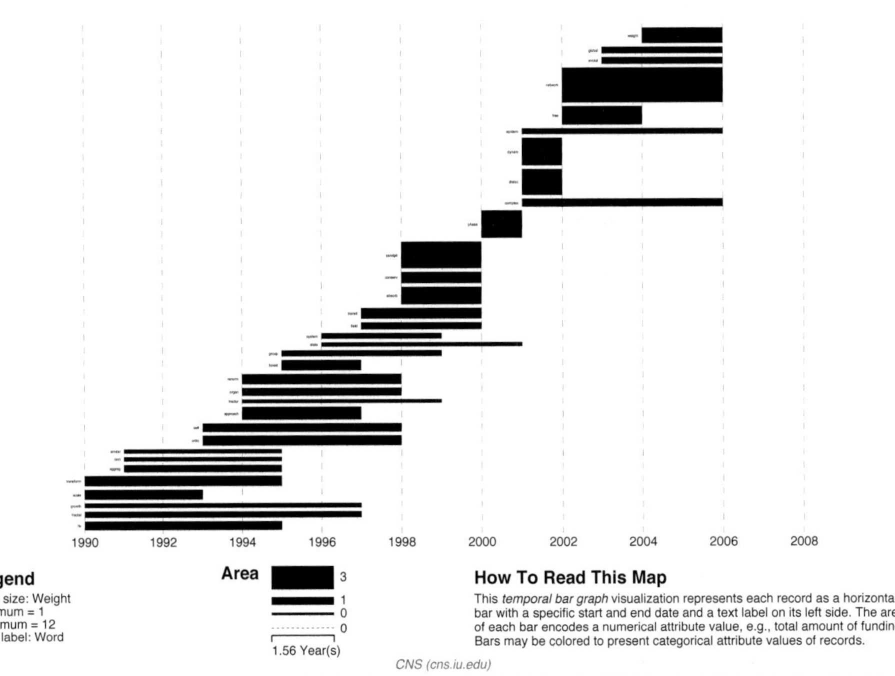

Figure 2.36 Temporal bar graph of burst detection in the titles of articles from Alessandro Vespignani (http://cns.iu.edu/ivmoocbook14/2.36.pdf)

weight than those depicted in the first graph. These smaller, more numerous bursting terms permit a more detailed examination of patterns and trends. The *protein* burst starting in 2003, for example, indicates the year in which Vespignani started to work with protein-protein interaction networks, while the burst *epidem*—also from 2001—is related to the application of complex network theory to the analysis of epidemic phenomena in biological networks.

 **Homework**

Register for and login to the Scholarly Database (http://sdb.cns.iu.edu). Once registration is completed, an email with login information will be sent.

Search for publications on "mesothelioma" a rare form of cancer that is most commonly caused by exposure to asbestos. In the 'Search' interface select the 'MEDLINE' dataset, all years (default), enter "mesothelioma" in the 'Title' field, and click on the 'Search' button (Figure 2.37).

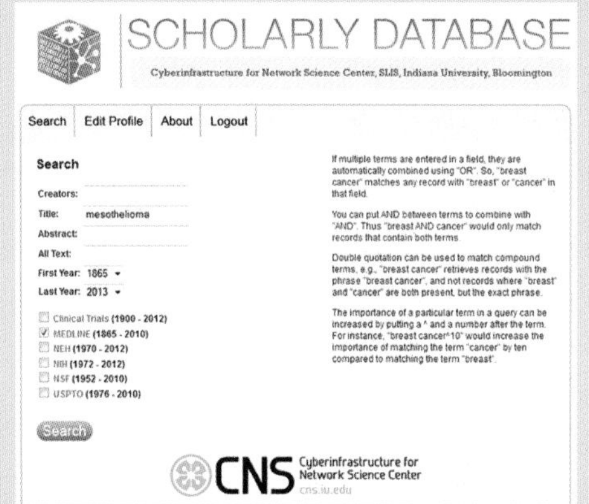

Figure 2.37 SDB 'Search' Interface

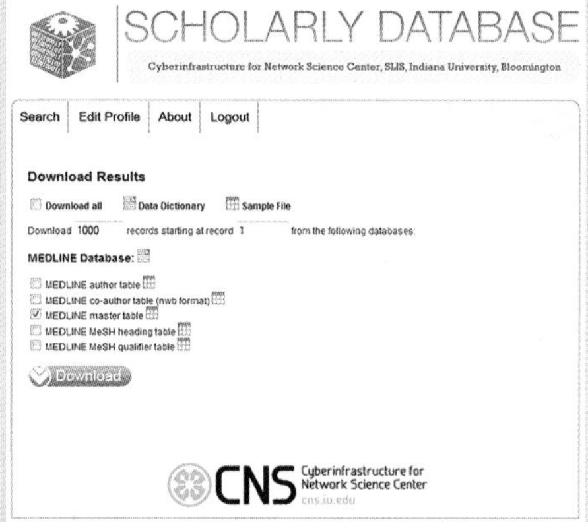

Figure 2.38 SDB 'Download Results' Interface

The results page, not shown here, will show a listing of relevant publications. Select 'Download' to bring up the 'Download Results' page (Figure 2.38) with a listing of available download formats. Click 'Download' to save the first thousand results, that is, the top 1,000 most relevant publications, and make sure the 'MEDLINE' master table is selected.

Unzip the folder and load the CSV file into Sci2 to conduct burst detection, analogous to the one conducted in the previous section. (Do not forget to normalize the 'article_title' column.) To interpret the visualization, you might want to consult the Wikipedia article on mesothelioma.[30]

30 http://en.wikipedia.org/wiki/Mesothelioma

Chapter Three

"WHERE": Geospatial Data

Chapter 3: Theory Section

In this chapter, we explore geospatial data analysis and visualization, which originated in geography and cartography but are increasingly common in statistics, information visualization, and many other areas of science. The analyses aim to answer "WHERE" questions that use location information to identify their position or movement over geographic space. For example, we might be interested to know where major experts are located, how they are interlinked via collaborations (Figure 1.17), or what career trajectory they took. Intangible entities, for example, an idea for a new product, might be born at a certain institution but might travel locally or abroad before being manufactured. Locations and movement can be explored at the micro (e.g., individual) to macro (e.g., country) levels.

Analogous to Chapter 2, the theory part starts with a discussion of exemplary visualizations, followed by an overview and definition of key terminology, and then an introduction and exemplification of workflow design. We will also discuss the usage of colors when designing visualizations.

3.1 EXEMPLARY VISUALIZATIONS

Geospatial visualizations have a rich history rooted in early maps. Although the early maps were imperfect, cartographers such as Herman Moll generated maps that illustrated the known world in astounding detail (Figure 3.1).[1] However, what is even more interesting is how these early cartographers handled the portions of the world that were unknown at the time, simply leaving them blank. For example, the world map created by Moll in 1736 leaves major portions of the coastline of Australia undrawn. Other map makers occluded unknown territories by big clouds or decorative elements.

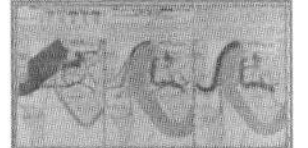

The next example shows three maps of European raw cotton imports (Figure 3.2).[2] They were created by Joseph Minard, the French civil engineer whose influential map of Napoleon's march to Moscow we examined in Chapter 2 (Figure 2.3). In his life, he created over 50 maps, looking at, among other things, differential price rates for the transport of goods, as shown here, but also at diffusion patterns of people over time and space. Shown below is the seventh and final version in a series of maps illustrating the impact of the American Civil War from 1861 to 1865 on European cotton trade. The flow of raw cotton prior to the war is shown on the left, during the war is shown in the middle, and after the

---

1 Moll, Herman. 1736. *Atlas Minor. Or a New and Curious Set of Sixty-Two Maps. . . .* London: Thos. Bowles and John Bowles.

2 Robinson, Arthur H. 1967. "The Thematic Maps of Charles Joseph Minard." *Imago Mundi: A Review of Early Cartography* 21: 95–108.

war is shown on the right. The different bands represent the different flows of cotton. For example, the blue band in the left map represents the enormous amount of cotton coming from America to Europe before the war. During the war (middle map) export blockades changed global trade patterns—Europe relied more on cotton from other countries, such as India and China (orange band) but also Egypt (brown band). Even after the war ended (right map), the flow of cotton from America is much smaller than before the war.

While many early cartographers faced challenges that included a lack of knowledge of certain parts of the world, modern researchers working in information visualization face a new set of challenges, such as data coverage and quality across the area that they would like to study, analyze, and visualize. For example, the map by Michael Hamburger and his team shows tectonic movements and earthquake hazard predictions (Figure 3.3).[3] In some cases, data coverage is poor, such as in Africa, where there are many blank spots. Conversely, in Japan, where there are many seismic sensors buried in the ground, the data coverage and quality are extremely high.

The goal of many visualizations is to aid in strategic decision making. An excellent example is the map shown in Figure 3.4. It was created to help realign the Boston maritime traffic separation scheme (TSS) so that right and other baleen whales have a lower risk of being struck by ships, ultimately having a major impact on survival rates in whales. The map shows the old TSS (dashed), or, the waterway where ships would travel—through areas of high baleen whale density. The newly proposed traffic corridor (solid line) actively avoids these high-density areas to decrease the number of encounters between whales and ships. The TSS shift was accepted by the United Nations' International Maritime Organization in December 2006 and became active in July 2007.

Another map that facilitates strategic decision making shows the impact of air travel on the global spread of infectious diseases (Figure 3.5).[4] On the top left, we see the spreading pattern of Black Death in the fourteenth century. The disease spread through personal contacts and at the rate that individuals moved across Europe. That is, the disease traveled in waves, represented on the map by lines, labeled with the corresponding dates. In the upper right-hand corner of the map, we see a very different, more rapid and global disease transmission pattern—via airport hubs. Sick people might board a plane, infecting some of the fellow passengers who may go on to spread the disease to another city or country. The problem is exacerbated even further because airports tend to be in urban areas with a high population density, thus facilitating the rapid spread of disease.

---

3 UNAVCO Facility. 2010. Jules Verne Voyager. http://jules.unavco.org (accessed July 31, 2013).

4 Colizza, Vittoria, Alain Barrat, Marc Barthélemy, and Alessandro Vespignani. 2006. "The Role of the Airline Transportation Network in the Prediction and Predictability of Global Epidemics." *PNAS* 103, 7: 2015–2020.

Figure 3.1 *A New Map of the Whole World with the Trade Winds According to the Latest and Most Exact Observations* (1736) by Herman Moll (http://scimaps.org/I.3)

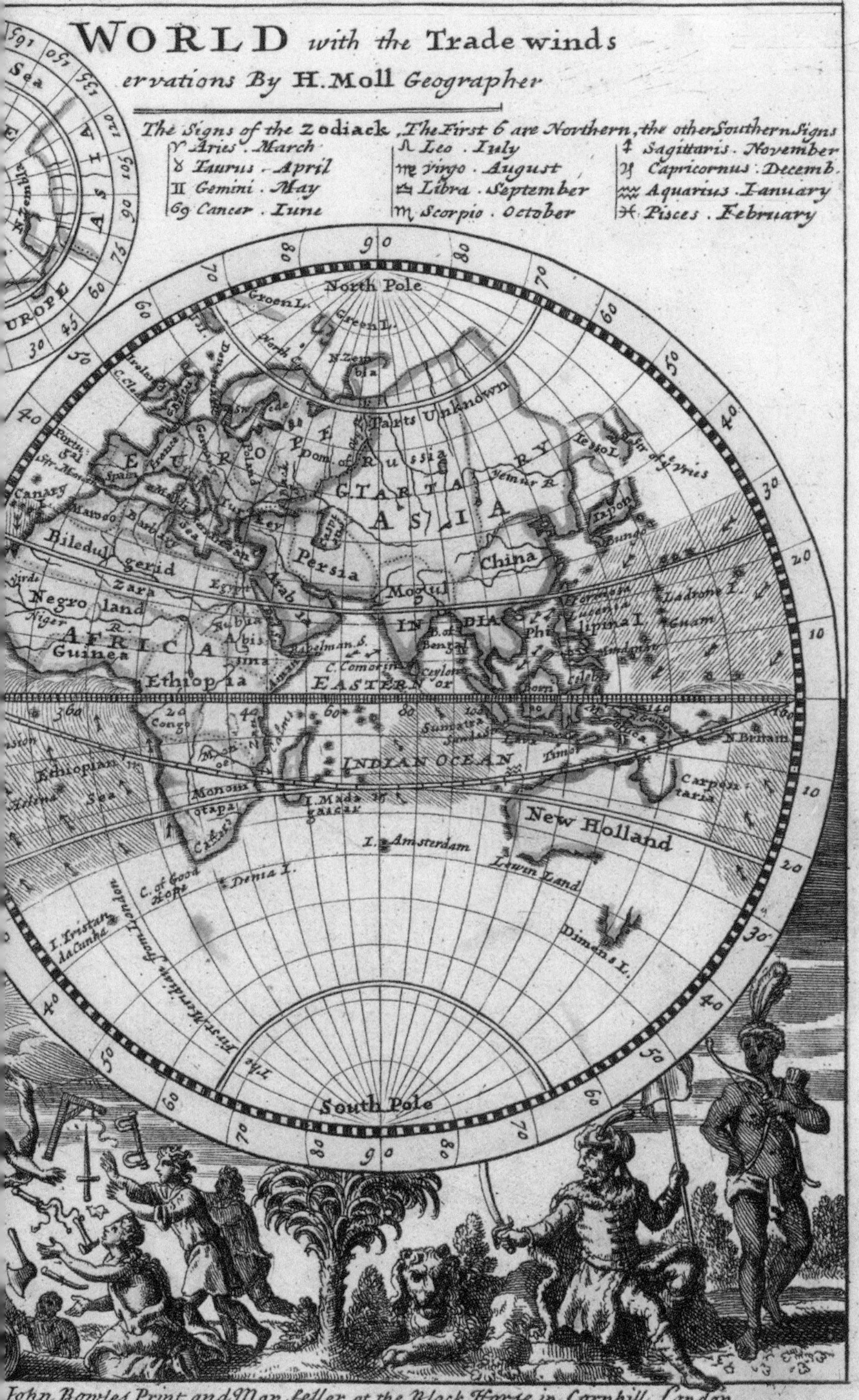
1
WORLD with the Trade winds
ervations By H.Moll Geographer
The Signs of the Zodiack, The First 6 are Northern, the other Southern Signs
Aries . March
Taurus . April
Gemini . May
Cancer . June
Leo . July
Virgo . August
Libra . September
Scorpio . October
Sagittaris . November
Capricornus . Decemb.
Aquarius . January
Pisces . February
North Pole
South Pole
EUROPE
ASIA
AFRICA
Persia
China
INDIAN OCEAN
New Holland
Ethiopian Sea
John Bowles Print and Map Seller at the Black Horse in Cornhill London

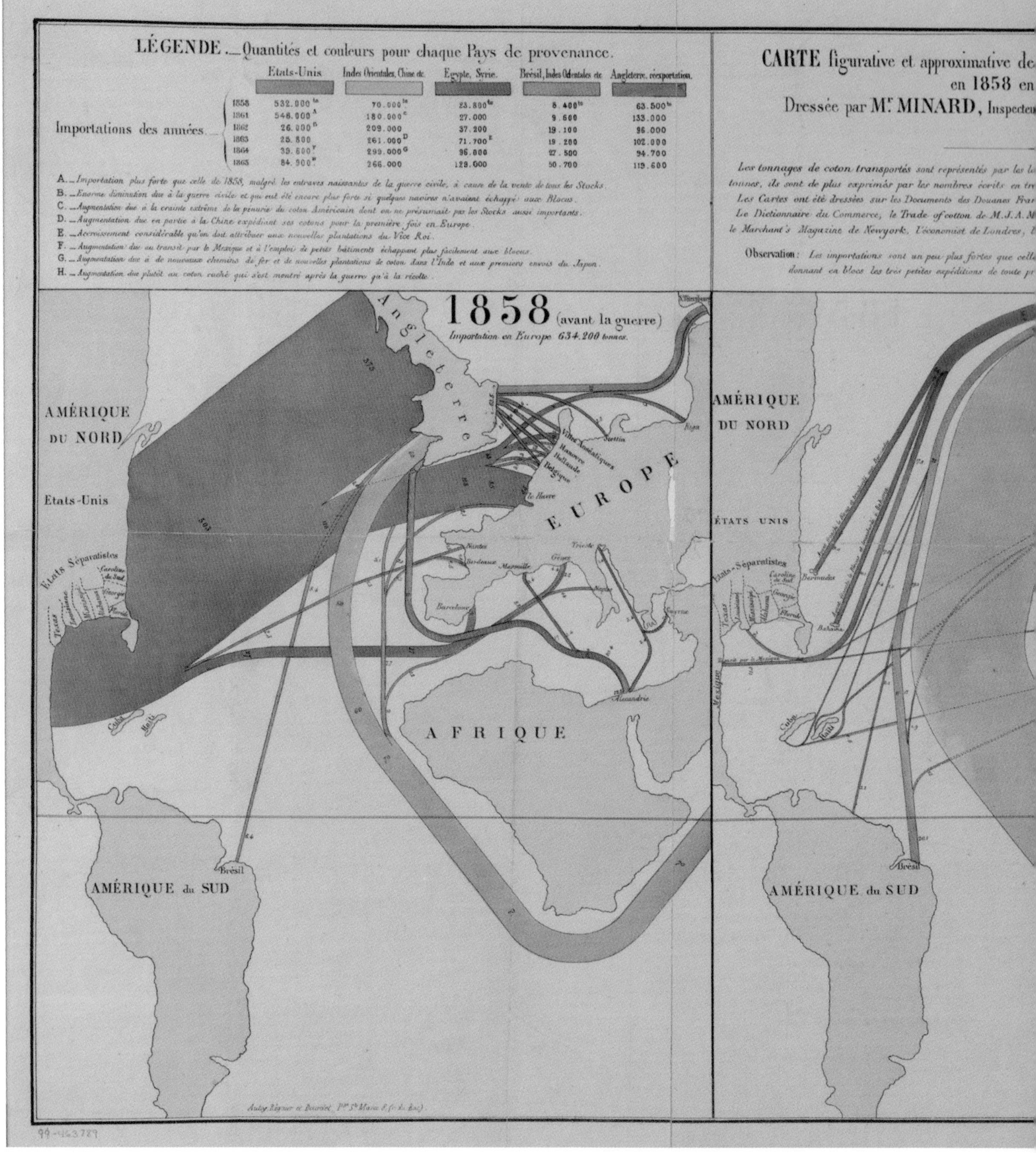

Figure 3.2 *Europe Raw Cotton Imports in 1858, 1864, and 1865* (1866) by Charles Joseph Minard (http://scimaps.org/IV.1)

s de **COTON BRUT** importées en Europe
n 1865,
Ponts et Chaussées en retraite.
is, *le 14 Mai 1866.*

nes colorées à raison d'un millimètre pour cinq milles
et dont l'unité est mille tonnes.
ses, Belges, Hollandaises, Italiennes, Autrichiennes,
circular et la publication Stolterfoht de Liverpool,
urpi d'Alexandrie etc.

arceque j'ai négligé celles d'une demie tonne et que les Douanes
'ai su à laquelle les rapporter.

De l'importation du Coton en 1865. — *La question Commerciale du coton entre dans des phases nouvelles depuis que la guerre civile des États-Unis d'Amérique a cessé.*

Toutes les parties du Globe qui envoyaient du coton en Europe en ont expédié plus en 1865 qu'en 1864, à l'exception de l'Inde et de la Chine; même des contrées méridionales de l'Europe ont cultivé plus de coton qu'ordinairement et en ont envoyé près de six mille tonnes à Marseille et à Trieste. Il y a donc aujourd'hui un surcroit d'activité générale pour la production de cette plante textile.

Toutes fois l'importation de 1865 est encore d'un sixième au dessous de ce qu'elle était avant la guerre.

Au milieu des importations diverses, un fait remarquable a lieu. Des cotons sont expédiés aujourd'hui de Bombay à Liverpool par la Mer Rouge, le chemin de fer de Suez à Alexandrie, la Méditerranée et l'Océan. La vapeur est l'unique moteur des mouvements sur les rails et sur les mers; ces transports sont indépendants de ceux de la Compagnie Péninsulaire Orientale et de la Compagnie des Messageries Impériales.

Cette voie insolite qui devance le Canal de l'Isthme de Suez, sera-t-elle encore suivie après l'exploitation du Canal? Indique-t-elle d'autres voies semblables pour le coton de l'Asie centrale traversant la Mer Noire et la Mer Caspienne? C'est ce qu'on ne peut dire.

En attendant nous assistons à la lutte opiniâtre des trois Pays grands producteurs de coton. 1° Les États-Unis qui cherchent à reconquérir le marché, mais dont le génie si actif et si entreprenant est singulièrement entravé par l'irrésolution et l'indolence des nègres affranchis qu'ils ne peuvent peut être plus employer; 2° l'Égypte qui abandonne peu à peu sa culture si ancienne du blé pour celle du coton; 3° l'Inde qui donnant une nouvelle impulsion aux plantations de coton, existant chez elle de temps immémorial, voudra à toute force se payer des énormes sacrifices qu'elle a faits en ouvrant des voies de terre, d'eau et de fer pour relier ses districts cotonniers avec ses ports maritimes.

Voila les grandes forces productives, quant aux débouchés consommateurs, qui se résument presqu'à l'Angleterre, il n'est pas probable que ce pays retombe dans la même faute d'avoir tiré d'une seule source la matière première indispensable à la vie de quatre millions de ses habitants. Sans doute il entretiendra entre les producteurs rivaux une concurrence si utile pour lui et pour l'Europe, et nous pouvons espérer de la voir continuer longtemps.

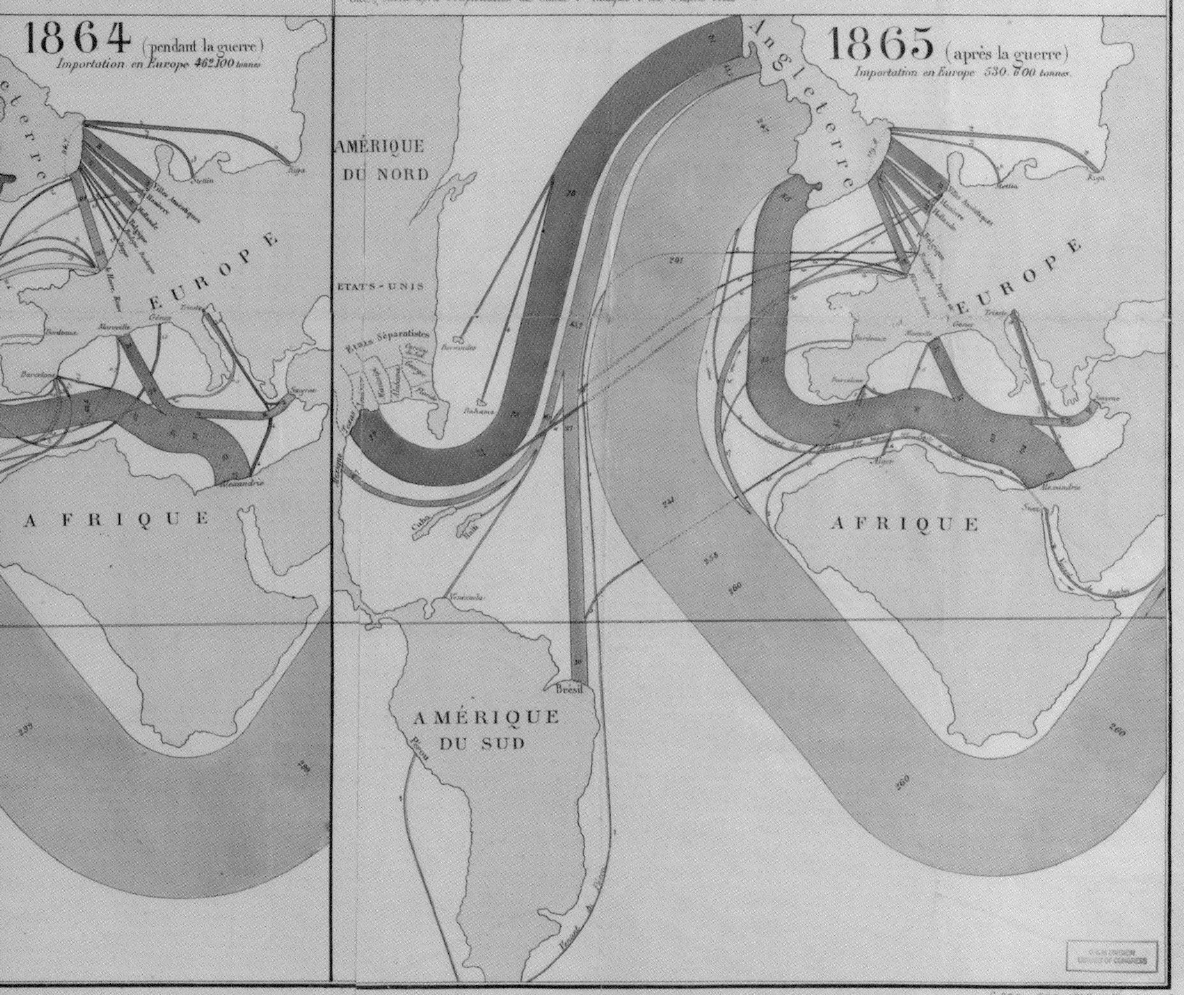

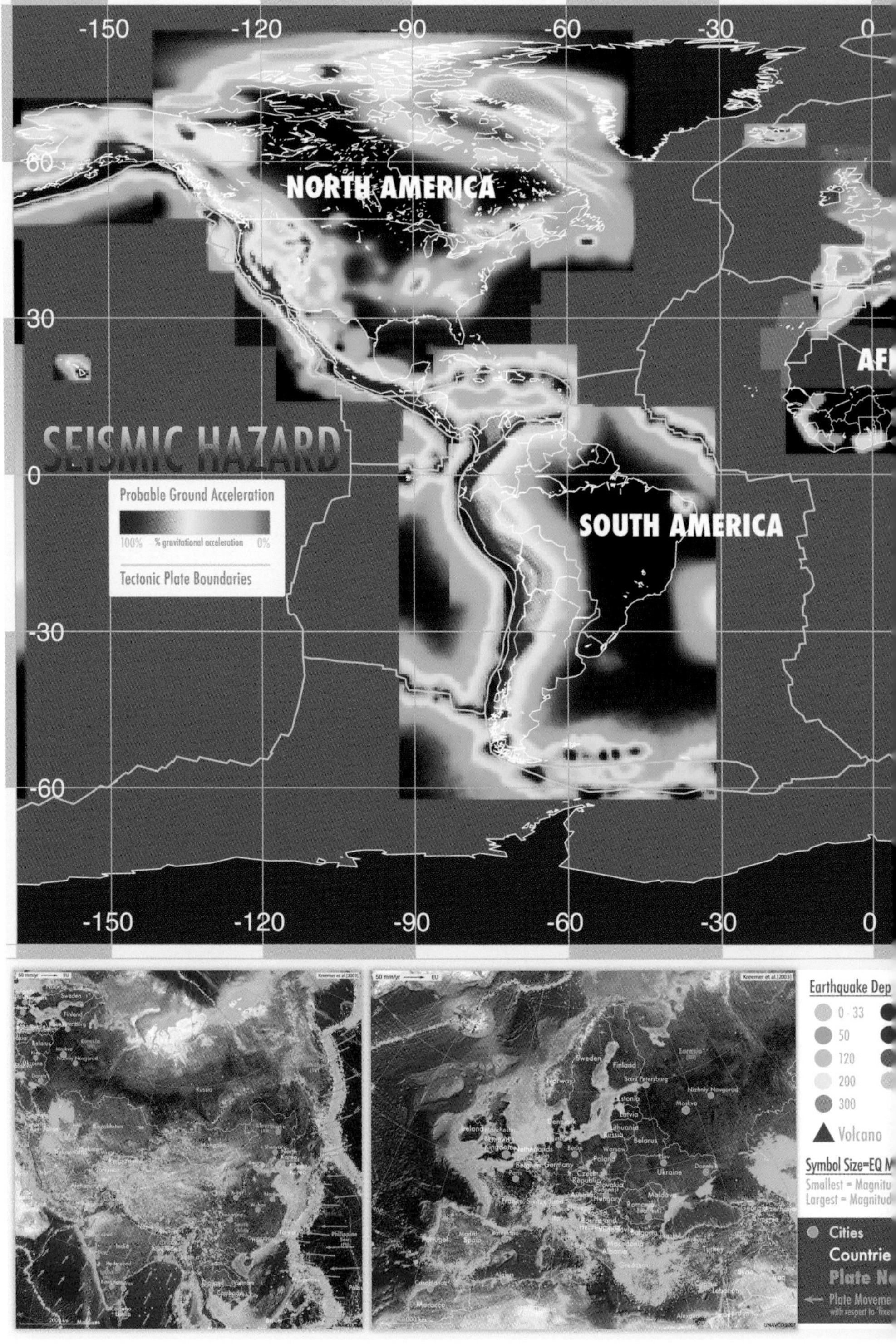

Figure 3.3 *Tectonic Movements and Earthquake Hazard Predictions* (2007) by Michael W. Hamburger, Chuck Meertens, and Elisha F. Hardy (http://scimaps.org/III.1)

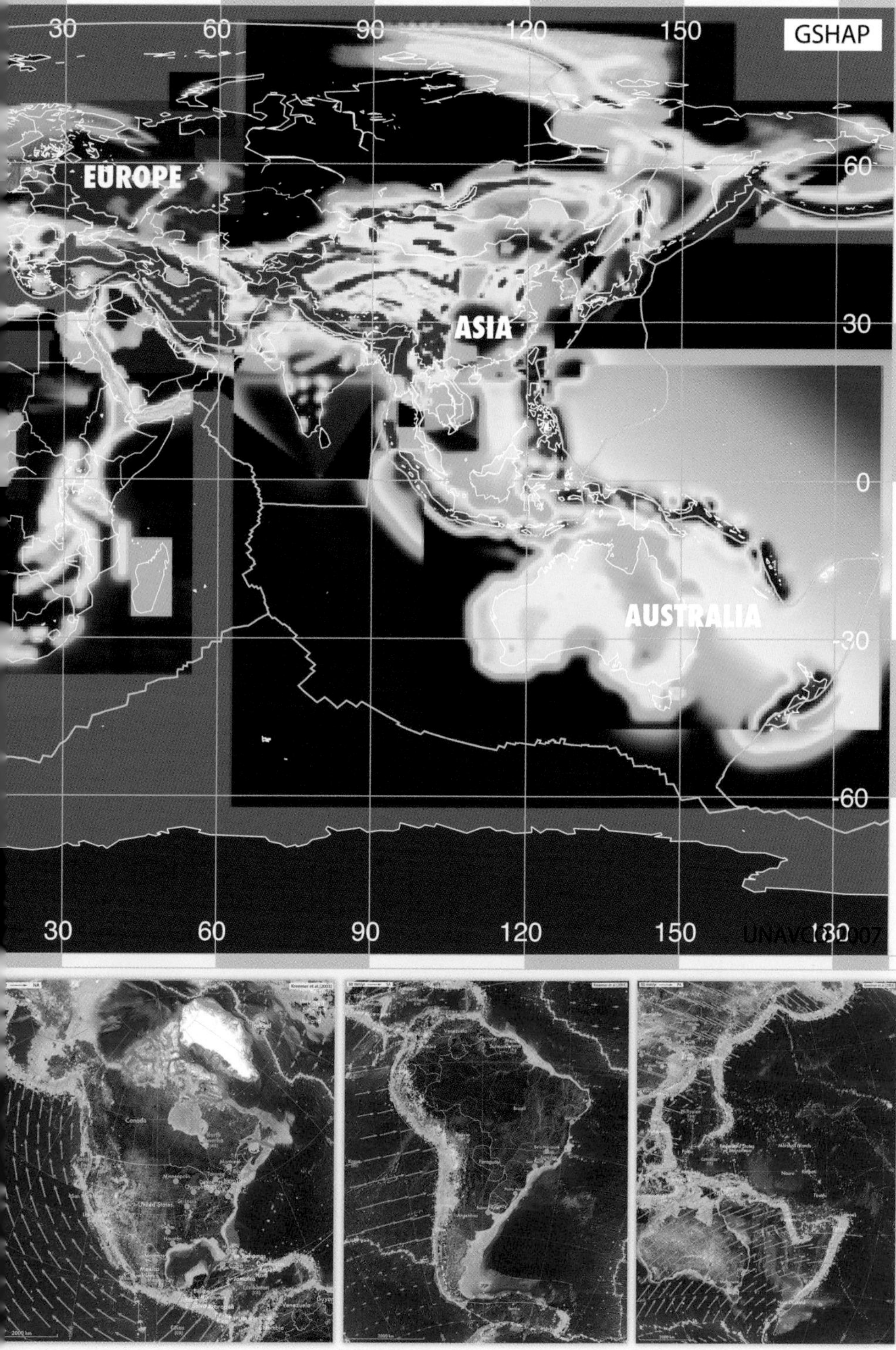
GSHAP
EUROPE
ASIA
AUSTRALIA
30
60
90
120
150
180
0
-30
-60
UNAVCO 2007

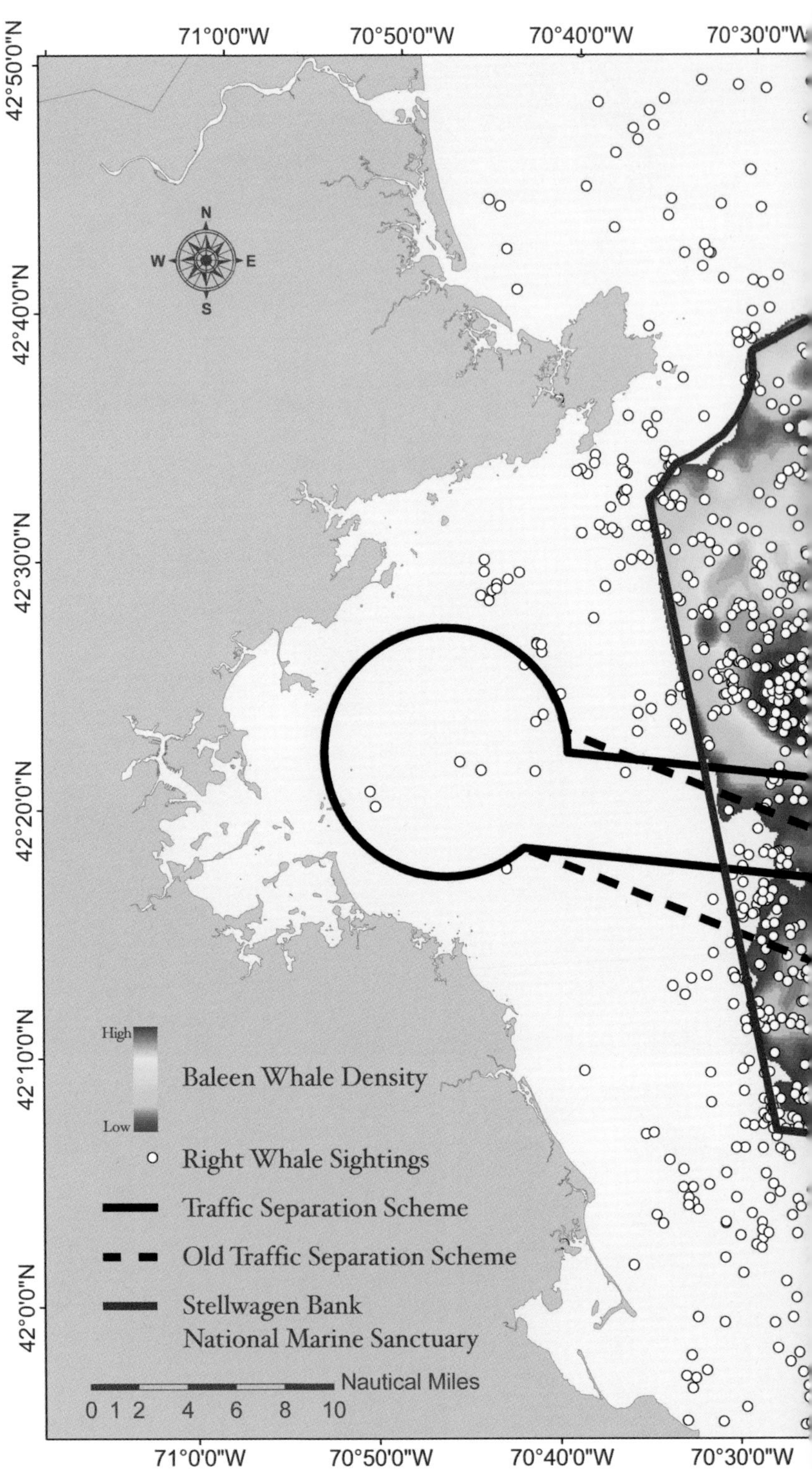

Figure 3.4 *Realigning the Boston Traffic Separation Scheme to Reduce the Risk of Ship Strike to Right and Other Baleen Whales* (2006) by David N. Wiley, Michael A. Thompson, and Richard Merrick (http://scimaps.org/V.3)

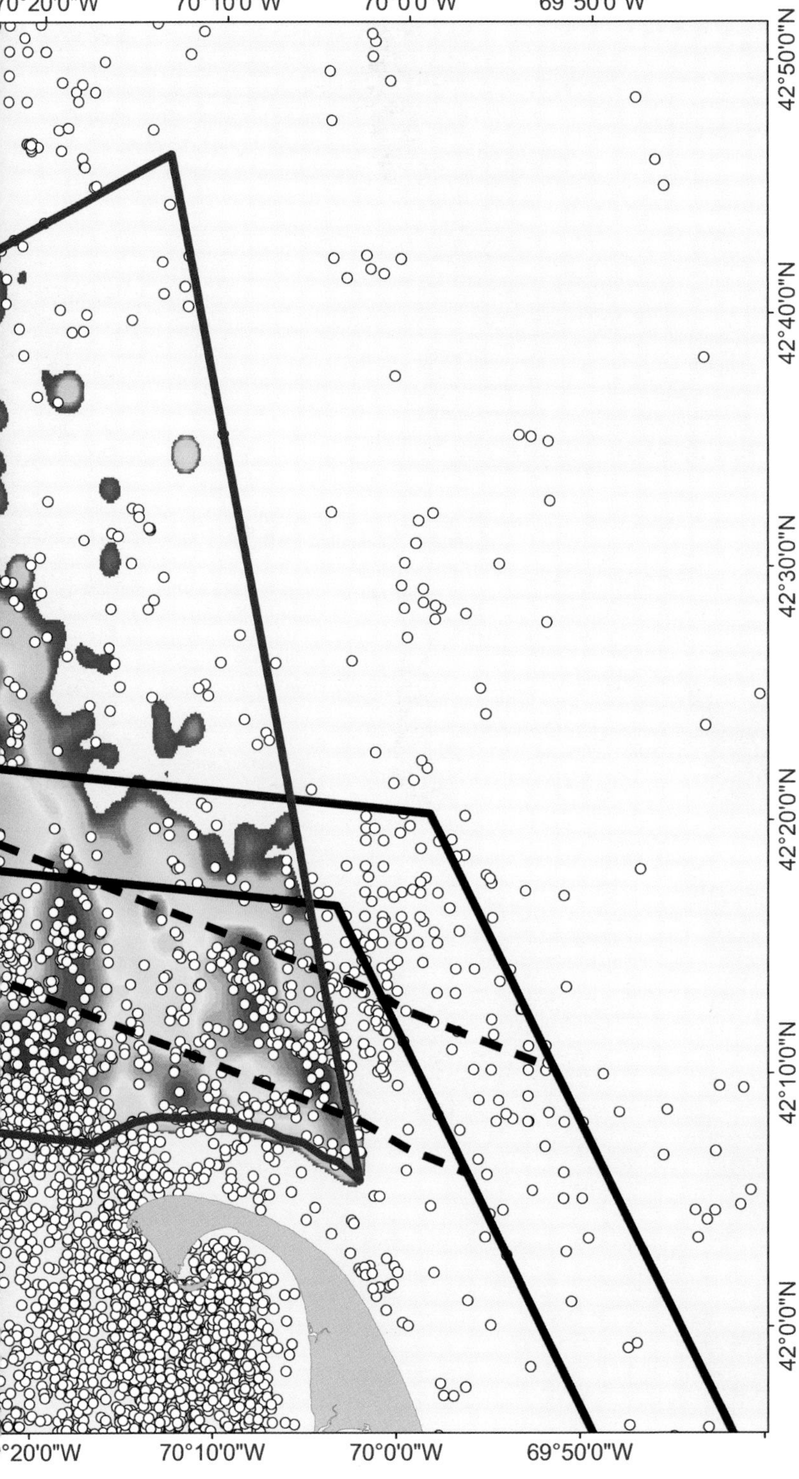

70°20'0"W
70°10'0"W
70°0'0"W
69°50'0"W
42°50'0"N
42°40'0"N
42°30'0"N
42°20'0"N
42°10'0"N
42°0'0"N
°20'0"W
70°10'0"W
70°0'0"W
69°50'0"W

Impact OF Air Travel ON Glob

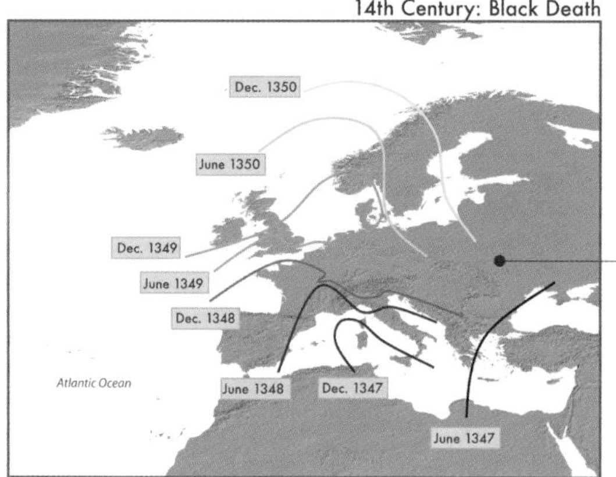

Epidemic spreading pattern changed dramatically after the development of modern transportation systems.

In pre-industrial times disease spread was mainly a spatial diffusion phenomenon. During the spread of Black Death in the 14th century Europe, only few traveling means were available and typical trips were limited to relatively short distances on the time scale of one day. Historical studies confirm that the disease diffused smoothly generating an epidemic front traveling as a continuous wave through the continent at an approximate velocity of 200-400 miles per year.

Forecasts OF THE N

Seasonal

Forecasts are obtained with a stochastic computational model which explicitly incorporates data on worldwide air travel and detailed census data to simulate the global spread of an influenza pandemic.

The modeling approach considers infection dynamics (i.e., virus transmission, onset of symptoms, infectiousness, recovery, etc.) among individuals living in urban areas around the world, and assumes that individuals are allowed to travel fom one city to another by means of the airline transportation network.

Numerical simulations provide results for the temporal and geographic evolution of the pandemic influenza in 3,100 urban areas located in 220 different countries. The model allows to study different spreading scenarios, characterized by different initial outbreak conditions, both **geographical** and **seasonal**.

The central map represents the cumulative number of cases in the world after the first year from the start of a pandemic influenza with R0=1.9 originating in Hanoi (Vietnam) in the Spring.

WORLD

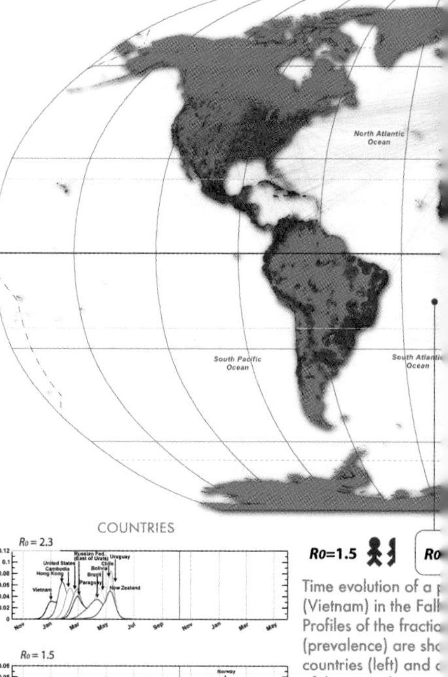

R0=1.5

Time evolution of a p (Vietnam) in the Fall Profiles of the fractio (prevalence) are sho countries (left) and c of the reproductive r consistently with the (top right), and R0=2 comparison with fas

Figure 3.5 *Impact of Air Travel on Global Spread of Infectious Diseases* (2007) by Vittoria Colizza, Alessandro Vespignani, and Elisha F. Hardy (http://scimaps.org/III.3)

Spread of Infectious Diseases

'he SARS outbreak on the other hand was :haracterized by a patched and heterogeneous ›patio-temporal pattern mainly due to the air ransportation network identified as the major channel ›f epidemic diffusion and ability to connect far apart 'egions in a short time period. The SARS maps are ›btained with a data-driven stochastic computational nodel aimed at the study of the SARS epidemic pattern ınd analysis of the accuracy of the model's predictions. ›imulation results describe a spatio-temporal evolution ›f the disease (color coded countries) in agreement with he historical data. Analysis on the robustness of the nodel's forecasts leads to the emergence and dentification of epidemic pathways as the most ›robable routes of propagation of the disease. Only ew preferential channels are selected (arrows; width ndicates the probability of propagation along that ›ath) out of the huge number of possible paths the nfection could take by following the complex nature of ıirline connections (light grey, source: IATA).

21st Century: SARS

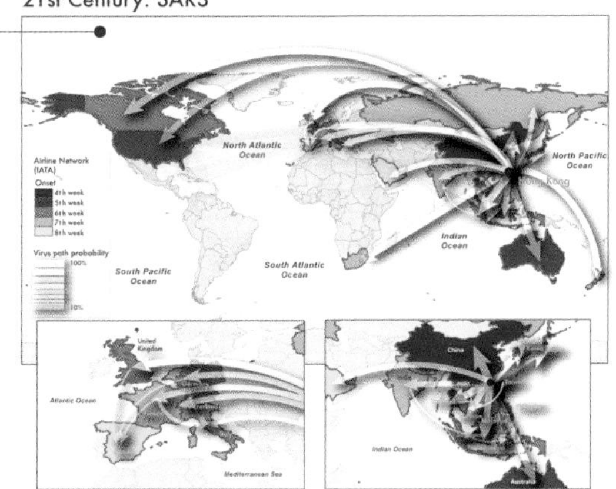

Pandemic Influenza

10⁶

0

The US maps focus on the situation in the US after one year, and show the effect of changes in the original scenario analyzed. Different color coding is used for the sake of visualization.

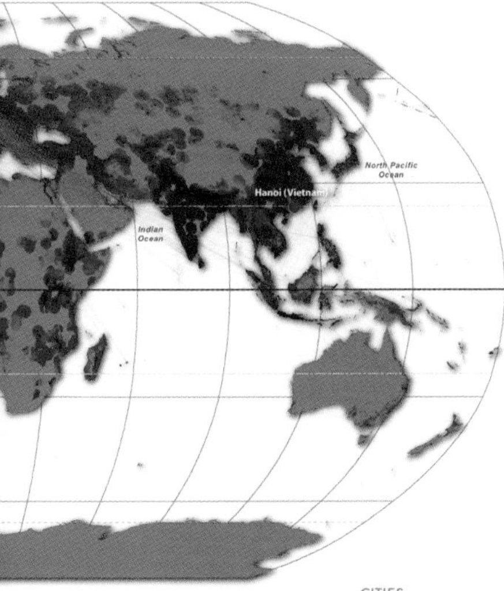

Ro=2.3

ırting in Hanoi ervention scenario. ıs individuals in time ə representative Two different values :onsidered: Ro=1.5, n for the US map to provide the g.

CITIES

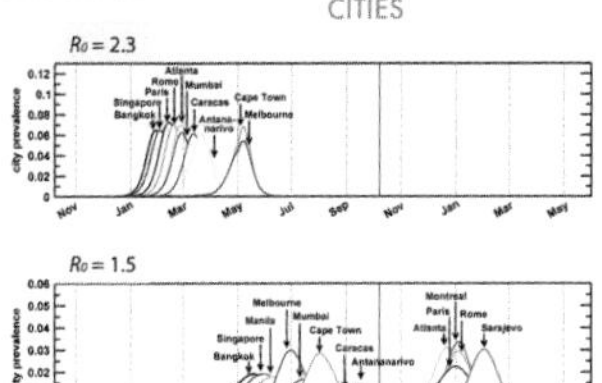

The model inlcudes the worldwide air transportation network (source: IATA) composed of 3,100 airports in 220 countries and E=17,182 direct connections, each of them associated to the corresponding passenger flow. This dataset accounts for 99% of the worldwide traffic and is complemented by the census data of each large metropolitan area served by the corresponding airport.

Additional spreading scenarios can be obtained by modeling different levels of infectiousness of the virus, as expressed in terms of the **reproductive number Ro**, representing the average number of infections generated by a sick person in a fully susceptible population.

Intervention strategies modeling the use of antiviral drugs can be considered. Two scenarios are compared: an uncooperative strategy in which countries only use their own stockpiles, and a cooperative intervention which envisions a limited worldwide sharing of the resources.

Reproductive Number (Ro)

1.7

1.5

Intervention

UNCOOPERATIVE

COOPERATIVE

Interested in forecasting the next pandemic influenza, Colizza et al. studied the effects of seasonality (when an epidemic starts), geography (where it starts), and reproductive number, R_0. The latter indicates how quickly the disease spreads (i.e., how many times you have to be in contact with an infected person before you yourself are infected with the disease). Different intervention strategies were examined as well—interestingly, they found that if U.S. vaccines are administered globally and strategically, then there will likely be fewer fatalities in the United States than if they are used to treat people in the United States exclusively.

3.2 OVERVIEW AND TERMINOLOGY

There are many different types of geographic maps. In all of them, the emphasis is naturally on location. There are general **reference** maps, **topographic** maps, which we might have used when hiking, and **thematic** maps, which overlay data on a geospatial substrate. In this section we will focus on thematic maps.

Within the category of thematic maps there are different types. There are **physio-geographical** maps, such as the seismic hazard map we examined in the previous section. Maps that show vegetation or soil patterns over a landscape are other examples. Then there are **socio-economic** maps that show political boundaries, population density, or voting behavior (Figure 3.9). Finally, there are **technical** maps, which show navigation routes, such as the whale population relative to shipping channels map (Figure 3.4).

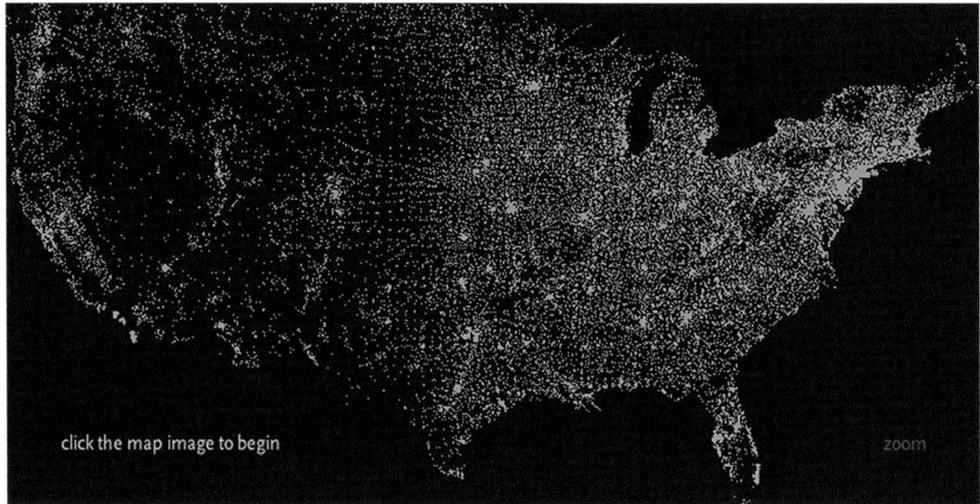

Figure 3.6 Interactive *Zipdecode* map by Ben Fry

Ben Fry's *Zipdecode* map[5] is shown in Figure 3.6. The interactive visualization allows users to type in all or a portion of zip codes to see the area covered by those numbers. Interestingly, the zip code 12345 happens to be Schenectady, New York. Even without typing in a zip code we can see right away that there are more zip codes in the eastern United States and around major urban areas relative to the western United States.

In order to understand geospatial visualizations, we will need some familiarity with basic terminology used in cartography and geography. One fundamental term in cartography and geography is **geocode**, which is the identification of a location of a record in terms of some geographic identifier, e.g., address or census tract. The next important term is **geographic coordinates set**. These are the latitude/longitude values for a certain point on the surface of the Earth. The term **geodesic** refers to the shortest distance between two points on the surface of a spheroid. Finally a **great circle** is the largest possible circle that can be drawn around a sphere, and in the case of the Earth both the equator and the prime meridian are examples of great circles. Another term we are likely to encounter is **gazetteers**, which allow us to take a list of geographic places, or geocodes, and get all geographic coordinates for those.

In the remainder of this section we introduce six different map types: proportional symbol maps, choropleth maps, heat maps (also called isopleth), cartograms (or value-by-area maps), flow maps, and space-time cubes.

Proportional symbol maps and **choropleth maps** are shown in Figure 3.7. Proportional symbol maps (left) allow for size, color, or shape code data overlays according to one or more data attribute values. Proportional symbol maps require that sets of data be aggregated to points within an area. For example, they can be used to show the total number of cancer cases per city. To render densities per area, do not use proportional symbol maps

Figure 3.7 Proportional symbol map (left) and choropleth map (right)

5 http://benfry.com/zipdecode

but choropleth maps that show an overall average within a defined area. An example is average population density per country or unemployment rate per U.S. county (Figure 3.7, right). Using choropleth maps, each artificial connection unit (e.g., states or census tracts) might be colored or shaded according to a data value.

Proportional symbol maps do not have to use abstract symbols (e.g., circles) to represent data. For example, the map of world country codes by John Yunker (Figure 3.8)[6] uses the codes at the end of every URL and email address. While .com is the world's most popular top-level domain (TLD), many others are country code TLDs. For example, .us stands for the United States, .cn for China, etc. Country letter codes are size-coded based on frequency of use. They are color-coded by continent, and a key in the lower right provides the full name of the country.

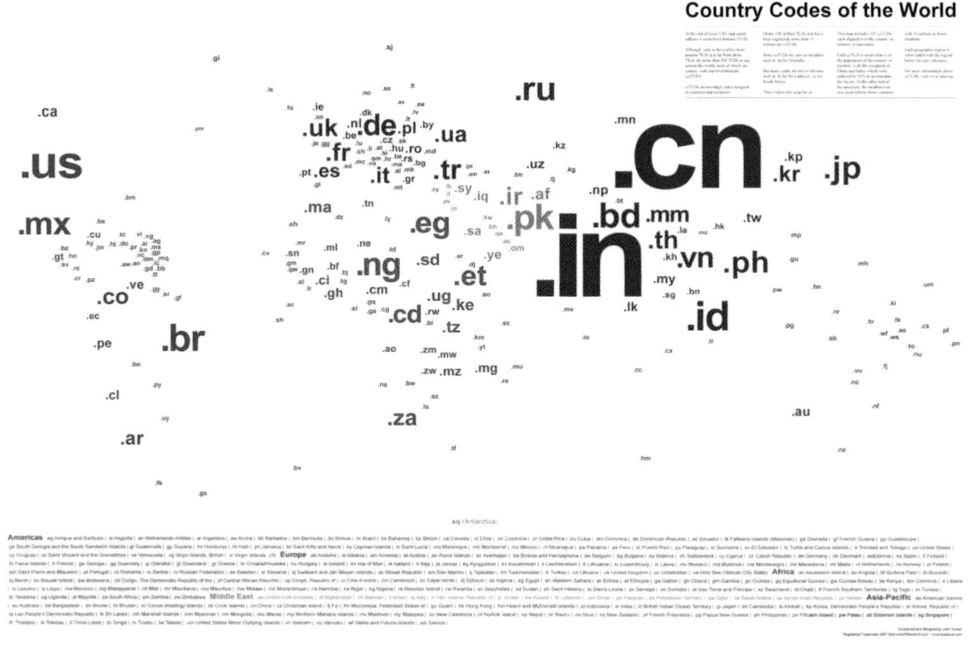

Figure 3.8 Country Codes of the World by John Yunker—an example of a proportional symbol map

Heat maps, also called **isopleth** maps, color-code areas according to data values. An example is the seismic hazard map (Figure 3.3). The green, or cooler, regions on this map correspond to areas of lower seismic activity, while the red, or hotter, regions correspond to areas of higher seismic activity. Contour lines might connect points of equal value.

6 See map online at http://www.bytelevel.com/map/ccTLD.html

Cartograms use data attribute values to distort the area and or shape of familiar maps (see *Ecological Footprint* in Figure 1.14 in Section 1.2). Another example is the 2012 U.S. presidential election map by Mark Newman[7] (Figure 3.9). The U.S. states are colored in red if the majority of votes (70%) went to the Republican candidate, Mitt Romney. They are color-coded in blue if the majority of the votes went to the Democratic candidate, Barack Obama. The maps on the left of Figure 3.8 (A and C) are undistorted. Maps on the right (B and D) are cartograms. The pair of maps at the top of the visualization (A and B) shows the results of the election based on the popular vote, with the map on the right (B) distorted based on state population. That is, states with a large population expand in area size while states with a low population decrease in area size. The maps on the bottom (C and D) show the election results at the more detailed county level based on the percentages of votes, with the map on the right (D) distorted based on county population.

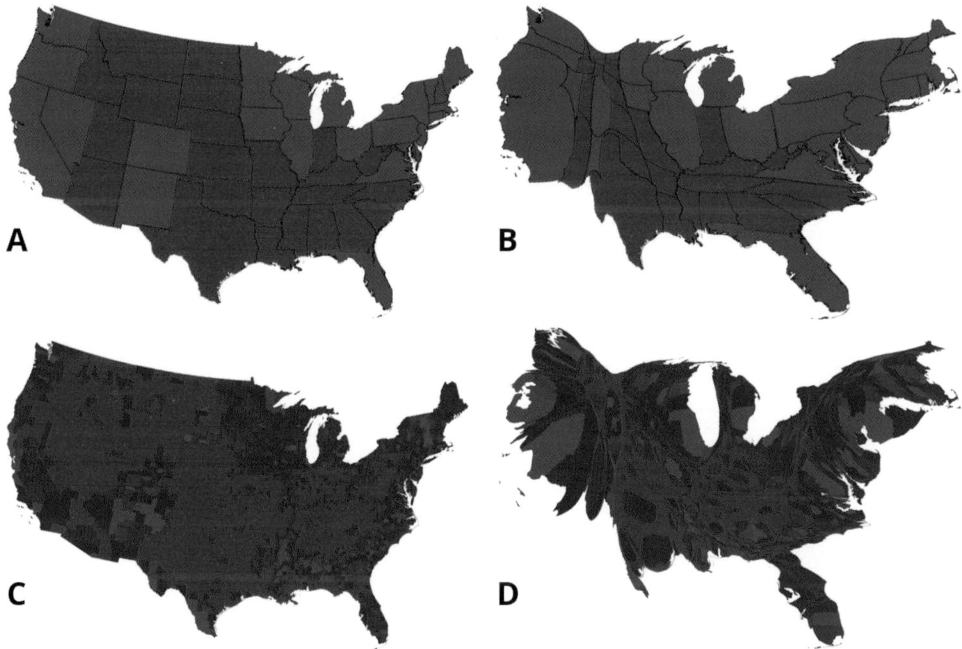

Figure 3.9 Mark Newman's cartograms of the 2012 U.S. presidential election results

7 Additional maps and detailed explanation is at http://www-personal.umich.edu/~mejn/election/2012/

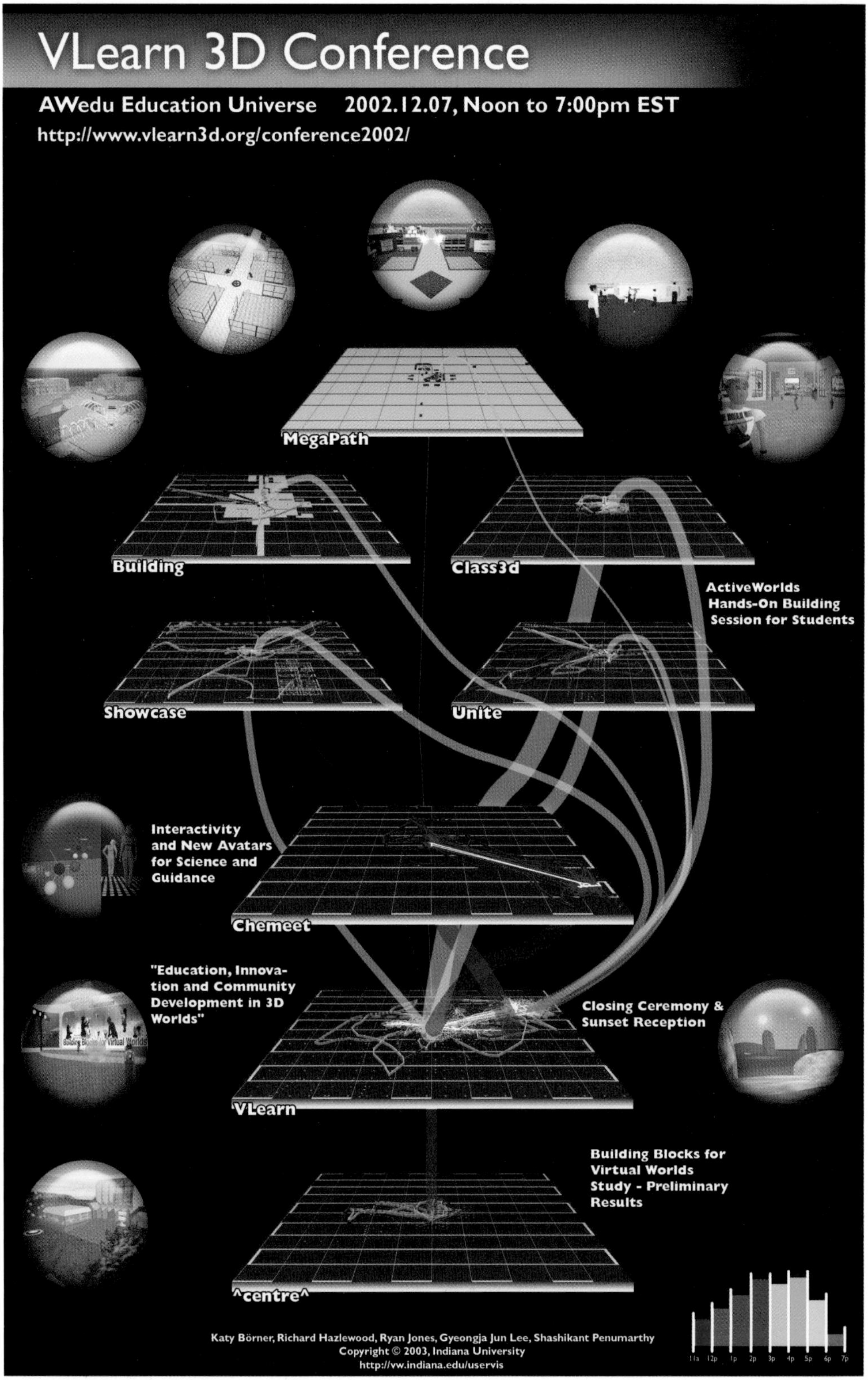

Figure 3.10 *VLearn 3D Conference* (2003) by AWedu Education Universe (http://cns.iu.edu/ivmoocbook14/3.10.jpg)

Looking at the bottom pair of maps, we can see how mixed the results are in some areas of the country. In many states there is not a clear majority for either candidate, and these areas are colored with shades of purple. Many of the strongly Democratic areas occur around larger urban areas, and many of the strongly Republican areas are spread across the rural areas of the country. These rural areas have a smaller population, and therefore end up appearing smaller when the map is distorted based on population.

Flow maps reduce visual clutter by merging edges. They are frequently applied to improve the legibility of linkages (e.g., collaborations, product transit routes) overlaid on geospatial maps or other reference systems. They reduce visual clutter by merging links. Links might be thickness coded to indicate capacity or speed. Another example is the map of worldwide collaborations by the Chinese Academy of Sciences discussed in Section 1.1 and shown in Figure 1.11.

Space-time cube maps show movement in space over time using a series of layers, typically arranged chronologically from the lowest layer to the upper layer. We can visually encode various data attributes in each layer, showing both the geospatial and temporal elements of the data. An example of a space-time cube is the VLearn 3D conference mapped over space and time (Figure 3.10).[8] Attendees at this conference start out in the VLearn world, a virtual learning environment, shown at the center of the map. Then participants disperse into the VLearn environment and enjoy breakout sessions in five different worlds, coming back to the VLearn world for a closing ceremony.

Trails of conference attendees are color-coded by time of the day. Early visitors appear between 11:00 a.m. and 12:00 p.m., explore the world, and try to find out where all the different talks are happening. The conference starts at noon, and a purple trail is used to show the movement of the many conference attendees to the VLearn world. Later on, people distribute across the breakout sessions, and then come back for the closing ceremony featuring virtual fireworks.

8 Zoomable map is at http://info.ils.indiana.edu/~katy/viswork/vlearn3d.jpg

3.3 WORKFLOW DESIGN

Using the general workflow introduced in the first chapter, we will now look at the types of data that are used to generate geospatial maps, the types of analysis, and also the visualization of geospatial data, comprising the selection of the visualization type, overlaying the data, and visually encoding this data (Figure 3.11). The three steps in VISUALIZE are exemplified using a proportional symbol map of the United States and a choropleth map of the world.

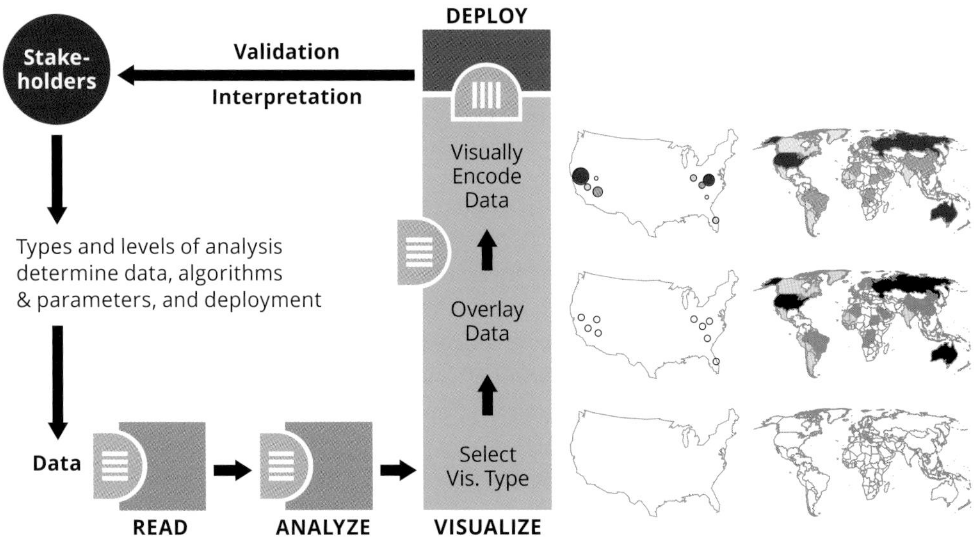

Figure 3.11 Visualization workflow for a proportional symbol map

Read & Preprocess Data

There are many free data sources that provide geospatial data. Among them are IBM Many Eyes[9] and the Scholarly Database[10] discussed in Chapter 2.

Geospatial data come in a variety of formats, including **vector** format, **raster** format, and **tabular** format, such as CSV files. Finally, there are software-specific formats, many of which are proprietary.

After obtaining the data, we need to perform preprocessing (i.e., geocoding, thresholding, unification, or aggregation). For example, when analyzing the diffusion of information among major U.S. research institutions[11] (see Figure 1.4), we need to determine the

9 http://www-958.ibm.com/software/data/cognos/manyeyes/datasets

10 http://sdb.cns.iu.edu

11 Börner, Katy, Shashikant Penumarthy, Mark Meiss, and Weimao Ke. 2006. "Mapping the Diffusion of Information among Major US Research Institutions." *Scientometrics* 68, 3: 415–426.

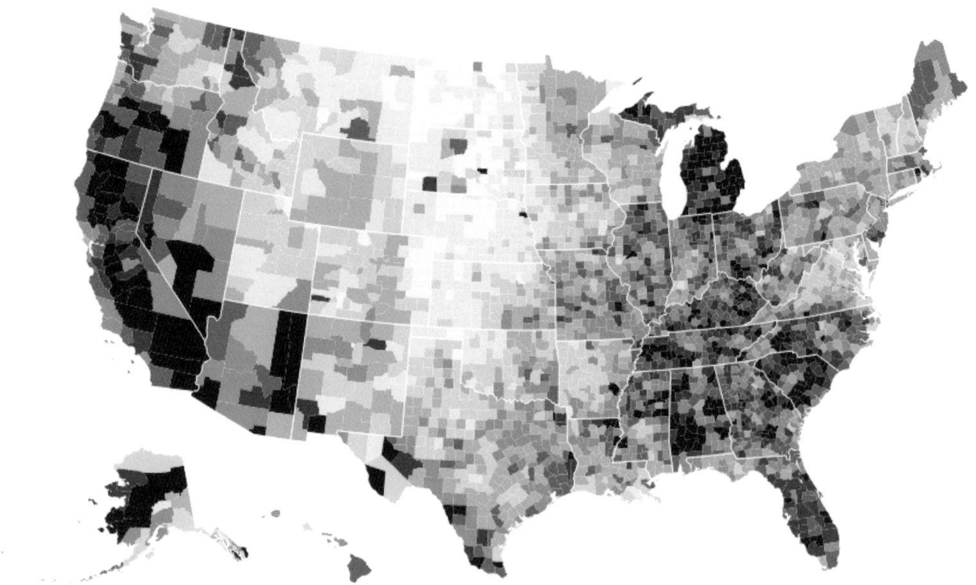

Figure 3.12 Choropleth map of U.S. unemployment data

number of unique institutions and their geolocations. As for Indiana University (IU), it has eight different campuses spread throughout the state. Should we represent IU as one data point or is it important to maintain the geographic identity of the different regional campuses? The decision has major consequences: If we keep eight separate instances then possibly none of them makes it into some of the top *n* lists. However, if we treat it as one instance, and aggregate all of the data of interest, then IU might be very visible on a research map of the United States. We need to find a compromise between geographic identity and statistical significance. An additional complication is the fact that IU Bloomington, the main campus, has two different zip codes. Which one should we use? Detailed user needs can guide this decision-making process but in some cases the stakeholders might have to be involved to arrive at the best solution.

Another general type of preprocessing is making sure that the data truly has the expected temporal, geospatial, or topical coverage. For example, if the data is supposed to cover the years 2000–2005 and the United States exclusively, make sure all data records fall into this time frame and no geolocation is positioned outside the United States. When overlaying linkage data (e.g., citation or collaboration links, over a geospatial map), make sure no link is longer than half the earth's circumference.

Figure 3.13 Proportional symbol with great arcs showing airport traffic data

Analyze & Visualize

With clean, geolocated data, we can use different types of geospatial reference maps and generate different types of data overlays. Figure 3.12 shows a choropleth map of U.S. unemployment data by county for 2008 rendered by Bostock.[12] Dark blue colors represent more severe levels of unemployment and light blue indicates low unemployment rates. Note, for example, the rather high levels of unemployment in California and Michigan.

The next visualization (Figure 3.13) shows airport traffic data using a proportional symbol map and linkage overlays as rendered by Bostock.[13] Major airports are represented by circles, area size-coded by the number of connections. The connections that can be made from Chicago O'Hare International Airport are represented by great circle arcs. As O'Hare is an international airport, a number of links go to places outside the United States, and thus off the map.

Figure 3.37 in the hands-on section shows a proportional symbol map that visually encodes three data variables using circle ring color, circle area color, and circle area size.

---

12 See large map and code at http://bl.ocks.org/mbostock/4060606

13 See interactive map and code at http://mbostock.github.io/d3/talk/20111116/airports.html

3.4 COLOR

In this section we introduce the use of color in visualizations. Color is not only important for geospatial visualizations, but also for all visualizations discussed throughout this book. It is very useful in conveying importance or attracting attention to specific elements of a visualization. Think, for example, of picking cherries from a tree. It is easy to spot those red cherries in a green-leafed tree. Similarly, in information visualization color can be helpful for labeling, for categorization, and for comparisons. We might use colors to imitate reality (e.g., blue is commonly used to color water on geographic maps). Appealing to these common frames of reference can help make visualizations more intuitive.

Color Properties

Color is one of the quantitative graphic variable types that we discussed in Chapter 1. All colors have three important properties: **value**, **hue**, and **saturation** (see Figure 1.19). **Color value** has many different names, including lightness, shade, tone, percent value, density, and intensity. It equals the amount of light coming from a source, or being reflected off of an object. Color value is defined along a lightness-darkness axis. We should use color value to create depth, convey lightness, create patterns, or to lead the eye and emphasize parts of a visualization. Poor contrast happens when two colors have very similarly perceived brightness. It's important to compare colors on a gray-scale to make sure they are obviously distinguishable.

The next element of color is **hue**, or tint, which is each color's individual wavelength of light. Hue is a qualitative variable and is therefore good for categorizing elements in a visualization but should not be used to encode a quantitative magnitude. Humans can name about 12 different colors, so if a task requires users to identify and communicate colors, we advise not to use more than that. The *Language Communities in Twitter* map (Figure 1.16 in Section 1.2) uses more than 30 different colors—one for each language. The colors are carefully selected to ensure that geospatially close languages are sufficiently different and distinguishable. As mentioned before, different hues should have a significant luminous difference in addition to color difference—simply print your visualization in black and white and make sure all colors are distinguishable.

The final element of color is **saturation**, which refers to the level of light intensity in a color, ranging from dull to bright. Highly saturated, purer color will appear in the foreground for a viewer, whereas low saturation colors will look dull and fade into the background. Simultaneous contrast with background colors can dramatically alter the color appearance of a graphic object.

Color Schemes

There are four commonly used color schemes: **binary**, **diverging**, **sequential**, and **qualitative** (Figure 3.14).[14]

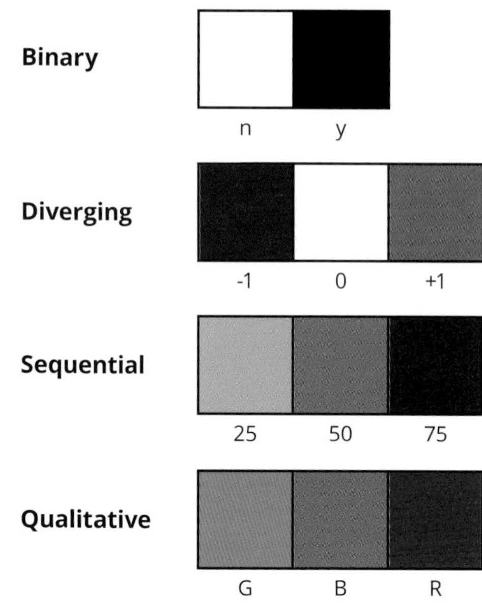

Figure 3.14 Color schemes

Binary schemes use two colors—for example, white and black, red and green, or yellow and blue.

Diverging color schemes, sometimes referred to as bipolar color schemes, are quantitative. The emphasis is on high and low values. The values that occur in the midrange between the high and low are typically assigned a black or white color.

Sequential color schemes are quantitative. They use a single hue, and they are best for ordered data as it progresses from low to high. Typically, light colors are used for low data values and dark colors are used for high data values (see the U.S. unemployment map in Figure 3.12).

Qualitative color schemes, as their name suggests, are qualitative and can be used to represent nominal or categorical data.

We provide an example of a diverging color scheme in the Money Market map (Figure 3.15). It shows the up and down of different stock prices. Up is green, which is good, and down is red, which is bad. The map on the left shows year-to-date (YTD) values, that is, the difference from starting from the beginning of the current year to the present day. While most stocks are colored green (i.e., they gained in value), the map has some red fields (e.g., Barrick Gold Corp lost 50.78% in value). Shown on the right is the change over the last 26 weeks—Facebook Inc. is one of the major winners with 79.23% in value; it gained 84.48% YTD.

---

14 Brewer, Cynthia A. "Color Use Guidelines for Mapping and Visualization." http://www.personal.psu.edu/faculty/c/a/cab38/ColorSch/SchHome.html (accessed September 4, 2013).

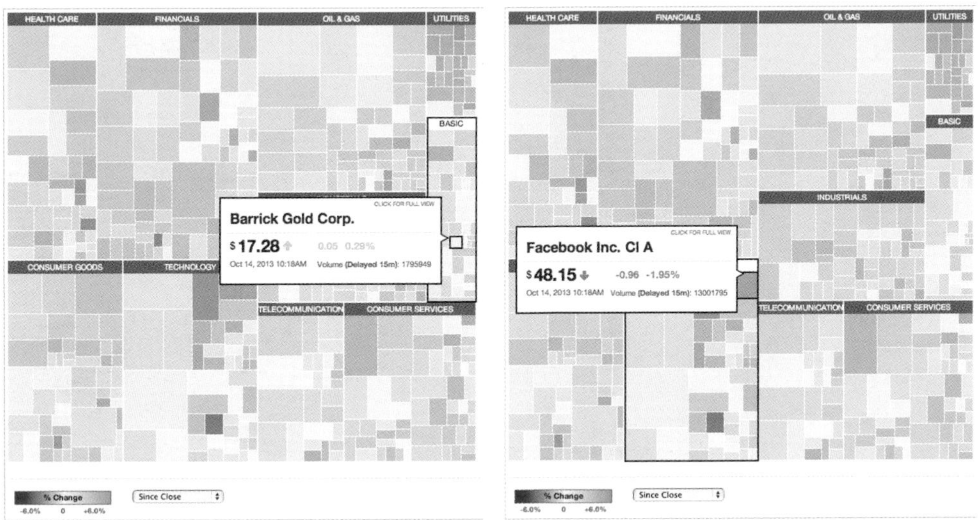

Figure 3.15 Money Market map displaying changes in the stock market with a diverging color scheme

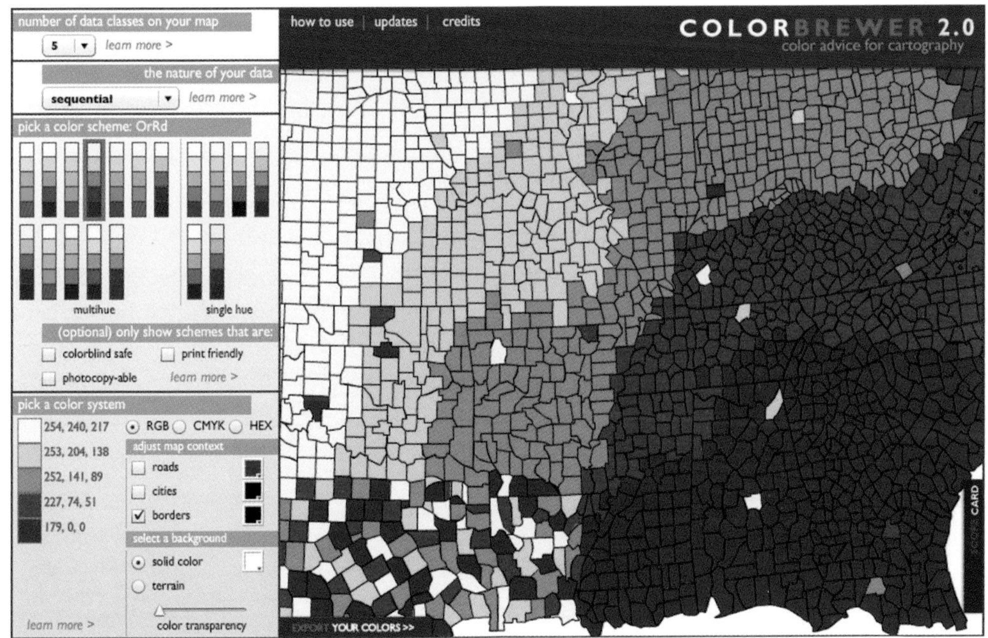

Figure 3.16 Color Brewer, a useful online tool for experimenting with different color schemes over geospatial data

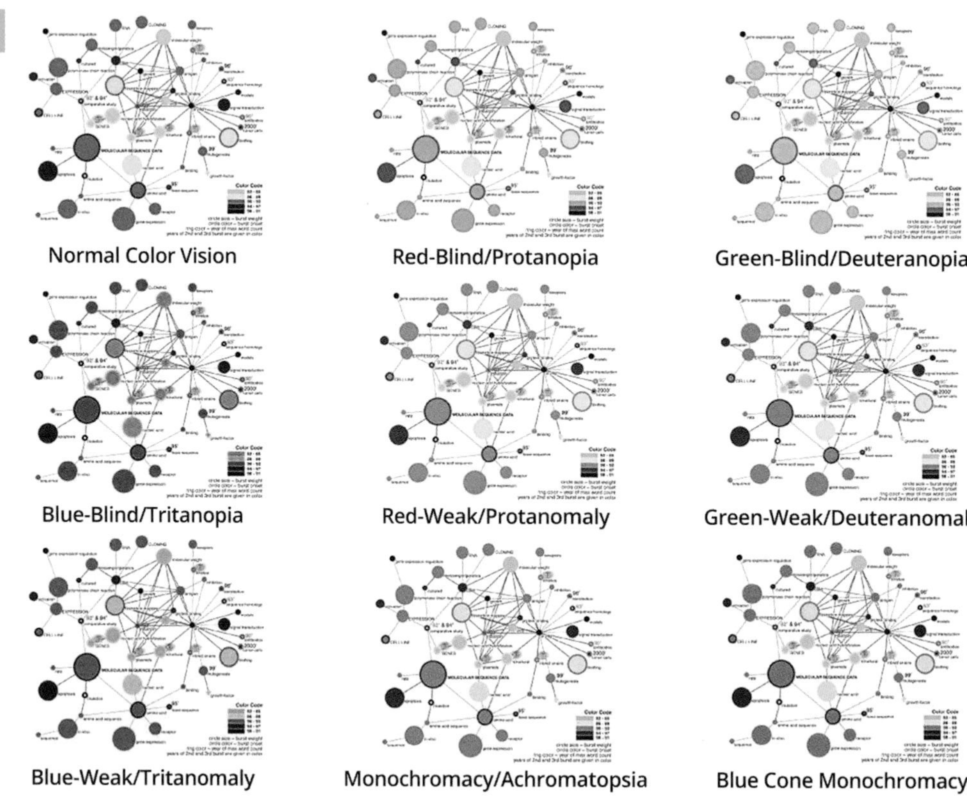

Figure 3.17 Original visualization (top left) and eight modifications that simulate different kinds of color blindness (http://cns.iu.edu/ivmoocbook14/3.17.jpg)

Additional information and examples of these different color schemes can be found at the Color Brewer web site[15] and in related publications.[16] The Color Brewer (Figure 3.16) is a very useful tool for learning about how different color schemes interact with each other on geospatial data. We can also to try out different combinations of data types and color schemes. Additionally, the Color Brewer allows us to experiment with colors that are color-blind safe, or photocopy and print friendly. Once we have settled on a color scheme and tested it using Color Brewer, we can obtain the RGB, CMYK, or HEX values to apply to our own visualization.

---

15 Interactive color selection interface is at http://colorbrewer2.org

16 Brewer, Cynthia A. 1994. "Color Use Guidelines for Mapping and Visualization." In *Visualization in Modern Cartography*, edited by Alan M. MacEachren and D.R. Fraser Taylor, 123–147. Tarrytown, NY: Elsevier Science.
Brewer, Cynthia A. 1994. "Guidelines for the Use of the Perceptual Dimensions of Color for Mapping and Visualization." In *Proceedings of the International Society for Optical Engineering*, edited by J. Bares, 54–63. San Jose, CA: SPIE.

Color Blindness

A considerable number of people has some kind of color blindness. If color is used to encode important information, make sure that people with different color blindness types can read the information. For some perspective, examine Figure 3.17 which shows in the top left corner "Mapping topic bursts in *PNAS* publications" (Figure 1.4). This is the original visualization—shown as somebody with normal color vision would perceive it. Next we provide eight versions of this figure to show how people with different color blindness types would perceive the same visualization; see figure labels for type of color blindness. To test our own visualizations, we can use any of the color blindness simulators on the web, such as Colblindor.[17]

Self-Assessment

1. Which map type should not be used to represent population density?
   A. Proportional symbol map
   B. Choropleth map
   C. Heat map

2. Given a data variable of type ratio, which graphic variable type is not appropriate to represent it?
   A. Size
   B. Shape
   C. Value (Lightness)

3. What image format is a JPEG file?
   A. Vector
   B. Raster

4. What format is a PostScript (.ps) file?
   A. Vector
   B. Raster

Chapter 3: Hands-On Section

3.5 VISUALIZING USPTO DATA WITH THE PROPORTIONAL SYMBOL MAP AND THE CHOROPLETH MAP

Data Types & Coverage	
Time Frame:	1865-2008
Region:	Multiple
Topical Area:	Influenza
Network Type:	Geospatial Analysis

Analysis Types/Levels	•	●	⬤
Temporal			
Geospatial			X
Topical			
Network			

This workflow shows how to use the Sci2 Tool for visualizing patents containing the term *influenza* with a proportional symbol map and a choropleth map. We compiled the file used in this workflow, *usptoInfluenza.csv*,[18] by downloading patents that contain the term *influenza* from the Scholarly Database (SDB). We then preprocessed the resulting file to include only the 'Country', the 'Longitude' and 'Latitude', the number of 'Patents' associated with a country, and the 'Times Cited', which indicates number of times those patents have been cited (Figure 3.18). Load the file using *File* > *Load* and select 'Standard csv format' when prompted. To see the raw data, right-click on the file in the 'Data Manager' and select 'View' (Figure 3.18).

	A	B	C	D	E
1	Country	Latitude	Longitude	Patents	Times Cited
2	Hungary	47.16116	19.504959	0.083333333	4
3	Belgium	50.500992	4.47677	3.017857143	11
4	Germany	51.090839	10.45424	4.783333333	4
5	Canada	62.35873	-96.582092	5.539285714	21
6	Russia	59.461479	108.831779	0.266666667	2
7	Austria	47.69651	13.34577	4.2	17
8	Netherlands	52.108089	5.33033	1	2
9	Switzerland	46.813091	8.22414	0.507575758	6
10	Taiwan	23.599751	121.023811	2	3
11	Australia	-24.916201	133.393112	1.617857143	23
12	United States	39.83	-98.58	73.9983889	220
13	France	46.712448	1.71832	2.201165501	9
14	South Africa	-28.483219	24.676991	0.333333333	1
15	Japan	37.487598	139.838287	15.99166667	39
16	Israel	31.389299	35.36124	3.5	3
17	United Kingdom	54.313919	-2.23218	3.85	12

Figure 3.18 USPTO influenza dataset as seen in Microsoft Excel

To visualize the data using a proportional symbol map, select the file in the 'Data Manager' and run *Visualization* > *Geospatial* > *Proportional Symbol Map*. Use the parameters to size the symbols based on the number of 'Patents' and color them based on the 'Times Cited' value as shown in Figure 3.19.

Sci2 will generate the visualization and output a PostScript file to the 'Data Manager'. Save the PostScript file (by right-clicking the file and selecting 'Save') and convert it to a PDF for viewing; see p. 286 in the Appendix for further instructions. The world map has 16 circles overlaid—one for each country in the dataset (Figure 3.20). The circles are areas size-coded (linearly) by the number of patents associated with the country and color-coded from yellow (one) to red (220) according to the number of citations. As we can see, the United States has by far the largest number of patents and citations.

[18] *yoursci2directory*/sampledata/geo

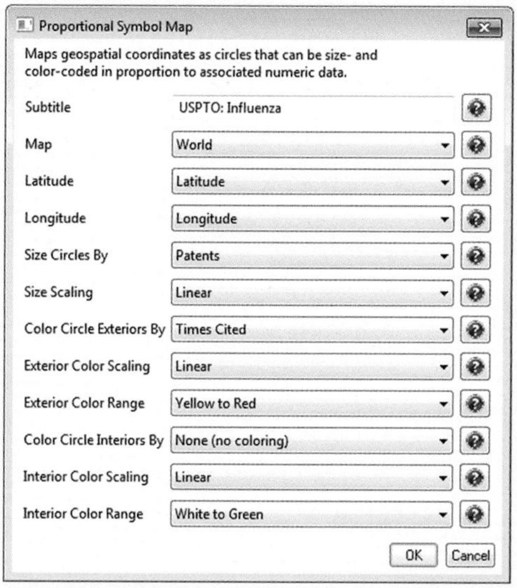

Proportional Symbol Map
Maps geospatial coordinates as circles that can be size- and color-coded in proportion to associated numeric data.
Subtitle: USPTO: Influenza
Map: World
Latitude: Latitude
Longitude: Longitude
Size Circles By: Patents
Size Scaling: Linear
Color Circle Exteriors By: Times Cited
Exterior Color Scaling: Linear
Exterior Color Range: Yellow to Red
Color Circle Interiors By: None (no coloring)
Interior Color Scaling: Linear
Interior Color Range: White to Green
OK Cancel

Figure 3.19 Parameters used with proportional symbol map to visualize USPTO influenza data

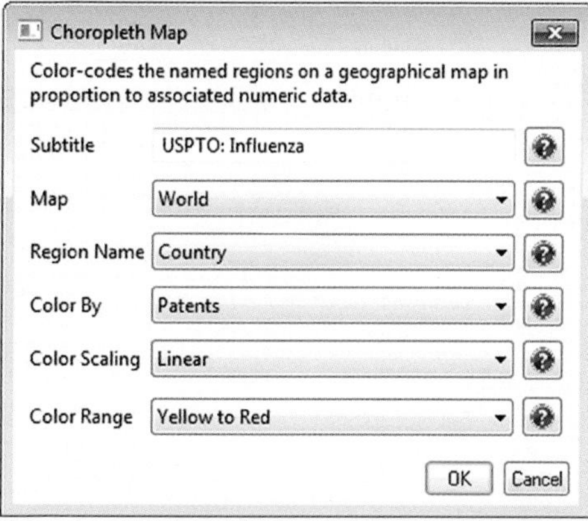

Figure 3.21 Parameters used with choropleth map to visualize USPTO influenza data

To create a geospatial map with region coloring of the very same file, run *Visualization* > *Geospatial* > *Choropleth Map* and set the parameters so that the countries are color-coded from yellow to red based on the number of patents (Figure 3.21).

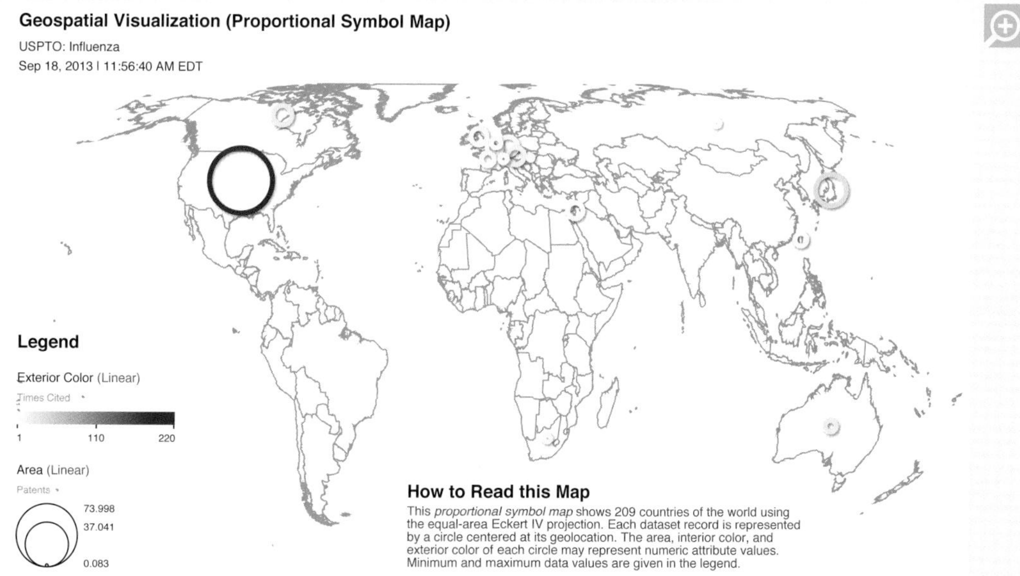

Figure 3.20 Proportional symbol world map of USPTO patents on influenza research (http://cns.iu.edu/ivmoocbook14/3.20.pdf)

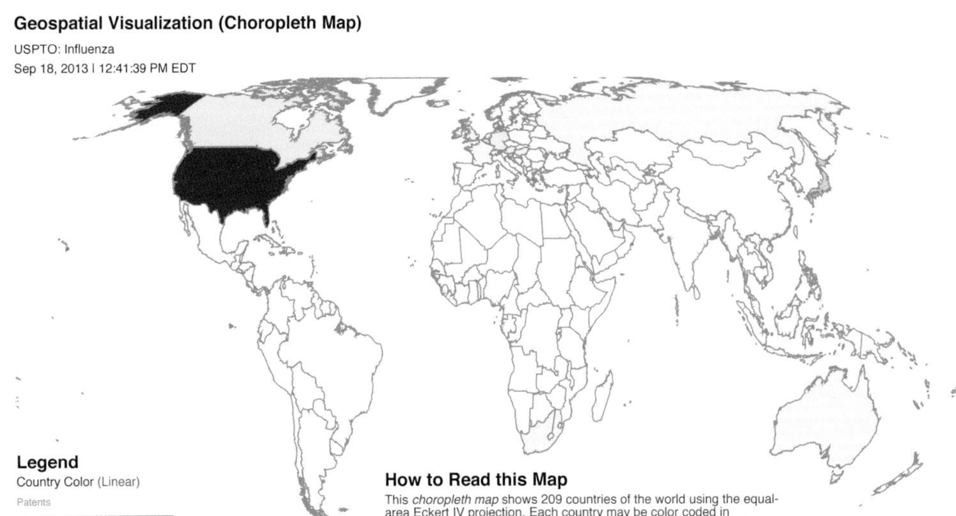

Figure 3.22 Choropleth world map of USPTO patents on influenza research (http://cns.iu.edu/ivmoocbook14/3.22.pdf)

Sci2 will output a PostScript file to the 'Data Manager'. Save it, convert it to a PDF, and open it to see that countries have been shaded from yellow to red according to the number of patents associated with that country (Figure 3.22).

Proportional symbol maps are best for visually encoding multiple attributes (up to three) of a dataset. Alternatively, if you wish to visually encode only one attribute of your data, then choropleth maps are an appropriate choice.

3.6 USING THE CONGRESSIONAL DISTRICT GEOCODER

Data Types & Coverage	
Time Frame:	2002-2018
Region:	United States
Topical Area:	Science of Science and Innovation
Network Type:	Not Applicable

Analysis Types/Levels	•	●	⬤
Temporal			
Geospatial		X	
Topical			
Network			

The Congressional District Geocoder is a plugin available for Sci2; download it from the Additional Plugins section of the Sci2 wiki.[19] Then, drag and drop the JAR file (*edu.iu.sci2.*

19 http://wiki.cns.iu.edu/display/SCI2TUTORIAL/3.2+Additional+Plugins

preprocessing.zip2district_0.0.1.jar) into the Sci2 plugins folder.[20] When Sci2 is re-launched, *Analysis > Geospatial > Congressional District Geocoder* is available for use in the top menu.

In this workflow we use a CSV file exported from the NSF Award Search,[21] a publicly available portal to search National Science Foundation funding. Please see the Sci2 Wiki[22] for step-by-step instructions on how to query for and download NSF data from that site. The *SciSIPFunding.csv* file has been made available on the IVMOOC Sample Data page in the Sample Datasets section on the Sci2 wiki.[23] Download the file and load it into Sci2 using *File > Load.* The file contains 253 awards made under NSF's Science of Science and Innovation Policy program.[24] One of the awards is entitled *TLS: Towards a Macroscope for Science Policy Decision Making*, which is the project that financed the development of the Sci2 Tool.

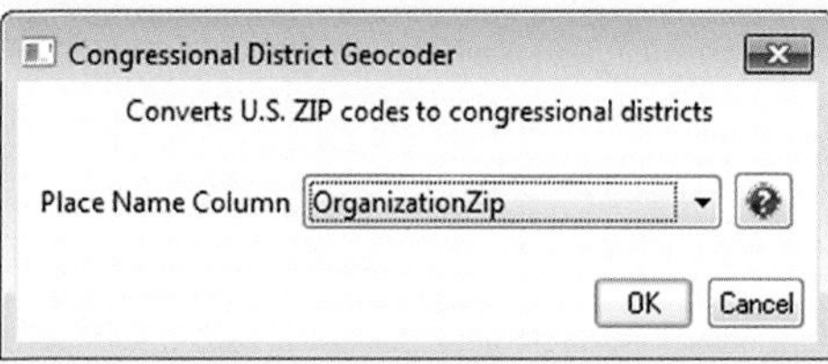

Figure 3.23 Use the zip code column to get the latitude and longitude data and congressional district data

Load the file as a 'Standard csv format'. Select the file in the 'Data Manager' and run *Analysis > Geospatial > Congressional District Geocoder* and set the 'Place Name Column' to 'OrganizationZip' (Figure 3.23). The Congressional District Geocoder requires nine-digit zip codes.

The result is a file in the 'Data Manager' titled "With Congressional District from 'OrganizationZip'". Any warnings or errors are listed in the console. The output table contains all columns of the input table with three additional columns appended: 'Congressional District', 'Latitude', and 'Longitude' (Figure 3.24). View the data by right-clicking on the file in the 'Data Manager' and selecting 'View'.

Z	AA	AB
Congressional District	Latitude	Longitude
KS-02	38.061244	-95.2888365
CA-23	34.916539	-120.5965215
PA-01	40.0076115	-75.1247195
MI-15	41.9815855	-83.4928825
AZ-05	33.6543055	-111.7402155
PA-14	40.3684875	-79.8622715
WA-07	47.66072	-122.336855
TX-26	33.2038595	-97.1703095
MA-08	42.351997	-71.0778455
MA-08	42.351997	-71.0778455
TX-26	33.2038595	-97.1703095

Figure 3.24 Data with 'Congressional District', 'Latitude', and 'Longitude' appended

Next, reformat the values in the 'AwardedAmountToDate' column. In Excel or some other spreadsheet program, select

20 *yoursci2directory*/plugins

21 http://www.nsf.gov/awardsearch

22 http://wiki.cns.iu.edu/display/SCI2TUTORIAL/4.2+Data+Acquisition+and+Preparation#id-42DataAcquisitionandPreparation-4221NSFAwardSearch4221NSFAwardSearch

23 http://wiki.cns.iu.edu/display/SCI2TUTORIAL/2.5+Sample+Datasets#id-25SampleDatasets-IVMOOCSampleDataIVMOOCSampleData

24 http://www.nsf.gov/funding/pgm_summ.jsp?pims_id=501084

the entire column, right-click on the column, and select 'Format Cells' (Figure 3.25). Reformat the values so they appear as integers, instead of monetary values, which will allow Sci2 to aggregate these values.

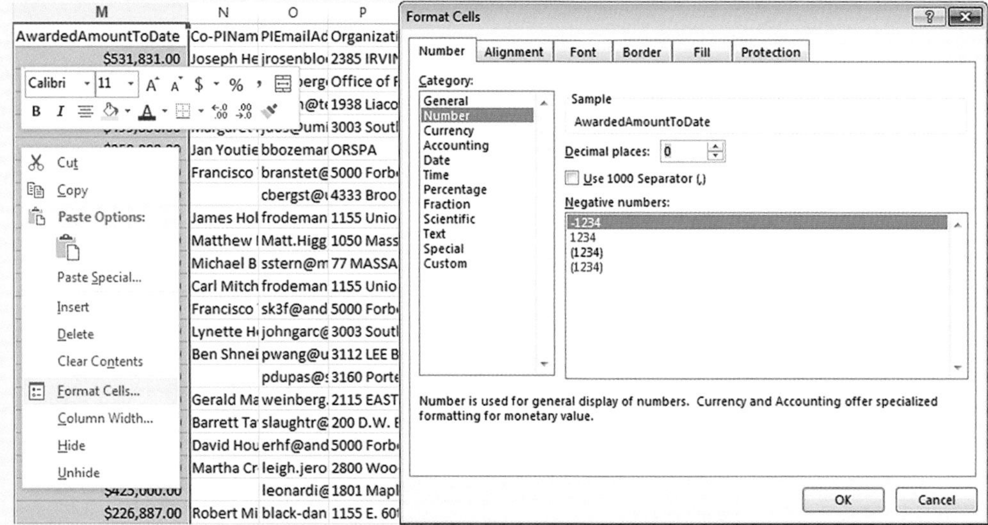

Figure 3.25 Formatting 'AwardedAmountToDate' cells as integers

Save the file as CSV file and reload it into Sci2. Now, aggregate the data based on 'Congressional District', sum the 'AwardedAmountToDate', report the max 'Latitude' value, and report the max 'Longitude' value by running *Preprocessing* > *General* > *Aggregate Data* (Figure 3.26).

The resulting file will be greatly simplified. Run *Visualization* > *Geospatial* > *Proportional Symbol Map* and enter the parameters shown in Figure 3.27.

The result is a PostScript file in the 'Data Manager'. Save the PostScript file, convert it to a PDF, and view; see p. 286 in the Appendix for further instructions. The map shows all of NSF SciSIP funding aggregated by congressional district and sized by the total number of awards and colored by the total amount of money per congressional district (Figure 3.28). The congressional district with the most awards is MA-08, but the district with the most money is DC-00.

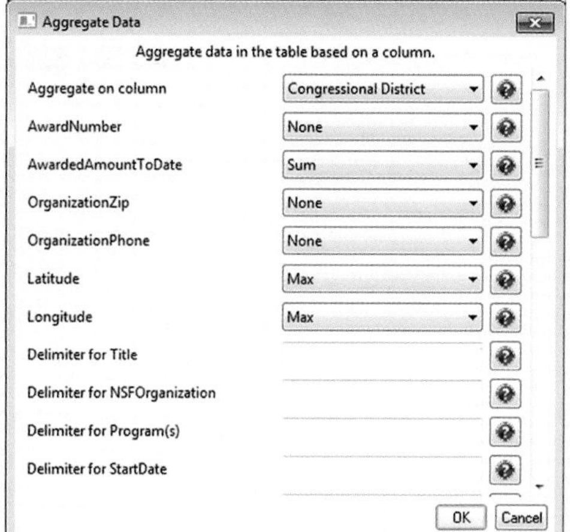

Figure 3.26 Aggregating dataset based on 'Congressional District' and summing the 'AwardedAmountToDate'

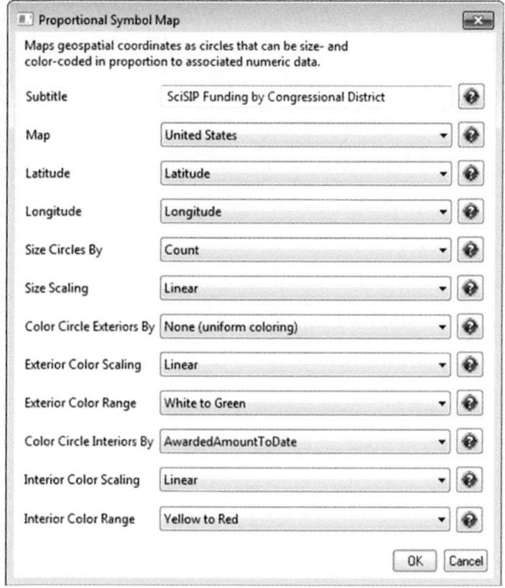

Figure 3.27 Parameters for creating a proportional symbol map with symbols sized by 'Count' and colored by 'AwardAmountToDate'

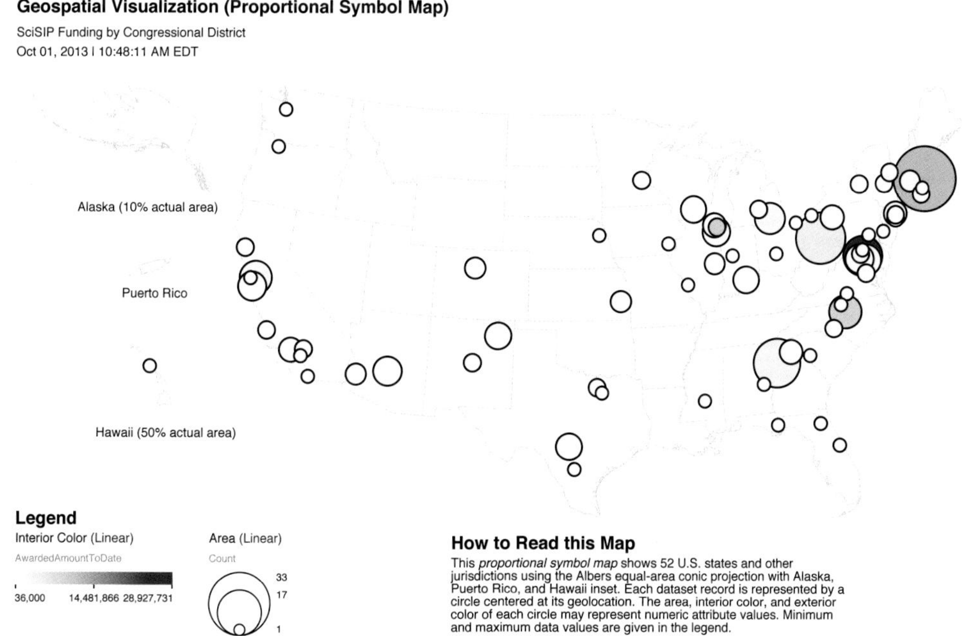

Figure 3.28 NSF SciSIP funding by congressional district (http://cns.iu.edu/ivmoocbook14/3.28.pdf)

3.7 GEOCODING NSF DATA WITH THE GENERIC GEOCODER

Data Types & Coverage	
Time Frame:	1959-2010
Region:	United States
Topical Area:	Science Education
Network Type:	Geospatial

Analysis Types/Levels	•	●	⬤
Temporal			
Geospatial		X	
Topical			
Network			

This workflow visualizes National Science Foundation funding, aggregated by state, for awards with the phrase "science education" in the title using a proportional symbol map. First, go to the Scholarly Database (SDB) (http://sdb.cns.iu.edu). If you are not registered for SDB you will need to do so before you can download data. Once you have completed the registration, you will be emailed a confirmation and you will be able to access the SDB Search interface. Next, enter the search term "science education" in the 'Title' field and make sure to select the 'NSF' database (Figure 3.29). Click 'Search'.

Figure 3.29 Scholarly Database 'Search' interface with "science education" entered in the 'Title' field and the 'NSF' database selected

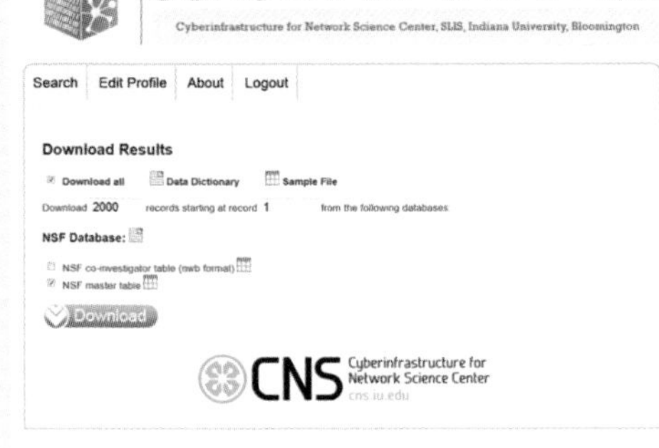

Figure 3.30 Scholarly Database 'Download Results' interface

To download the results, select 'Download'. In the 'Download Results' interface choose 'Download All' to get all 1,103 results and select the 'NSF master table' (Figure 3.30).

Unzip the dataset, and then load the *NSF_master_table.csv* file into Sci2 by selecting *File > Load*. Load the file in the 'Standard csv format'. Next, right-click on the file in the 'Data Manager' and select 'View'. As we are interested to see the amount of funding for states based on awards with the phrase "science education" in the title, along with the recency of this funding, all other data columns can be removed in the CSV file. Keep only the 'date_expires' column, the 'expected_total_amount' column, and the 'state' column.

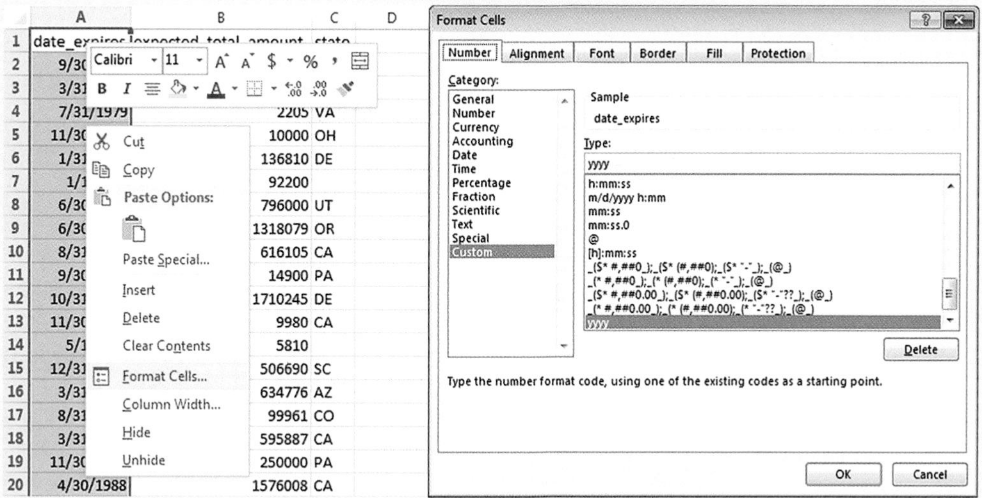

Figure 3.31 Changing the date format in Excel so that only the year appears in the 'date_expires' column

Change the 'date_expires' column to display only as the year to make input compatible with proportional symbol map visualization. Select the entire 'date_expires' column in Excel, right-click to format the cells, and then choose the custom option to format the date so that only the year appears (Figure 3.31). If the 'yyyy' date format is not already available, then type it in. The resulting file will contain the year that the NSF award expired (or expires), the total amount for those awards, and the U.S. state that corresponds with those awards (Figure 3.32).

Look through the awards and notice that not all awards are associated with a state. This is due to incomplete data, which typically occurs with older NSF grants. For the purposes of this workflow, remove these records from the dataset. Next, save the file and load it back into Sci2 in the 'Standard csv format'. Now, aggregate the data based on the state. To do this, run *Preprocessing > General > Aggregate Data*, selecting the 'Max' value in the 'date_expires' column and the 'Sum' values in the 'expected_total_amount' column (Figure 3.33).

	A	B	C
91	1993	57406	AK
92	2009	241630	AK
93	2010	335179	AK
94	2010	72354	AK
95	2012	474207	AK
96	2011	555285	AK
97	1976	100000	AL
98	1980	105700	AL
99	1980	135600	AL
100	1979	5000	AL
101	1979	5000	AL
102	1981	250000	AL
103	1979	20878	AL
104	1981	172400	AL
105	1979	5000	AL
106	1999	45000	AL
107	2000	30925	AL
108	2014	900000	AL
109	1980	123400	AR
110	1980	34800	AR

Figure 3.32 Simplified dataset that includes only the expiration date in years, the total award amount, and the state associated with the awards

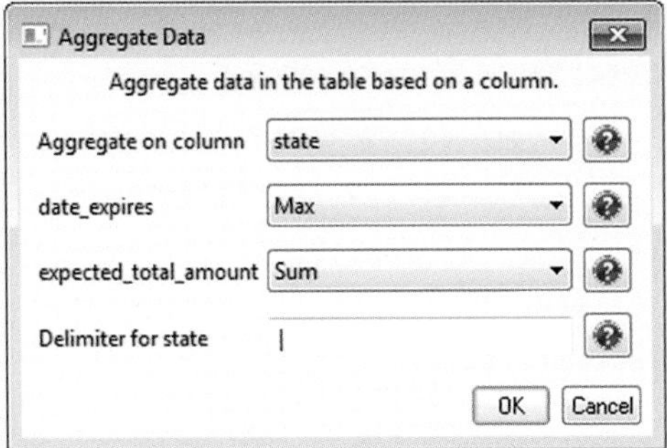

Figure 3.33 Aggregating based on the 'state' column

Click 'OK', and a new file will be generated in the 'Data Manager' called "Aggregation performed using unique values in 'state' column". In the new data file, the states have been aggregated: the 'date_expires' column will display the most recent year an award expires for each state, the 'expected_total_amount' for all awards associated with a state are summed, and a new column indicating how many times a state appeared in the dataset was created under the label 'Count' (Figure 3.34).

	A	B	C	D
1	date_expires	expected_total_amount	state	Count
2	2012	2007480	AK	7
3	2014	1775503	AL	12
4	1983	406912	AR	3
5	2013	10376771	AZ	21
6	2013	50227874	CA	114
7	2011	22518348	CO	30
8	2012	3397100	CT	11
9	2012	30963886	DC	31
10	2011	2718391	DE	5
11	2009	4805163	FL	14
12	2010	8252089	GA	19
13	2009	2907320	HI	11
14	2010	2900331	IA	17
15	2010	2042532	ID	6
16	2010	9554548	IL	32
17	2010	1909332	IN	12
18	1999	986302	KS	7
19	2010	943439	KY	9
20	2011	9764979	LA	17

Figure 3.34 The data after aggregation has been performed. 'Count' reports the number of instances of attribute upon which aggregation has been performed, in this case by state.

Next, select the new file in the 'Data Manager' and run *Analysis > Geospatial > Generic Geocoder* and input the following parameters to perform geocoding by state (Figure 3.35).

Generic Geocoder
Geocodes place names to geographic coordinates (latitudes and longitudes)
Place Type: US State
Place Name Column: state
OK Cancel

Figure 3.35 Using the Generic Geocoder to geocode NSF awards by state

The result is a file in the 'Data Manager' that has the title "With Latitude & Longitude from state". Select this file and run *Visualization > Geospatial > Proportional Symbol Map* and input parameters so that circles are sized by

Proportional Symbol Map
Maps geospatial coordinates as circles that can be size- and color-coded in proportion to associated numeric data.
Subtitle: NSF Funding for Science Education by State
Map: United States
Latitude: Latitude
Longitude: Longitude
Size Circles By: Count
Size Scaling: Linear
Color Circle Exteriors By: date_expires
Exterior Color Scaling: Linear
Exterior Color Range: Yellow to Orange
Color Circle Interiors By: expected_total_amount
Interior Color Scaling: Linear
Interior Color Range: Yellow to Red
OK Cancel

Figure 3.36 Parameter values used to generate proportional symbol map of NSF awards with "science education" in the title, aggregated by state the count, circle exteriors are colored from yellow to orange by 'date_expires', and circle interiors are colored from yellow to red by the 'expected_total_amount' (Figure 3.36).

The resulting map visualizes the level of funding in total for states based on NSF awards with the phrase "science education" in the title, displaying when the most recent award expired to give a sense of the time scale for this funding. The map also shows how many awards there are per state, reflected by the size of the symbols (Figure 3.37). Use this map to illustrate the concentration of science education funding in the United States; remember that for some geographic visualizations, it can be useful to divide total numeric values by each state's population in order to see whether the values are more or less than would be expected given the number of people per state.

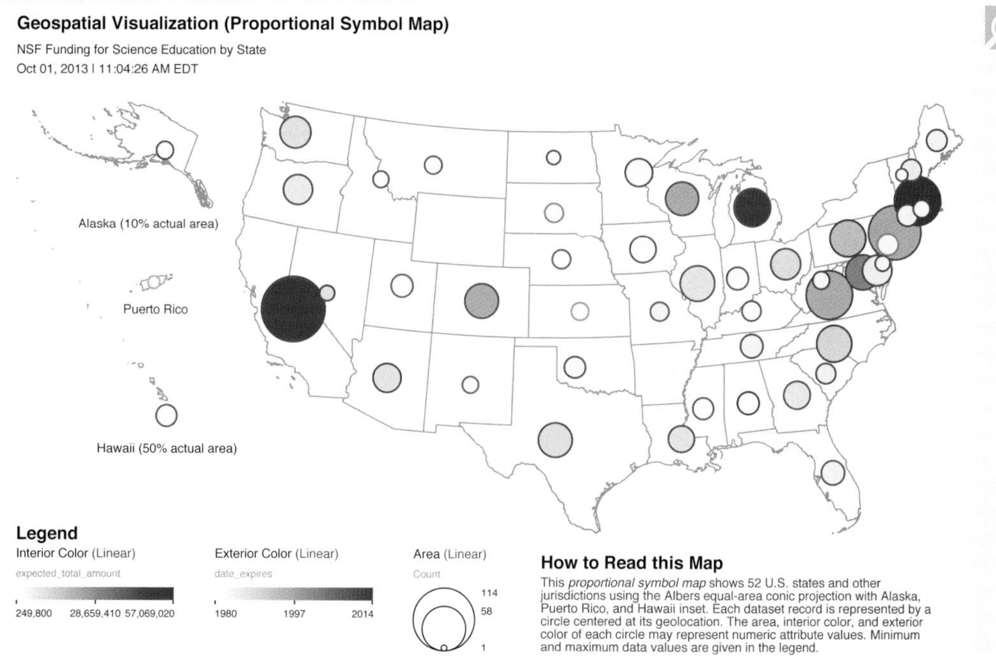

Figure 3.37 NSF funding by state for awards with the phrase "science education" in the title (http://cns.iu.edu/ivmoocbook14/3.37.pdf)

Homework

Download NSF data from the Scholarly Database (http://sdb.cns.iu.edu) and create a geospatial visualization of your choosing. For example, geocode the states associated with an NSF record file and use the proportional symbol map to visualize and understand the geospatial coverage of this funding.

LXIII

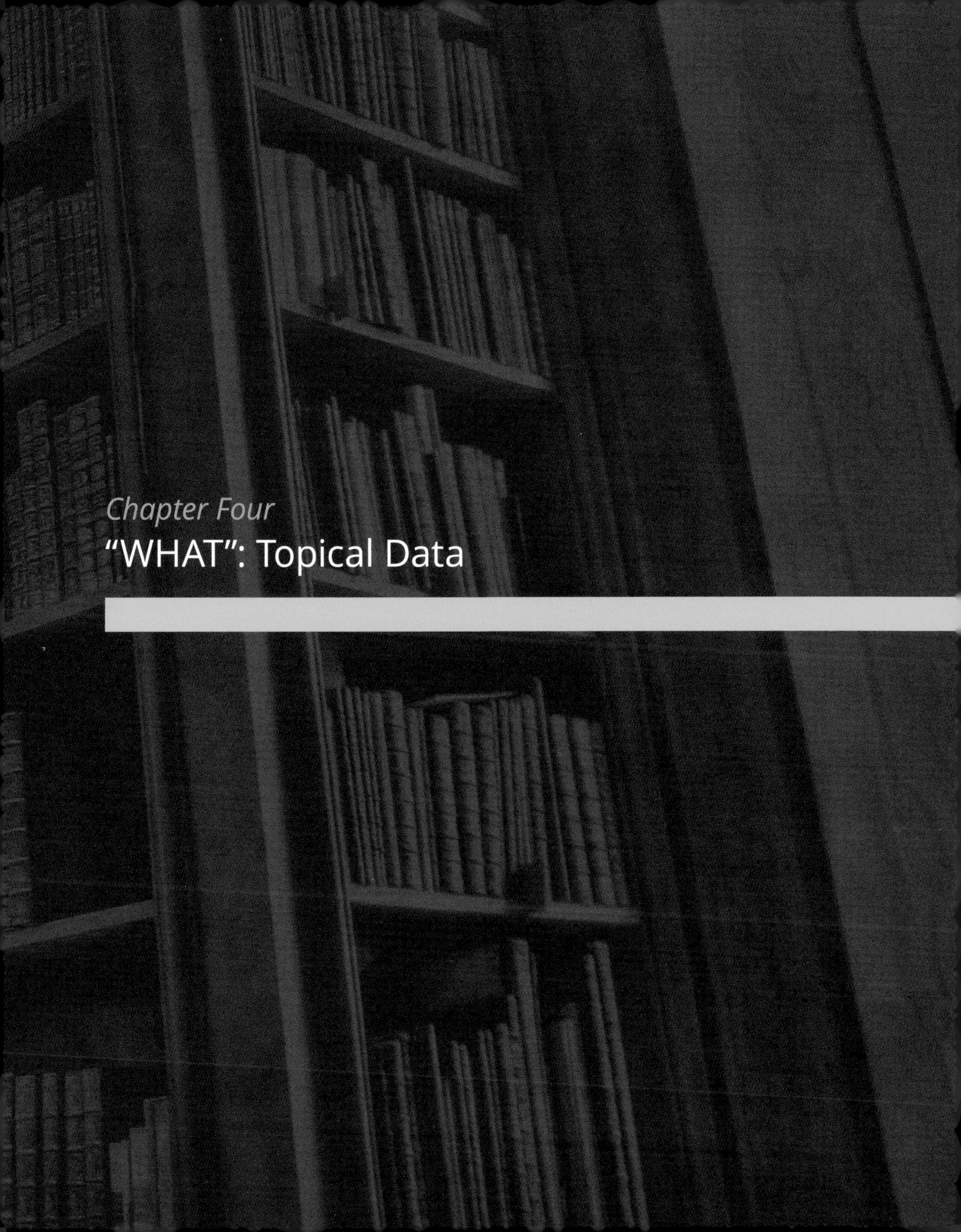

Chapter Four

"WHAT": Topical Data

Chapter 4: Theory Section

In this chapter, we will discuss topical (also called textural, linguistic, or semantic) data analysis and visualization to answer "WHAT" questions. The term *topic analysis* is used in a variety of ways, but for the purposes of this book it means extracting a set of unique words or word profiles and their frequencies to determine the topic coverage of a body of text. That is, we will be using texts (e.g., from article abstracts or grant titles) to identify major topics, their interrelations, and their evolution over time at different levels of analysis—micro to macro.

Just like the previous two chapters and the subsequent two chapters, we begin this section with a discussion of visualization examples, followed by an overview and explanation of key terminology and workflow design. In addition, we introduce two more advanced topics: the design and update of a topic map for all of science, also called the science map.

4.1 EXEMPLARY VISUALIZATIONS

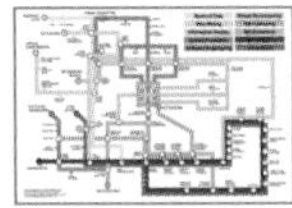

In this section we will discuss four maps. The first visualization (Figure 4.1) is by Keith V. Nesbitt, created when he was a PhD student in computer science at Sydney University. He had a hard time communicating his planned PhD work to his advisor, who questioned the validity of his dissertation topic. Initially, when trying to do this verbally, he had little success and almost gave up. As a last attempt, he visualized the many "trains of thought" that were contributing to his planned PhD work as a subway map. In the map, each line represents a certain line of research he hoped to conduct. The map itself communicates how all these different lines of research complement each other, what the main exchange points are, and how we can travel from one "station" to the next one. The map was effective in getting his advisor's approval, and it provided guidance during the dissertation project. Nesbitt's thesis[1] details and exemplifies each of color-coded lines of research shown in Figure 4.1, providing an even deeper understanding of their topical structure and interlinkage.

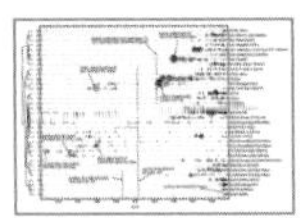

The second visualization (Figure 4.2) is an example of what is called a **cross map**. It was created by Steven A. Morris and shows a timeline of 60 years of anthrax research literature.[2] Time is represented on the *x*-axis from left to right, and topics are clustered in a hierarchical manner on the *y*-axis. Topic labels are given on the right-hand side. Each circle represents a publication on that topic for a certain year. Each is color-coded and size-coded according to additional attribute values, similar to a proportional symbol map (see Figure 3.13, Airport Traffic Map, in the previous chapter), but using a graph layout instead of a geographic layout. In particular, the number of citations is mapped onto the

1 Nesbitt, Keith V. 2003. "Multi-Sensory Display of Abstract Data." PhD diss., University of Sydney.

2 Morris, Steven A., and Kevin W. Boyack. 2005. "Visualizing 60 Years of Anthrax Research." In *Proceedings of the 10th International Conference of the International Society for Scientometrics and Informetrics*, edited by Peter Ingwersen and Birger Larsen, 45–55. Stockholm: Karolinska University Press.

area size of the circle, and those circles that are colored red have been cited more recently than those that are colored white. To provide context for this research, external events are overlaid on the graph. For example, the postal bioterrorist attacks generated a number of new research topics, as we can see in the lower right corner.

The visualization, in an easy-to-read format, quickly gives us a global overview of what research exists in a specific area, when it was published, on what topics, how recently it was cited, and how many citations certain papers received, which might help us identify papers we want to read first. Other cross map visualizations overlay linkages to indicate how papers cite each other or to show who's collaborating with whom in terms of co-authorship.

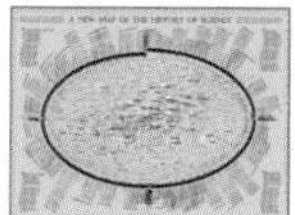

The third visualization, a map of *The History of Science*, was created by W. Bradford Paley and displays four volumes of Henry Smith Williams's *A History of Science*[3] arranged in a circle (Figure 4.3). The first volume starts at 12 o'clock (top) and turns right to 3 o'clock. Second volume is from 3 o'clock to 6 o'clock. The third volume goes from 6 o'clock (bottom) to 9 o'clock, and the final volume goes from 9 o'clock back to 12 o'clock. The preface for each volume is displayed in the four corners and corresponds to the position of the volume in the circular visualization. The text of the volumes is arranged so that it appears as the big bold band, creating an oval reference system. Words that appear in the four volumes are placed inside of the reference system based on where in the text they occur. As a metaphor, imagine each word is connected by rubber bands (indicated by fine white lines) to the places in the original text (in the big bold band) where it occurs. Words that appear throughout the texts, such as *system*, *known*, *various*, and *important*, end up in the middle of the oval. Words that occur mostly in the first volume such as *conception*, *scientific*, and *Greek* appear in the first, top-right quadrant, etc. To ease interpretation, all words with an uppercase first letter, typically proper nouns such as the names of people or places, appear in red.

Examining this map we begin to understand the people and places that were important to science in different centuries. Plus, we can trace changes in the focus of science over the centuries. For example, in the beginning, astronomy was a major focus, but later on physics became central, and scientists became interested in matter, head, form, and light. It wasn't until much later, around the 1770s, that we begin to see words indicating that chemistry has gained importance. Finally, near the top of the arc, medicine takes center stage.

The TextArc visualization connects directly to Project Gutenberg,[4] making it possible to render many different books in this way and to start exploring them in novel ways.

The fourth and final visualization (Figure 4.4) is by André Skupin, a cartographer who uses self-organizing maps (SOM) and geographic information systems (GIS) to render

[3] Williams, Henry Smith. 1904. *A History of Science*. New York: HarperCollins.

[4] http://www.gutenberg.org

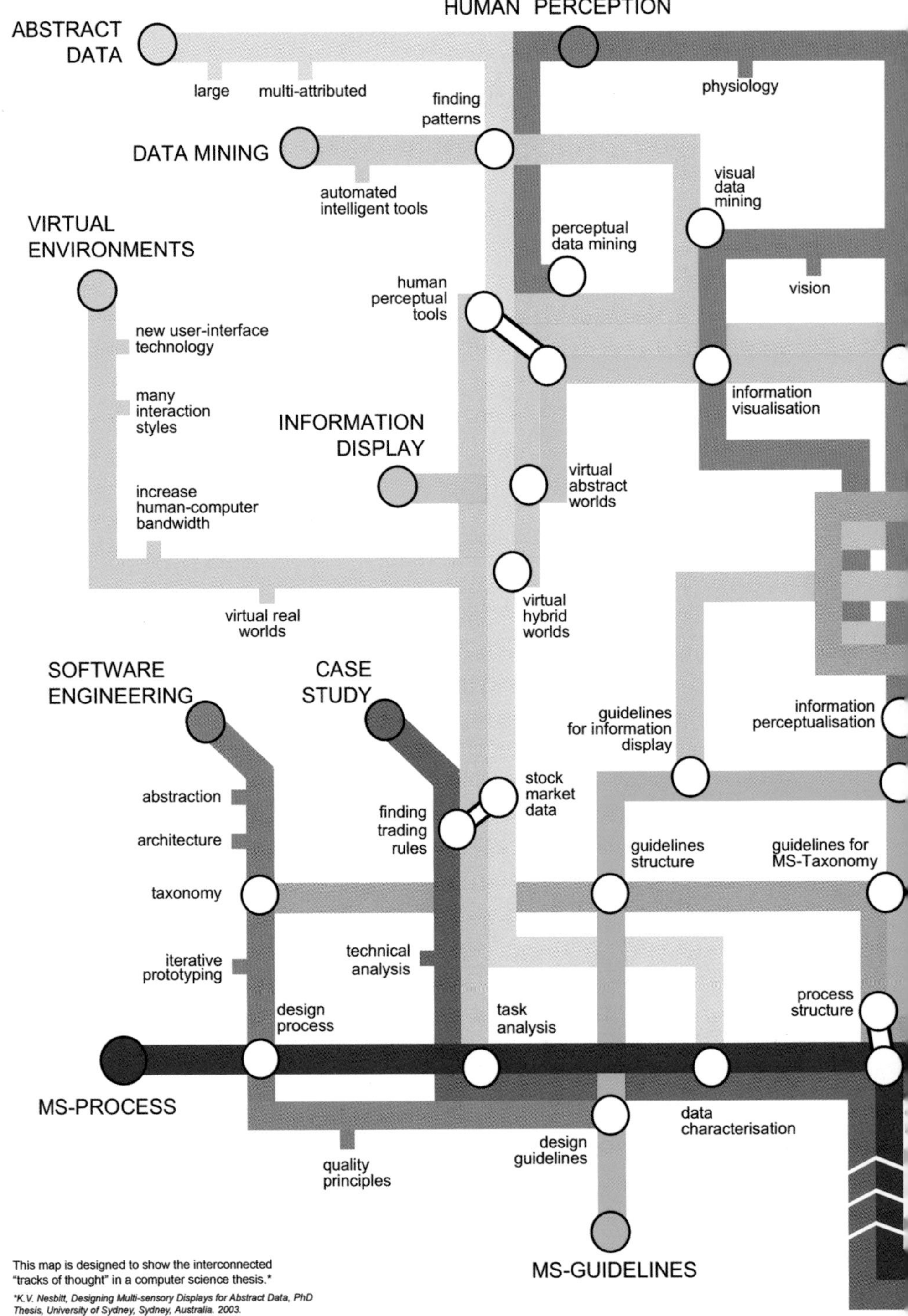

Figure 4.1 *PhD Thesis Map* (2004) by Keith V. Nesbitt (http://scimaps.org/I.6)

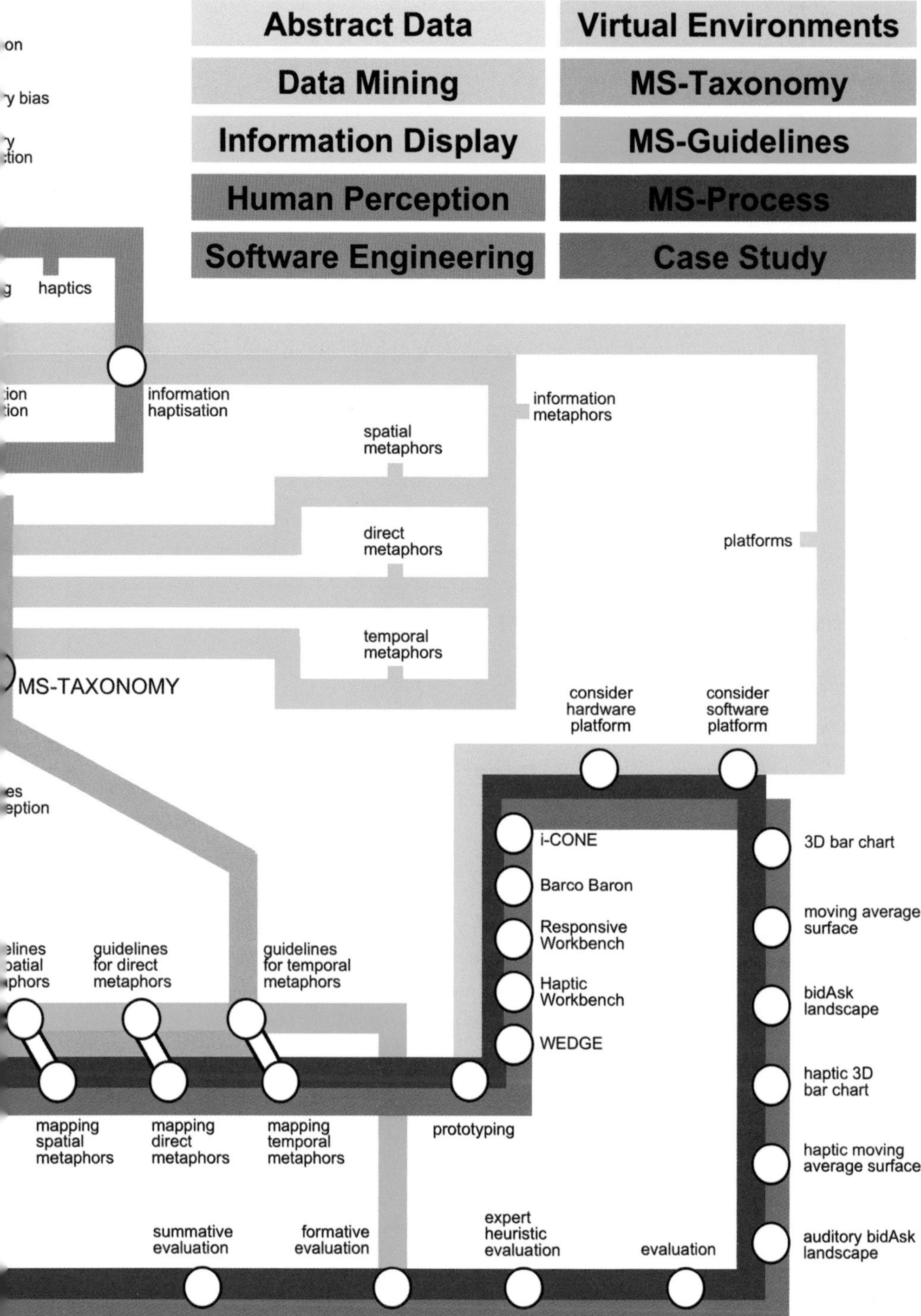

Abstract Data
Virtual Environments
Data Mining
MS-Taxonomy
Information Display
MS-Guidelines
Human Perception
MS-Process
Software Engineering
Case Study
haptics
information haptisation
information metaphors
spatial metaphors
direct metaphors
temporal metaphors
platforms
MS-TAXONOMY
consider hardware platform
consider software platform
i-CONE
Barco Baron
Responsive Workbench
Haptic Workbench
WEDGE
3D bar chart
moving average surface
bidAsk landscape
haptic 3D bar chart
haptic moving average surface
auditory bidAsk landscape
guidelines for direct metaphors
guidelines for temporal metaphors
mapping spatial metaphors
mapping direct metaphors
mapping temporal metaphors
prototyping
summative evaluation
formative evaluation
expert heuristic evaluation
evaluation

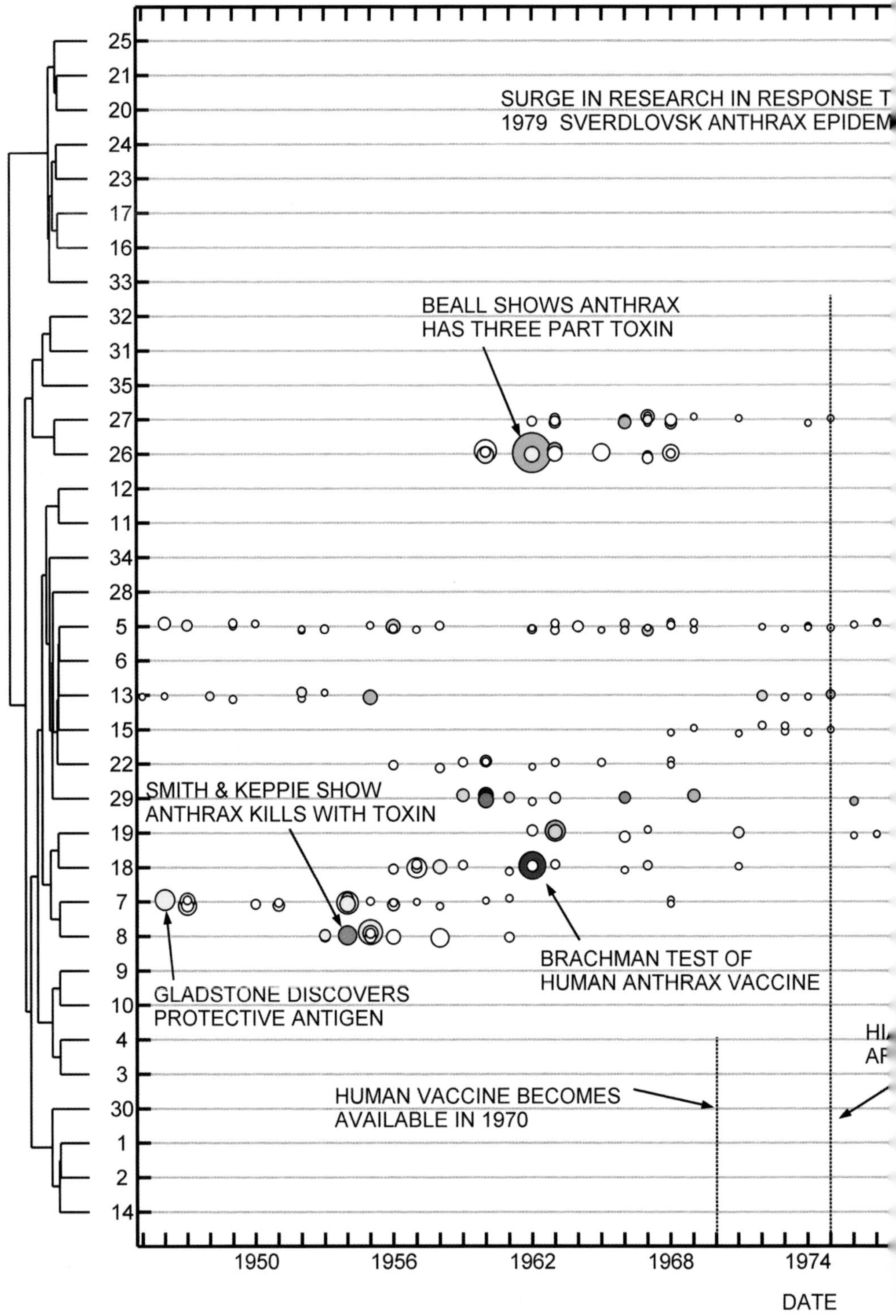

Figure 4.2 *Timeline of 60 Years of Anthrax Research Literature* (2005) by Steven A. Morris (http://scimaps.org/I.7)

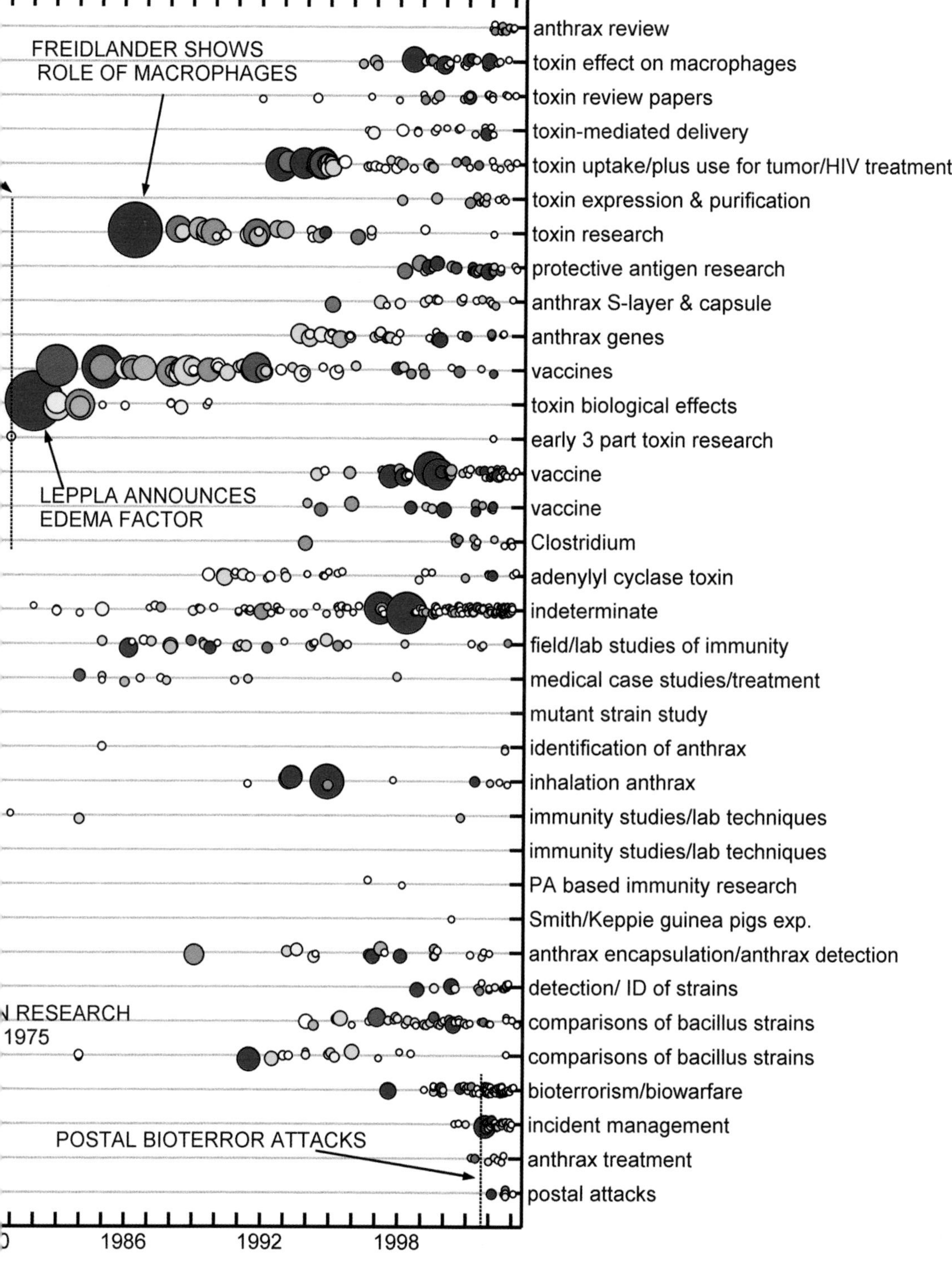
FREIDLANDER SHOWS
ROLE OF MACROPHAGES
LEPPLA ANNOUNCES
EDEMA FACTOR
N RESEARCH
1975
POSTAL BIOTERROR ATTACKS
anthrax review
toxin effect on macrophages
toxin review papers
toxin-mediated delivery
toxin uptake/plus use for tumor/HIV treatment
toxin expression & purification
toxin research
protective antigen research
anthrax S-layer & capsule
anthrax genes
vaccines
toxin biological effects
early 3 part toxin research
vaccine
vaccine
Clostridium
adenylyl cyclase toxin
indeterminate
field/lab studies of immunity
medical case studies/treatment
mutant strain study
identification of anthrax
inhalation anthrax
immunity studies/lab techniques
immunity studies/lab techniques
PA based immunity research
Smith/Keppie guinea pigs exp.
anthrax encapsulation/anthrax detection
detection/ ID of strains
comparisons of bacillus strains
comparisons of bacillus strains
bioterrorism/biowarfare
incident management
anthrax treatment
postal attacks
1986
1992
1998

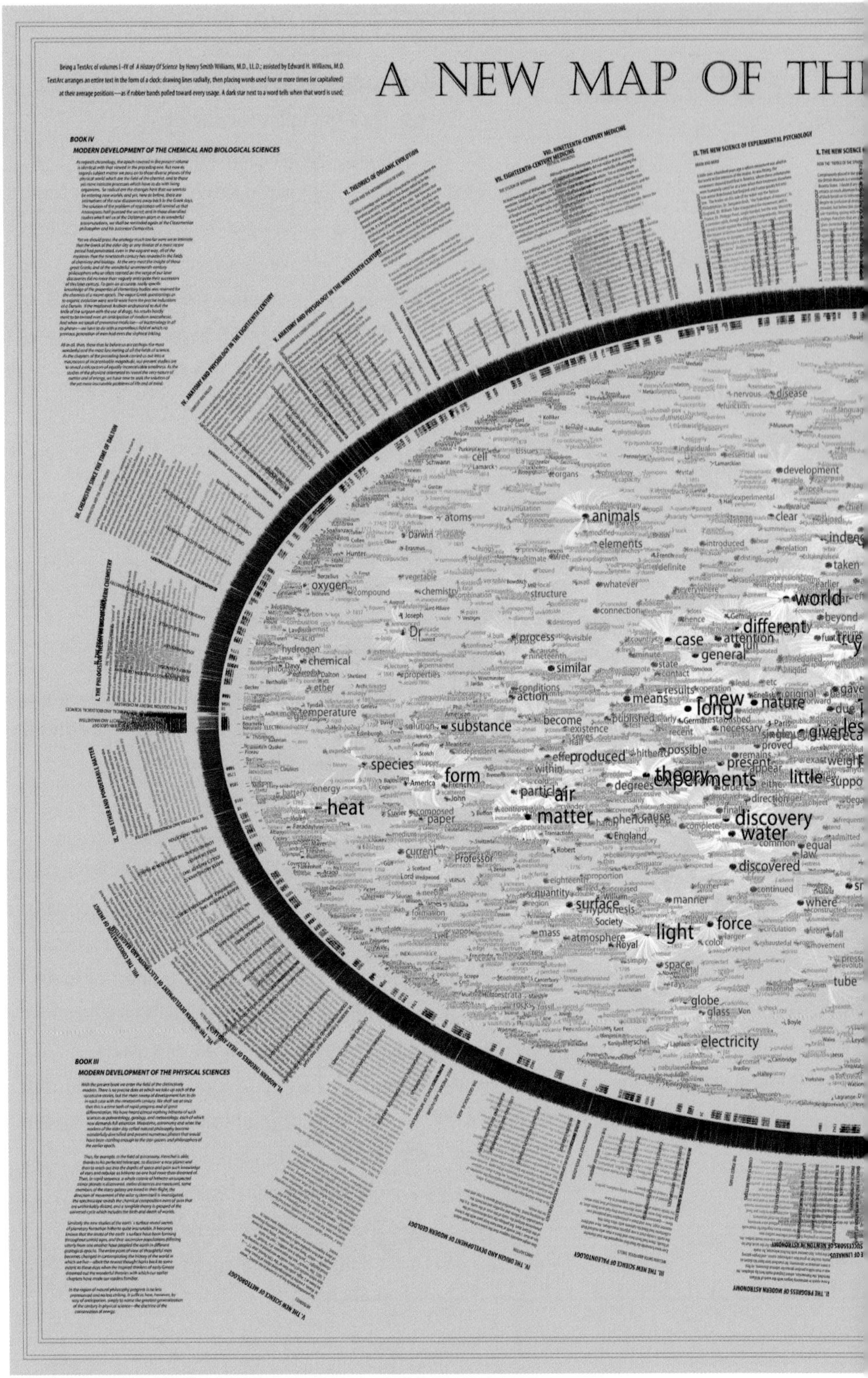

Figure 4.3 *TextArc visualization of The History of Science* (2006) by W. Bradford Paley (http://scimaps.org/II.7)

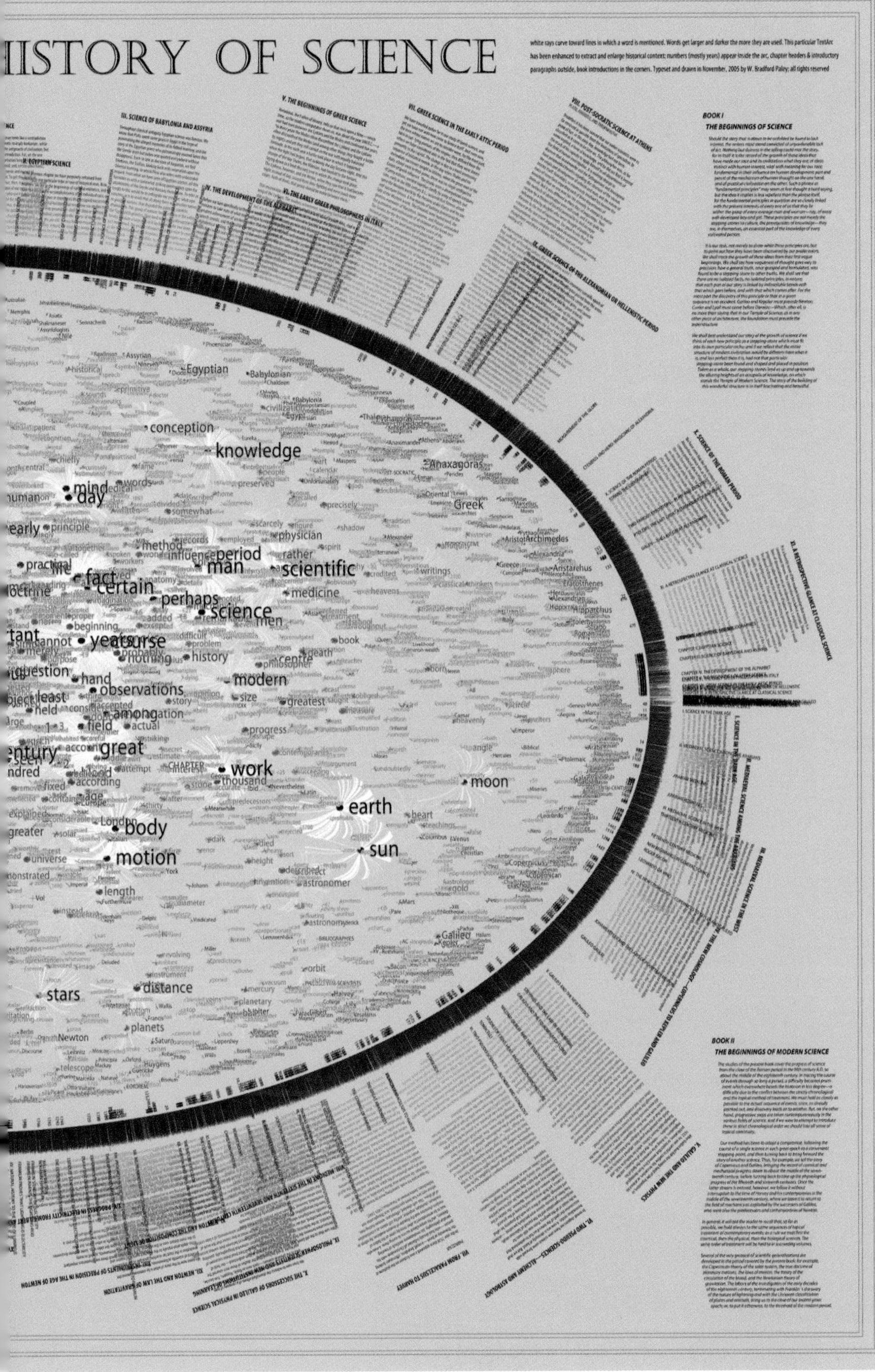

HISTORY OF SCIENCE
white rays curve toward lines in which a word is mentioned. Words get larger and darker the more they are used. This particular TextArc has been enhanced to extract and enlarge historical context: numbers (mostly years) appear inside the arc, chapter headers & introductory paragraphs outside, book introductions in the corners. Typeset and drawn in November, 2005 by W. Bradford Paley; all rights reserved
III. SCIENCE OF BABYLONIA AND ASSYRIA
V. THE BEGINNINGS OF GREEK SCIENCE
VII. GREEK SCIENCE IN THE EARLY ATTIC PERIOD
VIII. POST-SOCRATIC SCIENCE AT ATHENS
IV. THE DEVELOPMENT OF THE ALPHABET
VI. THE EARLY GREEK PHILOSOPHERS IN ITALY
IX. GREEK SCIENCE OF THE ALEXANDRIAN OR HELLENISTIC PERIOD
X. SCIENCE OF THE ROMAN PERIOD
XI. A RETROSPECTIVE GLANCE AT CLASSICAL SCIENCE
BOOK I
THE BEGINNINGS OF SCIENCE
BOOK II
THE BEGINNINGS OF MODERN SCIENCE
conception
knowledge
mind
day
early
principle
method
period
man
scientific
fact
certain
perhaps
science
men
years
course
history
modern
observations
great
work
earth
moon
sun
body
motion
stars
distance
Newton
Anaxagoras
Greek
Egyptian
Babylonian

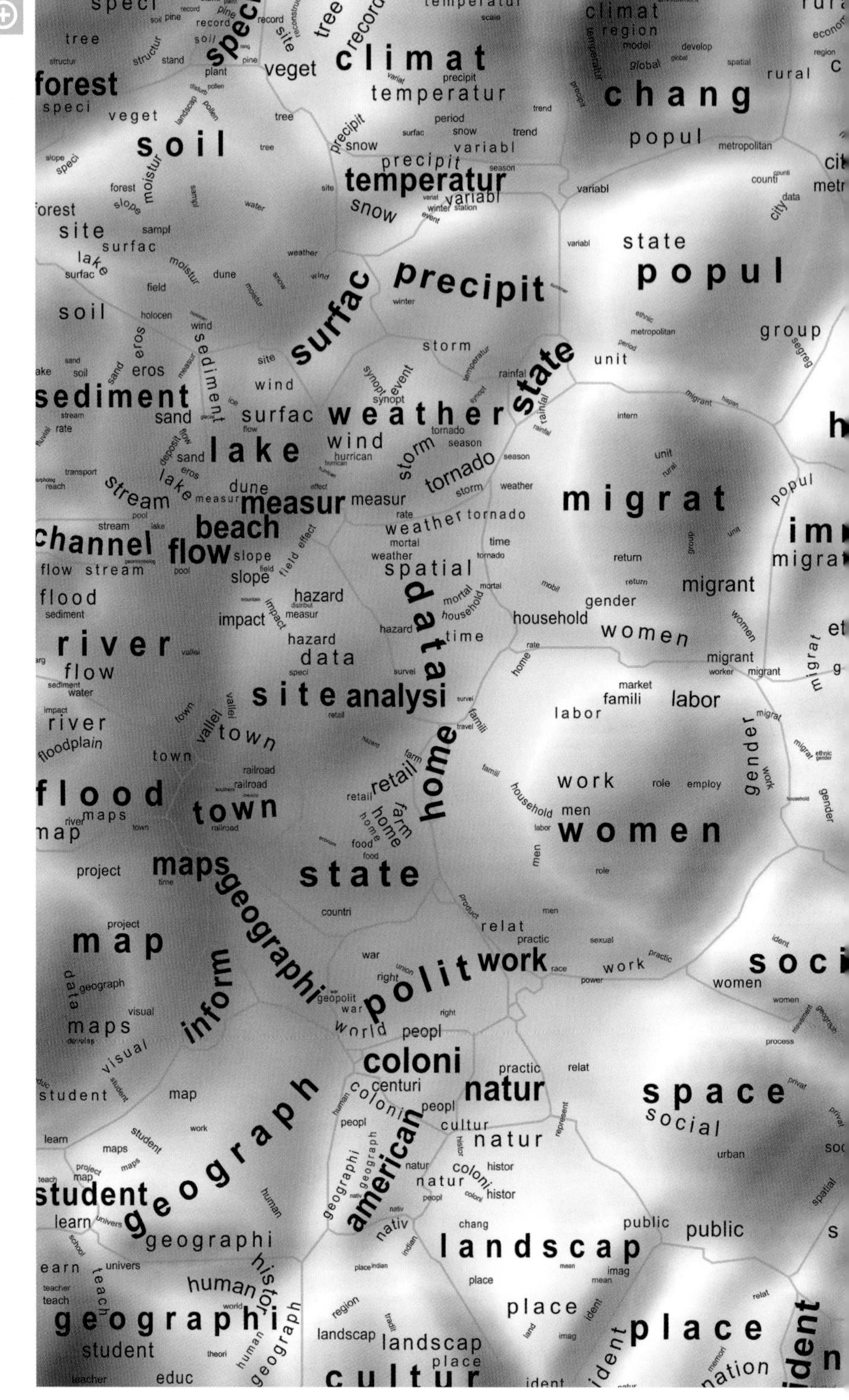

Figure 4.4 *In Terms of Geography* (2005) by André Skupin (http://scimaps.org/I.9)

growth
develop
urban
plan
transport
transit
network
travel
simul
process
model
system
scale
spatial
gis
method
inform
space
econom
city
hous
neighborhood
social
inner
public
transport
plan
transit
rail
inform
decis
data
gis
remot
gis
system
health
geographi
residenti
medic
social
servic
health
hous
commun
provid
popul
water
suppli
qualiti
river
water
use
problem
wetland
sens
imag
remot
satellit
veget
wetland
spectral
cover
sens
remot
land
system
use
manag
migr
immigr
health
local
commun
resourc
watersh
resourc
water
protect
plan
ecolog
manag
land
park
natur
environment
risk
justic
resourc
sustain
land
develop
econom
tourism
tourist
organ
polit
polici
govern
issu
industri
local
polici
environment
local
econom
impact
local
industri
nation
polici
region
industri
invest
product
state
economi
manufactur
global
world
intern
trade
economi
polit
space
parti
power
nation
market
trade
labor
intern
servic
firm
produc
product
technolog
process
industri
restructur
financi
sector
market
state
territori
unit
regul

textual data.[5] It shows ten years of abstracts submitted to the annual conference for the Association of American Geographers (AAG). The data comprises 22,000 abstracts submitted to the annual meetings of the AAG during a ten-year period from 1993 to 2002. Skupin used a SOM arranged in a honeycomb pattern to derive a two-dimensional landscape of geography research. The brown mountains indicate areas of homogeneous research (i.e., if we were able to zoom in on one of the brown areas, we would see hundreds of small pixels, each pixel representing a single abstract, and all abstracts deal with similar topics). Major topics are GIS, health, water, community, woman, migration, or population studies. In Skupin's visualization we can also see valleys, represented by the blue areas on the map. Valleys denote areas with a high level of heterogeneity (i.e., abstracts are rather different from each other). This is the realm of interdisciplinary research, and the question becomes: Are these valleys the land of the lost and confused researchers? Or are they among the most fertile research environments as they are fed by the "sediments" that trickle down from the surrounding mountains? To answer these questions, we could create a similar visualization using more recent data, 2003 to the present, and see if researchers originally working in these low-lying areas were able to climb up existing mountains or if they created new mountains of emerging research.

While self-organizing maps are useful for mapping textual data, they are time and computationally intensive to create. Map labeling was done automatically, using the most common term in the subset of abstracts. If these labels seem strange, that is because they have been stemmed, a concept we will discuss later in this chapter.

4.2 OVERVIEW AND TERMINOLOGY

In this section, we will look at different representations of topical data and discuss terminology used in the analysis and visualization of this data. The main goals in topical analysis, or text analysis, are to understand the topical distribution of a dataset—what topics are covered and how much of each topic is covered. Topical analysis is also interested in how topics emerge, merge, split, or die, something especially interesting for the detection of new research areas. Many people are also interested in topic bursts (see Section 2.4).

Topical analysis is performed across different levels of analysis from the micro to the macro. For example, we might look at a single document, or a single individual's research output, an example of micro-level topical analysis. Or, we can look at journal and book volumes, or scientific disciplines, examples of meso-level analysis.

---

5 Skupin, André. 2004. "The World of Geography: Visualizing a Knowledge Domain with Cartographic Means." *PNAS* 101 (Suppl. 1): 5274–5278.

When conducting a topical analysis, the first most basic term is **text**, a sequence of written or spoken words (e.g., the full text of a book, paper, email, or something much shorter, such as a tweet). Most of the time, we would not just analyze one piece of text, but we would analyze an entire **text corpus** instead. For example, we might analyze all of the tweets from one user. We have seen Bradford Paley's visualization of four books in the TextArc visualization (Figure 4.3), but typically we would analyze many books or abstracts, like in André Skupin's visualization of the 22,000 AAG abstracts (Figure 4.4). One of the goals of topical analysis is to identify **topics** in unstructured texts, whether through the identification of noun-phrases that appear verbatim in the text or through the identification of latent terms. Another term we will likely encounter in the area of topical analysis is **n-gram**, which is a sub-sequence of *n* items from a given sequence of text or speech. **Stop words** are loosely defined as very commonly used words in a body of text, such as *a, the, in, and,* etc. When analyzing a corpus of text, we will want to remove these words as they add little meaning. **Stemming** is another step in the preprocessing stage of topical analysis. It refers to a process for reducing inflected words to their stem, base, or root form. So, for instance, if we have *playing, playful, player,* stemming would reduce these words to *play.* That is, all three original words would map to *play,* resulting in fewer words to analyze, which makes analyzing large amounts of text more feasible.

Two major issues that are frequently encountered when conducting topical analysis are **synonymy** and **polysemy**. Synonymy refers to the fact that there exist words and phrases that are alike in meaning or significance, but are actually two distinct words. Examples would be *happy, joyful, elated*, which all mean roughly the same thing. Another example might be *close* and *shut*, again words that have a similar meaning. Polysemy means one word can have different meanings. For instance, there is a *bank* where we could sit on and a *bank* where we put our money. A *crane* could be a machine used in the construction of buildings or it could be a bird. There are many examples of words that are polysemic, and these words will require disambiguation for accurate topical analysis. Typically, disambiguation can be done by analyzing the context in which those words appear.

When working with different types of topical representations, charts, tables, graphs, geospatial maps, and network graphs are widely used.

Charts, such as word clouds, have no well-defined reference system. Figure 4.5 is an example of a word cloud of movie titles from the Internet Movie Database (IMDb). It was created using the online service Wordle,[6] which allows us to easily create word clouds from text data. The more often the word appears in movie titles, the larger it appears in the word cloud. Larger words tend to be placed in the middle of the cloud, but there is no real spatial reference system involved.

---

6 http://www.wordle.net

Figure 4.5 Word cloud of movie titles from the Internet Movie Database (IMDb) created using Wordle (http://cns.iu.edu/ivmoocbook14/4.5.jpg

Tables are easy to read and they scale to large datasets. Tools such as the Graphical Interface for Digital Libraries (GRIDL),[7,8] developed at the Human-Computer Interaction Lab (HCIL) at the University of Maryland, allow users to view several thousand documents at once using a two-dimensional tree display (Figure 4.6). GRIDL allows users to navigate through the use of categorical and hierarchical axes called hieraxes. We can actually click on Egypt and see cities inside of Egypt displayed along the bottom. The farther we move down on the categorical axes, the more granular the categories become, allowing us to explore topics and their subtopics. There is also an information column that tells us how many more data points exist in Egyptian classification, in Greece, etc. If the dataset contains more documents than can be displayed in a cell, then GRIDL offers a way to visually aggregate those documents into bars. This way, we can view up to 10,000 records at once to quickly identify patterns and distributions. GRIDL also supports the color-coding of additional data attributes (not shown in Figure 4.6).

Graphs are commonly used to visualize the results of a topical analysis. Examples are plots that show how often a word/topic occurs over time, circular visualizations (e.g., TextArc visualization in Figure 4.3), or cross maps (e.g., the timeline of anthrax research literature in Figure 4.2).

We can use **geospatial maps** to indicate which topics occur in what spatial location (e.g., we can use a proportional symbol map to indicate how many authors have published on nanotechnology in U.S. institutions). That is, we would use area-sized coding to represent

---

7 Shneiderman, Ben, David Feldman, Anne Rose, and Xavier Ferré Grau. 2000. "Visualizing Digital Library Search Results with Categorical and Hierarchial Axes." In *Proceedings of the 5th ACM International Conference on Digital Libraries (San Antonio, TX, June 2–7)*, 57–66. New York: ACM.

8 http://www.cs.umd.edu/hcil/west-legal/gridl

the number of papers published in nanotechnology. The visualization of the diffusion of information among major U.S. research institutions[9] (see Figure 1.4) overlays key U.S. institutions that perform biomedical research on a map of the United States. The Illuminated Diagram display (Figure 7.2) discussed in Chapter 7 provides an interactive means to explore what research is conducted where in the world.

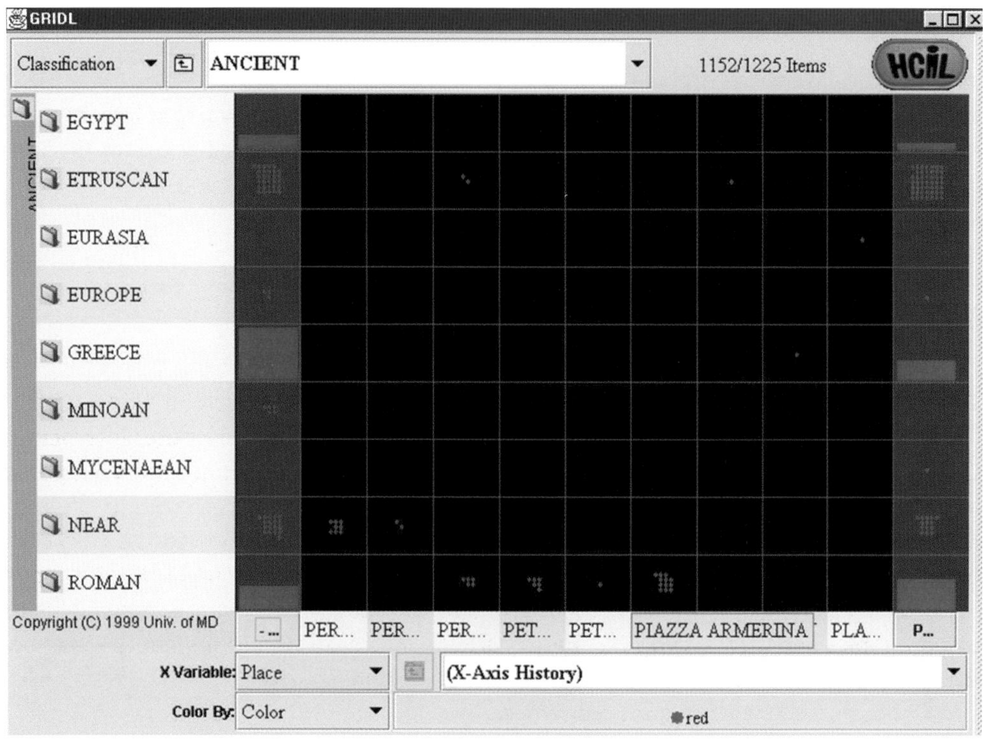

Figure 4.6 Graphical Interface for Digital Libraries (GRIDL) with hieraxes

Alternatively, we can create an abstract two-dimensional space that uses geospatial metaphors. An example is the self-organizing map (SOM) of geography research created by André Skupin (Figure 4.4). Here, each of the 22,000 abstracts is associated with a specific cell in the SOM. A new abstract is added to the map based on topical similarity between the new abstract and the abstracts already existing in the cells. The rather time-consuming similarity comparison of all abstracts in each cell to the new abstract can be sped up through lockup tables or smart indexes. Ultimately, the new abstract is placed in the SOM cell with the most similar abstracts.

---

9 Börner, Katy, Shashikant Penumarthy, Mark Meiss, and Weimao Ke. 2006. "Mapping the Diffusion of Information among Major U.S. Research Institutions." *Scientometrics* 68, 3: 415–426.

Network graphs, such as tree visualizations of hierarchical data (see topical hierarchy on left of timeline of anthrax research literature in Figure 4.2), word co-occurrence networks (see Section 4.8), concept maps, and science map overlays (see Section 4.4) are all used to represent topical analysis results.

4.3 WORKFLOW DESIGN

In this section we will examine the basic workflow used to analyze and visualize topical data (Figure 4.7). Using the workflow introduced in Chapter 1, we will first look at data and how they are read—what kind of data formats text data typically comes in, how to analyze it, and how to visualize it. In terms of visualization, we will, again, look at different reference systems, at different ways to overlay data, and at different ways to graphically encode data variables. Finally, via the deployment of the visualization, it becomes possible for us to validate the maps and to interpret them. As we know now, this often leads to additional data acquisition, additional data analysis, etc. Figure 4.7 exemplarily shows a word cloud and a map of science reference system with a proportional symbol data overlay where circle size denotes the number of papers published and circle color indicates major disciplines of science.

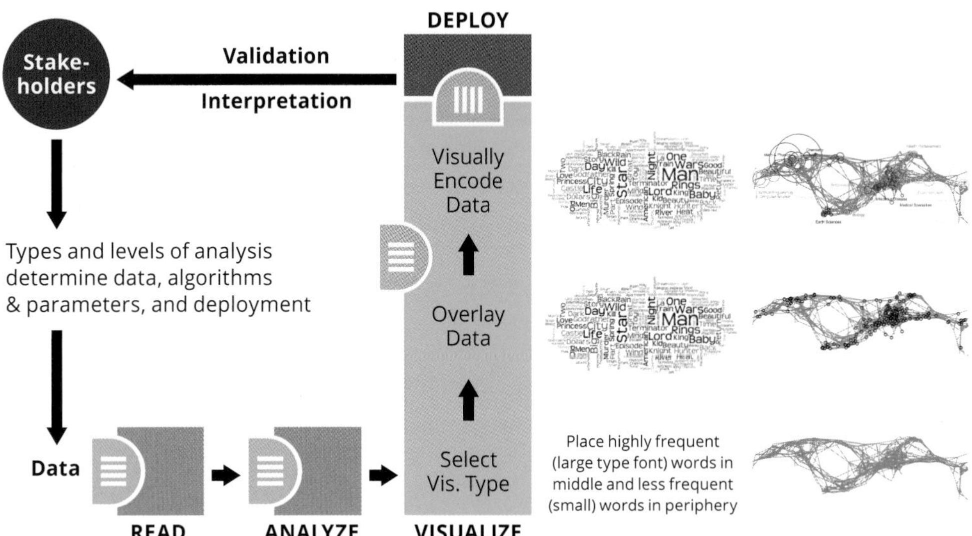

Figure 4.7 Visualization workflow for the UCSD Map of Science reference system

Read & Preprocess Data

We can acquire text data from many sources. Simply copy text from any document or download it from online sources. Examples include the Google Ngrams dataset[10] with text from millions of books scanned by Google, free e-books from Project Gutenberg,[11] the WordNet lexical database for English,[12] KD datasets,[13] the previously mentioned Scholarly Database,[14] or any of the many data repositories listed on the Digging into Data site.[15] Most text data will be in text (.txt) or tabular format (.csv).

After obtaining the data, we will likely need to preprocess the data. For example, we might want to **lowercase** all letters. This way capitalized words used in a title or at the beginning of a sentence will be not be treated differently than those that are lowercase. Next, we **tokenize** the text. Here, we split text into a list of individual words, separated by a text delimiter. We treat each word as a distinct token, which allows it to be processed programmatically. Then, we might **stem** tokens. Here, we remove prefixes and suffixes, leaving the root and helping to identify the core meaning of a word. Finally, we might remove **stop words**, such as "of" and "in" from the text. Figure 4.8 shows an example of the text normalization process using the title of the Albert-László Barabási and Albert Réka publication, "Emergence of Scaling in Random Networks."[16] Despite normalization, we have to deal with synonymy and polysemy, as discussed earlier in this chapter.

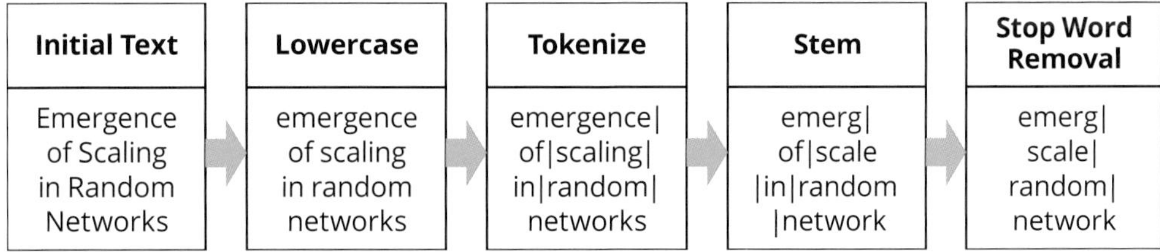

Figure 4.8 Exemplary text normalization process

10 http://books.google.com/ngrams
11 http://www.gutenberg.org
12 http://wordnet.princeton.edu
13 http://www.kdnuggets.com/datasets
14 http://sdb.cns.iu.edu
15 http://www.diggingintodata.org/Repositories/tabid/167/Default.aspx
16 Barabási, Albert-László, and Albert Réka. 1999. "Emergence of Scaling in Random Networks." *Science* 286: 509–512.

Analyze & Visualize

In terms of topical analysis, there are several distinct types of analysis that we can use, including frequency analysis, clustering and classification, or sentiment analysis, such as trying to identify if a piece of text is in favor of or against a certain topic. We can also use burst analysis, which we examined in Chapter 2 as a means for analyzing temporal data, in topical analysis.

Topical analysis typically means breaking down a highly dimensional topical space. For example, we may want to analyze all the documents appearing in Project Gutenberg, which has over 42,000 items. If we are conducting a topical analysis of the entire collection, we would need to analyze all the words appearing in those books, most likely more than 100,000 unique words. The resulting term-by-document matrix would have more than 42,000 book rows and more than 100,000 word columns. The value in each cell of the matrix indicates how often a certain term occurs in the book. Despite working with this high-dimensional topic space, we have only two dimensions to actually represent that space (e.g., as a topic map). **Dimensionality reduction**, such as self-organizing maps or multidimensional scaling, help reduce the dimensionality of the space; for a review of different techniques see Börner et al.[17] The aim of dimensionality reduction is to preserve the most important semantic structure in this high-dimensional space so that it can be represented using two or three dimensions.

Figure 4.9 The VocabGrabber visual thesaurus interface

When performing text analysis, we can use dictionaries and thesauri to identify the meaning of words. Some of these are online, such as the VocabGrabber service,[18] which offers a visual interface for determining the context of the words in a whole piece of text. Figure 4.9 shows an example where the titles of the top 250 most highly rated movies from the Internet Movie Database (IMDb) site are fed into VocabGrabber. The VocabGrabber automatically creates a list of vocabulary from the given text, and we can sort, filter, and save this list for use in other types of analysis. As for the IMDb data, the service returns a list of terms sorted by frequency of occurrence. *Man* is the word used most often, followed by *life*, *ring*, and *star*. In addition to sorting words by frequency, this service also allows us to see which words are relevant for geography (displayed in blue), which ones might refer to

[17] Börner, Katy, Chaomei Chen, and Kevin W. Boyack. 2003. "Visualizing Knowledge Domains." Chap. 5 in *Annual Review of Information Science & Technology*, edited by Blaise Cronin, 37: 179-255. Medford, NJ: American Society for Information Science and Technology.

[18] http://www.visualthesaurus.com/vocabgrabber

people (purple), which ones might apply to social studies (gold), and which ones apply to science (green); *terminator* might not be perfectly classified.

We can filter the results by category, such as geography (Figure 4.10), reducing the list of words to geography-relevant terms. Two words are given in other colors, as they are also relevant for other categories. In addition, we can use VocabGrabber to visualize the semantic network—showing *man* connected to *Isle of Man, human being, human, homo,* etc.

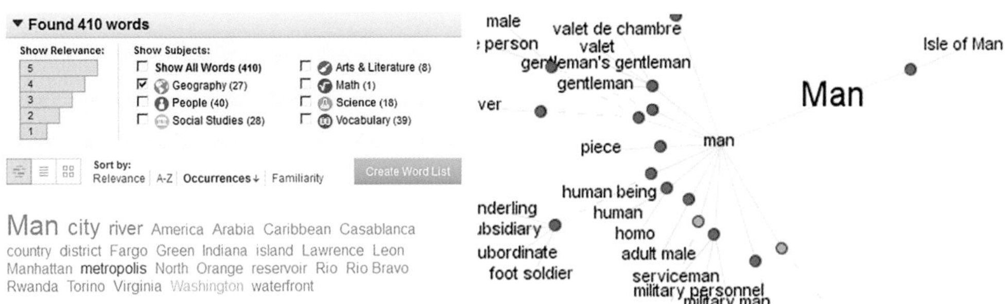

Figure 4.10 VocabGrabber supports filtering by category (left) and creating semantic networks (right)

Another example of a common topical visualization is **word clouds**, such as the one made with Wordle.net[19] that we examined in Figure 4.5. For this visualization we used the same dataset of the top 250 IMDb movies. The layout tries to fill the existing space, and frequently appearing words are placed closer to the center. The size of the font is proportional to the frequency with which those words appear, and the color has no meaning other than to help legibility in dense word clouds. The layout is non-deterministic, so we will get a slightly different layout every time we compute it. The service allows for users to select from a variety of layouts and color schemes.

Another example of a topical visualization is the Google Books Ngram Viewer,[20] which displays word counts over time (Figure 4.11). In this particular case, we see the results for three comma-separated phrases—"Albert Einstein," "Sherlock Holmes," and "Frankenstein." What the Google Books Ngram Viewer does is identify how often these terms appear in books between 1800 and 2000. We can see that Frankenstein has quite a bit of coverage in those books, followed by Sherlock Holmes, and then later, Albert Einstein.

This next visualization shows a network graph science map. We created this map using the UCSD Map of Science and Classification System. It shows a two-dimensional representation of 554 different subdisciplines of science. The 13 major disciplines of science are color-coded and labeled. We can use this base map to overlay the number of publications

---

19 http://wordle.net

20 http://books.google.com/ngrams

Google books Ngram Viewer

Figure 4.11 Google Ngram Viewer interface

Topical Visualization

Generated from 361 Unique ISI Records
90 out of 112 records were mapped to 182 subdisciplines and 13 disciplines.
September 19, 2013 | 00:32 PM EDT

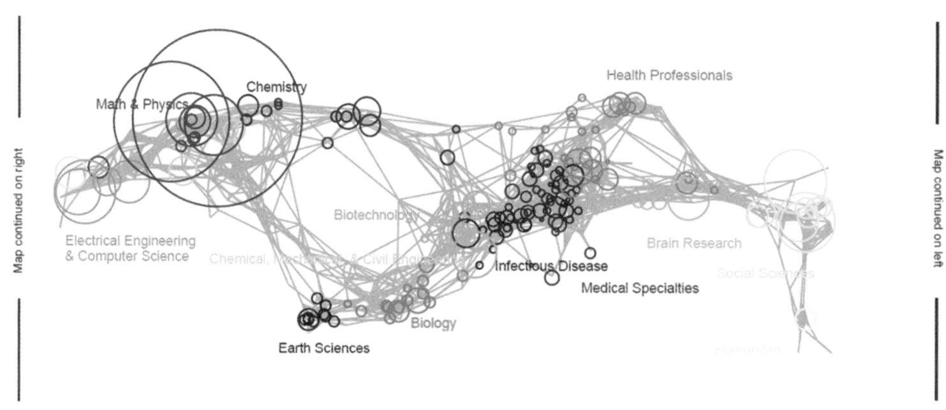

2008 The Regents of the University of California and SciTech Strategies.
Map updated by SciTech Strategies, OST, and CNS in 2011.

Legend

Circle area: Fractional record count
Unclassified = 22
Minimum = 0
Maximum = 98
Color: Discipline
See end of PDF for color legend.

Area

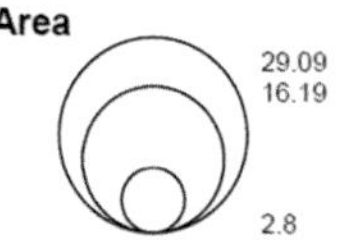

How To Read This Map

The *UCSD map of science* depicts a network of 554 subdiscipline nodes that are aggregated to 13 main disciplines of science. Each discipline has a distinct color and is labeled. Overlaid are circles, each representing all records per unique subdiscipline. Circle area is proportional to the number of fractionally assigned records. Minimum and maximum data values are given in the legend.

CNS (cns.iu.edu)

Figure 4.12 UCSD Map of Science with overlay of publications by four network science researchers (http://cns.iu.edu/ivmoocbook14/4.12.pdf)

or the number of citations by a researcher, institution, or country, for example. Here we show an overlay of the publications by four network science researchers. As we can see in Figure 4.12, many of the publications are in Math & Physics (purple) but quite a few were also published in the Social Sciences (yellow). To add a publication to the map, its journal publication venue is identified; using a journal-subdiscipline lookup table that associates more than 25,000 journals with the 554 subdisciplines, the publication is then added to the correct node. Given a larger set of publications, it makes sense to identify all unique journal venues and their frequency before doing this lookup. Note that there are 95 publications that are unclassified. Those might be books or papers published in venues that are not covered by the UCSD Map of Science.

There are many other tools that we can use to run text analysis, to identify topics, and to map topics. Among them are Textalyser,[21] TexTrend,[22] which is OSGi/CIShell compliant, and VOSviewer,[23] designed for creating, visualizing, and exploring bibliometric maps of science.

4.4 DESIGN AND UPDATE OF A CLASSIFICATION SYSTEM: THE UCSD MAP OF SCIENCE

In this section we introduce the UCSD Map of Science and Classification System, originally funded by the University of California, San Diego.[24] We discuss the design of the original map, the initial update using Elsevier Scopus data, the final updated map that uses Thomson Reuters' Web of Science and Scopus data, map validation, and the application of this map in different tools and services.

The original map was created using 7.2 million publications and their references from Scopus database. The original map also uses Web of Science data, including the Social Science and the Arts and Humanities Citation Indices. This dataset captures data from 2001 to 2004 and includes about 16,000 unique journals combined for the two datasets.

To calculate the similarity between millions of publications, a combination of bibliographic coupling and keyword vectors was used.[25] Clusters of similar publications were then aggregated to 554 subdisciplines of science, which were labeled and linked to relevant journals and keywords. The subdisciplines were further aggregated into thirteen main scientific disciplines (e.g., math or biology), which are labeled and color-coded in the map.

---

21 http://textalyser.net

22 http://textrend.org

23 http://vosviewer.com

24 Börner, Katy, Richard Klavans, Michael Patek, Angela Zoss, Joseph R. Biberstine, Robert P. Light, Vincent Larivière, and Kevin W. Boyack. 2012. "Design and Update of a Classification System: The UCSD Map of Science." *PLoS One* 7, 7: e39464. http://dx.doi.org/10.1371/journal.pone.0039464

25 Klavans, Richard and Kevin W. Boyack. 2006. "Quantitative Evaluation of Large Maps of Science." *Scientometrics* 68, 3: 475-499.

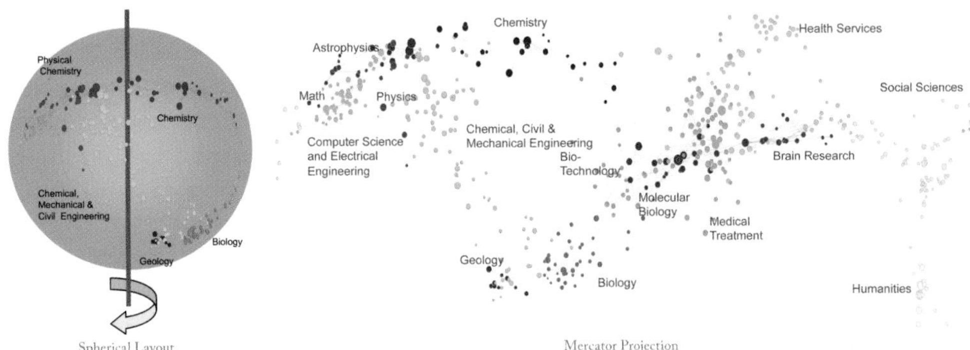

Figure 4.13 Original Map of Science covering five years of Scopus and Web of Science data

The network of 554 subdisciplines and their major similarity linkages was then laid out on the surface of a sphere. Subsequently, it was flattened using a Mercator projection resulting in a two-dimensional map (Figure 4.13). Just like the map of the world, this UCSD Map of Science wraps around horizontally (i.e., the right side connects to the left side of the map).

In order to do proportional symbol data overlays, a new dataset is "science-coded" using the journals and keywords associated with each of the 554 subdisciplines. For example, a paper published in the journal *Pharmacogenomics* has the science-location Molecular Medicine, as the journal is associated with this subdiscipline in the discipline Health Professionals. A table listing all unique journal names and their subdisciplines and disciplines is freely available online.[26] If non-journal data (e.g., patents, grants, or job advertisements) need to be science-located then the keywords associated with each subdiscipline are used to identify the science location for each record based on textual similarity.

A full update of the UCSD Map of Science was completed two years ago using 2006–2008 data from Scopus and 2005–2010 data from Web of Science, increasing the number of source titles to 25,000. Before performing the update, desirable features of a continuously updated Map of Science were identified, and these features were used to guide the update process.[27] In order to update the map, a strategic process was applied. For each of the more than 4,000 new journals, the number of outgoing and incoming citations for each journal and subdiscipline were calculated. The fact that some disciplines publish more papers was accounted for, and the counts were then normalized by the number of papers published among all journals assigned to a subdiscipline. Each new journal was then assigned to the top subdiscipline

26 http://sci.cns.iu.edu/ucsdmap

27 Börner, Katy, Richard Klavans, Michael Patek, Angela Zoss, Joseph R. Biberstine, Robert P. Light, Vincent Larivière, and Kevin W. Boyack. 2012. "Design and Update of a Classification System: The UCSD Map of Science." *PLoS ONE* 7, 7: e39464. http://dx.doi.org/10.1371/journal.pone.0039464

citing it. In terms of multidisciplinary journals such as *PLOS ONE,* the highest combined relative importance across subdisciplines was used. It was decided to assign highly interdisciplinary journals to exactly one subdiscipline because people often have a hard time dealing with the fact that if *Science* or *Nature* publications get added to the Map of Science, then all the many nodes associated with these two journals highlight (or change proportionally in size).

The new UCSD Map of Science is widely used in different displays, services, and tools. Among others it is used in the Illuminated Diagram Display (see Section 7.2), which supports the interactive exploration of geospatial and topical expertise profiles. It is also employed in the VIVO International Researcher Networking Service (Section 7.2) to facilitate the exploration and comparison of expertise profiles for different organizations/ institutions. The Map of Science has been deployed in the MAPSustain interactive web site,[28,29] which provides a visual interface[30] to seven different publication, funding, and patent data sources. The web site helps researchers, industry, and government staff to understand activities and results on sustainability, particularly biofuel and biomass. Finally, the UCSD Map of Science is available in the Sci2 Tool (see workflow in Section 4.6). Sci2 provides extensive information on how many paper records were mapped to what subdiscipline. A listing of unclassified records is provided in support of data cleaning.

The science map has been validated as part of a study to identify a consensus Map of Science.[31] In that study, 20 maps of science were examined and found to have a very high level of correspondence. Some are paper-level maps and some are journal-level maps. Some are created just by externalizing what one expert thought the structure of science looks like. Others use large-scale datasets and advanced data mining and visualization algorithms. We examine and compare the 20 maps in Figure 4.14.

New global maps of science are coming into existence every year. In order to understand their accuracy and utility for answering different types of questions, more evaluation studies are needed.

---

28 http://mapsustain.cns.iu.edu

29 Stamper, Michael J., Chin Hua Kong, Nianli Ma, Angela M. Zoss, and Katy Börner. 2011. "MAPSustain: Visualising Biomass and Biofuel Research." In *Proceedings of Making Visible the Invisible: Art, Design and Science in Data Visualization, University of Huddersfield, UK*, edited by Michael Hohl, 57–61.

30 Börner, Katy, and Chaomei Chen, eds. 2002. *Visual Interfaces to Digital Libraries. Lecture Notes in Computer Science* 2539. Berlin: Springer-Verlag.

31 Boyack, Kevin W., David Newman, Russell Jackson Duhon, Richard Klavans, Michael Patek, Joseph R. Biberstine, Bob Schijvenaars, André Skupin, Nianli Ma, and Katy Börner. 2011. "Clustering More Than Two Million Biomedical Publications: Comparing the Accuracies of Nine Text-Based Similarity Approaches." *PLoS ONE* 6, 3: 1–11.

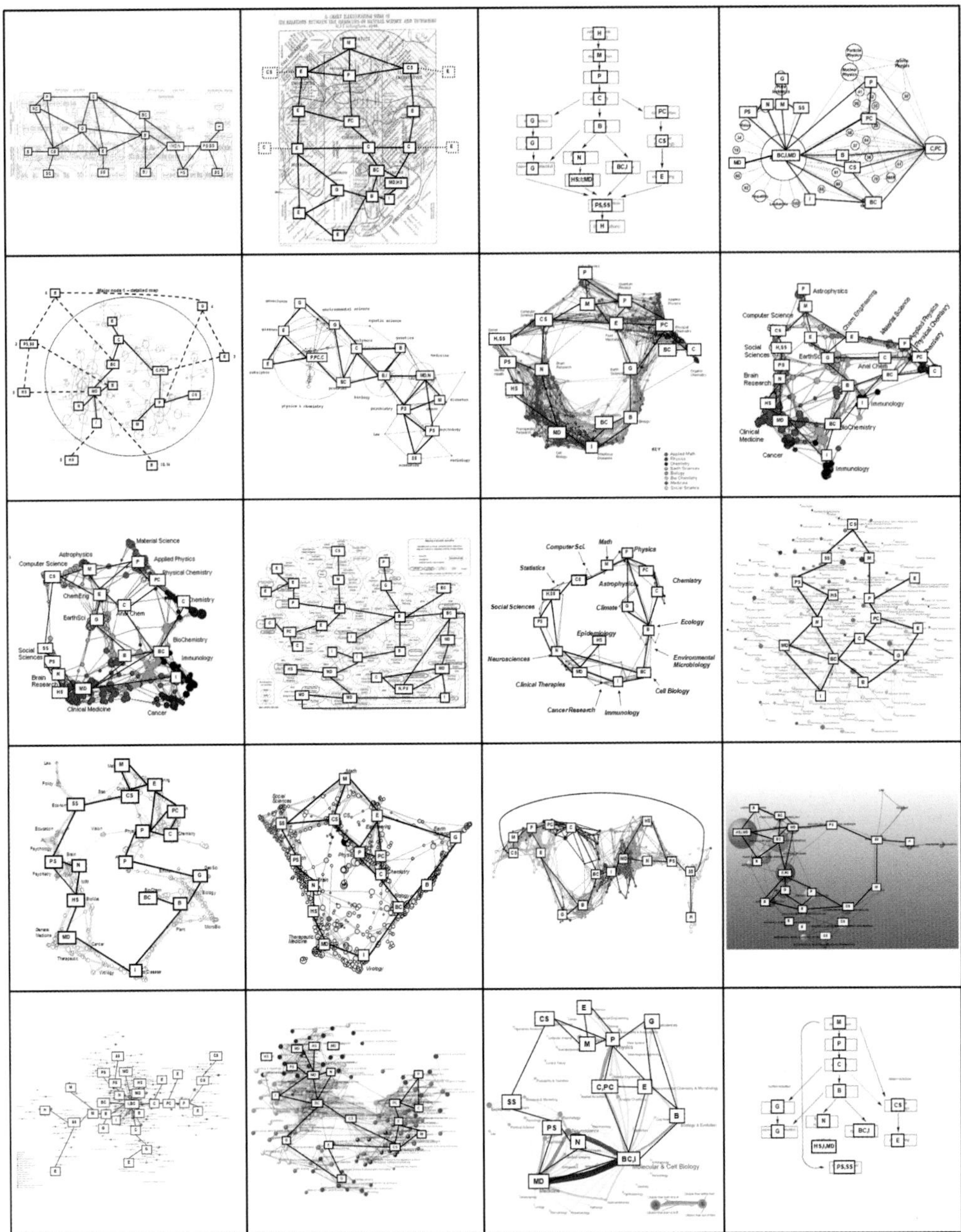

Figure 4.14 Twenty different maps of science compared to arrive at a consensus map

Self-Assessment

1. What visualization type is a word cloud?
   a. Chart
   b. Graph
   c. Map

2. In text normalization, "tokenize" refers to the . . .
   a. Removal of low-content prefixes and suffixes
   b. Removal of low-content tokens
   c. Breaking a stream of text up into words or phrases

3. Which of the below steps is not relevant for text normalization in preparation for topical analysis and visualization?
   a. Lowercase words
   b. Remove stop words
   c. Stemming
   d. Extract co-occurrence network
   e. Tokenization

4. When is text normalization not needed?
   a. To determine word similarity
   b. To determine record similarity
   c. To extract word co-occurrence
   d. To perform controlled vocabulary search

Chapter 4: Hands-On Section

4.5 MAPPING TOPIC BURSTS IN *PROCEEDINGS OF NATIONAL ACADEMY OF SCIENCES (PNAS)*

Data Types & Coverage	
Time Frame:	1982-2001
Region:	Worldwide
Topical Area:	Mostly Biomedical
Network Type:	Word Co-Occurence

Analysis Types/Levels	•	●	⬤
Temporal		X	
Geospatial			
Topical		X	
Network		X	

Co-word analysis identifies the number of times two words are used together (e.g., in the title, keyword set, abstract and/or full text of a publication). The weighted and undirected word co-occurrence networks can be visualized providing a unique view of the topic coverage of a dataset.

In this workflow we explain how to combine burst detection and word co-occurrence analysis to visualize topics and topic bursts in biomedical research using papers published in the *Proceedings of the National Academy of Sciences* (*PNAS*) from 1982 to 2001.[32] The complete dataset of 47,073 papers was made available to participants of the Arthur M. Sackler Colloquium on "Mapping Knowledge Domains" in 2003 but cannot be shared. Instead, we use the smaller dataset of the top 50 most frequent and most bursting keywords from the original dataset. This word co-occurrence network has 50 nodes and 1,082 edges that represent the co-occurrence of the words. The network is extremely dense and so we applied the pathfinder network scaling algorithm (PFNet)[3] (see description in Section 6.4) to reduce the large number of edges to 62. We then visualized the network using the free tool Pajek.[33] While Pajek was originally developed only for Windows it can be run on a Mac by setting up an instance of Darwine.[34]

The workflow comprises the following steps: Download *PNAS_top50-words.net* file from the Sample Datasets section on the Sci2 wiki.[35] Download, install, and run Pajek. Load the file into Pajek by clicking on the open folder icon in the 'Networks' portion of the Pajek interface. The resulting load report will tell how many lines of the file have been read, 132 lines in this

---

[32] Mane, Ketan K., and Katy Börner. 2004. "Mapping Topics and Topic Bursts in *PNAS*. *Proceedings of the National Academy of Sciences of the United States of America* 101 (Suppl. 1): 5287–5290. doi:10.1073/pnas.0307626100.

[33] http://mrvar.fdv.uni-lj.si/pajek

[34] http://vlado.fmf.uni-lj.si/pub/networks/pajek/howto/PajekOSX.pdf

[35] http://wiki.cns.iu.edu/display/SCI2TUTORIAL/2.5+Sample+Datasets

case. Next, select *Draw* > *Network* from the top menu of Pajek. The graph renders in a separate window without any formatting. Follow these steps in the graph window:

1. Run *Layout* > *Energy* > *Fruchterman Reingold* > *2D*.
2. Select *Options* > *Size* > *of Vertices Defined in the Input File*.
3. Select *Options* > *Colors* > *Vertices* > *As Defined on Input File*. After resizing and coloring the nodes, move the nodes around slightly to eliminate overlapping by clicking and dragging.
4. Select *Options* > *Colors* > *Vertices Border* > *As Defined on Input File*.
5. Select *Options* > *Lines* > *Grey Scale*.

The final visualization shows the most frequently occurring and bursting terms, how often they are used together, and the date for the start of the burst (Figure 4.15). The nodes are sized based on the maximum burst level, the color corresponds to the year in which the words are most often used, the node borders are colored based on the starting year of the burst, and the edges are colored based on how often these words appear together. See also description of original map in Figure 1.4.

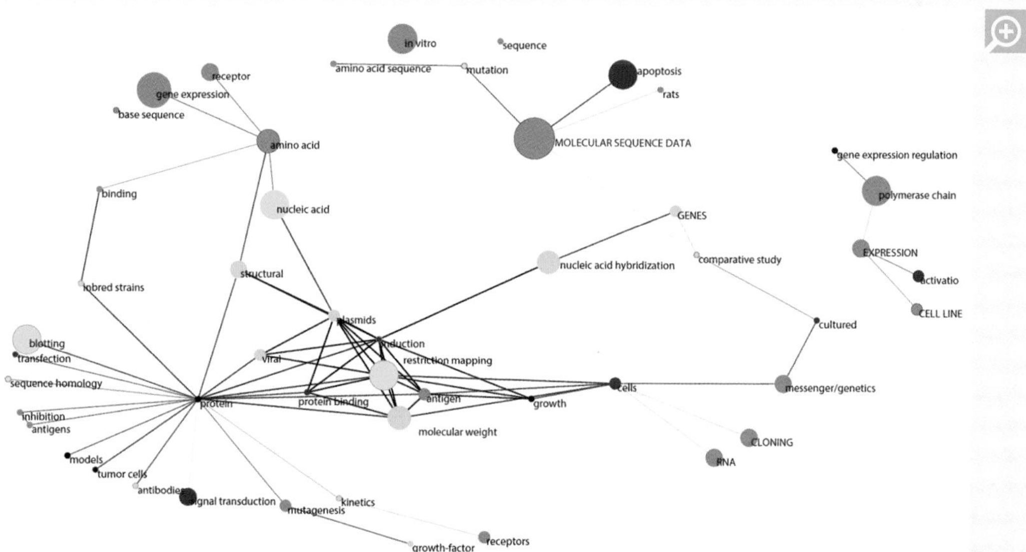

Figure 4.15 Co-word space of the top 50 highly frequent and bursty words used in the top 10% of the most highly cited *PNAS* publications from 1982 to 2001 (http://cns.iu.edu/ivmoocbook14/4.15.jpg)

4.6 UCSD MAP OF SCIENCE

Data Types & Coverage	
Time Frame:	1955-2007
Region:	Miscellaneous
Topical Area:	Network Science
Network Type:	Not Applicable

Analysis Types/Levels	●	●	●
Temporal			
Geospatial			
Topical		X	
Network			

The UCSD Map of Science is a visual representation of 554 subdisciplines within 13 disciplines of science and their relationships to one another, shown as lines connecting to points (see Section 4.4 for design, update, and usage of the map). This workflow uses publication data for four major network science researchers: Stanley Wasserman, Eugene Garfield, Alessandro Vespignani, and Albert-László Barabási. The data were downloaded from the Web of Science (WoS) in 2007.

Load the *FourNetSciResearchers.isi* file[36] into Sci2 using *File* > *Load*. The file will show in the 'Data Manager' titled '361 Unique ISI Records'. Select this file and run *Visualization* > *Topical* > *Map of Science via Journals* and use the default parameters (Figure 4.16).

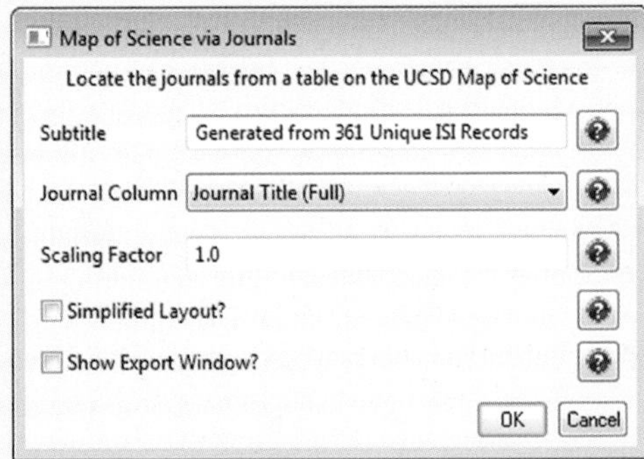

Figure 4.16 Parameters used to overlay *FourNetSciResearchers.isi* publications on the UCSD Map of Science

Upon selecting 'OK', three files appear in the 'Data Manager'. One lists the 'Journals located' on the Map of Science. The other lists 'Journals not located'. Review the latter file and correct any spelling errors so that more journals can be mapped if possible. The third file is a PostScript file. Save the PostScript file, convert it to a PDF (see p. 286 in the Appendix for instructions), and view it (Figure 4.17). The visualization shows the topic coverage of the four researchers—subdisciplines in which any of them published are indicated by circles. The circles are size-coded by the number of citations and color-coded by the 13 disciplines. There exists a major topical concentration in Math & Physics (large purple circle), but also in Computer Science and Social Science. Reading the legend reveals that 22 publications could not be science located—those should be checked for spelling errors.

We will also use the *FourNetSciResearchers.isi* data to extract and visualize an author co-occurrence (co-author) network in Section 6.6.

---

36 *yoursci2directory*/sampledata/scientometrics/isi

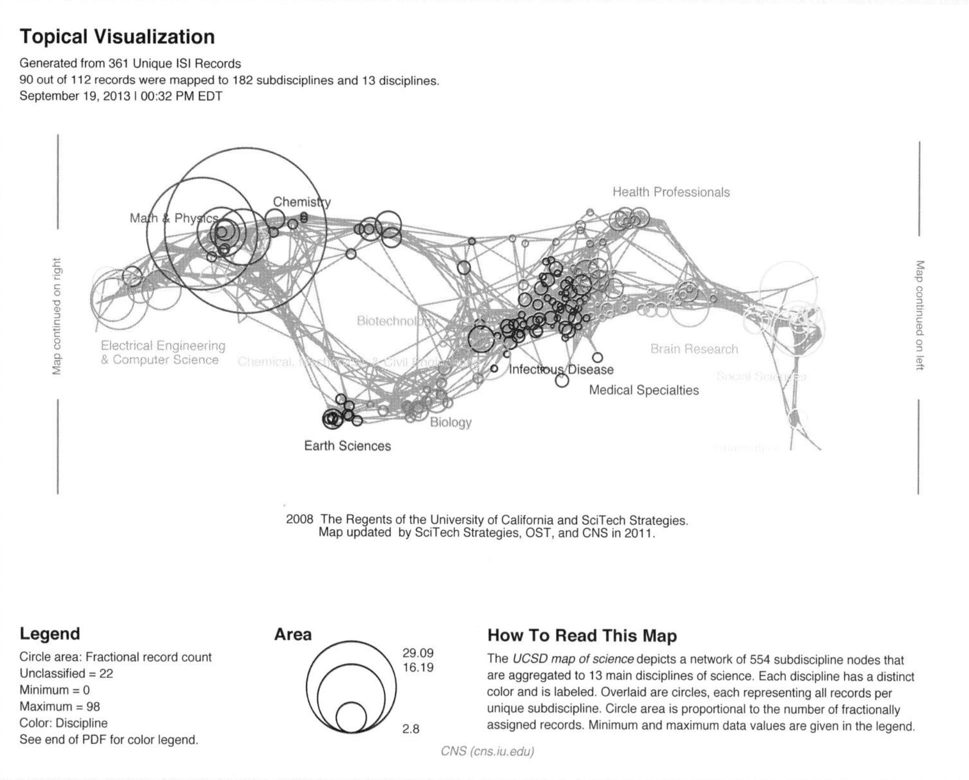

Figure 4.17 *FourNetSciResearchers.isi* over the Map of Science (http://cns.iu.edu/ivmoocbook14/4.17.pdf)

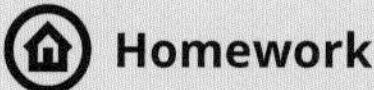

Homework

Download some citation data that you find interesting, make sure the data contain journal titles. Take this data and overlay it on the Map of Science using the journal titles, similar to the workflow performed in Section 4.6. See if the map matches your expectations based on the areas of research covered by your dataset.

Chapter Five
"WITH WHOM": Tree Data

Chapter 5: Theory Section

This chapter provides an introduction on how to use tree data to answer "WITH WHOM" questions. Tree datasets, such as directory structures, organizational hierarchies, branching processes, genealogies, or classification hierarchies are commonly organized and displayed using tree visualizations: for example, tree views, treemaps, or tree graphs.

This section discusses exemplary visualizations, relevant terminology, and different approaches to visualize hierarchical data.

5.1 EXEMPLARY VISUALIZATIONS

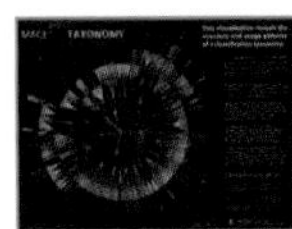

Here we will discuss four examples of tree visualizations. The first example was designed by Moritz Stefaner. It depicts a classification taxonomy developed and used in the Metadata for Architectural Contents in Europe (MACE) project (Figure 5.1).[1] This project aims to provide better access to digital resources for teaching and learning about architecture. The map shows a visual representation of this classification of architecture resources. The visualization is comprised of over 2,800 terms available in different languages—English, Spanish, German, Italian, and Dutch. Starting from the most general term, which is placed at the center, each pass to the outside displays terms that are more specific to certain areas of architecture.

The circle overlays indicate the number of associated resources for each class, helping us understand the structure and usage of the taxonomy. For subject matter experts in the project, this visualization has shown to be useful for quality control and the iterative refinement of the taxonomy. This map is a good example of a **radial tree graph**, a type of visualization that we will discuss in more detail later in this chapter. There's also an interactive version available at the MACE portal.[2]

The next visualization, *The Tree of Life* (Figure 5.2),[3] is another example of a radial tree graph. This visualization was created by researchers at the European Molecular Biology Laboratory. It shows the phylogeny of 191 species for which genomes have been fully sequenced. There are three sub-trees that correspond to the three domains of cellular organisms: Archaea, Eukaryota, and Bacteria. These domains are indicated by the three colored bands around the outside of the graph, and within these bands are listed the 191 species names. The tree

---

1 Wolpers, Martin, Martin Memmel, and Moritz Stefaner. 2010. "Supporting Architecture Education Using the MACE System." *International Journal of Technology Enhanced Learning* 2 (½): 132–144.

2 http://portal.mace-project.eu/BrowseByClassification

3 Ciccarelli, Francesca, Tobias Doerks, Christian von Mering, Christopher J. Creevey, Berend Snel, Peer Bork. 2006. "Toward Automatic Reconstruction of a Highly Resolved Tree of Life." *Science* 311, 5765: 1283–1287.

structure at the center of the graph was created based on orthologs, which are genes in different species that share a common ancestral gene by speciation.

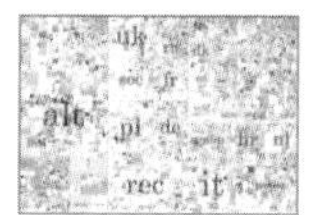

In the next visualization, we see a **treemap** view of Usenet's returnees (Figure 5.3).[4] This map was created by two Microsoft engineers, Marc Smith and Danyel Fisher, a sociologist and computer scientist respectively. They created this portrait of activity of about 190,000 newsgroups, which generated 257 million postings in 2004. The visualization uses the treemap layout originally introduced by Ben Shneiderman at the University of Maryland.[5] Each newsgroup is represented by a square. For instance, all newsgroups that start with UK would be inside of the square labeled with *uk*. Within the *uk* newsgroup there are sub-categories for other newsgroups including *tv* for television and *rec* for recreation, among many others. The treemap is a space-filling layout. It is sorted—all the larger categories are in the lower left corner and become smaller toward the top right corner.

The final example, *Examining the Evolutions and Distribution of Patent Classifications,* shows a map of patent classifications and how they increase over time (Figure 5.4).[6] It shows the enormous increase in the number of patents over time for the two time slices, 1983–1987 and 1998–2002. The map displays inserts for the slow-growing classes of patents, which are mechanical, chemical, and other areas. The map also displays the fast-growing classes of patents, which include electrical & electronic, computers & communications, and drugs & medical. This map employs a treemap layout, color-coded green for areas of growth, black if the area is stagnant, and red if it is declining. There are two treemaps for each class of patents across the two time slices so we can see how these patent classes have grown. On the right is a listing of the top 10 sub-classes and their number of patents. Class 514, for example, is drug, bio-affecting, and body treating compositions.

In the lower part of the map, the patent portfolios for Apple Computers and Jerome Lemelson are displayed. We can see that Apple's patents have mostly increased over time, with only some decline. Lemelson has fewer patents but basically a similar number each year. Apple's portfolio spans 1980–2002 and Lemelson's portfolio spans 1976–1980. The color-coding is done in a way that whenever there was no patent granted in a class for the last five years, then this class is highlighted in yellow. We can see that from time to

---

4 Fiore, Andrew, and Marc A. Smith. 2001. "Tree Map Visualizations of Newsgroups." Technical Report MSR-TR-2001-94, October 4. Microsoft Corporation Research Group. http://research.microsoft.com/apps/pubs/default.aspx?id=69889 (accessed July 31, 2013).

5 Shneiderman, Ben. 1992. "Tree Visualization with Tree-Maps. 2-D Space-Filling Approach." In *ACM Transactions on Graphics* 11:92–99. New York: ACM Press.

6 Kutz, Daniel O. 2004. "Examining the Evolution and Distribution of Patent Classifications." In *Proceedings of the 8th International Conference on Information Visualisation,* 983–988. Los Alamitos, CA: IEEE Computer Society.

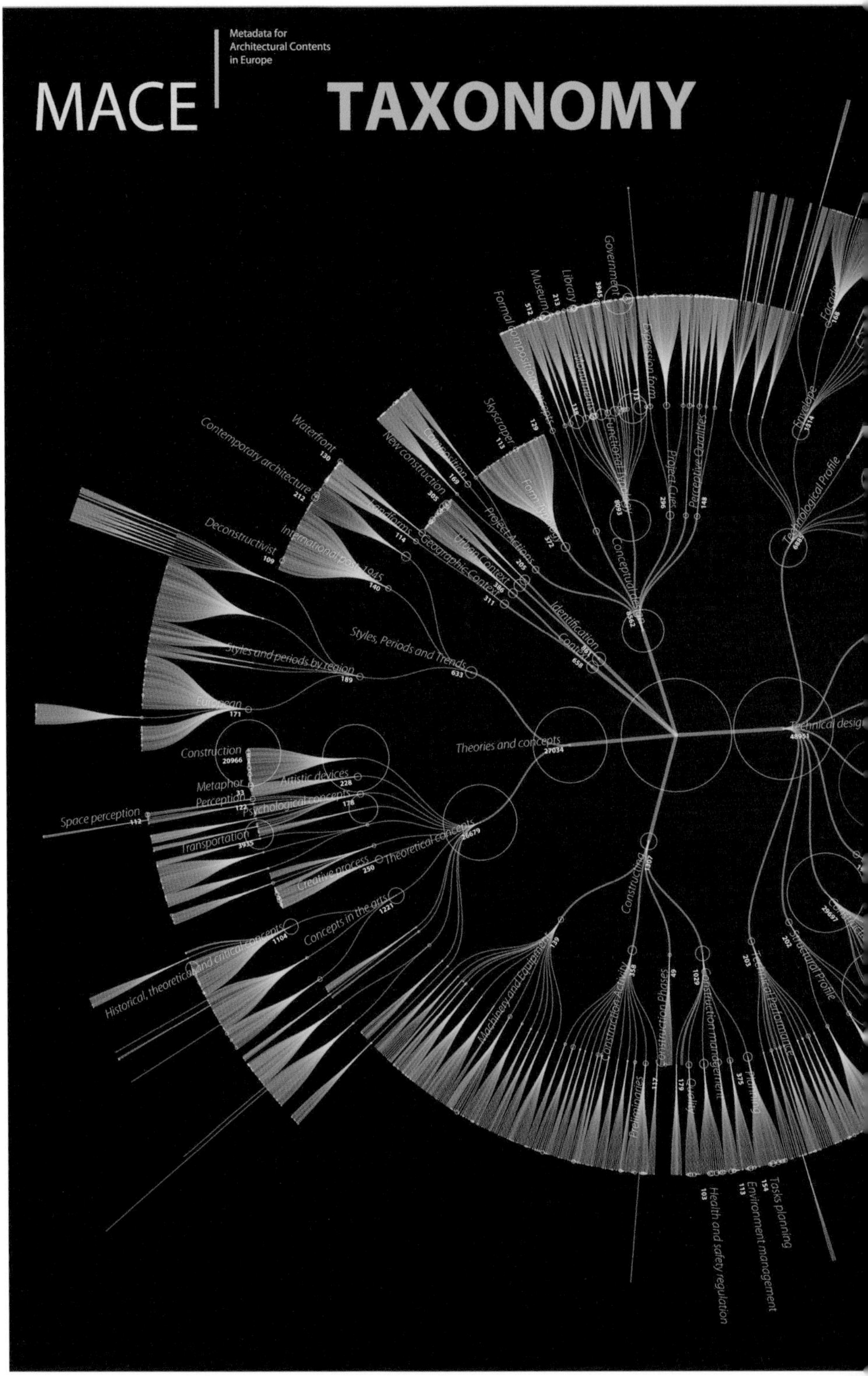

Figure 5.1 *MACE Classification Taxonomy* (2011) by Moritz Stefaner (http://scimaps.org/VII.9)

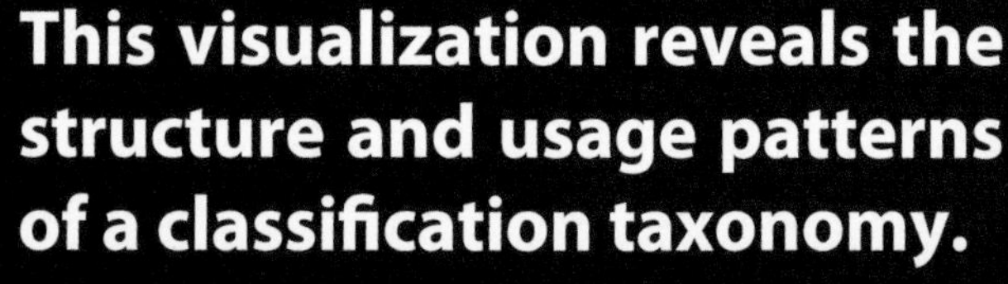

This visualization reveals the structure and usage patterns of a classification taxonomy.

It is developed and used in the MACE project, which aims at providing better access to digital resources for teaching and learning about architecture.

The diagram shows the structure of the vocabulary used for tagging resources. Currently, it comprises over 2800 concepts, many of which have labels in German, English, Spanish, French, and other languages.

The layout is based on the radial layout mechanism introduced in [1], and provides a birds-eye view of the whole taxonomy tree, with the root placed at the center of the graphic, and each path to the outside representing one "route of specialization".

Accordingly, we can see how the vocabulary is organized in broad categories like *Technical Design, Conceptual Design*, or *Theories and Concepts* closer to the center, which contain multiple levels of sub-categories located on rings on the periphery.

In addition, circle overlays indicate the number of resources tagged with the respective term (or any child term), providing hints about the usage patterns of the taxonomy. The exact number of resources for some selected concepts can be found below the text label.

http://www.mace-project.eu

[1] Yee, K-P., Fisher, D., Dhamija, R. and Hearst, M. (2001) 'Animated exploration of dynamic graphs with radial layout', IEEE Symposium on Information Visualization, INFOVIS' 01, San Diego, USA, pp.43–50.

Thanks to the MACE team for compiling the taxonomy and providing the technical infrastructure as well as the MACE users for providing the metadata.

The MACE project was co-funded by the European commission under contract number ECP 2005 EDU 038098 in the eContentplus programme.

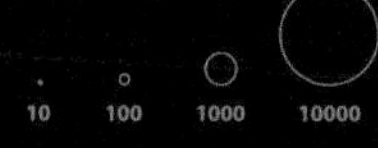

Number of resources

Visualization designed and developed by
Moritz Stefaner *(http://moritz.stefaner.eu)*
while working at the Interaction Design Lab, FH Potsdam

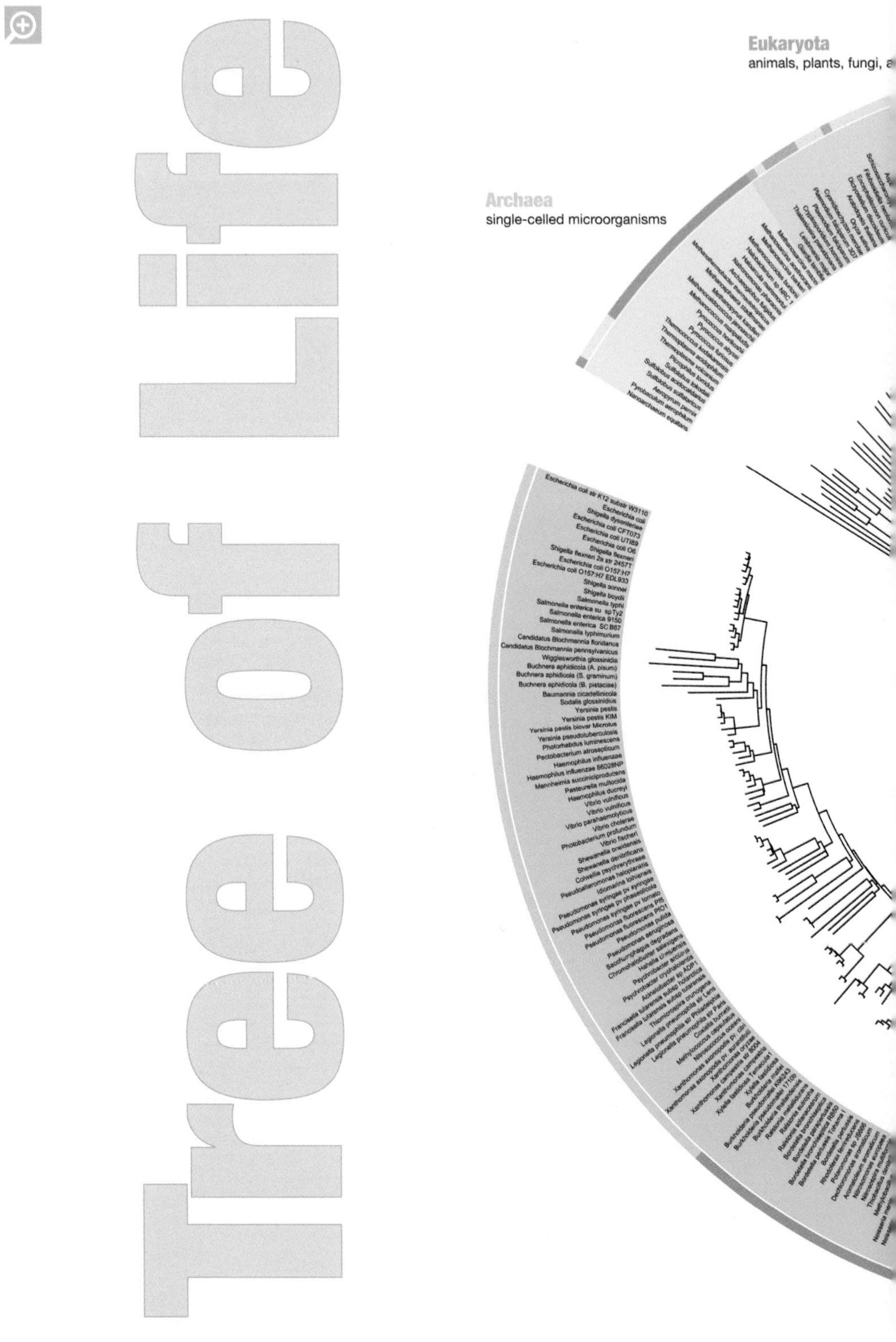

Figure 5.2 *Tree of Life* (2006) by Peer Bork, Francesca Ciccarelli, Chris Creevey, Berend Snel, and Christian von Mering (http://scimaps.org/VI.1)

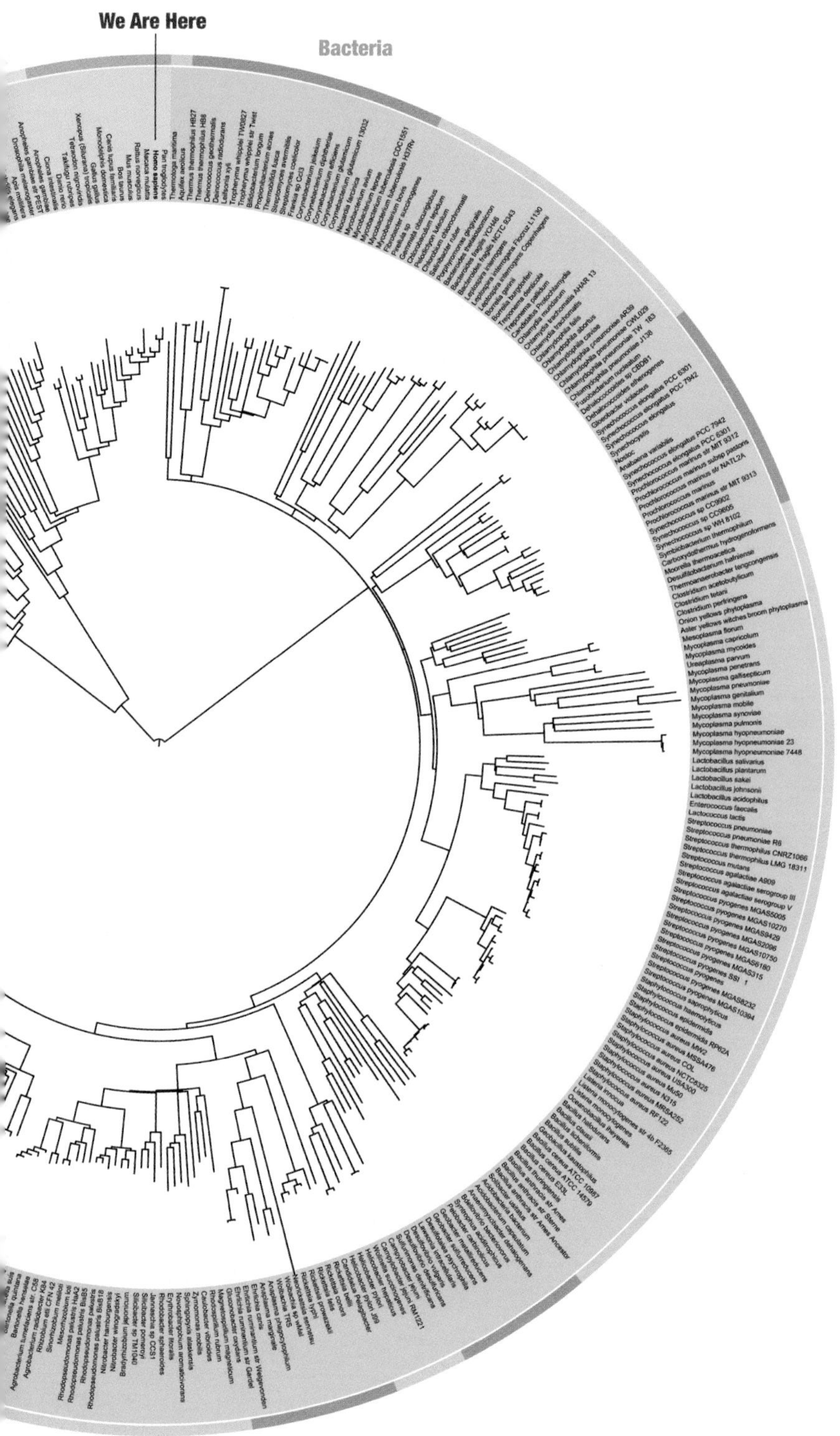
We Are Here
Bacteria

Figure 5.3 *Treemap View of 2004 Usenet Returnees* (2005) by Marc Smith and Danyel Fisher (http://scimaps.org/I.8)

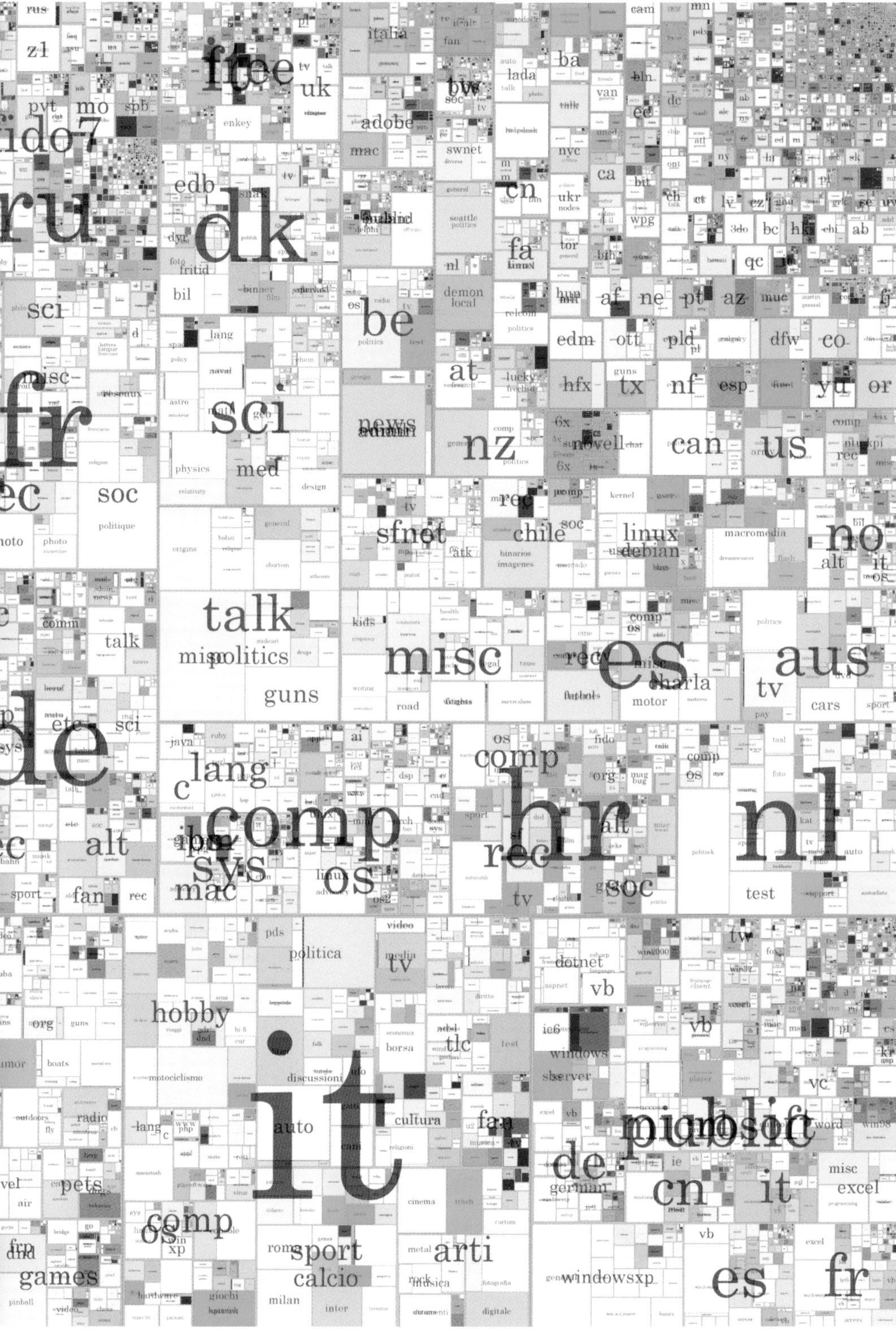

rus
z1
free
uk
italia
fan
cam
mn
ba
lada
van
adobe
pvt
mo
spb
enkey
mac
swnet
nyc
ca
ru
dk
edb
cn
ukr
bit
wpg
seattle
fa
tor
3do
bc
chi
ab
qc
bil
fritid
sci
be
demon
local
af
ne
pt
az
edm
ott
pld
dfw
co
fr
misc
lang
at
hfx
tx
nf
esp
or
sci
news
nz
can
us
astro
physics
med
design
soc
politique
photo
origins
abortion
sfnet
rec
chile
linux
debian
macromedia
no
alt
talk
politics
guns
misc
es
aus
tv
cars
road
motor
comp
lang
comp
os
sys
mac
hr
nl
rec
soc
tv
test
alt
fan
rec
sport
java
ruby
c
politica
pds
video
tv
dotnet
vb
hobby
org
guns
boats
motociclismo
borsa
ie6
windows
it
auto
cultura
cinema
public
microsoft
word
de
german
cn
it
misc
excel
radio
pets
comp
os
xp
sport
calcio
arti
rock
metal
windowsxp
es
fr
games
pinball
roma
milan
inter
musica
digitale

Examining the Evolution & Dist

Managing Growing Patent Portfolios

Organizations, businesses, and individuals rely on patents to protect their intellectual property and business models. As market competition increases, patenting innovation and intellectual property rights becomes ever more important.

Managing the staggering number of patents demands new tools and methodologies. Grouping patents by their classifications offers an ideal resolution for better understanding how intellectual borders are established and change over time.

The charts below show the annual number of patents granted from January 1, 1976 to December 31, 2002 in the United States Patent and Trademark Office (USPTO) patent archive; slow and fast growing patent classes; the top-10 fast growing patent subclasses; and two evolving patent portfolios.

The Structure and Evolution of th

The United States Patent and Trademark (
more than 450 classes covering broad ap
class 514 encompasses all patents dealin
Treating Compositions.' Classes are furth
have hierarchical associations. As one ex
99 entitled "with vehicle."

The top-10 fast growing patent classes fo
the number of patents granted. Most com
Communications' and the 'Drugs and Me

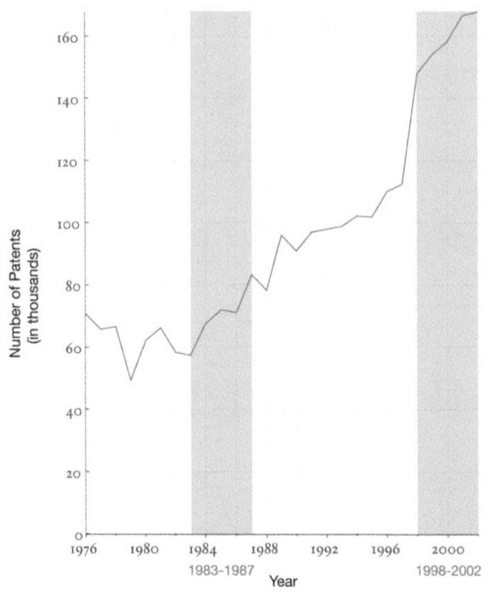

Slow Growing Classes

Mechanical

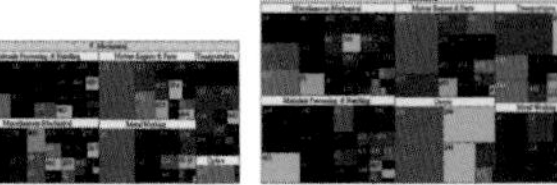

Others

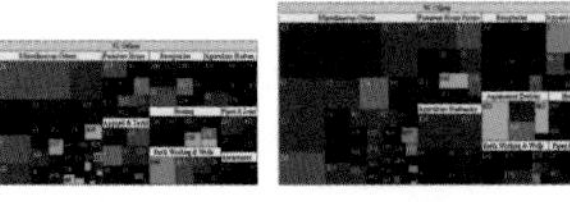

Chemical

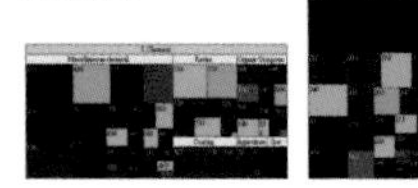

1983 - 1987   1998 - 2002

Patent Portfolio Analysis

A longitudinal analysis of portfolios reveals different patenting strategies. For each year (given in gray above each treemap), a treemap of all new patents granted to the assignee is shown. The number of patents is given below each treemap. The same size and color coding as above was used. In addition, yellow indicates that no patent has been granted in that class in the last 5 years.

Apple Computer, Inc.

Apple Computer, Inc.'s portfolio starts in 1980 and increases considerably in size over time. In most years, more than half of Apple Computer's patent filings were placed into four classes, namely '395 Information Processing System Organization', '345 Computer Graphics Processing, Operator Interface Processing, and Selective Visual Display Systems', '382 Image Analysis', and '707 Data Processing: Database and File Management or Data Structures'. These four classes are an integral part of Apple Computer, Inc.'s patent portfolio, receiving patents every year.

2 1 1 2 3 3 3 3 9 7 23 24 35 49 55

Jerome Lemelson

The patent portfolio of Jerome Lemelson shows a very different activity pattern. Starting in 1976, he publishes between 6-20 patents each year. However, the predominance of yellow shows that there is little continuity from previous years in regards to the classes into which patents are filed. No class dominates. Instead, more and more new intellectual space is claimed.

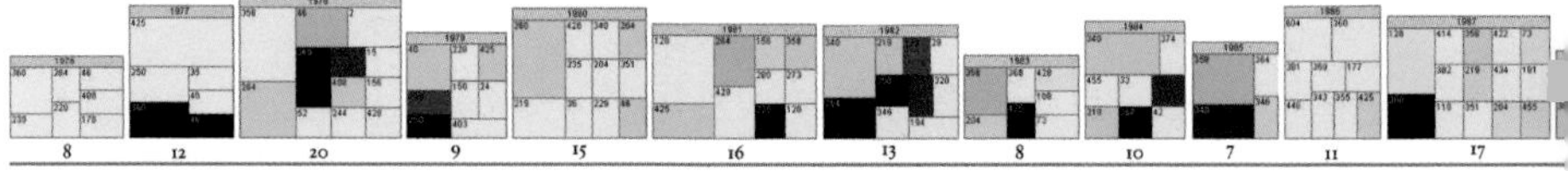

Figure 5.4 *Examining the Evolution and Distribution of Patent Classifications* (2004) by Daniel O. Kutz, Katy Börner, and Elisha F. Hardy (http://scimaps.org/IV.5)

-ution of Patent Classifications

t Space

gns each patent to one of omains. For example, ıg, Bio-Affecting and Body down by subclasses that ss 455 features subclass

2 are listed together with 'Computer and

The evolving hierarchical structure of patent classes and their sizes is represented using treemaps, a space-filling visualization technique developed by Ben Shneiderman at the University of Maryland. A treemap presents a hierarchy as a collection of nested rectangles—demarcating a parent-child relationship between nodes by nesting the child within the parent rectangle. The size and color of each rectangle represent certain attributes of the nodes.

Here, each rectangle represents a class and the area size denotes the total number of patents in that class. The rectangle's color corresponds to percentage increase (**green**) or decrease (**red**) in the number of patent granted in that class from the previous interval.

Growing Classes

cal & Electronic

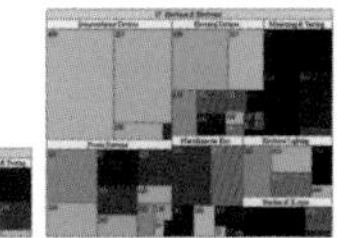

uters & Communications

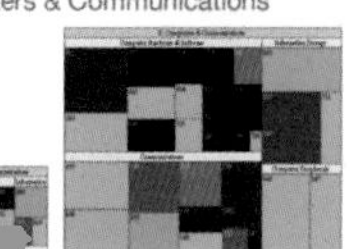

& Medical

1987 1998 - 2002

Top-10 Subclasses

Class	Title	# of Patents
514	Drug, Bio-Affecting and Body Treating Compositions	18,778
438	Semiconductor Device Manufacturing:Process	17,775
435	Chemistry: Molecular Biology and Microbiology	17,474
424	Drug, Bio-Affecting and Body Treating Compositions	13,637
428	Stock Material or Miscellaneous Articles	13,314
257	Active Solid-State Devices (e.g., Transistors, Solid-State Diodes)	12,924
395	Information Processing System Organization	9,955
345	Computer Graphics Processing, Operator Interface Processing, and Selective Visual Display Systems	9,510
359	Optical: Systems and Elements	9,151
365	Static Information Storage and Retrieval	8,392
	Total	13,0910

1998 - 2002

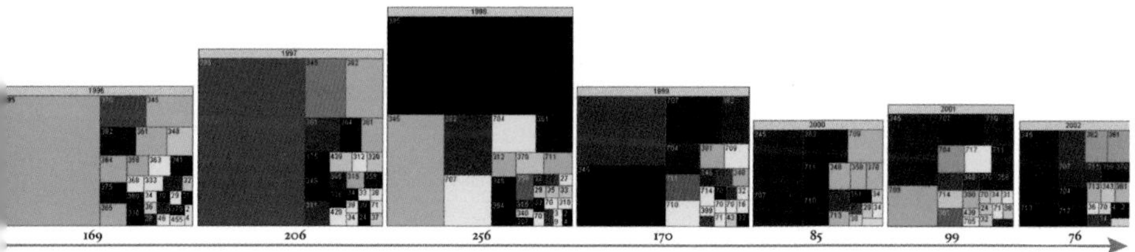

1980 - 2002

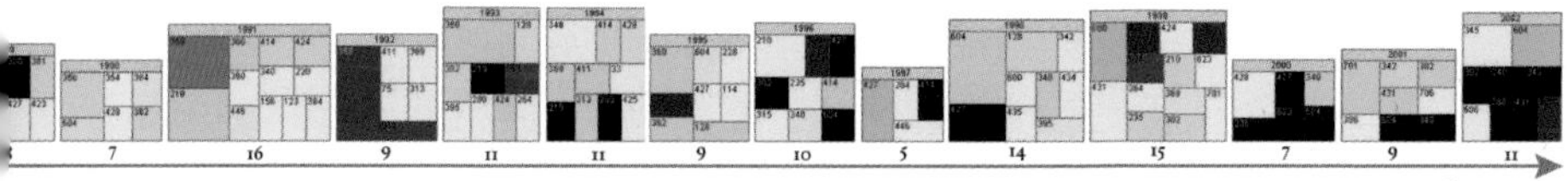

1976 - 2002

time Apple has patents in a new class where it didn't have any patents in the previous five years. However, Jerome Lemelson seems to patent mostly in new classes as if he is trying to cover more and more intellectual space.

5.2 OVERVIEW AND TERMINOLOGY

This section introduces key terminology and properties of trees. An exemplary tree is shown in Figure 5.5. It consists of nodes that are interconnected by edges. As it is a **rooted tree**, it has a designated **root node** and all other nodes are descendants of this root node. Think of the root node, here the node labeled A, as the "great-great-grandmother" in a family tree. The node labeled E has one **parent node** B, one **sibling node** D, and two **children nodes** G and H. The last node on a branch of the hierarchy is called a **leaf node**.

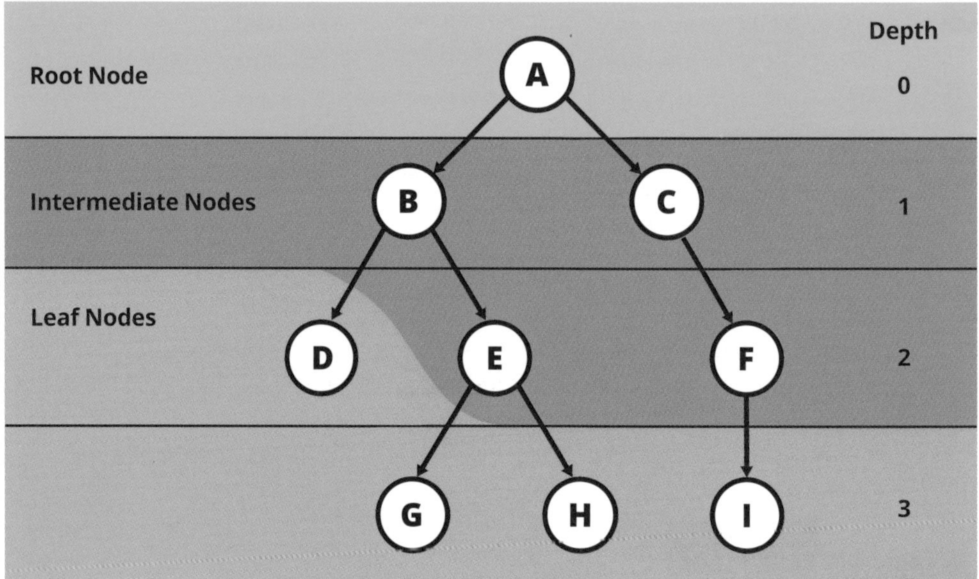

Figure 5.5 A tree with different node types at different depths

Some trees are **un-rooted trees**, where any node can be chosen as a root node. Some trees are **binary trees**, like in Figure 5.5, where each node has at most two children nodes. There are **balanced trees**, which are rooted trees where no leaf node is much farther away from the root than any other leaf node. Another type of tree is called a **sorted tree** (Figure 5.6), where children of each node have a designated order, not necessarily based on their value, and they can be referred to specifically. In this example, we go from A to I using a so-called pre-order traversal along the dashed lines, picking up nodes left, top, and right in a recursive fashion. Taken together, the tree shown in Figure 5.6 is binary, unbalanced, and sorted; and if we say that A is a designated root node, then it's rooted as well.

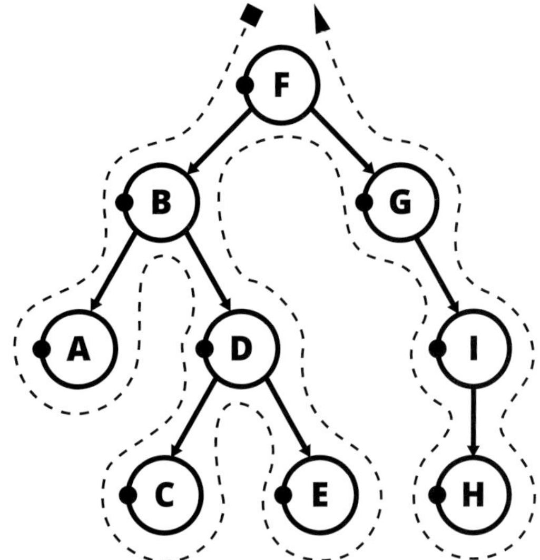

Figure 5.6 A sorted, binary, unbalanced, and rooted tree

In terms of **node properties**, there is an **in-degree** for each node, which is the number of edges arriving at that node, and an **out-degree**, the number of edges leaving—pointing to children nodes. The root is the only node in the tree that has an in-degree of zero. All leaf nodes have an out-degree of zero. The **depth** of a node in a tree is the length of the path from the root to that node, where the root node is at depth zero. Each node, but also each edge, can have additional properties. For example, in a family tree, a person may have a name, age, gender, hair and eye color, etc.

In terms of **tree properties**, trees are typically analyzed in order to calculate their **size**, which is the number of nodes; and their **height** (also called their depth), which is the length of the path from the root to the deepest node in the tree. The trees in Figures 5.5 and 5.6 both have a size of 9 and a depth of 3.

5.3 WORKFLOW DESIGN

Let's look at the workflow design for the analysis and study of tree data. As introduced in Chapter 1, we are using an iterative process (see Figure 5.7) of identifying stakeholder needs to gain a detailed understanding of the types and levels of analysis that are needed. We then try to get our hands on the best data, READ and ANALYZE this data, then VISUALIZE the data—a process that involves selecting the visualization type, overlaying the data, and visually encoding the data—and finally DEPLOY visualizations for interpretation and validation by stakeholders.

Figure 5.7 exemplifies this process for tree data. This one is special as most tree visualizations don't have a set reference system, but here the reference system is generated from the data itself. For example, a file directory structure (e.g., a set of nodes and their edges) might be laid out using different algorithms such as force-directed layouts or treemaps discussed in Section 5.5. Additional node, edge, and tree attributes, calculated during the ANALYZE phase, might be visually encoded.

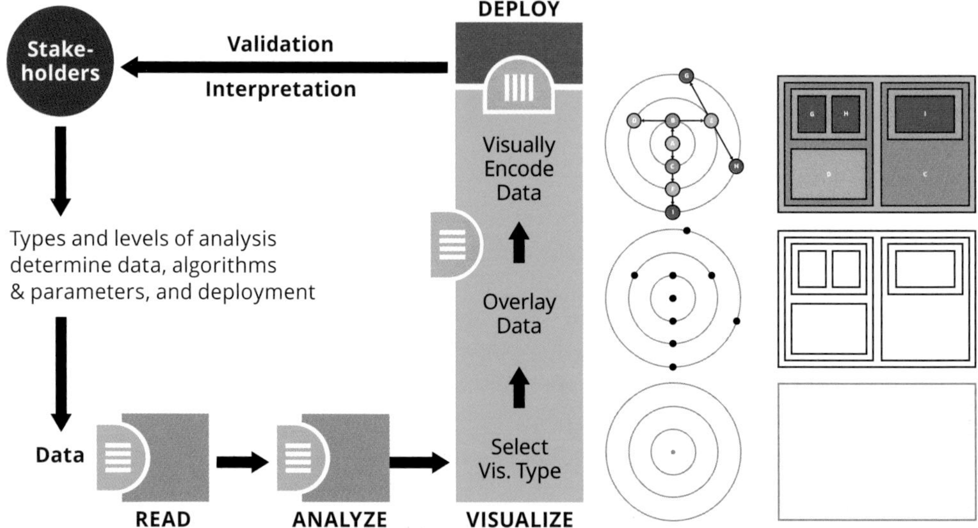

Figure 5.7 Visualization workflow for tree data with two tree layout examples

Read & Preprocess Data

During this phase we can download tree data from repositories such as IBM's Many Eyes,[7] Pajek Datasets,[8] Stanford's Large Network Dataset Collection,[9] Tore Opsahl's Datasets,[10] TreeBASE Web,[11] or Sci2 Tool Datasets.[12] We can use software programs like the Sci2 Tool to read directory structures (see Section 5.5) or to extract networks from tabular data (see Section 6.3, Network Extraction). We can run web crawlers to read web content.[13]

7 http://www-958.ibm.com/software/data/cognos/manyeyes/datasets

8 http://vlado.fmf.uni-lj.si/pub/networks/data

9 http://snap.stanford.edu/data

10 http://toreopsahl.com/datasets

11 http://treebase.org

12 http://sci2.wiki.cns.iu.edu/display/SCI2TUTORIAL/2.5+Sample+Datasets

13 Thelwall, Mike. 2004. "Web Crawlers and Search Engines." In *Link Analysis: An Information Science Approach*, 9–22. Bingley, UK: Emerald Group Publishing.

There are a variety of data formats for representing tree data, but data typically come in network formats, such as GraphML, an XML schema created to represent graphs. Pajek is also widely used, as is the NWB (Network Workbench) format. Other data formats include TreeML, another XML schema; Edgelists, a simple text file that shows connections between nodes; and CSV, comma delimited data.

Analyze & Visualize

Tree analysis and visualization aims to maximize the exploration and communication of the structure (e.g., size, height) and content information (node and edge attributes) while utilizing display space efficiently. Interactivity might be used to support search, filter, clustering, zoom and pan, or details on demand (see Chapter 7).

Analysis is commonly used to calculate additional node, edge, and tree attributes (see Section 5.2 and Hands-On part of this chapter). We can also perform tree simplification (e.g., use Pathfinder Network Scaling discussed in Section 6.4), subtree extraction, and tree comparisons.

Visualization starts with the calculation of a tree layout. An example of how to visualize a file directory structure using five different layout algorithms: circular layout, tree view, radial tree, balloon graph, and treemap, is given in Section 5.5 as part of the Hands-On Section of this chapter. Here we will detail two exemplary tree layout algorithms: radial trees and treemaps.

A **radial tree layout** was used for visualizing the *MACE Classification Taxonomy* (Figure 5.1) and *The Tree of Life* (Figure 5.2). Using this layout, the root node is placed at the center of the graph, and the children are placed in concentric circles fanning out from the root node. Children are evenly distributed on concentric circles and branches of the tree do not overlap. That is, the algorithm must take into consideration how many children exist in order to effectively lay out the graph.

Specifically, the algorithm reads a tree data structure and information on the maximum size circle that can be placed, for example, on the screen or printout. We can use this maximum size circle to place nodes from the deepest level in the tree (it might have to be reduced in size if nodes are size coded like in Figure 5.1). The distance between levels (d) equals the radius of the maximum circle size divided by the depth of the graph. Then, we place our root node in the center of the graph, and all nodes that are children of the root node are distributed evenly over the 360 degrees of the first circle (L1). Then we divide 2π by the number of nodes at level 1 to get the angle space (Θ) between the nodes on the circle. We basically try to estimate how many nodes have to be placed so there will be no overlap, and we place these parent nodes accordingly. For all subsequent levels—level 2 and level 3 in this example—we use information on their parents, their location, and the space needed for their children to place all the remaining nodes. For each of the nodes, we move through the list of parents and then look through all the children for that parent to calculate the child's location relative to the parents.

By determining the bisector limits (green lines in Figure 5.8), the algorithm will divide the available space for nodes. The bisector lines will allow the nodes to be spaced evenly so that the children of one node will not overlap the children of an adjacent node. To determine the bisector limits we must first find the tangent lines, which go at a right angle to the parent and the circle on which it lies (blue lines in Figure 5.9). Where those blue lines cross, this is where the green bisector line goes through to the root node. Basically, the radial tree layout algorithm considers three cases: Case 0 places the root node; Case 1 places the nodes at level one so that they are all equal distance from each other, and calculates the bisector and tangent limits for each node; Case 2 takes care of all other levels, the nodes in level 2 and higher. It loops through all the nodes at that level and gets a list of parent nodes, then finds the number of children for each parent, and calculates the angle space for those parents. Then, for each parent the code loops through all the nodes to calculate the position for their children.

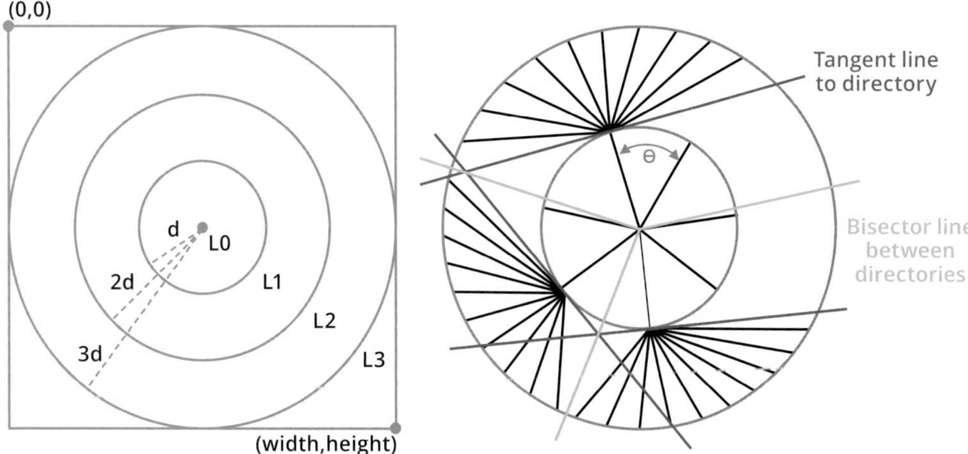

Figure 5.8 Placing concentric circles, tangent lines, and bisector limits

A simple example is shown in Figure 5.9. On the left is the tree of size 9 and depth 3 that we examined previously. The right part shows the three concentric circles that will be needed to place all nine nodes. The root node will be placed in the center, all other nodes on the concentric circles—according to their depth. Tangent lines and bisector limits are used to ensure that children of one node do not overlap the children of an adjacent node. As this tree is rather small, tangent lines do not cross, making this layout rather trivial.

A **treemap layout** can be seen in the *Treemap View of 2004 Usenet Returnees* (Figure 5.3) and *Examining the Evolution and Distribution of Patent Classifications* (Figure 5.4). Treemap visualizations are not immediately intuitive and can take some practice to read successfully. Figure 5.10 shows a treemap next to a tree view of the same data for comparison. To lay out a treemap, two pieces of information are required: a rooted tree data structure and the size of the area available for layout. The rectangular area is commonly defined by specifying the coordinates for the upper-left and the lower-right points of the treemap. The algorithm itself is recursive. It takes the root node as input, together with the area available for layout and a partition direction (e.g., horizontally). Then, the code takes the "active" node, which in the beginning is the root node, and determines the number *n* of outgoing edges from this active

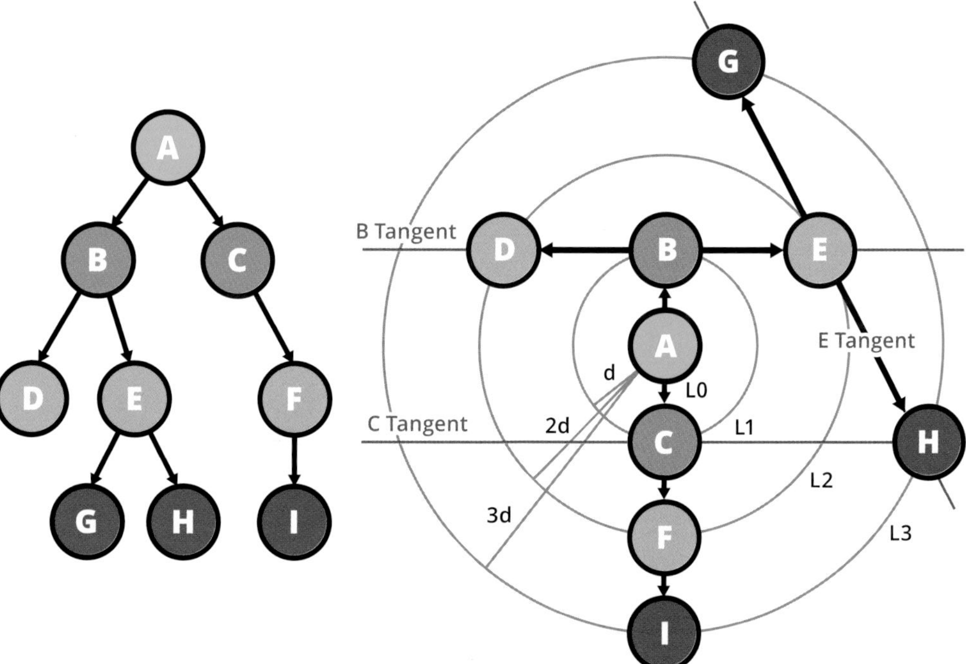

Figure 5.9 Radial tree graph layout sample

node. If *n* is less than one, then the code stops. However, if *n* is larger than one the region gets divided in the partitioning direction by that number. The region is divided so that the size of each child area corresponds to its value (e.g., the number of bytes in a file directory or some other attribute of the data). Once this is done, the partition direction is changed; for example, if it used to be done horizontally, it will now be done vertically, and the algorithm re-run with a new "active" node, new area size, and updated partition direction.

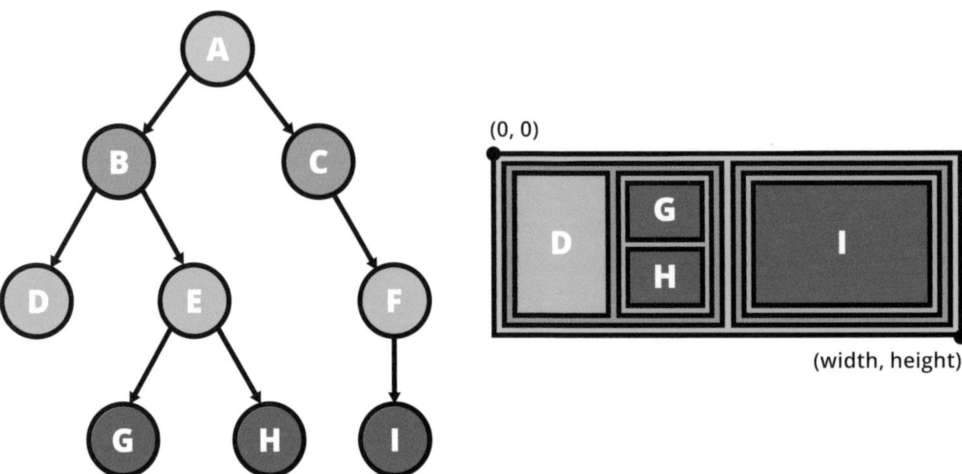

Figure 5.10 A tree view (left) compared with a treemap (right) of the same data

That is, while the radial tree assigned the largest circle to highest level nodes, the treemap algorithm assigns it to the root node at level 0. Next, this space is further divided into areas according to the number of children of the green root node. In the example shown in Figure 5.10, the root node has two children nodes, colored in gray. In the treemap layout, each of these two nodes gets an equal amount of space (see right depiction). Furthermore, node B has two children (D, E), and node E has two children (G, H). Correspondingly, within blue B box on the left, there are two orange boxes, and one of them is further divided into two more boxes. Node C has one child node (F), which itself has another child and leaf node (I). Consequently, the area on the right shows this nested structure with I as the leaf node.

The strength of the treemap layout is that it utilizes 100% of the display space and is scalable to datasets containing millions of records. It shows the nesting of the hierarchical levels and can represent several leaf node attributes. However, treemaps have some drawbacks. Comparing the size of two areas (e.g., a long and thin rectangle versus a square) or labeling non-leaf nodes and showing their attribute values is difficult. We can leave space for labeling and visual encoding, but that takes away from the space we have to lay out the data. Furthermore, the rectangles can get very small, making them difficult for users to see.

Force-directed layouts such as Kamada-Kawai, Fruchterman-Reingold, or Generalized Expectation-Maximization (GEM) can also be applied to layout tree data (see Chapter 6 on networks for examples).

Self-Assessment

1. What tree visualization(s) would be most effective to visualize space consumed by files in a file system
   a. Tree view
   b. Radial tree
   c. Tree map
2. What tree visualization(s) would be most effective to visualize decision trees
   a. Tree view
   b. Radial tree
   c. Tree map
3. What tree visualization(s) would **not** be effective to visualize a family genealogy
   a. Tree view
   b. Radial tree
   c. Tree map
4. For the tree shown here, identify attributes for
   a. Node B: in-degree, out-degree, and depth
   b. Tree: size, height, balanced, binary, sorted

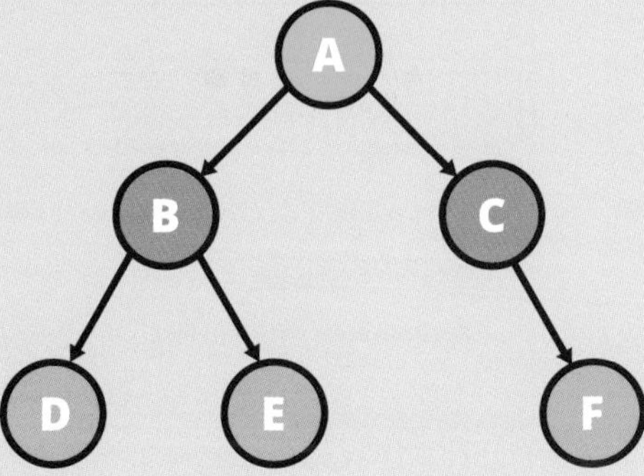

Chapter 5: Hands-On Section

5.5 VISUALIZING DIRECTORY STRUCTURES (HIERARCHICAL DATA) WITH SCI2

Data Types & Coverage	
Time Frame:	Not Applicable
Region:	Not Applicable
Topical Area:	Sci2 Directory
Network Type:	Directory Hierarchy

Analysis Types/Levels	● (small)	● (medium)	● (large)
Temporal			
Geospatial			
Topical			
Network	X		

Sci2 provides diverse algorithms to read, analyze, and visualize tree data. For example, you can read any directory on your computer or any network drive you have mapped to your machine. Simply run *File > Read Directory Hierarchy* and a parameter window will be displayed, as shown in Figure 5.11. Select a root directory on your machine; for example, the Sci2 directory that might be right on your Desktop. Then enter the number of levels to recurse (i.e., the depth up to which the directory structure should be read). If you want to read all subdirectories simply check 'Recurse the entire tree'. Next, decide if you just want to see the file directories or also the names of all files in the directory structure and check/uncheck the last box.

Note that reading a very large directory (e.g., your entire hard disk) can be extremely time consuming. The result of scanning the Sci2 directory will be added a 'Directory Tree – Prefuse (Beta) Graph' in the 'Data Manager' (Figure 5.12).

This file is formatted in an XML schema called TreeML, using *Prefuse (Beta) Graph*. TreeML files consist of a list of declarations and a series of branches ending in leaves. Figure 5.13 shows the beginning of the Sci2 Directory Structure TreeML file. The `<branch>` tag indicates a node that has children in the hierarchy, whereas the `<leaf>` tag indicates a node that has no children, or, a node at the end of a branch.

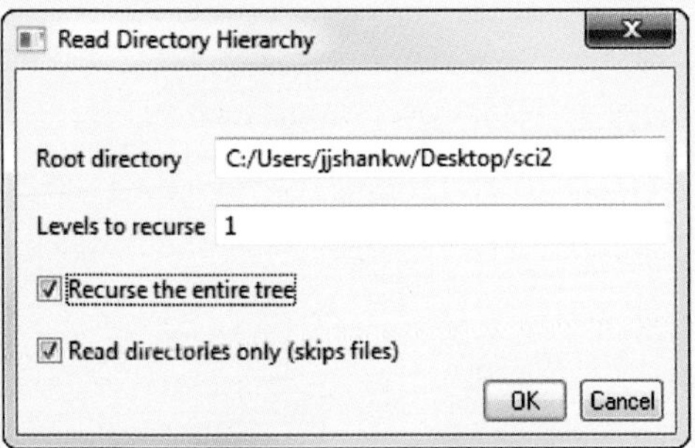

Figure 5.11 Read Directory Hierarchy parameter window. The Sci2 directory, recursing the entire tree, and skipping the files that were input.

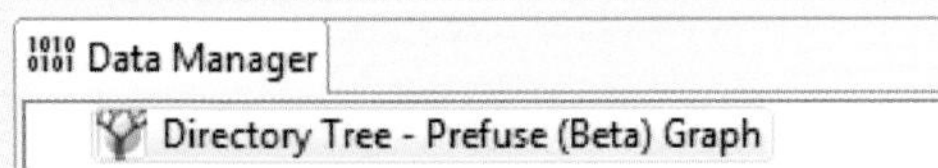

Figure 5.12 Directory Tree displayed in the 'Data Manager'

```
<tree>
  <declarations>
    <attributeDecl name="label" type="String"/>
  </declarations>
  <branch>
    <attribute name="label" value="sci2"/>
    <branch>
      <attribute name="label" value="configuration"/>
      <leaf>
        <attribute name="label" value=".settings"/>
      </leaf>
      <branch>
        <attribute name="label" value="org.eclipse.core.runtime"/>
        <leaf>
          <attribute name="label" value=".manager"/>
        </leaf>
      </branch>
      <branch>
        <attribute name="label" value="org.eclipse.equinox.app"/>
        <leaf>
          <attribute name="label" value=".manager"/>
        </leaf>
      </branch>
```

Figure 5.13 The top portion of the Sci2 directory represented as a TreeML file

To view the whole TreeML file, right-click on the 'Directory Tree - Prefuse (Beta) Graph' file in the 'Data Manager' and save it as a 'TreeML (Prefuse)' file in a directory location of your choice. You can open and edit XML files with a variety of free programs, such as Notepad, or proprietary programs, such as Adobe Dreamweaver and oXygen XML Editor.

Subsequently, we will use five different algorithms to visualize this exemplary tree structure: circular layout, tree view, radial tree, balloon graph, and treemap.

To visualize a tree structure with the **circular layout** you need to save the 'Directory Tree – Prefuse (Beta) Graph' file from the 'Data Manager' as a 'Pajek.net' file. Then, reload the Pajek.net file into Sci2 and you will be able to visualize the network using GUESS (*Visualization* > *Networks* > *GUESS*). Once the network has fully loaded into GUESS, apply the Circular layout (*Layout* > *Circular*). Finally, add the node labels by setting the Object to 'all nodes' and clicking 'Show Label' (Figure 5.14). The result quickly shows you the **size** of the tree and its **density** (i.e., the number of nodes and edges). Tree attribute values could be visually encoded. A circular layout does not show you the nested structure of the tree.

To visualize the tree structure in **tree view**, select 'Directory Tree - Prefuse (Beta) Graph' in the 'Data Manager' and run *Visualization* > *Networks* > *Tree View (prefuse beta).*

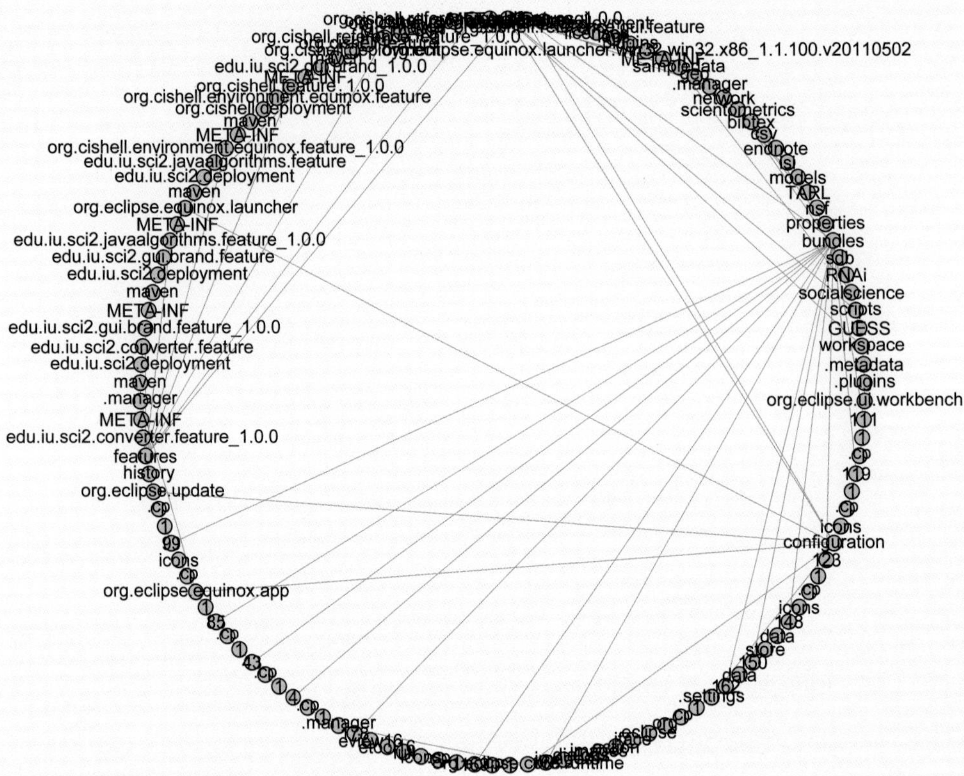

Figure 5.14 Circular layout visualization of the Sci2 directory

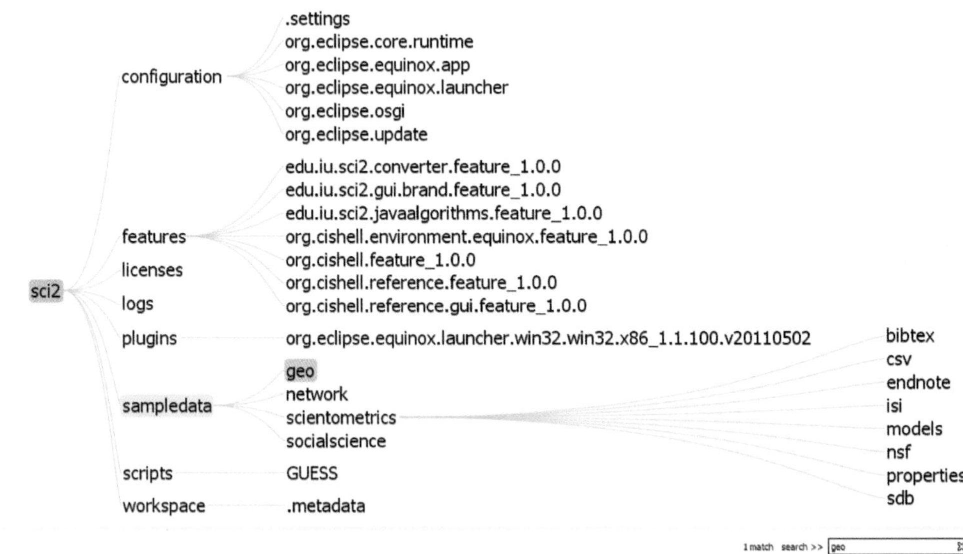

Figure 5.15 Tree View visualization of the Sci2 directory

The initial visualization displays the first three levels of the directory structure (Figure 5.15). If you want to explore deeper in the structure, click on any directory in that level to see the directories nested below the node you have selected. If you are searching for a particular directory in a large hierarchy there is a search bar in the lower left-hand side of the 'Prefuse' screen that allows users to find exact matches for search terms entered, which is why you see "geo" highlighted in red in the visualization.

You can also view the Sci2 directory structure as a **radial graph**; see explanation in Section 5.3. Simply run *Visualization > Networks > Radial Tree/Graph (prefuse alpha)* to see the directory structure in this layout (Figure 5.16). By selecting a node in the graph (e.g., "scientometrics"), each of its children in the hierarchy will be highlighted. Anytime a node is selected, the graph will rearrange to show the nodes directly beneath that node in the hierarchy. Note, the radial tree view can be difficult to read for large directory structures.

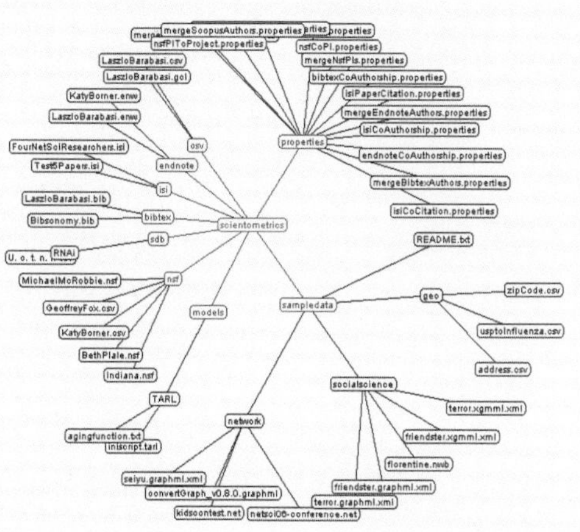

Figure 5.16 Radial tree graph visualization of the Sci2 'scientometrics' directory

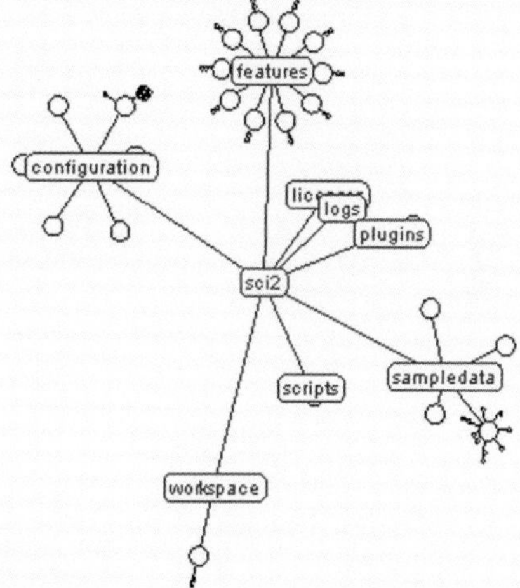

Figure 5.17 Balloon graph visualization of the Sci2 directory

In order to visualize tree data as a **balloon graph**, you will have to install an additional plugin, *BalloonGraph.zip*, that can be obtained from Section 3.2 on the Sci2 wiki.[14] After restarting Sci2, read the Sci2 directory again and select the 'Directory Tree– Prefuse (Beta) Graph' file from the 'Data Manager' and then select *Visualization > Balloon Graph (prefuse alpha)*. The result is shown in Figure 5.17.

In addition, you can visualize a tree using a **treemap** (see explanation in Section 5.3). Simply select the 'Directory Tree - Prefuse (Beta) Graph' and run *Visualization > Networks > Tree Map (prefuse beta)*. The result is shown in Figure 5.18 (left). If the Sci2 directory structure is read with files, then the plugin directory becomes the largest (see Figure 5.18, right). Basically, Sci2 is composed of many plugins. This treemap interface also supports

14 http://wiki.cns.iu.edu/display/SCI2TUTORIAL/3.2+Additional+Plugins

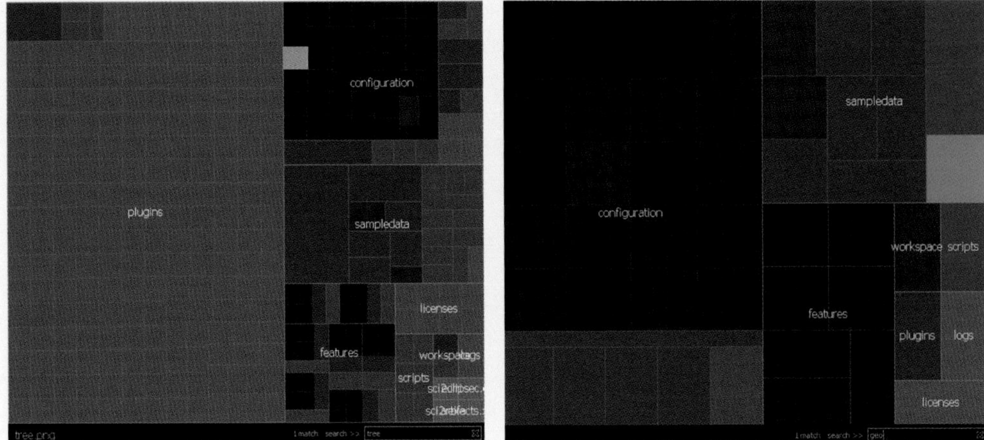

Figure 5.18 Treemap visualization of Sci2 directories including all files (left), and directories only (right).

search (see lower right corner and results for "tree" highlighted on the right).

Creating a TreeML File

It is possible to create and edit smaller TreeML files manually, and for this process it helps to understand XML. Before you start any XML encoding, it is a good idea to sketch the hierarchical structure you wish to display. For example, you might like to encode the sim-

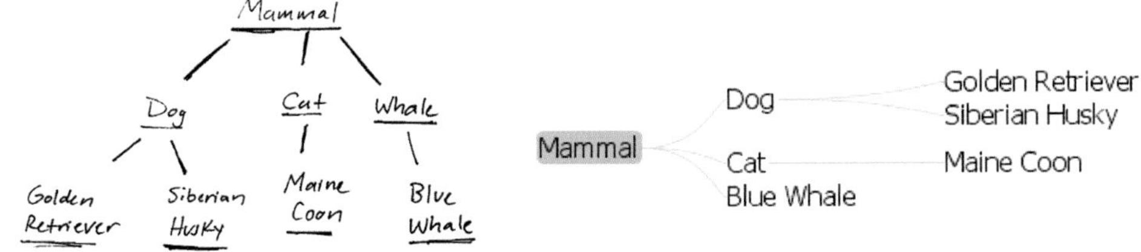

Figure 5.19 Sketch (left) and tree view (right) of simple TreeML file

ple tree shown in Figure 5.19 (left).

You can create a TreeML file by using any text editor, such as Notepad, or a proprietary program, such as Adobe Dreamweaver or oXygen XML Editor (Figure 5.20).

```
<?xml version="1.0" encoding="utf-8"?>
<tree>
<declarations>
<attributeDecl name="label" type="String"/>
</declarations>
<branch>
```

```
<attribute name=”label” value=”Mammal”/>
    <branch>
    <attribute name=”label” value=”Dog”/>
        <leaf>
        <attribute name=”label” value=”Golden Retriever”/>
        </leaf>
        <leaf>
        <attribute name=”label” value=”Siberian Husky”/>
        </leaf>
    </branch>
    <branch>
    <attribute name=”label” value=”Cat”/>
        <leaf>
        <attribute name=”label” value=”Maine Coon”/>
        </leaf>
    </branch>
    <branch>
    <attribute name=”label” value=”Blue Whale”/>
    </branch>
</branch>
</tree>
```

Figure 5.20 Custom TreeML file

Save the file as an XML (.xml) file and load it into Sci2 as 'PrefuseTreeMLValidation' (Figure 5.21). After loading the file, you can visualize the hierarchy by running *Visualization > Networks > Tree View (prefuse beta)*. Figure 5.19 (right) shows a **tree view** rendering of this tree hierarchy.

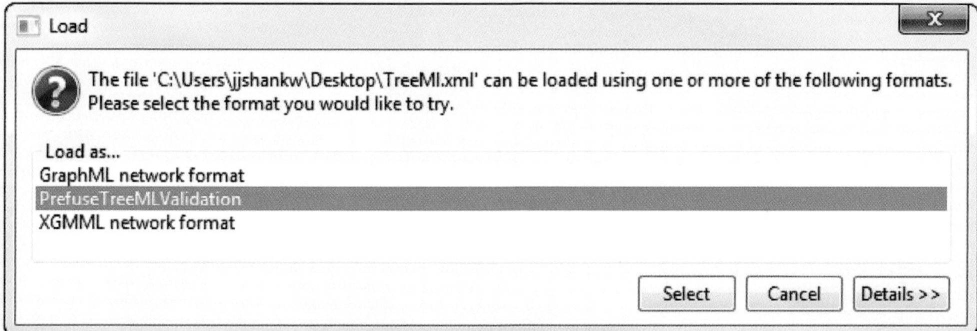

Figure 5.21 Loading TreeML file as 'PrefuseTreeMLValidataion'

Homework

1. Read a directory on your computer and visualize it using at least three different layout algorithms.
2. Manually create a TreeML file and visualize it.

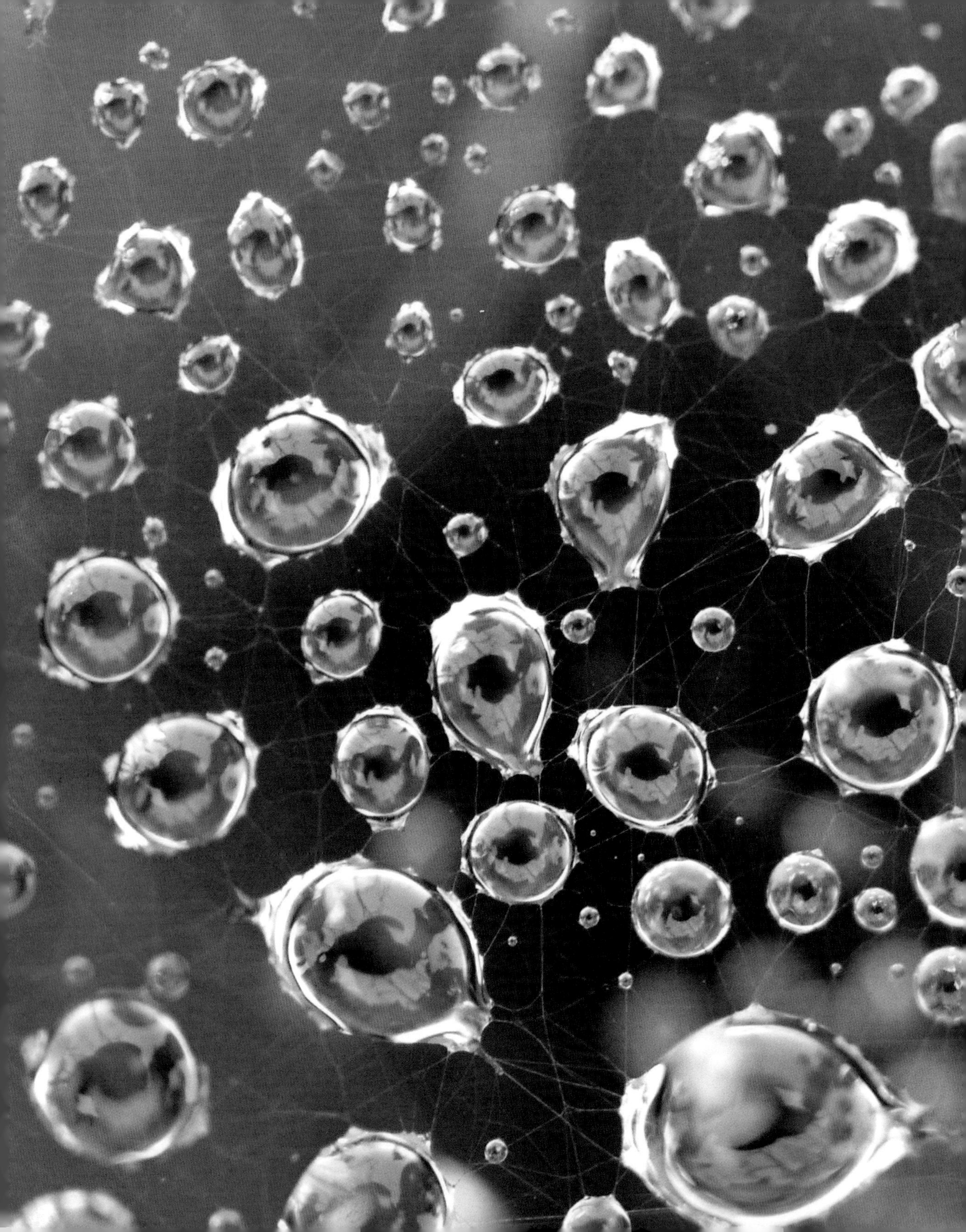

Chapter Six

"WITH WHOM": Network Data

Chapter 6: Theory Section

In this chapter, we will look at the analysis and visualization of network data. The study of networks aims to increase our understanding of natural and manmade networks. It builds on social network analysis, physics, information science, bibliometrics, scientometrics, econometrics, informetrics, webometrics, communication theory, sociology of science, and several other disciplines.[1,2,3] Networks might represent collaborations between authors, business and marriage ties between families, or citation linkages between papers or patents. The goal of network studies is to identify highly connected authors (or papers), i.e., those with many collaboration (or citation) links; network properties such as size and density; structures such as clusters and backbones; among others.

Networks exist at the micro to macro level, and their structure and dynamics are studied in many scientific disciplines. As in previous chapters, we start with a discussion of examples, provide important terminology, and then explain the general workflow for the analysis and visualization of networks.

6.1 EXEMPLARY VISUALIZATIONS

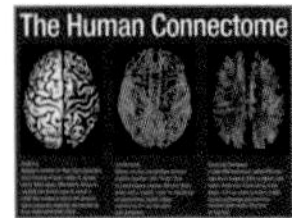

The Human Connectome map (Figure 6.1)[4] shows three renderings of the human brain. The image on the left shows a dissection of postmortem brain tissue. The special preparation reveals major anatomical areas and features of the brain but does not reveal the brain's connections. Shown on the right-hand side is a complete map of major anatomical connections that link distinct regions of the cerebral cortex. In its entirety, the brain consists of 10^{11} neurons and 10^{15} synaptic links, and the total wiring of the brain is estimated to span thousands of miles. The map was created by biomedical engineer and neuroscientist Patric Hagmann in 2008 using magnetic resonance imaging (MRI) data acquired from a living person.

The map in the middle shows the human connectome, the interconnections of different areas of the brain. It was created by computational cognitive neuroscientist Olaf Sporns using network science tools. Network analysis revealed robust small-world attributes, the existence of multiple modules interlinked by hub regions, and a structural core comprised of a set of brain regions that are highly interconnected. As multiple datasets from

1 Börner, Katy, Soma Sanyal, and Alessandro Vespignani. 2007. ""Network Science."" Chap. 12 in *Annual Review of Information Science & Technology*, edited by Blaise Cronin, 537–607. Medford, NJ: Information Today, Inc./American Society for Information Science and Technology.

2 Newman, Mark E.J.. 2010. *Networks: An Introduction*. New York: Oxford University Press.

3 Easley, David, and Jon Kleinberg. 2010. *Networks, Crowds, and Markets: Reasoning About a Highly Connected World*. New York: Cambridge University Press.

4 Hagmann, Patric, Leila Cammoun, Xavier Gigandet, Reto Meuli, Christopher J. Honey, Van J. Wedeen, and Olaf Sporns. 2008. "Mapping the Structural Core of Human Cerebral Cortex." *PLoS Biology* 6, 7: 1479–1493.

different patients were analyzed, it became clear that individual connectomes display unique structural features that might also explain differences in cognition and behavior.

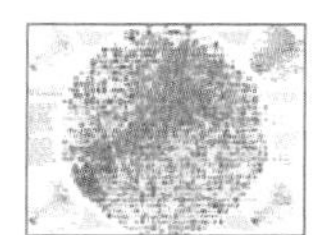

In the next visualization (Figure 6.2), we see a map of Wikipedia activity related to science.[5] The map shows Wikipedia entries that are categorized as math (blue), as science (green), and as technology (yellow), which are laid out in a two-dimensional space. An invisible 37 x 37 half-inch grid was drawn underneath the network and filled with relevant images from key articles.

In the four corners, we have smaller versions of the same 2-D layout with articles size-coded according to article edit activity (top left), number of major edits from January 1, 2007 to April 6, 2007 (top right), number of bursts in edit activity (bottom right), and the number of times other articles link to an article (bottom left).

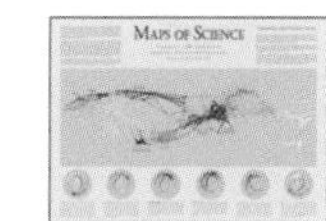

The third visualization (Figure 6.3) entitled *Maps of Science: Forecasting Large Trends in Science*[6] was compiled using 7.2 million publications in over 17,000 separate journals, proceedings, and series from a five-year period of 2001 to 2005 (see Section 4.6 for a detailed description of this map and its update). The 13 major disciplines of science are color-coded and labeled. Down below the large map we see six smaller maps that show us how the different areas of science are evolving, pushing, and pulling on each other over this five-year time frame.

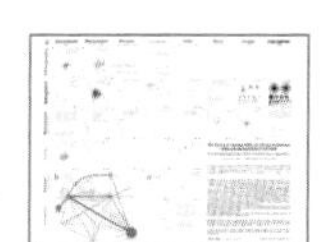

The fourth visualization (Figure 6.4) presents a global view of an entire scholarly database—the Census of Antique Works of Art and Architecture Known in the Renaissance, 1947–2005[7]—to communicate the types of records covered as well as their interlinkage. The different record types (e.g., document, monument, person, location, date) are organized in a matrix. Row and column headers give the record type names and the number of total records per type. In each cell, we see a description of the data in terms of a network, but also in terms of distributions, which gives you a good understanding of the coverage and interlinkage of record types. The inset (b) in the lower left shows how different record types are interlinked with each other. This network visualization can also be produced for relational databases or linked open data in other domains.

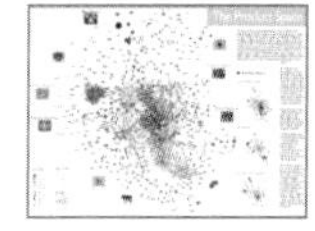

The fifth visualization (Figure 6.5) shows the product space of exported goods and its impact on the development of nations.[8] If a country exports two goods together, it is assumed that these two products have something in common. In the 2-D layout, each node represents

5 Holloway, Todd, Miran Božičević, and Katy Börner. 2007. "Analyzing and Visualizing the Semantic Coverage of Wikipedia and Its Authors." *Complexity* 12, 3: 30–40.

6 Börner, Katy, Richard Klavans, Michael Patek, Angela Zoss, Joseph R. Biberstine, Robert P. Light, Vincent Lariviére, and Kevin W. Boyack. 2012. "Design and Update of a Classification System: The UCSD Map of Science." *PLoS One* 7, 7: e39464.

7 Schich, Maximilian. 2010. "Revealing Matrices." In *Beautiful Visualization: Looking at Data through the Eyes of Experts*, edited by Julie Steele and Noah Lilinsky, 227–254. Sebastopol, CA: O'Reilly.

8 Hausmann, Ricardo, César A. Hidalgo, Sebastián Bustos, Michele Coscia, Sarah Chung, Juan Jimenez, Alexander Simoes, Muhammed A. Yildirim. 2011 *The Atlas of Economic Complexity.* Boston, MA: Harvard Kennedy School and MIT Media Lab.

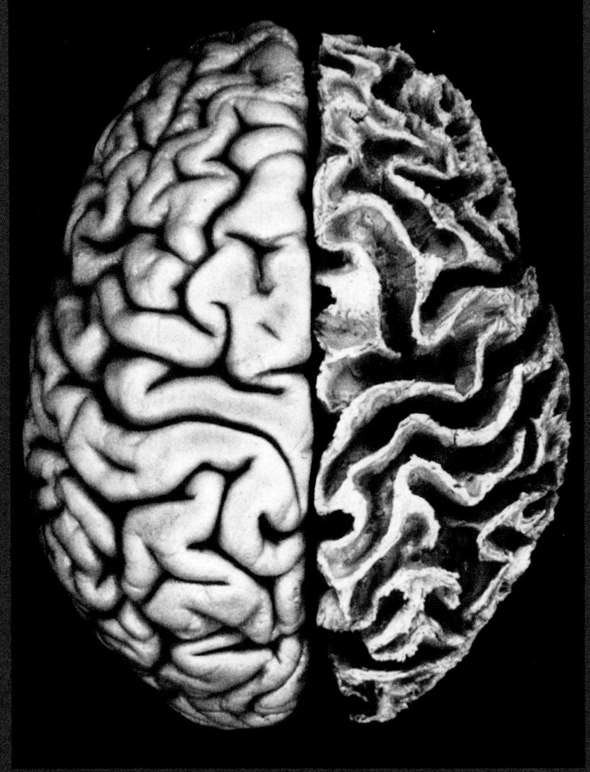

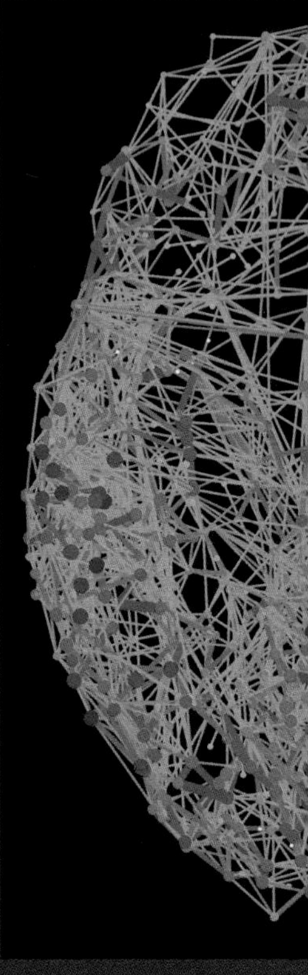

Figure 6.1 *The Human Connectome* (2008) by Patric Hagmann and Olaf Sporns (http://scimaps.org/VI.2)

Connectome

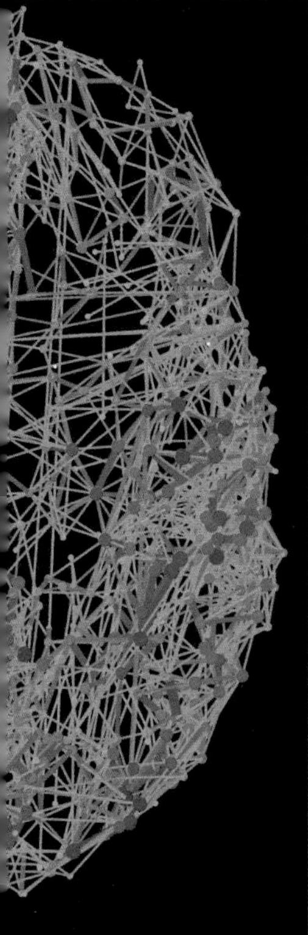

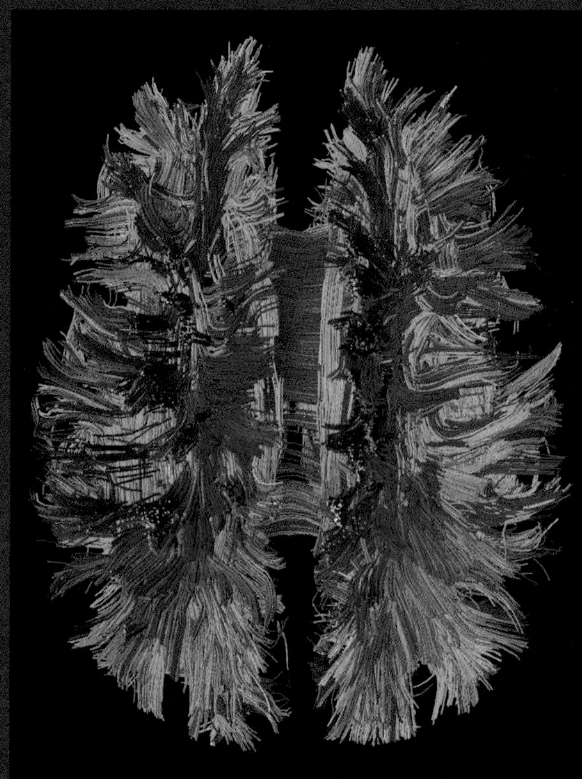

tions of brain
hubs" that
different brain
re" or backbone
relays
ughts

Neuronal Pathways
A new MRI technique called diffusion spectrum imaging (DSI) analyzes how water molecules move along nerve fibers. DSI can show a brain's major neuron pathways and will help neurolo-gists relate structure to function.

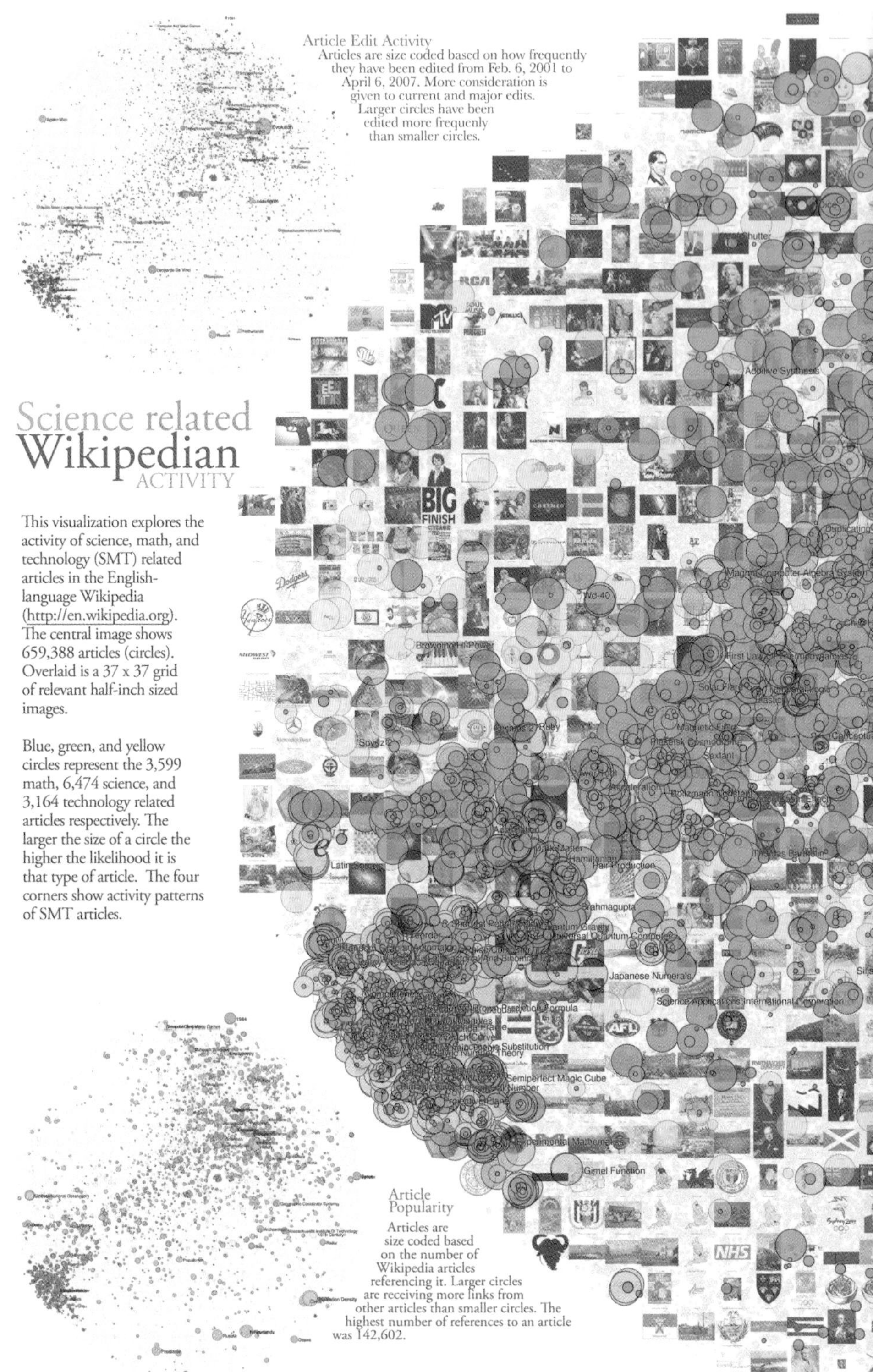

Figure 6.2 *Science-Related Wikipedia Activity* (2007) by Bruce W. Herr II, Todd M. Holloway, Elisha F. Hardy, Kevin W. Boyack, and Katy Börner (http://scimaps.org/III.8)

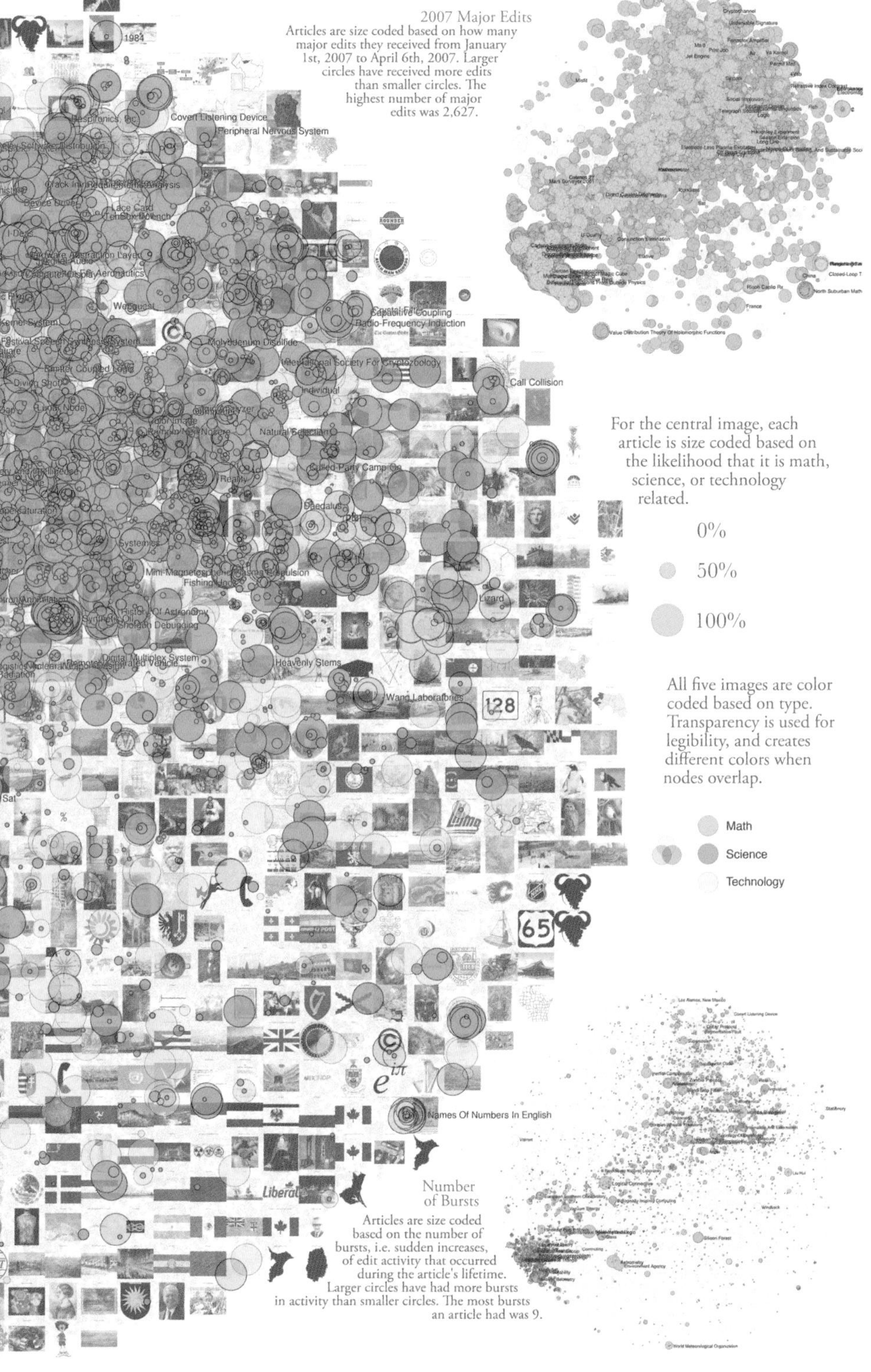

2007 Major Edits

Articles are size coded based on how many major edits they received from January 1st, 2007 to April 6th, 2007. Larger circles have received more edits than smaller circles. The highest number of major edits was 2,627.

For the central image, each article is size coded based on the likelihood that it is math, science, or technology related.

0%

50%

100%

All five images are color coded based on type. Transparency is used for legibility, and creates different colors when nodes overlap.

Math

Science

Technology

Number of Bursts

Articles are size coded based on the number of bursts, i.e. sudden increases, of edit activity that occurred during the article's lifetime. Larger circles have had more bursts in activity than smaller circles. The most bursts an article had was 9.

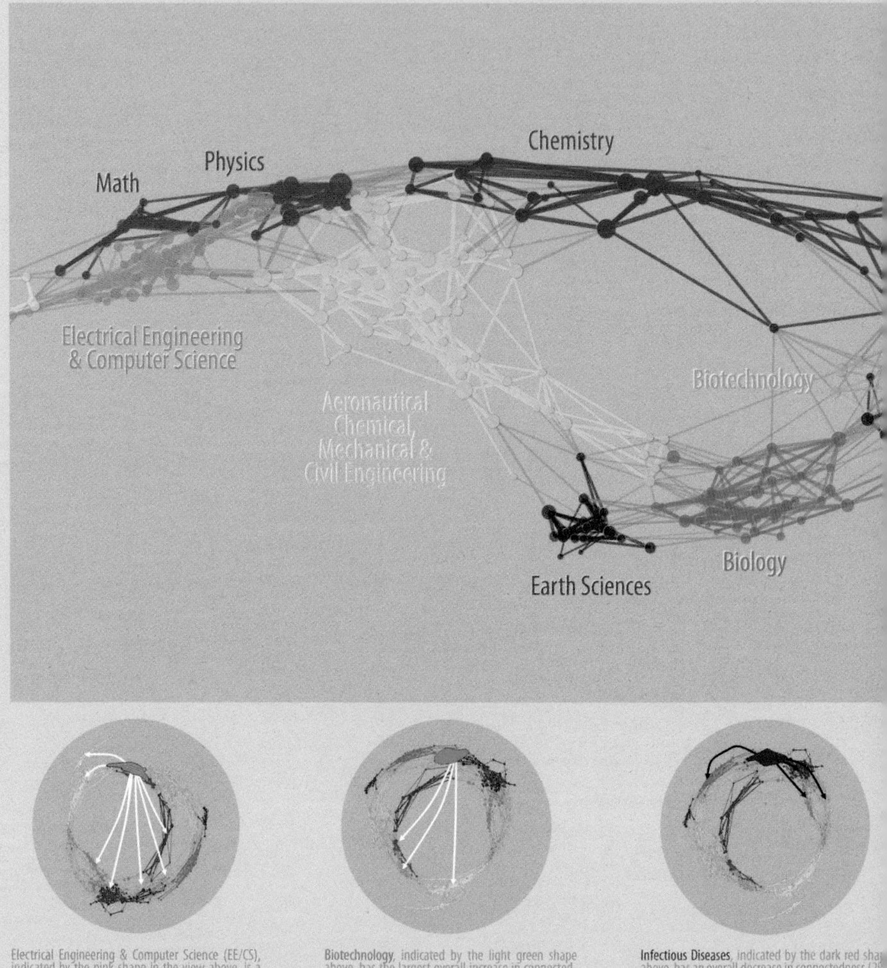

Figure 6.3 *Maps of Science: Forecasting Large Trends in Science* (2007) by Richard Klavans and Kevin W. Boyack (http://scimaps.org/III.9)

SCIENCE

scholarly documents
, proceedings or symposia
nd Dec, 2005

Forecasting Large Trends in Science

Calculations were performed using the large colored groupings of disciplines (fields) to determine if any of them were likely to cause large scale changes in the structure of science over time. Connectedness coefficients between fields were calculated for each individual year, 2001-2005. A simple regression analysis was conducted to see if there were significant changes in these connectedness coefficients from year-to-year.

If the structure of science shown below is moving toward stability, we would expect connectedness between neighboring fields to increase, and connectedness between distant fields to decrease. We found the opposite, suggesting that the underlying structure is unstable and likely to change dramatically over the next decade.

Six stories, representing how the structure is likely to change, are provided below. Maps with white arrows represent instances of distant fields that are likely to be pulled closer to each other in the future. Maps with dark arrows represent fields that are currently close-knit, that are likely to become more dispersed. We expect that future maps of science will show changes in stucture corresponding to these observations. Medicine will disperse slightly, while the physical sciences will tighten and draw closer to the medical fields.

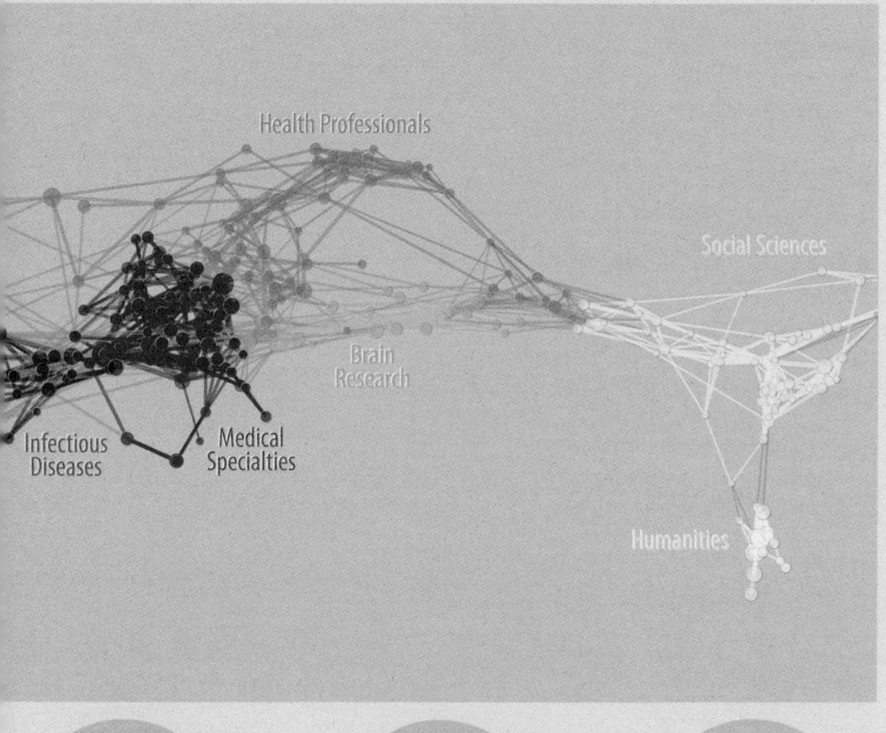

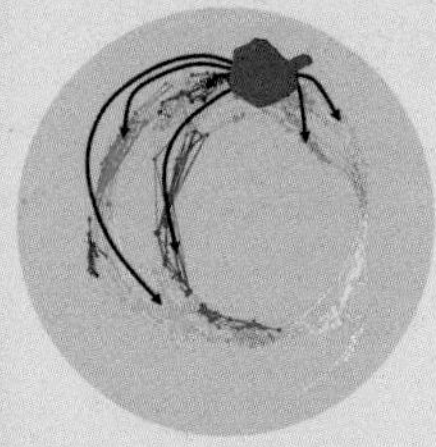

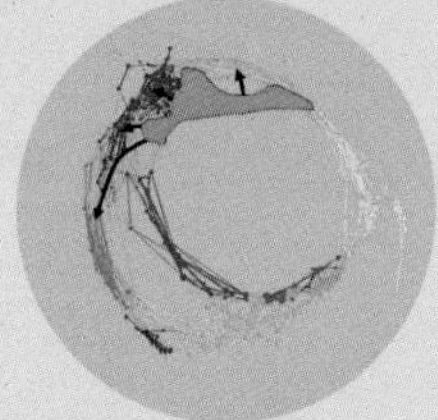

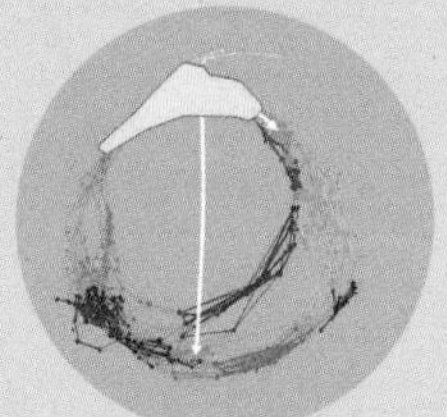

edical Specialties, indicated by the red shape above, s an overall decrease in connectedness (2%) with her fields. This is dominated by decreasing connecn strength to the other medical fields and biology, shown by the black arrows. The only connection creasing in strength is the one to EE/CS, which is not own here, but was shown as a white arrow in the st story.

The Health Professionals field, indicated by the orange shape above, has the largest overall decrease in connectedness (4%) to other fields. As with the other medical fields, its connection strength with medicine and biology is decreasing in all cases, as shown by the black arrows. With the decreasing connection strengths throughout medicine, we expect the map structure in these areas to relax slightly over time.

The Social Sciences, indicated by the yellow shape above, had an overall increase in connectedness (9%) with other fields. Although its greatest connectedness gains were with EE/CS and Biotechnology (see white arrows), it also had consistent connection increases with nearly all the other fields. In general the fields of EE/CS, Biotechnology, and the Social Sciences are become more connected, and are pulling on the physical sciences as well.

g methodology and descriptive text by Dick Klavans, President, SciTech Strategies, Inc., and Kevin Boyack, Sandia National Laboratories. Graphics & typography by Ethan Meillier and Mike Patek.

all.

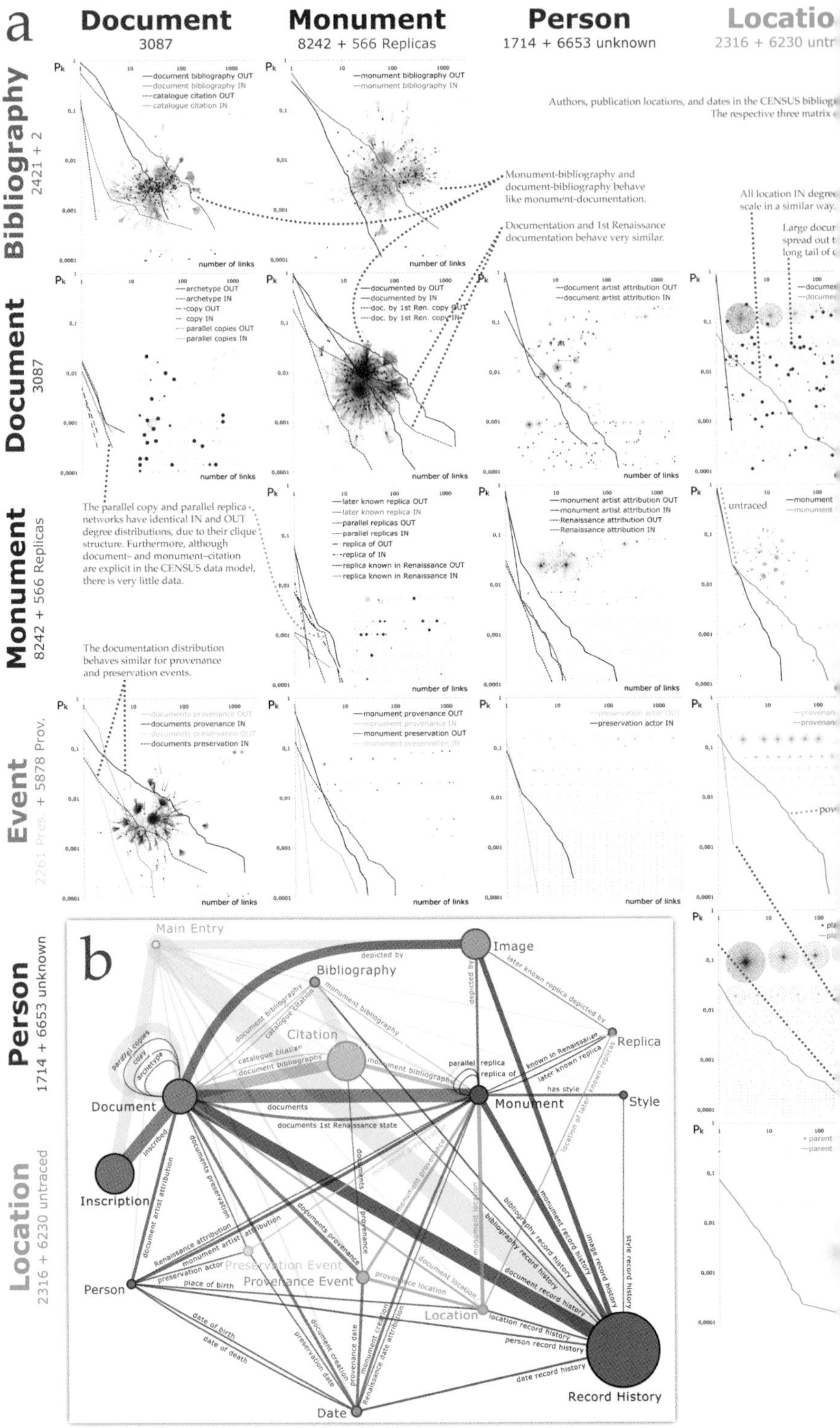

a

Document 3087 | **Monument** 8242 + 566 Replicas | **Person** 1714 + 6653 unknown | **Locatio** 2316 + 6230 untr

Bibliography 2421 + 2

Document 3087

Monument 8242 + 566 Replicas

Event 2261 Pres. + 5878 Prov.

Person 1714 + 6653 unknown

Location 2316 + 6230 untraced

Monument-bibliography and document-bibliography behave like monument-documentation.

Documentation and 1st Renaissance documentation behave very similar.

The parallel copy and parallel replica networks have identical IN and OUT degree distributions, due to their clique structure. Furthermore, although document- and monument-citation are explicit in the CENSUS data model, there is very little data.

The documentation distribution behaves similar for provenance and preservation events.

b

Figure 6.4 *The Census of Antique Works of Art and Architecture Known in the Renaissance, 1947–2005* (2011) by Maximilian Schich (http://scimaps.org/VII.7)

Date
3583 + 2777 unknown

Style
27 + 2465 unknown

Image
25865

Inscription
37324

d implicitly in unstructured text.

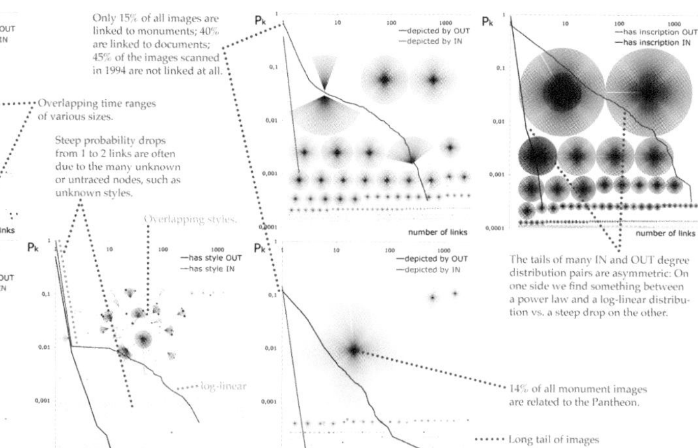

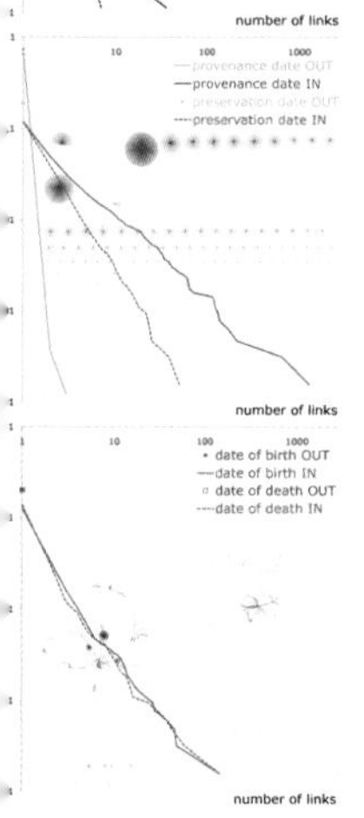

Quasi 1:n relation: Less than 0.1% of all provenance events have more than one date.

1:n relation indicates star or tree network structure – here, only one birth date per person, i.e. stars of persons around single dates.

The location node for Rome, has far more subdivisions, than expected by the remaining power law distribution.

The Census of Antique Works of Art and Architecture Known in the Renaissance 1947-2005

Revealing emergent complex structure within the data model definition of a scholarly database

Dr. Maximilian Schich CCNR, Northeastern University, Boston

The *Census of Antique Works of Art and Architecture Known in the Renaissance* at the time of analysis comprises 8,242 antique Monuments with 12,688 parts, and 3,087 Renaissance Documents with 31,197 parts. Additional record types include Person, Location, Date range, Style period, Image, document Inscription, monument Replica, Bibliography as well as Preservation and Provenance Events.

Part (a) shows a matrix of record types where rows denote link sources, while columns act as link targets, and actual records and their interrelations appear in the respective matrix cell. The number of total records per type is given below each row/column header, e.g., there are 8,242 Monuments plus 566 Replicas. A cell in the 6 x 8 matrix is filled, if links between the respective source and target exist, e.g., many Documents have a Bibliography. Each filled cell represents the network structure as well as the IN- and OUT-degree distributions for the mostly bi-modal networks. For example, the Document-Bibliography cell shows a rather large connected network and few small sub-networks. The corresponding distributions plot the cumulative probability Pk that nodes have at least a certain degree, e.g., the document bibliography OUT distribution shows a probability close to 1 for nodes that may have at least one link and a much lower probability to have at least 50 to 70 links. Annotations are provided to guide the exploration of the map.
Part (b) depicts the data model definition as a labeled node-link diagram. Node area size coding denotes the number of records for each record type while edge width reflects the total number of connections between respective records.
Link colors in (a) and (b) correspond to each other. Distribution plot colors equal the node type to which the respective link type is adjacent to in (b).

References: This map was first published by the author in the book chapter *Revealing Matrices. in: Beautiful Visualization. Looking at Data through the Eyes of Experts. Edited by Julie Steele and Noah Iilinsky. Sebastopol, CA: O'Reilly 2010. ISBN: 978-1-4493-7986-5* *URL: http://revealingmatrices.schich.info*

Acknowledgments: Special thanks go to German Research Foundation DFG and Albert-László Barabási for making this research possible, and to Projekt Dyabola/Stiftung Archäologie for providing the data.

Author contact: maximilian@schich.info

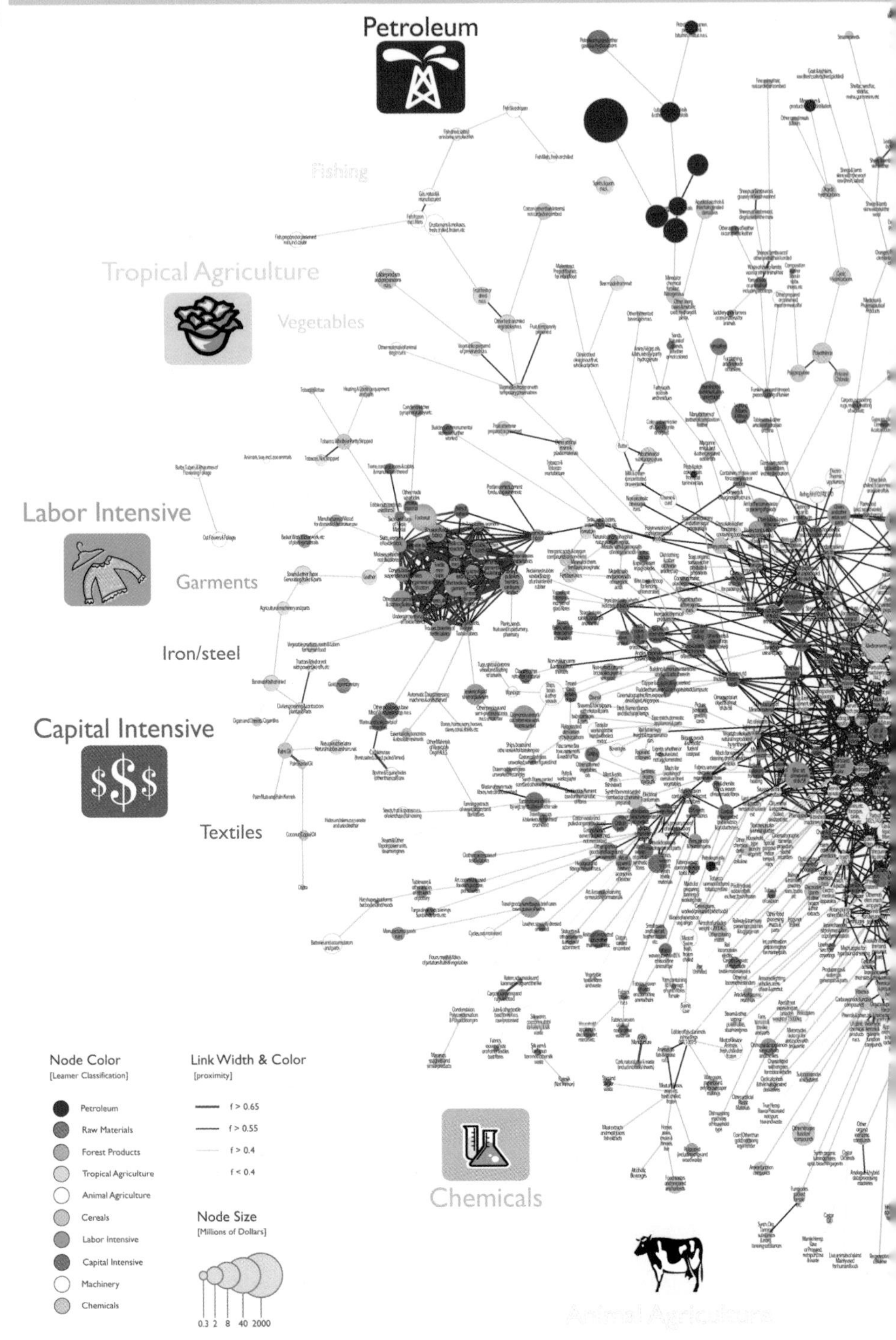

Figure 6.5 *The Product Space* (2007) by César A. Hidalgo, Bailey Klinger, Albert-László Barabási, and Ricardo Hausmann (http://scimaps.org/IV.7)

The Product Space

World trade flow data compiled by Feenstra et al. and available at the National Bureau of Economic Research were used to identify the complete co-export matrix of 775 industrial products for 1998-2000. A Maximum Spanning Tree (MST) algorithm was used to reduce the complete co-export matrix to less than 1% of the links. The resulting network, which combines the MST plus all links with a co-export frequency of at least 0.55, was laid out using a force-directed layout algorithm. Node sizes represent the value of traded products in millions of U.S. dollars. Their color corresponds to ten product groups identified using the Leamer classification. Each product class is labeled by an icon. Link color and width indicate the frequency of joint exports.

Economic Footprint

■ Indicate Relevant Exports

Industrialized Countries

East Asia Pacific

Latin America & the Caribbean

The network has a core-periphery structure with higher value product classes, e.g., machinery, and chemicals, in the core and lower quality classes, e.g., fishing and garments, in the periphery. Products at the core of the network are highly interconnected while products in the periphery are sparsely interlinked.

Each country has a certain product export footprint. Relevant exports by 'Industrialized Countries', 'East Asia Pacific' and 'Latin America & the Caribbean' are given on the right.

Traditional growth theory assumes that there is always a more sophisticated product within reach. However, given the core-periphery structure of the product space, the distances between products differ considerably.

Countries that operate at the core have capabilities to develop and manufacture a wide range of products. Yet, countries that mostly operate in the periphery of the product space have much fewer opportunities for diversification. A country's current footprint and the structure of the product space have a major impact on a country's future development.

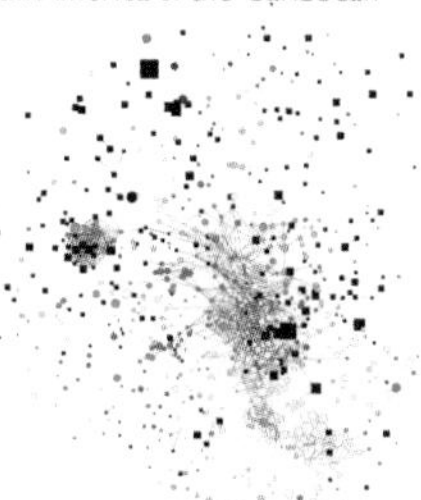

a type of product and node proximity denotes the number of times products are co-exported. Nodes are categorized and color-coded into raw materials, forest products, cereals, petroleum, etc. For example, all the petroleum nodes are colored in a dark reddish color.

Interestingly, all high technology, advanced manufacturing requiring products are in the middle, whereas tropical agriculture, garments, or textiles are in the outer periphery of the network. Developing countries typically export goods, which are in the periphery of the network, and it's actually hard for them to change their product offerings to the inner core with the more lucrative and technologically advanced products.

On the right-hand side, the same map is used to show the economic footprint of different regions. In the top map, black dots represent products that are typically exported by industrialized countries. Below, we see a data overlay for East Asia Pacific and below this one for Latin America and the Caribbean. It is easy for us to see that industrialized countries have far more products in the inner, more lucrative core of the product space network. We can also see that the products in the inner core potentially use expertise and manufacturing technology that occur closer to each other in the network. So if one of those products is not in demand anymore on the international market, it's rather easy to retrain labor force to generate other products like it. However, if you are operating in the fringes of the network, it's rather hard to retrain labor. Plus, there are much fewer products in close proximity.

6.2 OVERVIEW AND TERMINOLOGY

There are many research disciplines that study networks. In fact, network science has a long tradition in graph theory and discrete mathematics, in sociology and communication research, and also in bibliometrics, scientometrics, webometrics, and cybermetrics. More recently, many biologists and physicists have also started to adopt network science principles, and in doing so have actively advanced network science theory and practice. Conducting network science research can often be confusing, as different research areas use very different terms for the same artifacts. For instance, mathematicians and physicists might use the term "adjacency matrix" for a matrix that represents the node linkages between different nodes. However, in statistics and social network analysis, this matrix is called a "sociomatrix." Similarly, the "average shortest path length" or "diameter" is called "characteristic path length" in other disciplines. "Clustering coefficient" is sometimes called a "fraction of transitive triples." This lack of consistency in terminology makes it hard to transfer concepts developed in one area of research to another. For a review of key terminology, approaches and applications, see the network science review.[9]

In general, a network is composed of a set of nodes (sometimes called vertices), and a set of edges (sometimes called links) (see Figure 6.6). **Nodes** can be **isolated**. In this

9 Börner, Katy, Soma Sanyal, and Alessandro Vespignani. 2007. "Network Science." Chap. 12 in *Annual Review of Information Science & Technology*, edited by Blaise Cronin, 537–607. Medford, NJ: Information Today, Inc./American Society for Information Science and Technology.

particular example, C is isolated as it is not connected to any of the other nodes. Nodes can be **labeled**, and they can have quantitative or qualitative **attributes** (e.g., degrees that are commonly represented by the nodes' area size).

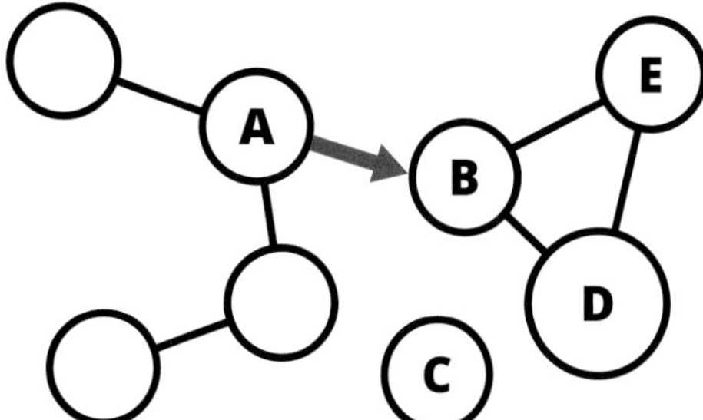

Figure 6.6 Example network

Edges can be undirected (e.g., two words co-occur), or directed (e.g., one paper cites another). In Figure 6.6, all black lines are undirected, and the red line is directed. Edges can be labeled (e.g., weights, attributes), and they can have additional attributes. Edges can also be **signed**, meaning they can have a positive or a negative meaning, such as friend or foe, or trust and distrust. Edges that start and end at one and the same node are called **self-loops**, see green edges in Figure 6.7.

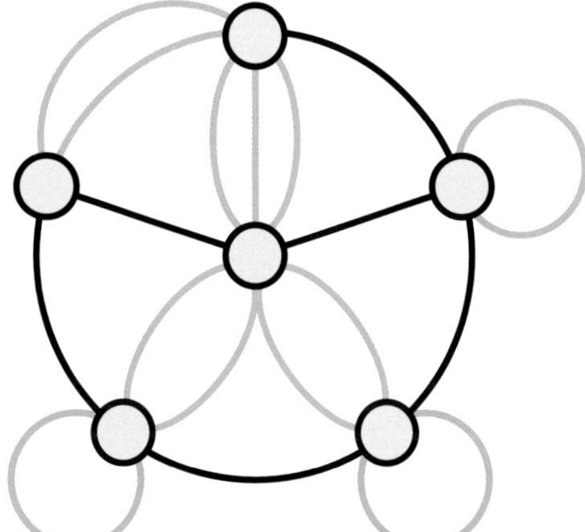
Figure 6.7 Multigraph with multiple edges in orange

Networks can be labeled, that is, nodes and/or edges have labels (weights, attributes). They can have a **temporal** component, meaning there is a timestamp associated with each node and edge in the network (e.g., indicating when it appeared in the network). Networks can be **undirected**, meaning that relations between pairs of nodes are symmetric. They can be **directed**, also called a **digraph**, where the directionality in the link represented directionality in the relationship. Networks with multiple edges between a pair of nodes are called **multigraph** (Figure 6.7).

Networks can be **bipartite**; that is, there exist two disjointed sets of nodes U, V that represent two distinct types of entities, and every link connects a node in U to a node in V (Figure 6.8).

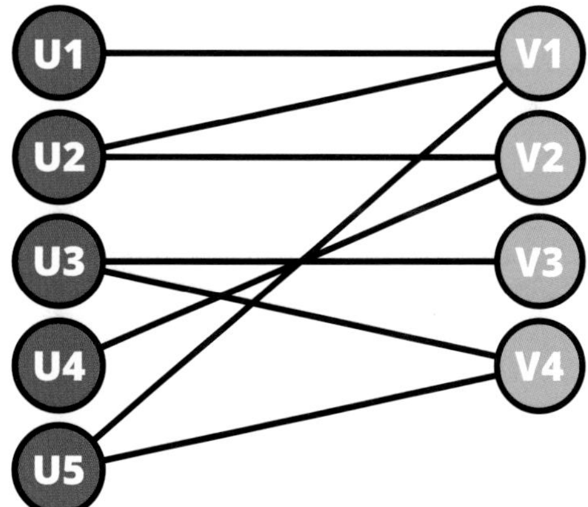

Figure 6.8 Bipartite network with two node types

Node and Edge Properties. Diverse algorithms exist to calculate additional properties of nodes, edges, and networks.[10] The **degree** of a node refers to the number of edges connected to it. In the sample network in Figure 6.6, node E has a degree of 2, and C has a degree of 0. Another commonly used measure for nodes is called **betweenness centrality**, which makes it possible to identify nodes that keep the network together, or that have a brokerage role in the network. **Betweenness centrality of a node** is the number of **shortest paths** between pairs of nodes that pass through a given node. Analogously, the **betweenness centrality of an edge** is the number of shortest paths among all possible node pairs that pass through the edge. The **shortest path length** is the lowest number of links to be traversed to get from one node to another node.

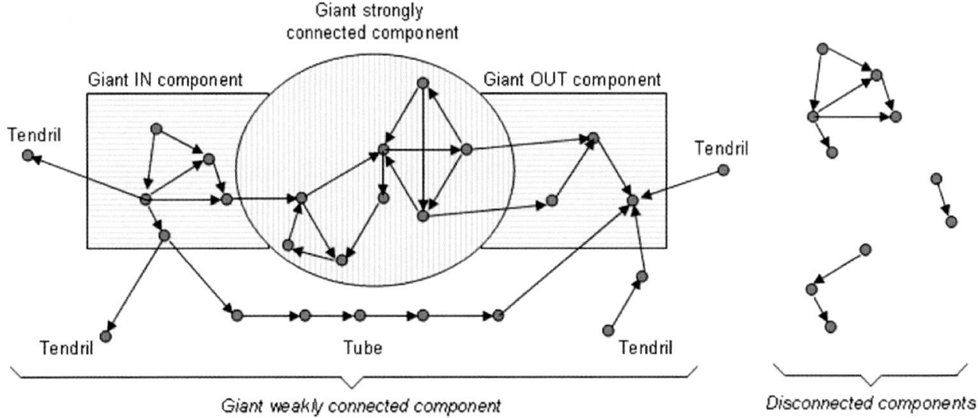

Figure 6.9 A network that shows a strongly connected component in the center, tendrils, and disconnected components

Network Properties. In a network, we can count the number of nodes and edges. For example, the network in Figure 6.6 has eight nodes and seven edges. Similarly, we can count the number of isolated (unconnected) nodes, or the number of self-loops (i.e., links that start from and end at the same node). The **size** of a network equals the number of nodes in a network. Network **density** equals the number of edges in a network divided by the number of edges in a fully connected network of same size (i.e., in a network that has the same number of nodes *n* and each node is connected to any other node; calculated by *n* multiplied by *n-1* and divided by 2). We can also calculate **average total degree** for nodes. And we can identify and count **weakly connected components** (i.e., sub-networks) and **strongly connected components** (i.e., sub-networks with a directed path from each node in the network to every other node). The Network Analysis Toolkit in Sci2 calculates all of these properties for a given network.[11]

10 Börner, Katy, Soma Sanyal, and Alessandro Vespignani. 2007. "Network Science." Chap. 12 in *Annual Review of Information Science & Technology*, edited by Blaise Cronin, 537–607. Medford, NJ: Information Today, Inc./American Society for Information Science and Technology.

11 http://wiki.cns.iu.edu/pages/viewpage.action?pageId=1245863#id-49NetworkAnalysisWithWhom-492ComputeBasicNetworkCharacteristics492ComputeBasicNetworkCharacteristics

The **diameter** of a network is as long as the longest of all shortest paths among all possible node pairs in a network (i.e., the number of links to be traversed to connect the most distant node pairs in a fully connected network). Interestingly, even very large networks, such as the World Wide Web or Facebook comprised of millions of nodes, have very short shortest path lengths. Basically within a few steps, any node in the network is connected to every other node—except for those nodes that are in unconnected sub-networks.

The **clustering coefficient** measures the average probability that two neighbors of a node *i* (i.e., two nodes connected to *i*) are also connected. Evidence suggests that in most real-world networks (e.g., social networks) nodes tend to create tightly knit groups characterized by a relatively high density of ties.

Many networks have a structure like the one shown in Figure 6.9. There is a giant, **strongly connected component**, a giant OUT component, and a giant IN component creating a bow-tie-like shape. There might be 'tubes', that is, pathways of nodes and edges, that connect nodes from the "Giant IN component" to nodes in the "Giant OUT component" and "tendrils" that interconnect single nodes or node trails to nodes in the "Giant IN or OUT component". The entire network is called the "giant **weakly connected component**." In addition, there might be disconnected components, as shown on the left in Figure 6.9.

6.3 WORKFLOW DESIGN

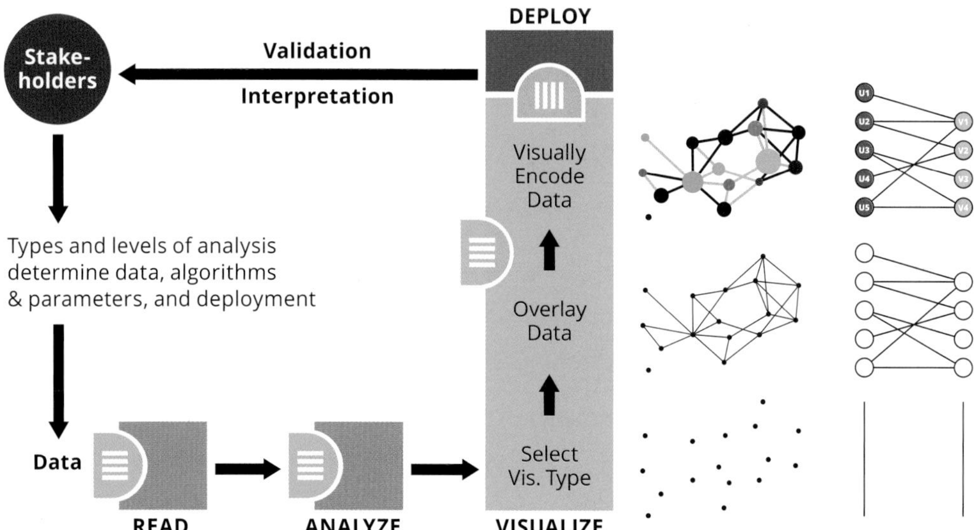

Figure 6.10 Needs-driven workflow design for network data

In this section we discuss the general workflow for the analysis and visualization of networks (Figure 6.10). Visualizing networks is difficult as many network layouts do not have a well-defined reference system—nodes and edges are laid out to represent similarity or distance relationships among nodes. Most network layouts are non-deterministic, that is, each new run of the layout algorithm results in a slightly different layout. Figure 6.10 shows a sample of a force-directed (or spring-embedded) layout of network nodes on the left and a bipartite network layout with two listings of the two node types on the right.

Read & Preprocess Data

There are many online sites and repositories that provide easy access to diverse types of network data. Examples are datasets from UCINET,[12] Pajek,[13] Gephi,[14] CASOS,[15] Stanford Large Network Dataset Collection,[16] Tore Opsahl,[17] and Sci2.[18] Other samples are listed in the Sci2 Tool wiki.[19]

Network data comes in a variety of formats such as GraphML or XGML formats, or in .NET format. There are different scientometrics formats, as defined and provided by major publishers and funding agencies. There are other formats, such as matrix formats, or simple CSV files, which can be used to extract networks.

Standard output formats comprise the above input formats, but they can also be image formats such as JPG, PDF, or PostScript, which we can use to add visualizations to presentations or publications.

Data preprocessing commonly involves unification, for example, to identify all unique nodes in a dataset. If we use textual data, the text might need to be tokenized, stemmed, stop worded, etc. (see Chapter 4). We might need to extract networks from tabular data (see "Network Extraction" on p. 187).

Given a network, we might need to remove **isolated** nodes or **self-loops**. We might also need to merge two networks, for example, to create a **multigraph** of social and business relationships (edges) for a set of people (nodes). If a network is large, we might apply thresholds to reduce the number of nodes and/or edges. For example, in a publication citation network, we might keep only those papers that have been cited at least once. Alternatively, we might apply clustering or backbone identification to make sense of complex networks (see details in Section 6.4).

---

12 http://sites.google.com/site/ucinetsoftware/datasets

13 http://pajek.imfm.si/doku.php?id=data:index

14 http://wiki.gephi.org/index.php/Datasets

15 http://www.casos.cs.cmu.edu/computational_tools/datasets

16 http://snap.stanford.edu/data

17 http://toreopsahl.com/datasets

18 http://sci2.wiki.cns.iu.edu/display/SCI2TUTORIAL/2.5+Sample+Datasets

19 http://sci2.wiki.cns.iu.edu/display/SCI2TUTORIAL/8.1+Datasets

Network Extraction

Much data comes in tabular format. For example, publication data might be stored in a table where each row represents a paper and columns represent unique paper IDs, a listing of all authors, a listing of all references, and publication year (Figure 6.11, top left). A key preprocessing step is the extraction of networks from tables.

In general, we can use columns with multiple values to extract co-occurrence networks. For example a column with names of all authors on a paper can be used to extract co-author networks. We can use a column with all references to extract co-reference (also called bibliographic coupling) networks.

We can use multiple columns to extract bipartite networks (e.g., authors and their papers). If two columns contain data of the same type, then we can extract direct linkage networks. For example, references refer to other papers and paper-reference networks resemble paper-citation networks.

Given the four-column table in Figure 6.11 (top left), we can extract many different networks. Using only the B column, we can extract a co-author network. We show the resulting undirected and weighted network below the data table. It has one node type: authors. There are as many nodes as there are unique authors. Edges represent co-occurrence—here co-author, relations. Edge weights denote the number of times two authors co-occur. For example, A2 and A6 co-occur on papers P2 and P6, and their link is twice as thick. The network can also be represented in textual format as a listing of nodes (vertices) and edges (see lower left). The node list assigns a unique identifier (ID) to each node and lists all node attributes, here the node label. The edge list represents each link

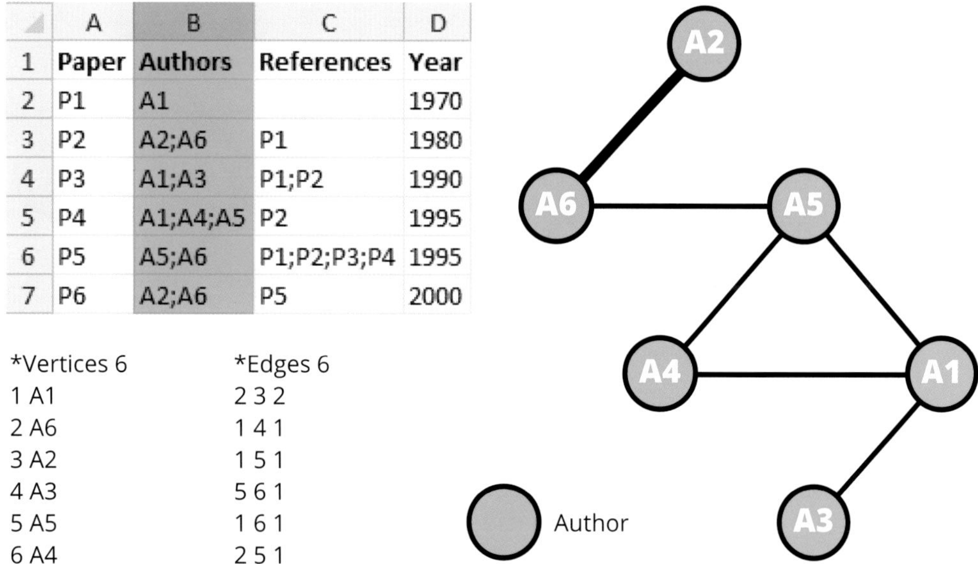

	A	B	C	D
1	Paper	Authors	References	Year
2	P1	A1		1970
3	P2	A2;A6	P1	1980
4	P3	A1;A3	P1;P2	1990
5	P4	A1;A4;A5	P2	1995
6	P5	A5;A6	P1;P2;P3;P4	1995
7	P6	A2;A6	P5	2000

*Vertices 6	*Edges 6
1 A1	2 3 2
2 A6	1 4 1
3 A2	1 5 1
4 A3	5 6 1
5 A5	1 6 1
6 A4	2 5 1

Figure 6.11 Weighted, undirected co-author network

by the identifiers of the two nodes the edge connects plus a weight attribute. Note that the edge from node ID two (A6) to ID three (A2) has a weight of two. All the other edges have a weight of one. In the Sci2 Tool, this type of network extraction is called "Extract Co-Occurrence Network" or "Extract Co-Author Network" (see Section 6.6).

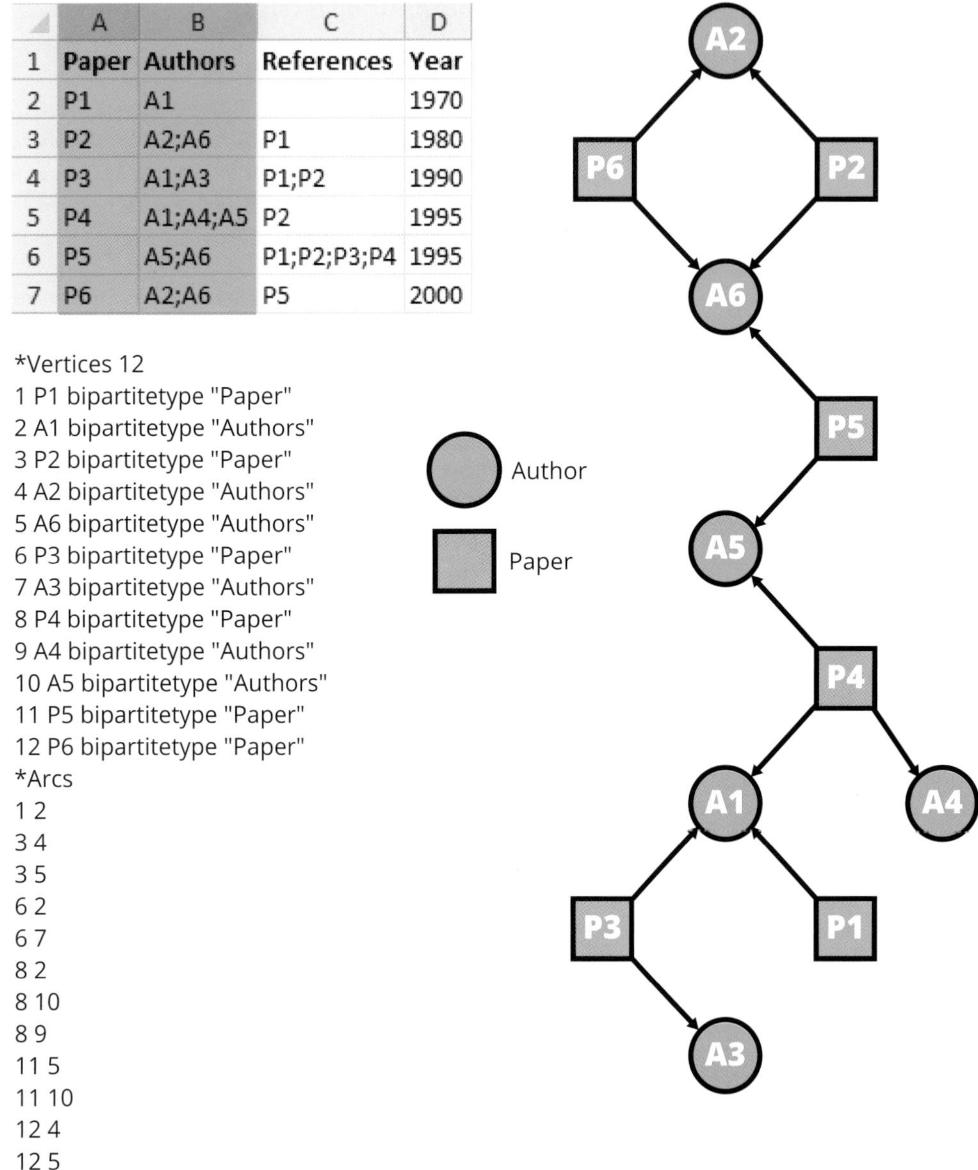

	A	B	C	D
1	**Paper**	**Authors**	**References**	**Year**
2	P1	A1		1970
3	P2	A2;A6	P1	1980
4	P3	A1;A3	P1;P2	1990
5	P4	A1;A4;A5	P2	1995
6	P5	A5;A6	P1;P2;P3;P4	1995
7	P6	A2;A6	P5	2000

```
*Vertices 12
1 P1 bipartitetype "Paper"
2 A1 bipartitetype "Authors"
3 P2 bipartitetype "Paper"
4 A2 bipartitetype "Authors"
5 A6 bipartitetype "Authors"
6 P3 bipartitetype "Paper"
7 A3 bipartitetype "Authors"
8 P4 bipartitetype "Paper"
9 A4 bipartitetype "Authors"
10 A5 bipartitetype "Authors"
11 P5 bipartitetype "Paper"
12 P6 bipartitetype "Paper"
*Arcs
1 2
3 4
3 5
6 2
6 7
8 2
8 10
8 9
11 5
11 10
12 4
12 5
```


Figure 6.12 Unweighted, directed bipartite author-paper network with bipartite type node property

Using two columns, we can extract a bipartite network from the same table (Figure 6.12). For example, using two node types—papers and authors—an unweighted, directed network can be derived. In Figure 6.12, author nodes are colored green and paper nodes are square and colored in orange. A paper might have multiple authors (e.g., P6 is pointing to authors A2 and A6, as does P2). The textual representation on the right lists an additional

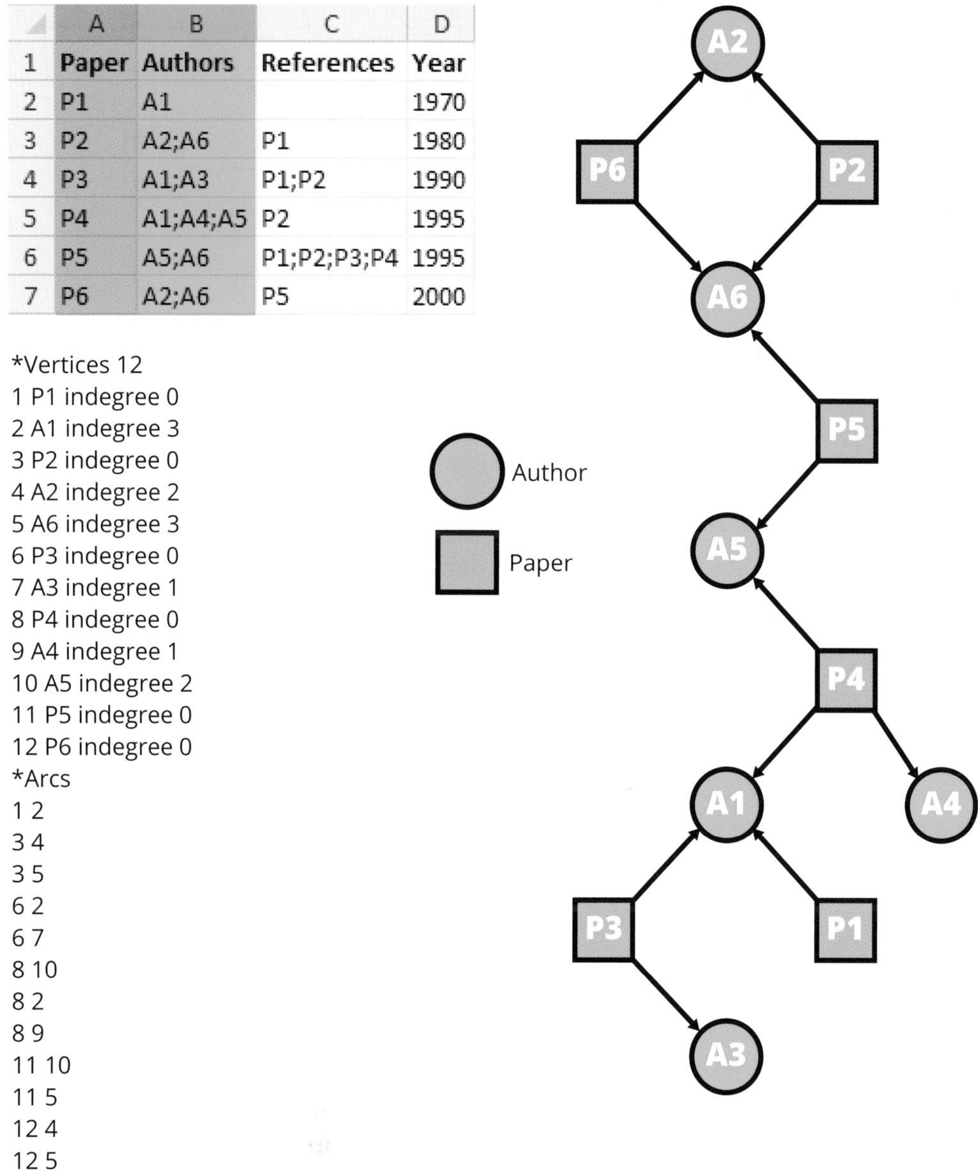

	A	B	C	D
1	**Paper**	**Authors**	**References**	**Year**
2	P1	A1		1970
3	P2	A2;A6	P1	1980
4	P3	A1;A3	P1;P2	1990
5	P4	A1;A4;A5	P2	1995
6	P5	A5;A6	P1;P2;P3;P4	1995
7	P6	A2;A6	P5	2000

*Vertices 12
1 P1 indegree 0
2 A1 indegree 3
3 P2 indegree 0
4 A2 indegree 2
5 A6 indegree 3
6 P3 indegree 0
7 A3 indegree 1
8 P4 indegree 0
9 A4 indegree 1
10 A5 indegree 2
11 P5 indegree 0
12 P6 indegree 0
*Arcs
1 2
3 4
3 5
6 2
6 7
8 10
8 2
8 9
11 10
11 5
12 4
12 5

Figure 6.13 Unweighted, directed bipartite author-paper network with indegree values for nodes

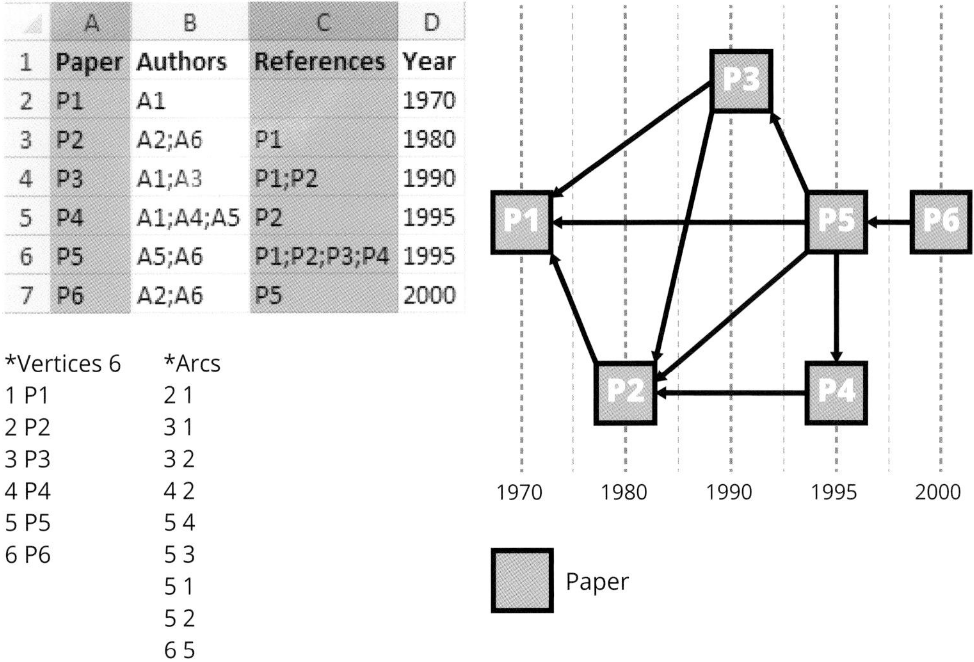

	A	B	C	D
1	Paper	Authors	References	Year
2	P1	A1		1970
3	P2	A2;A6	P1	1980
4	P3	A1;A3	P1;P2	1990
5	P4	A1;A4;A5	P2	1995
6	P5	A5;A6	P1;P2;P3;P4	1995
7	P6	A2;A6	P5	2000

*Vertices 6
1 P1
2 P2
3 P3
4 P4
5 P5
6 P6

*Arcs
2 1
3 1
3 2
4 2
5 4
5 3
5 1
5 2
6 5

Figure 6.14 Unweighted, directed paper-citation network, nodes laid out by year

node attribute bipartite type that identifies if a node is an author or a paper. We can use this node attribute to visually encode the different node types using graphic variable types. In the Sci2 Tool, this type of network extraction is called "Extract Bipartite Network" (see Section 6.8).

Using two columns, we can extract an unweighted, directed network of two node types (Figure 6.13). For example, if we use the same paper and author columns, the resulting network is identical to the one shown in Figure 6.12. However, the textual representation does not feature the bipartite type property. Instead we might calculate the indegree and outdegree of each node, and all nodes with an indegree of zero must be papers and those with an indegree of one or higher must be papers. In the Sci2 Tool, this type of network extraction is called "Extract Directed Network" (see Section 6.7).

Directed network extraction is particularly useful when different columns contain data of the same type and direct linkage networks can be extracted. For example, we can extract a paper-citation network from the paper and reference columns shown in Figure 6.14. The network is unweighted as each paper links to each reference exactly once; no reference is listed twice in the references section of a paper. It is directed as papers point to references, backwards in time. The network might be laid out in time (e.g., from the oldest paper published in 1970 on the left to the youngest paper published in 2000 on the right) to show how papers cite and build on each other. The listing of nodes and edges is given in the lower left. In the

Sci2 Tool, this type of network extraction is called "Extract Directed Network" (see Section 6.7).

We should never use bipartite network extraction to compute paper-citation networks (Figure 6.15). It would assume that papers and references are two different types of nodes, which is not the case.

When studying the diffusion of knowledge via paper-citation networks, it is desirable to direct citation linkages from older papers to younger papers. In the Sci2 Tool, simply apply "Extract Paper Citation Network" (see Section 6.7).

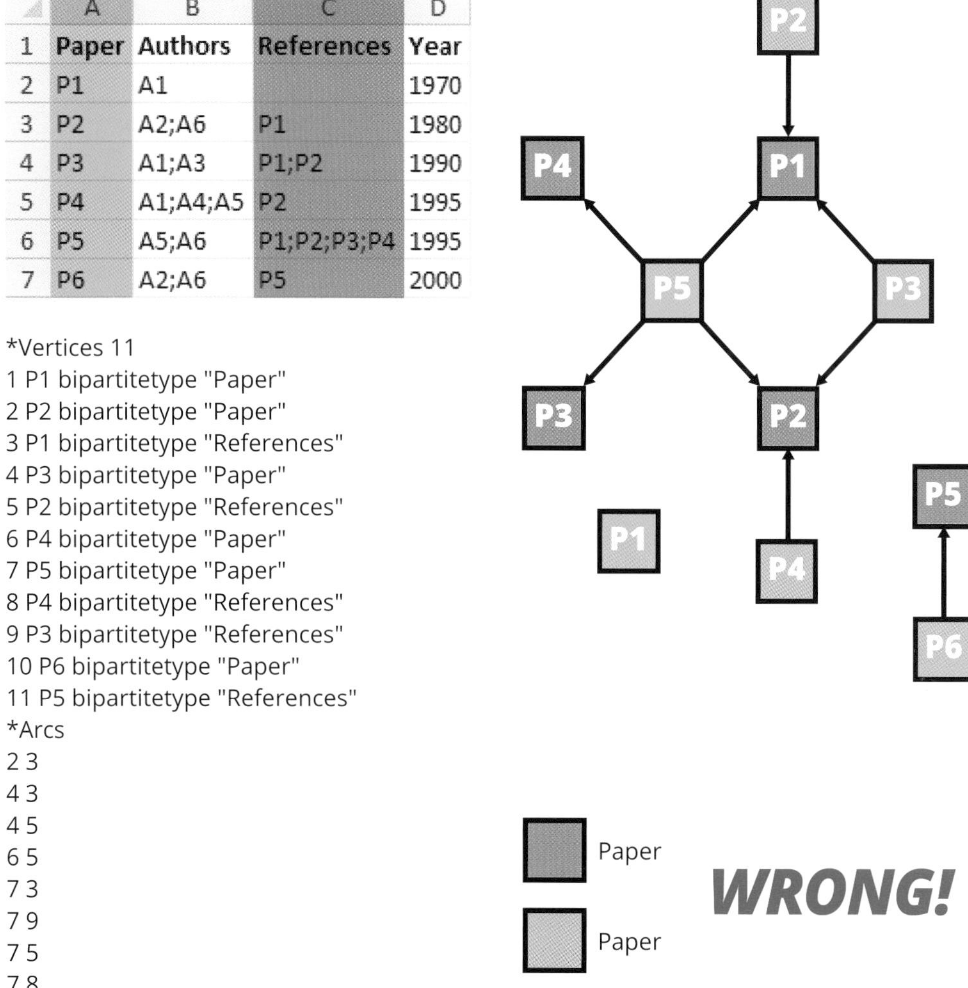

	A	B	C	D
1	Paper	Authors	References	Year
2	P1	A1		1970
3	P2	A2;A6	P1	1980
4	P3	A1;A3	P1;P2	1990
5	P4	A1;A4;A5	P2	1995
6	P5	A5;A6	P1;P2;P3;P4	1995
7	P6	A2;A6	P5	2000

```
*Vertices 11
1 P1 bipartitetype "Paper"
2 P2 bipartitetype "Paper"
3 P1 bipartitetype "References"
4 P3 bipartitetype "Paper"
5 P2 bipartitetype "References"
6 P4 bipartitetype "Paper"
7 P5 bipartitetype "Paper"
8 P4 bipartitetype "References"
9 P3 bipartitetype "References"
10 P6 bipartitetype "Paper"
11 P5 bipartitetype "References"
*Arcs
2 3
4 3
4 5
6 5
7 3
7 9
7 5
7 8
10 11
```


Figure 6.15 Erroneous application of bipartite network extraction to derive paper-citation network

Analyze & Visualize

We might apply diverse network analysis algorithms to calculate node, edge, and network properties such as those discussed in Section 6.2 or to cluster a network or identify its backbone (see Section 6.4). We can use resulting additional attribute values to place nodes (e.g., on relevant geolocations or topical locations) or to map them onto graphic variable types during visualization. In general, network layouts aim to use the display area effectively, to minimize node occlusions and edge crossings, and to maximize symmetry. These criteria might be relaxed to speed up the layout process. Subsequently, we discuss different standard layouts that exist for networks: random, circular, and force-directed placement.

Random layout (Figure 6.16) takes the dimensions of the available display area and a network (e.g., represented as a listing of nodes and edges plus their attributes) as input. It then assigns each node a random *x* and *y* position ensuring that this position is in the predefined display area. Layout is fast, and while the structure of the network cannot be identified, seeing the number of nodes and edges gives a first impression of the size and density of a network.

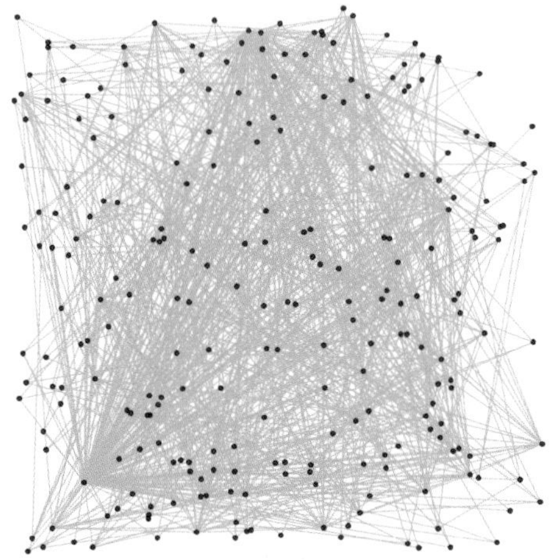

Figure 6.16 Random layout

Circular layout (Figure 6.17) takes the dimensions of the available display area and a network as input. It then calculates a circle as a reference system for node placement, keeping in mind any node size-coding. All nodes are placed on the circle exclusively. Node sequence might be alphabetical or sorted by node attributes (e.g., degree), by node similarity (i.e., more similar nodes are closer), or by network clustering (i.e., highly interlinked nodes are closer). Layout is relatively fast but slower than random as additional node attributes might have to be calculated, and node attributes might be used to determine node sequence along the circle. Circular layouts with meaningful node sequences can be extremely informative (e.g., see circular hierarchy visualization in Section 6.6).

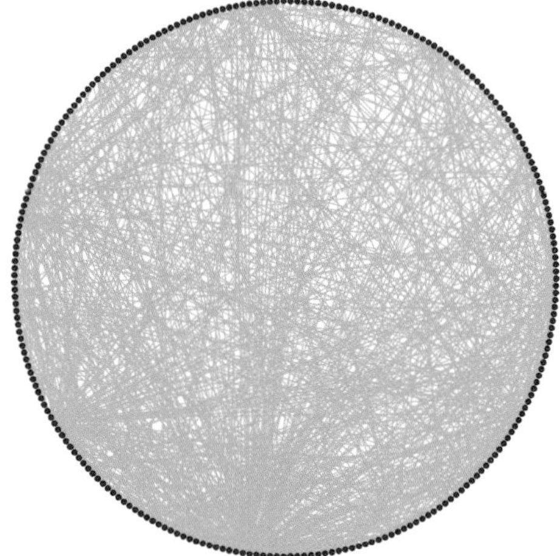

Figure 6.17 Circular layout

Force directed layout (Figure 6.18) takes the dimensions of the available display area and a network as input. Using information on the similarity/distance relationships among nodes—for example, co-author link weights—it calculates node positions so that similar nodes are in close spatial proximity. This layout is computationally expensive as all node pairs have to be examined and layout optimization is performed iteratively.

Running the Generalized Expectation Maximization (GEM) layout available in Sci2 via running GUESS on the very same network results in the layout shown in Figure 6.18. We can see the sub-networks, their size, density, and structure.

We can use node attributes to size-code, color-code, and label nodes (e.g., by the number of papers, citations, or co-authors). We might use edge attributes to size- and color-code edges (e.g., by the number of times two authors have co-authored). We must create a legend to communicate the mapping of data to graphic variable types (Figure 6.19 and Section 6.6).

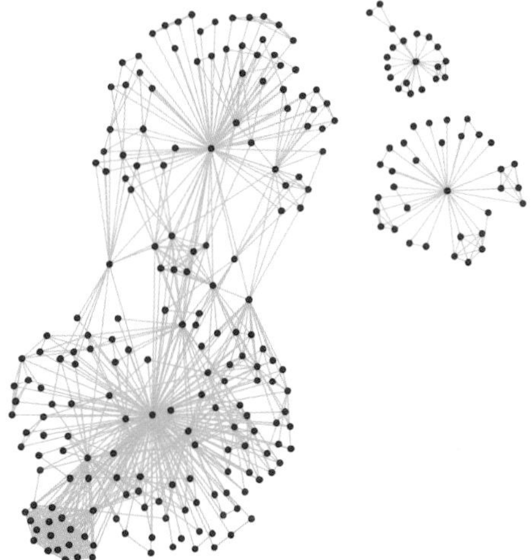

Figure 6.18 Force-directed layout

We discuss a number of other layouts and provide examples in other parts of this book:

Bipartite layout (Section 6.8) renders networks with two node types as two lists. The lists might be sorted alphabetically, by node attributes (e.g., degree), by node similarity (i.e., more similar nodes are closer), by network clustering (i.e., highly interlinked nodes are closer), etc. Edges connect nodes of one type to nodes of another type and might be width- and color-coded according to additional edge attributes.

Subway map layouts (Figure 4.1 in Section 4.1) aim for evenly distributed nodes, uniform edge lengths, and orthogonal drawings. They minimize area, bends, slopes, angles, and they maximize consistent flow direction in directed networks.

Figure 6.19 GEM layout of co-author network

Network overlays on geospatial maps (Figure 3.13 in Section 3.3) use a geospatial reference system to place nodes (e.g., based on address information).

Science maps (Figure 4.17 in Section 4.6) use a predefined reference system that might be a network to layout data (e.g., expertise profiles or career trajectories).

When visualizing extremely large networks, it is beneficial to discover and highlight landmark nodes, backbones, and clusters. We might need interactivity to support search, panning, zooming, or for details on demand and information requests, such as hovering over a node to bring up additional details (see Chapter 7).

6.4 CLUSTERING AND BACKBONE IDENTIFICATION

In this section we introduce two common approaches used to make sense of complex network visualizations. The first, clustering, identifies communities in networks (i.e., each node is assigned to one or more clusters and this additional node attribute can be used to visually encode nodes). The second, backbone identification, identifies the most important edges and deletes all other edges.

Clustering

Many different algorithms have been developed to cluster networks. A detailed review of network clustering, also called **community detection**, was recently compiled by Santo Fortunato.[20] The goal of clustering is to identify modules using the information encoded in the graph topology (i.e., the geometric position of and the spatial relations between nodes). Results might be visualized using graphic variable types (Section 1.2) or by adding additional cluster boundaries. This is exemplified in Figure 6.20. On the left we show nodes that are color-coded to indicate their correspondence to three different clusters. On the right we show the very same network but additional ellipsoids are used to visually depict a cluster hierarchy.

Divisive clustering algorithms detect inter-community nodes or links and remove them from the network (e.g., using thresholding on node and edge properties such as betweenness centrality discussed below). Agglomerative algorithms merge similar nodes recursively. An example is Blondel community detection, also discussed below. Optimization methods maximize an objective function. Details are discussed by Fortunato[21] but are not covered in this book.

Using node betweenness centrality to cluster networks. Betweenness centrality (BC) measures a node's centrality, load, or importance in a network. It equals the number

---

20 Fortunato, Santo. 2010. "Community Detection in Graphs." *Physics Reports* 486: 75–174. Accessed September 5, 2013. http://arxiv.org/pdf/0906.0612.pdf.

21 Ibid.

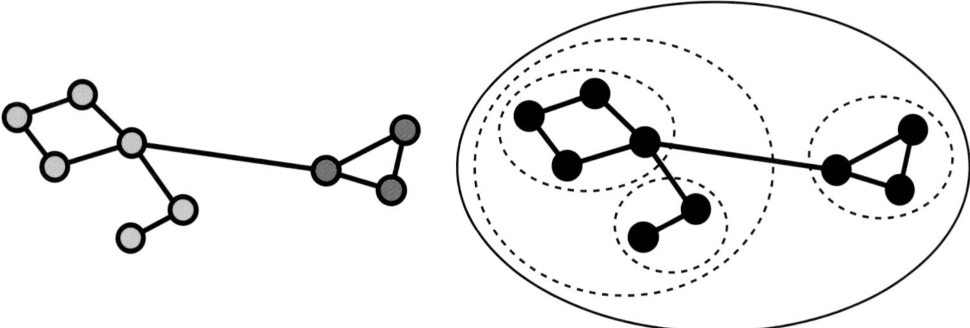

Figure 6.20 Visual representation of network clusters

of shortest paths from all nodes to all others that pass through that node. That is, nodes with higher betweenness occur on more paths between other nodes. The BC of a node *n* in a network is computed by (1) computing for each pair of nodes, the shortest paths between them; (2) for each pair of the node pairs, determining the fraction of shortest paths that pass through node *n*; (3) summing this fraction (calculated in step 2) over all pairs of nodes. In Figure 6.21 the BC of each node is represented by color hue, from red (minimum) to blue (maximum).

Figure 6.22 shows the collaboration network of Alessandro Vespignani and Albert-László Barabási with nodes sized and color-coded by their betweenness centrality. Five nodes have a BC of larger than 10 (red) and are labeled. The yellow nodes have a high BC but less so than the red ones. Then, the black nodes have a rather low BC. If high BC nodes are deleted (e.g., all red nodes), then the network disassembles into different sub-networks.

Alternatively, the BC of edges can be calculated and edges with high BC can be deleted. Similarly, nodes and edges might be deleted based on other attribute values, e.g., authors with few papers or citations might be omitted. However, it is often problematic to delete nodes and edges. This is why alternative methods have been developed.

Using Blondel community detection to cluster networks. Blondel's algorithm[22] aims to partition a network into communities of densely connected nodes, where nodes belonging to different communities are only sparsely connected. The quality of these communities within a cluster partition is then measured by the modularity of the partition. Here, modularity is a scalar value between -1 and 1 that matches the density of links within a community as compared to links between communities. Modularity is used as an objective function to arrive at the best cluster solution but also to compare Blondel's with other community detection approaches.

[22] Blondel, Vincent D., Jean-Loup Guillaume, Renaud Lambiotte, and Etienne Lefebvre. 2008. "Fast Unfolding of Communities in Large Networks." *Journal of Statistical Mechanics* P10008. http://dx.doi.org/10.1088/1742-5468/2008/10/P10008.

The Blondel algorithm reads a weighted network of *N* nodes. Initially, each node is assigned to a different community; each community has exactly one node. In phase one, for each node *i*, the gain in modularity that would take place by removing *i* from its community and by placing it in the community of one of its neighbors is calculated. This is computationally expensive as it is performed for each node in the network. The node *i* is then placed in the community for which the gain is maximum. If there's a tie, a tie-breaking rule is applied. If there are no positive gains, then *i* stays in its original community. This process is applied repeatedly and sequentially for all nodes in the network until a local maximum modularity is reached. In phase two, the algorithm aggregates the found communities in order to build a new network of communities. Here, the weights of the links between the new nodes are given by the sum of the weights of the links between nodes in the corresponding two communities. Links between nodes in the same community lead to self-loops for this community in the new network. These two phases are repeated iteratively until no increase of modularity is possible.

Figure 6.21 Node betweeness centrality shown in color with red representing the lowest and blue the highest

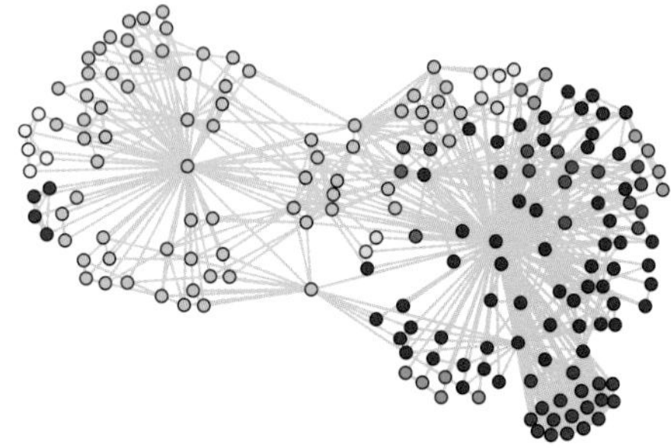

Figure 6.22 Co-authorship network with nodes colored based on community membership as identified by the Blondel community detection algorithm

The algorithm outputs additional cluster attributes for each node, up to three community levels. No edge attributes are added and no nodes or edges are deleted. As an example, we show Alessandro Vespignani and Albert-László Barabási's collaboration network with nodes color-coded by cluster membership in Figure 6.22; we show only the lowest clustering level.

To represent the complete clustering hierarchy, we can visualize the network using the **circular hierarchy visualization** (see Figure 6.41 in Section 6.6). Using this visualization, all node labels are listed in a circle. Nodes are interlinked by edges, here representing co-authorship. The outer circles represent the hierarchical grouping of communities. The color-coding in this example indicates the number of co-authored works. See workflow in Section 6.6 on how to run Blondel's algorithm and visualize results using the circular hierarchy visualization.

Backbone Identification

The main structure of a network (e.g., the part of a network that handles the major traffic and/or has the highest-speed transmission paths) is also called the **backbone** of a network. Backbone identification is particularly valuable when dealing with networks that are very dense, for example, where individual nodes and edges can no longer be seen and the layout resembles a big hairball.

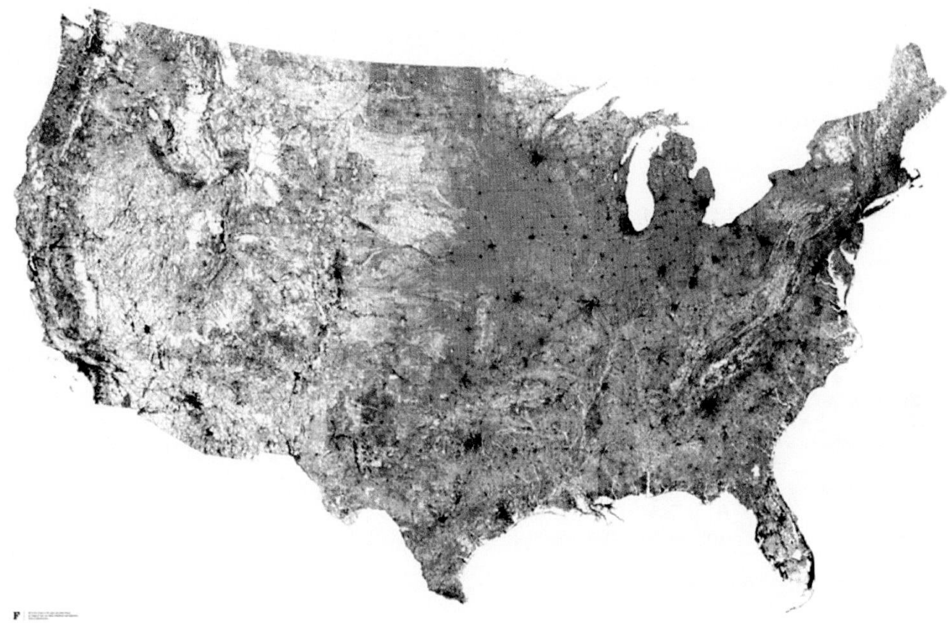

Figure 6.23 U.S. road network: map of 240 million individual road segments

An example is the U.S. road network. The All Streets[23] visualization by Ben Fry (Figure 6.23) shows all the 240 million individual road segments in the United States. The road network backbone made available by Wikipedia[24] (Figure 6.24) shows the U.S. interstate highways within the 48 contiguous states, giving us a much better understanding of how quickly we can make it from one point to the next.

Figure 6.24 Map of the U.S. interstate backbone

23 http://fathom.info/allstreets

24 http://en.wikipedia.org/wiki/Interstate_Highway_System

There are different approaches to identifying backbones. The simplest approach is to use node and/or edge properties to delete links that are less relevant. DrL, one of the most scalable layout algorithms in the Sci2 Tool, manages to layout large and dense networks by only keeping the top *n* highest weight edges per node. Another approach is Pathfinder Network Scaling discussed in more detail here.

Pathfinder Network Scaling[25] takes a matrix as input that represents the similarity or distance between each node pair. It then extracts the network that preserves only the most important links relying on triangle inequality to eliminate redundant or counterintuitive links. That is, if two nodes are connected by many different pathways, then only the path that has a greater weight as defined by the Minkowski metric is preserved. Basically, the most important edges are preserved. The output is a network with the same number of nodes but fewer links; it's much more of a tree-like structure.

To give an example, let's use the Alessandro Vespignani and Albert-László Barabási co-authorship network (see Figure 6.25, left). Pathfinder Network Scaling with default parameters reduces the network to the structure shown on the right.[26]

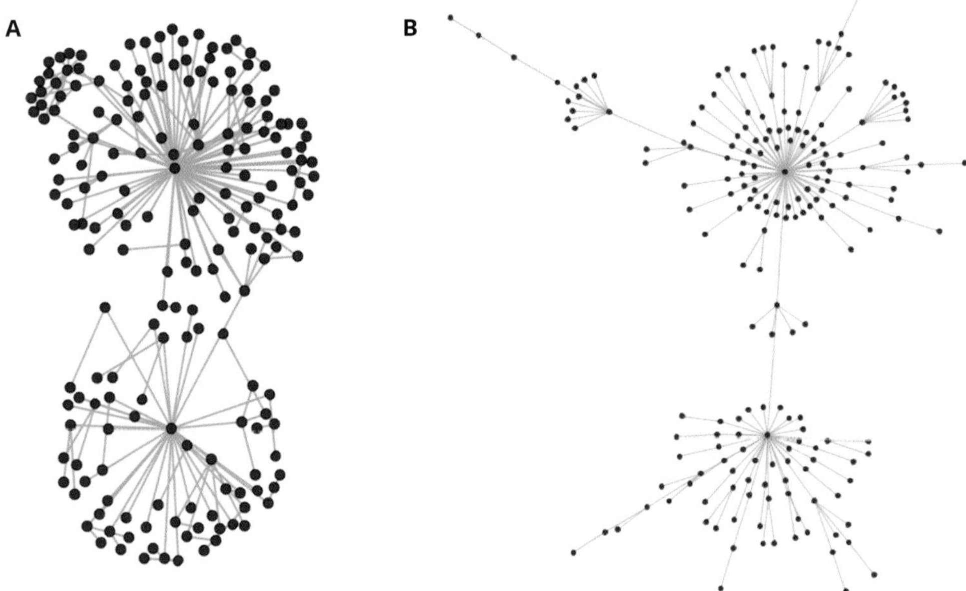

Figure 6.25 Alessandro Vespignani and Albert-László Barabási co-authorship network with complete network (A) and backbone via Pathfinder Network Scaling (B)

---

25 Schvaneveldt, Roger W., ed. 1990. *Pathfinder Associative Networks: Studies in Knowledge Organization*. Norwood, NJ: Ablex.

26 http://wiki.cns.iu.edu/display/SCI2TUTORIAL/5.1.4+Studying+Four+Major+NetSci+Researchers+(ISI+Data)

Self-Assessment

For the network shown here, identify attributes for:

1. Nodes
   a. degree for node E and D
   b. label of isolated node

2. Network
   a. size, number of edges, number of components
   b. is it directed, weighted, fully connected, labeled, multigraph

3. Giant component
   a. density
   b. diameter

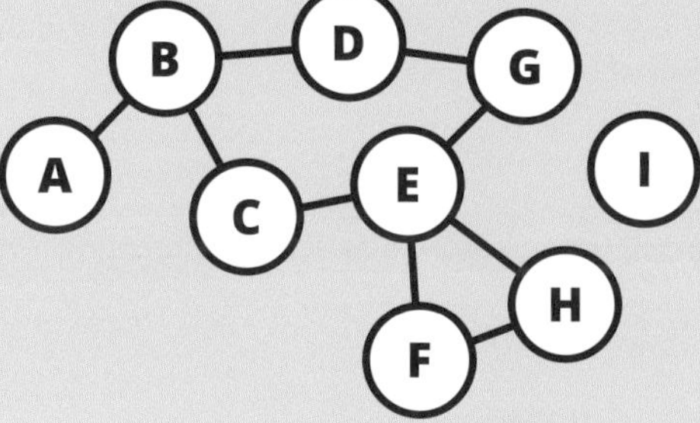

Chapter 6: Hands-On Section

6.5 VISUALIZING THE FLORENTINE NETWORK

Data Types & Coverage	
Time Frame:	Early 15th Century
Region:	Italy
Topical Area:	History, Politics
Network Type:	Marriage and Business

Analysis Types/Levels	•	●	⬤
Temporal			
Geospatial			
Topical			
Network		X	

This workflow uses John Padgett's Florentine families dataset, which includes 16 Italian families from the early fifteenth century. Each family is represented by a node in the network and is connected by edges that represent either marriage or business/lending ties. Each node (family) has several attributes: wealth (in thousands of lira), number of priorates (seats in the civic council), and total ties (total number of business ties and marriages in the dataset).

First, load *florentine.nwb*[27] into Sci2 using *File* > *Load*. After the file is loaded it will appear in the 'Data Manager' (Figure 6.26).

Figure 6.26 Sci2 'Data Manager' with *florentine.nwb* loaded

We will skip straight to the visualization step since the network file already contains all the node and edge attributes to be visualized. Select the file from the 'Data Manager' and choose *Visualization* > *Networks* > *GUESS* from the menu (Figure 6.27).

When the network loads in GUESS it will have a random layout (Figure 6.28).

Select *Layout* > *GEM* from the GUESS menu to layout the network using a force-directed placement algorithm. Notice that the GEM layout is non-deterministic—that

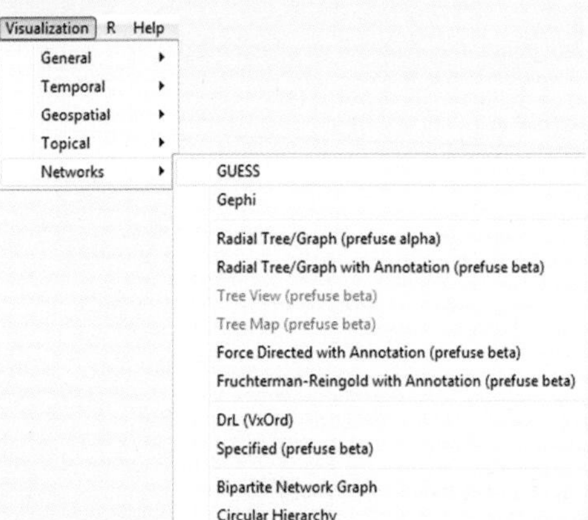

Figure 6.27 Selecting 'GUESS' from the *Visualization* > *Networks* menu

27 *yoursci2directory*/sampledata/socialscience

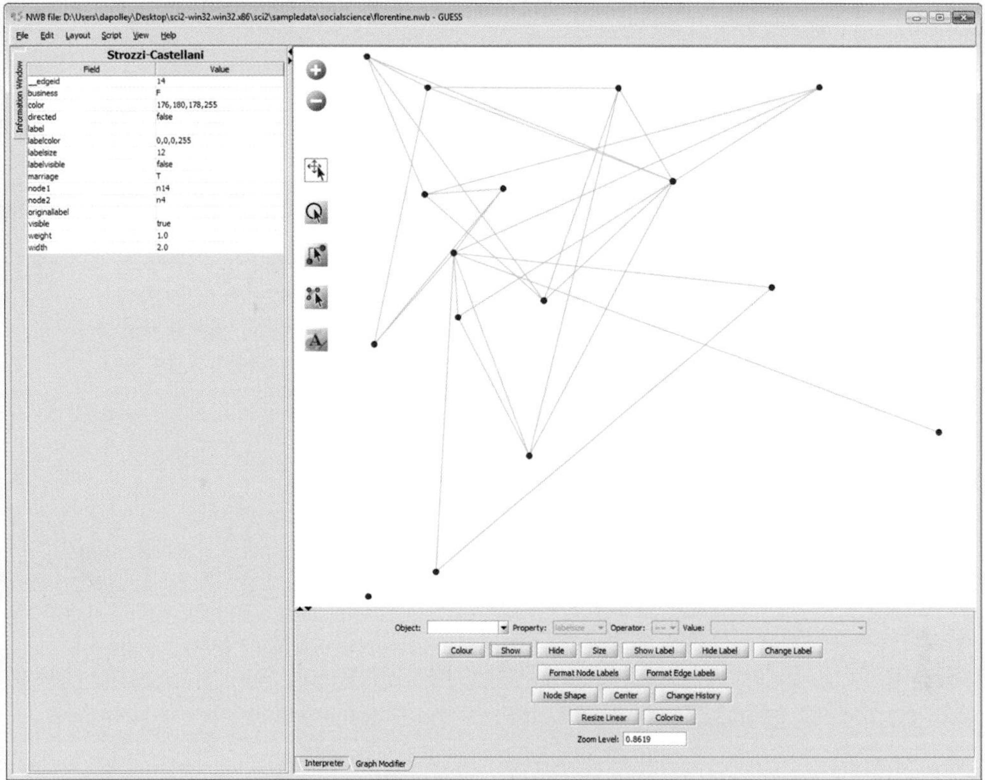

Figure 6.28 Florentine families network laid out randomly in 'GUESS'

is, each run results in a slightly different layout. To bring the nodes close together, run *Layout* > *Bin Pack* (Figure 6.29).

Next, resize the nodes based on the wealth attribute. In the 'Graph Modifier' window (Figure 6.28) select the 'Resize Linear' button and set the parameters to 'Nodes', 'wealth', and 'From: 5 To: 20' (Figure 6.30). Click 'Do Resize Linear'.

Next, 'Colorize' the nodes by selecting 'Nodes', 'priorates', and setting the color range 'From: black To: green' (Figure 6.31). To set the color, simply click on the square and a color palette will appear.

Then, color the edges to show the type of relationship between the families. Select the 'Object: edges based on ->', set the 'Property'

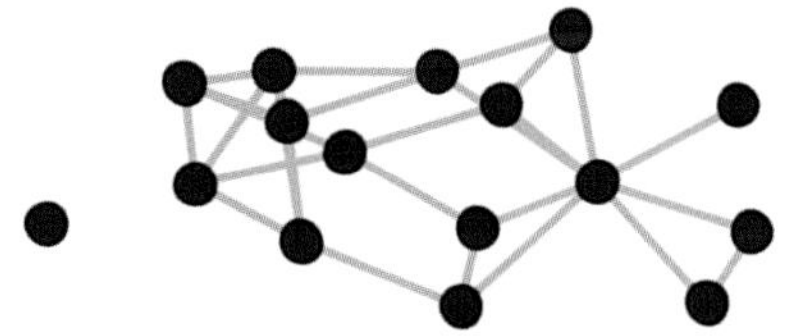

Figure 6.29 Florentine families network with GEM network layout applied

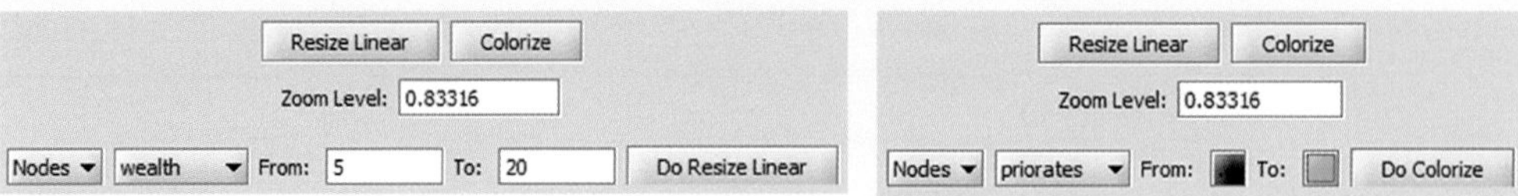

Figure 6.30 Resizing the nodes on a linear scale from 5 to 20 based on the wealth of each family

Figure 6.31 The Florentine families network with nodes colored on a spectrum from black to green based on the priorates

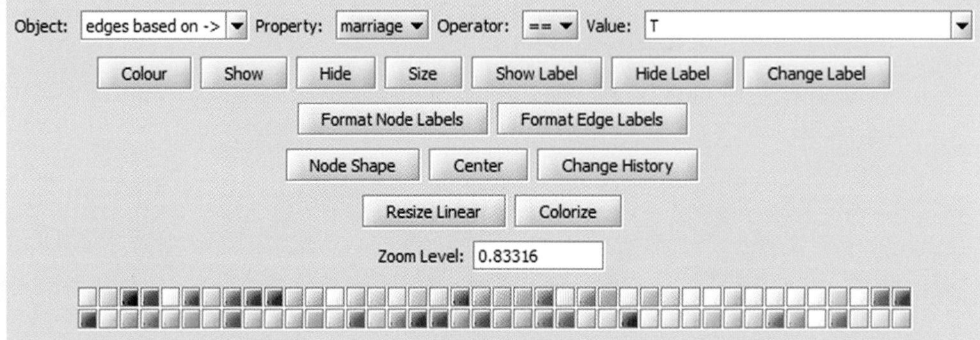

Figure 6.32 Coloring the edges based on relationship type

to 'marriage', the 'Operator' to '==', and the 'Value' to 'T'. Click the 'Colour' button and choose 'red' from the pallet that appears at the bottom of the 'Graph Modifier' pane (Figure 6.32).

Repeat this process to color the business ties, and color them blue. Next, color the edges that connect families through both business and marriage ties a different color. To do this, switch to the 'Intepreter' view at the bottom of the screen. Enter the following commands:

```
>>> for e in g.edges:
...   if(e.marriage=="T" and e.business=="T"):
...          e.color=purple
...
...
>>>
```

Make sure to hit the tab key once after the first line and twice after the second line. This will ensure that the code is properly nested. These commands tell GUESS that for all edges (`e`) in this graph (`g.edges`), if there is an edge that connects two families by marriage (`e.marriage=="T"`) and business (`e.business=="T"`), then color that edge purple (`e.color=purple`).

Next, switch back to the 'Graph Modifier' at the bottom of GUESS. Label all the nodes with the family names. Select the 'Object: all nodes', and then click the 'Show Label' button; the node labels will appear in the visualization. Two more changes will make the network look more presentable. Adjusting the spacing between nodes will make their labels visible. We can do this automatically by rerunning the GEM layout, or manually by adjusting individual nodes using the node selection icon in the graph window and clicking on nodes to drag them around.

Finally, as the size of our network increases it can become difficult to read it with thick black borders around every node. To resolve this, color borders the same as the node. Go to the 'Interpreter' tab at the bottom of the GUESS window and type the following commands:

```
>>> for n in g.nodes:
...   n.strokecolor = n.color
...
...
>>>
```

Again, make sure to hit the tab key before entering the second line. This code tells GUESS that for every node (*n*) in this graph of nodes (*g.nodes*) make the border color of the nodes (*n.strokecolor*) equal to the node color (*n.color*). The borders will no longer be visible in the final visualization (Figure 6.33). Please see "Creating Legends for Visualizations" section of the Appendix (p. 284) for how to represent the mapping of data variables to graphic variable types by means of a legend.

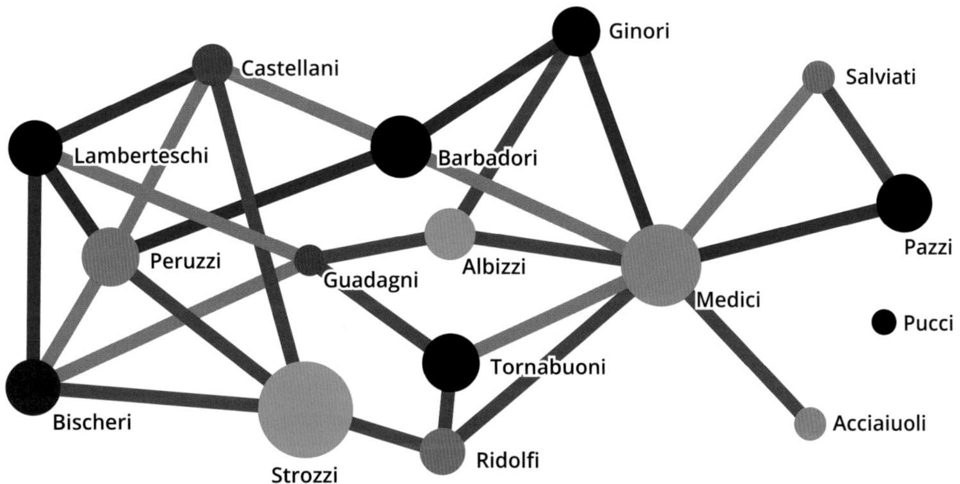

Figure 6.33 Final visualization of the Florentine families network

The resulting visualization reveals that two major families, the Medici and Strozzi, connected all the other families in the network. It also shows that the Medici family linked the majority of the network to three other families, thus placing themselves in a vital mediating role within the community.

6.6 AUTHOR CO-OCCURRENCE (CO-AUTHOR) NETWORK

Data Types & Coverage	
Time Frame:	1955-2007
Region:	Miscellaneous
Topical Area:	Network Science
Network Type:	Co-Author Network

Analysis Types/Levels	•	●	⬤
Temporal			
Geospatial			
Topical			
Network		X	

The Four Network Science Researchers file contains publications retrieved from the Web of Science (WoS) in 2007 for four major network science researchers: Stanley Wasserman, Eugene Garfield, Alessandro Vespignani, and Albert-László Barabási. In this workflow we cover the creation of an author co-occurrence network, commonly called a co-author network.

First, load the *FourNetSciResearchers.isi* file[28] into the Sci2 Tool. Then, select '361 unique ISI records' in the 'Data Manager' and run *Data Preparation > Extract Co-Author Network* and indicate that you are working with ISI data. The result is two derived files in the 'Data Manager': the 'Extracted Co-Authorship Network' and an 'Author information' table, which lists unique authors.

	A	B	C	D	E
1	label	number_of_authored_works	times_cited	uniqueIndex	combineValues
2	Abt, Ha	1	3	142	*
3	Alava, M	1	26	195	*
4	Albert, I	5	207	65	*
5	Albert, L	1	6	69	*
6	Albert, R	17	7741	60	*
7	Albet, R	1	16	60	
8	Alippi, A	2	107	214	*

Figure 6.34 'Author information' table modification to merge two author nodes

Open the 'Author information' table by right-clicking on the file and selecting 'View'. The file will open in your default spreadsheet editing program. Sort the data alphabetically by the author name and make sure the other columns are sorted as well. Identify names that refer to the same person and should only be represented by one node in the network. When you find two names that you want to merge, delete the asterisk (*) in the 'combineValues' column of the duplicate node's row. Then, copy the 'uniqueIndex' of the name that should be kept and paste it into the cell of the name that should be deleted. An example is shown in Figure 6.34, here 'Albet, R' is a misspelling of 'Albert, R' and the table was modified to keep the 'Albert, R' node and to add all 'number_of_authored_works' and 'times_cited' from 'Albet, R' to that node.

---

[28] *yoursci2directory*/sampledata/scientometrics/isi

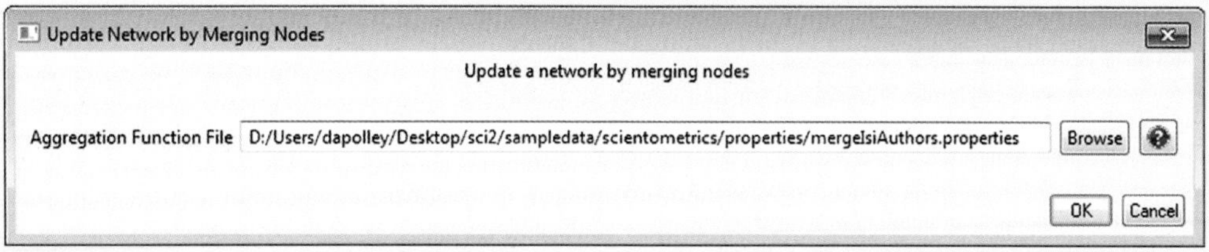

Figure 6.35 Select 'Aggregation Function File'

Save the revised table as a CSV file and reload it into Sci2. Select both the newly loaded 'Author Information' table and the co-author network by holding down the CTRL key while making the selection. With both files selected, run *Data Preparation > Update Network by Merging Nodes* (Figure 6.35). Make sure to use the proper aggregate function file, *mergeIsiAuthors.properties*[29] to ensure the merge node has the sum values for the 'number_of_authored_works' and 'times_cited' of both original nodes. For more information about aggregate function files, see the "Property Files" section of the Appendix (p. 288).

The result is an updated network as well as a report describing which nodes were merged. Visualize the updated co-authorship network by selecting *Visualization > Networks > GUESS.* Run *Layout > GEM and Layout > Bin Pack* (Figure 6.36) to see four clusters of nodes, two of which are connected, that represent the co-authorship networks of the four main authors in the dataset.

To encode additional node and edge properties using graphic variable types, enter the following commands into the 'Graph Modifier':

1. *Resize Linear > Nodes > number_of_authored_works > From: 10 To: 50*
2. *Colorize > Nodes > times_cited > From: To: >*
3. *Resize Linear > Edges > number_of_coauthored_works > From: .25 To: 8*
4. *Colorize > Edges > number_of_coauthored_works > From: To:*
5. Type in the interpreter:

```
>>> nodesbynumworks=g.nodes[:]
>>> def bynumworks(n1,n2):
...        return cmp(n1.number _ of _ authored _ works,
           n2.number _ of _ authored _ works)
...
>>> nodesbynumworks.sort(bynumworks)
>>> nodesbynumworks.reverse()
>>> for i in range(0,50):
...        nodesbynumworks[i].labelvisible=true
...
>>>
```

In the resulting visualization (Figure 6.36), author nodes are size-coded by the number of papers per author and color-coded by the total times these papers are cited. Edges are

29 *yoursci2directory*/sampledata/scientometrics/properties

color-coded and weighted by the number of times two authors collaborate. The remaining commands identify the top 50 authors by number of authored works and label those nodes.

The network shows three weakly connected components. The largest component shows the nodes for Barabási and Vespignani, who have co-authored together and share several co-authors. Vespignani and Stefano Zapperi have the strongest collaboration link in the network. The other two components are rather small, exemplifying the different collaboration patterns in physics (Barabási and Vespignani are physicists), social science (Wasserman), and information science (Garfield).

In order to identify author nodes that bridge different communities (see Section 6.4), calculate the betweenness centrality (BC) for each node. Select the 'Extracted Co-Authorship Network' file in the 'Data Manager' and run *Analysis > Weighted and Undirected > Node Betweenness Centrality*, and set the parameter to 'Weight' that represents the number of times two authors wrote a paper together (Figure 6.37).

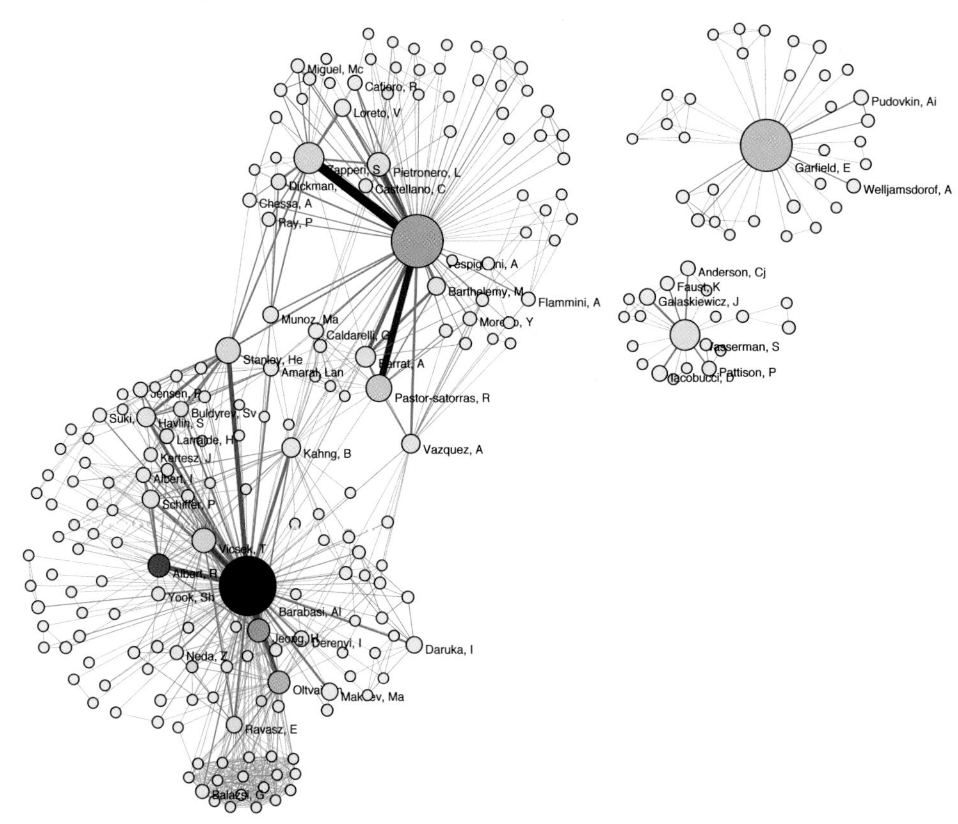

Figure 6.36 Four network science researchers' co-authorship network with nodes sized based on the number of authored works (http://cns.iu.edu/ivmoocbook14/6.36.pdf)

This will append a BC value to each node. Select the resulting network and visualize it by running *Visualize > Networks > GUESS* and layout using *Layout > GEM* and *Layout > Bin Pack*.

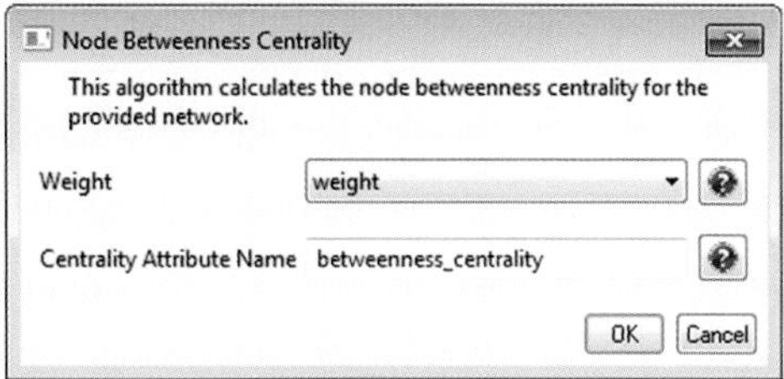

Figure 6.37 Calculating the node betweenness centrality based on weight

Now, repeat the commands listed above, which results in Figure 6.36. However, there is one small difference. In this network we size the nodes based on their BC value.

Resize Linear > Nodes > betweenness centrality > From: 10 To: > 50

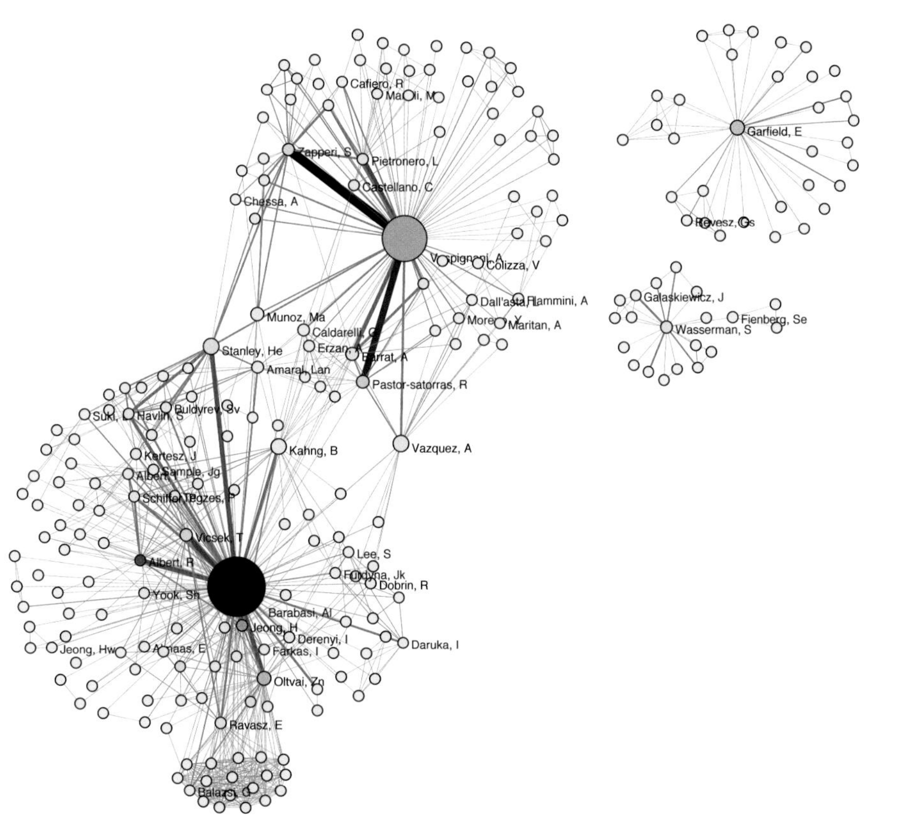

Figure 6.38 Four network science researchers' co-authorship network with the nodes sized based on betweenness centrality (http://cns.iu.edu/ivmoocbook14/6.38.pdf)

To label the top 50 nodes based on their BC, enter the following commands in the interpreter:

```
>>> nodesbybc=g.nodes[:]
>>> def bybc(n1,n2):
...         return cmp(n1.betweenness _ centrality,
            n2.betweenness _ centrality)
...
>>> nodesbybc.sort(bybc)
>>> nodesbybc.reverse()
>>> for i in range(0,50):
...         nodesbybc[i].labelvisible=true
```

The resulting network will have a different layout but the general structure of the three networks is similar. It shows the nodes have been sized based on their betweeneess centrality (Figure 6.38). The largest, highest betweenness centrality nodes are Albert-László Barabási and Alessandro Vespignani. This is not surprising as they are two of the four main scholars in this dataset, and they have the highest number of co-authors in this dataset. Both have backgrounds in physics, which may be part of the reason they share so many collaborators.

Now, take the co-authorship network and run the Blondel Community Detection to calculate a hierarchical clustering of authors (see Section 6.4).[30] Run the algorithm using *Networks > Weighted and Undirected > Blondel Community Detection*. Set the 'Weight' attribute to 'weight' (Figure 6.39).

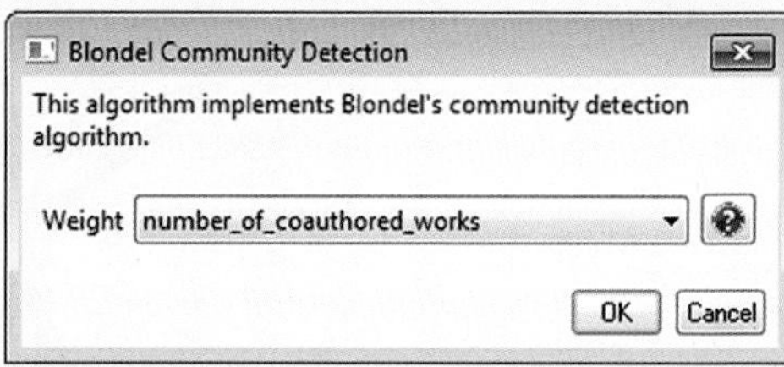

Figure 6.39 Calculating Blondel communities based on weight

The result is a new network, with community attributes added to each node (same network shown in 6.22). Visualize this network and the cluster hierarchy with the Circular Hierarchy Visualization. Run *Visualize > Networks > Circular Hierarchy* using the default parameters (Figure 6.40).

Circular Hierarchy
Provides Circular Hierarchy Visualization on the network.
Degree of Edge Bundling 0.75
Node Strength Column No Strength
Level 0 blondel_community_level_0
Level 1 blondel_community_level_1
Level 2 blondel_community_level_2
Level 3 No Level
Edge Weight Column number_of_coauthored_works
Node Color Column No Node Color
Node Color Range Yellow to blue
OK Cancel

Figure 6.40 Parameters for the circular hierarchy visualization

The result is a PostScript file in the 'Data Manger'. Save the file, convert it into a PDF, and view it (Figure 6.41). For more information on converting PostScript files to PDFs, see p. 286 in the Appendix.

In the circular hierarchy visualization, author names are displayed in a circular band, connected based on their

30 Blondel, Vincent D., Jean-Loup Guillaume, Renaud Lambiotte, and Etienne Lefebvre. 2008. "Fast Unfolding of Communities in Large Networks." *Journal of Statistical Mechanics* P10008.

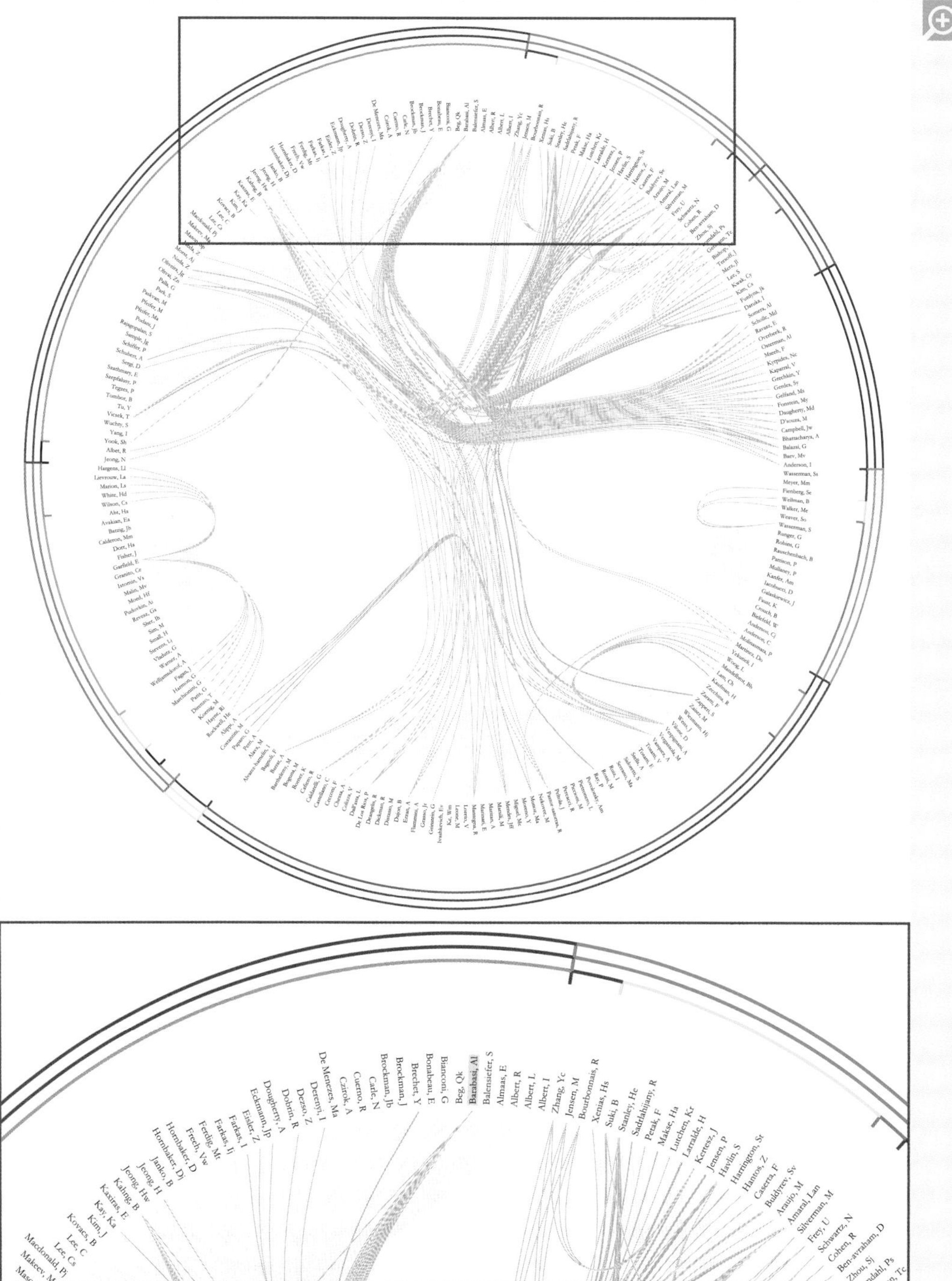

Figure 6.41 Circular hierarchy visualization of Blondel community detection result for four network science researchers' co-authorship network (A) and zoom in of Albert-László Barabási, his community, and his collaborators (B) (http://cns.iu.edu/ivmoocbook14/6.41.pdf)

co-authorship ties. Edges are bundled to make the network easier to read. Around the outside of the network are three circles. The innermost circle represents the communities identified at level 0, and each community includes the names within the tic marks on the circle. The next circles represent the communities identified at levels 1 and 2. For example, in the zoomed version, Barabási's node is clustered with the authors in the pink-colored community, but he has many connections to other authors in other communities.

6.7 DIRECTED NETWORKS: PAPER-CITATION NETWORK

Data Types & Coverage	
Time Frame:	1955-2007
Region:	Miscellaneous
Topical Area:	Network Science
Network Type:	Paper Citation Network

Analysis Types/Levels	•	●	⬤
Temporal			
Geospatial			
Topical			
Network		X	

In this workflow we show how to extract a paper-citation network from the *FourNetSciResearchers.isi* file[31] used in the last section. When loading the ISI file, Sci2 creates a 'Cite Me As' attribute for each publication in the '361 Unique ISI Records' file. This 'Cite Me As' attribute is constructed from the first author, publication year (PY), journal abbreviation (J9), volume (VL), and beginning page (BP) fields of its original ISI record and is used when matching papers to their references. To extract the paper-citation network, select the '361 Unique ISI Records' table and run *Data Preparation > Extract Directed*

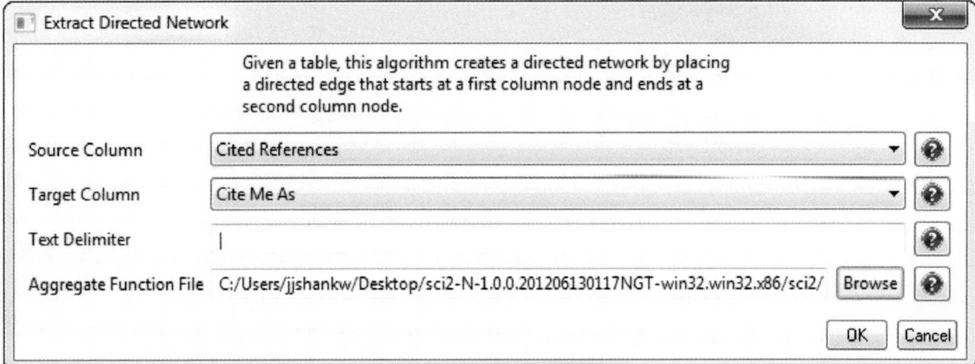

Figure 6.42 Extracting a directed network from the 'Cited References' column to the 'Cite Me As' column

---

31 *yoursci2directory*/sampledata/scientometrics/isi

Network, setting the 'Source Column' to 'Cited References', the 'Target Column' to 'Cite Me As', and the 'Aggregate Function File' to *isiPaperCitation.properties*[32] (Figure 6.42).

The result is a directed network of 5,342 papers, 361 from the original set plus references, and their 9,612 citation links. Each paper node has two citation counts. The local citation count (LCC) indicates how often a paper was cited by papers in the dataset. The global citation count (GCC) equals the times cited (TC) value in the original ISI file, according to Web of Science's records. Only references from other ISI records count towards an ISI paper's GCC value. Currently, the Sci2 Tool sets the GCC of references to -1 to allow users to prune the network to contain only the original ISI records. To view the complete network, select the 'Network with directed edges from Cited References to Cite Me As' in the 'Data Manager' and run *Visualization* > *Networks* > *GUESS*. Because the *FourNetSciResearchers.isi* dataset is so large, the visualization will take some time to load. A GEM layout of this network will take several minutes to calculate. Operation such as turning on and off node labels will take time, as GUESS needs to check each of the 9,612 nodes. The complete network with 15 weakly connected components and node labels for papers with equal or more than 500 citations is shown in Figure 6.43. Note the large size of the giant component.

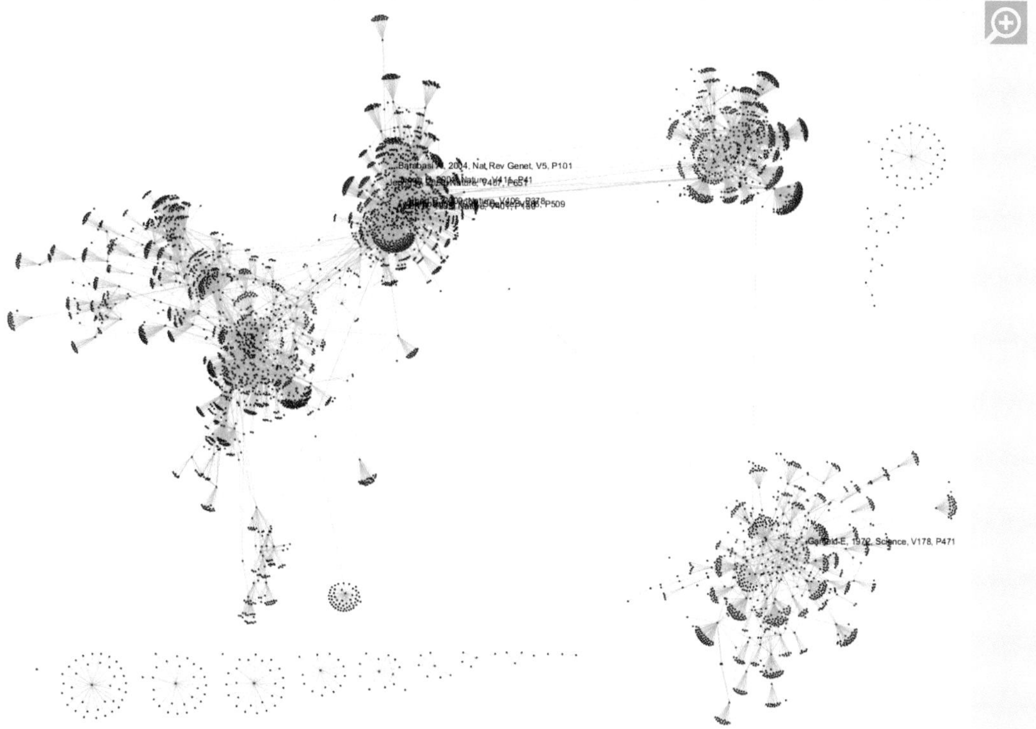

Figure 6.43 Paper-references network for *FourNetSciResearchers.isi* file (http://cns.iu.edu/ivmoocbook14/6.43.tif)

6.8 BIPARTITE NETWORKS: GEOFFREY FOX'S NSF AWARDS

Data Types & Coverage	
Time Frame:	1978-2010
Region:	Indiana University
Topical Area:	Informatics, Miscellaneous
Network Type:	Bipartite Investigator-Project

Analysis Types/Levels	●	●	●
Temporal	X		
Geospatial			
Topical			
Network			

Geoffrey Fox is the Associate Dean for Graduate Studies and Research and a Distinguished Professor of Computer Science and Informatics at Indiana University. The *GeoffreyFox.csv* file[33] contains information on his 26 National Science Foundation (NSF) grants, totaling $10,806,925, which were active from 1978 to 2010. Load the *GeoffreyFox.csv* file into Sci2. Extract a bipartite network using *Data Preparation > Extract Bipartite Network*, setting the 'First column' to 'All Investigators' and the 'Second column' to 'Award Number' (Figure 6.44). Do not specify any 'Aggregate Function File'.

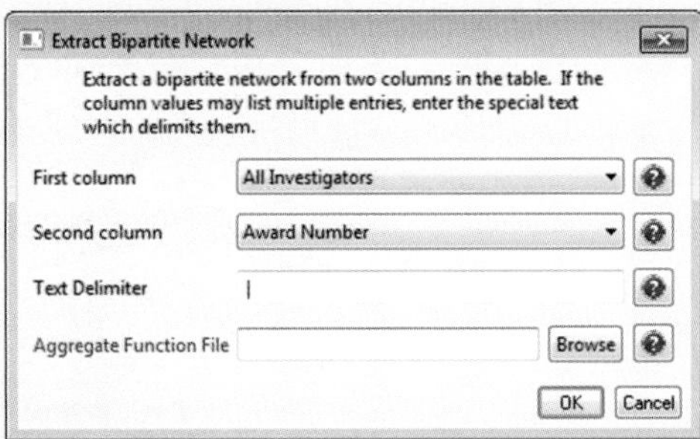

Figure 6.44 Extract a bipartite network connecting the award number to all project investigators

Next, calculate the degree of each node in the network using *Analysis > Networks > Unweighted and Undirected > Degree*. Running this analysis determines the total degrees of all nodes. Visualize the resulting network by running *Visualization > Networks > Bipartite Network Graph* and enter the parameters shown in Figure 6.45.

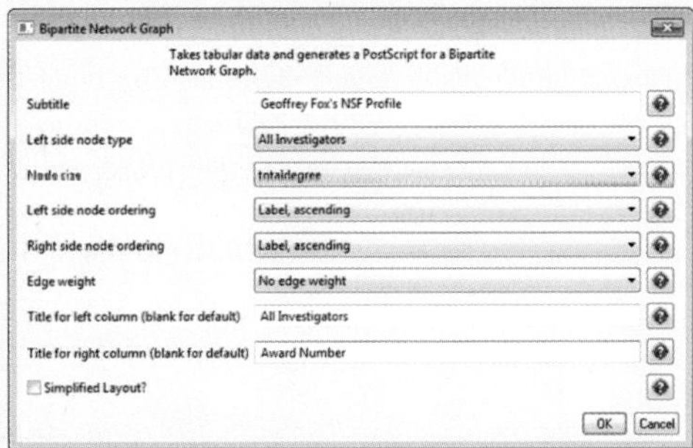

Figure 6.45 Visualizing the Geoffrey Fox bipartite network with the Bipartite Network Graph

The result is rendered into a PostScript file available in the 'Data Manager'. Save the PostScript file, convert it to a PDF file (see Appendix for instructions), and view (Figure 6.46). The visualization shows all the investigators in the left column and the titles of the awards with which they are affiliated in the right column. As the dataset contains exclusively projects by Fox, the Fox node is connected to all 26 awards; for example,

[33] *yoursci2directory*/sampledata/scientometrics/nsf

the maximum degree shown in the legend is 26. Gannon, Pierce, and Prince collaborated on three projects each with Fox. Six projects have five investigators—the maximum number of investigators allowed by the NSF.

Bipartite networks are useful for visualizing the connections between two different types of entities, in this case researchers and their NSF awards.

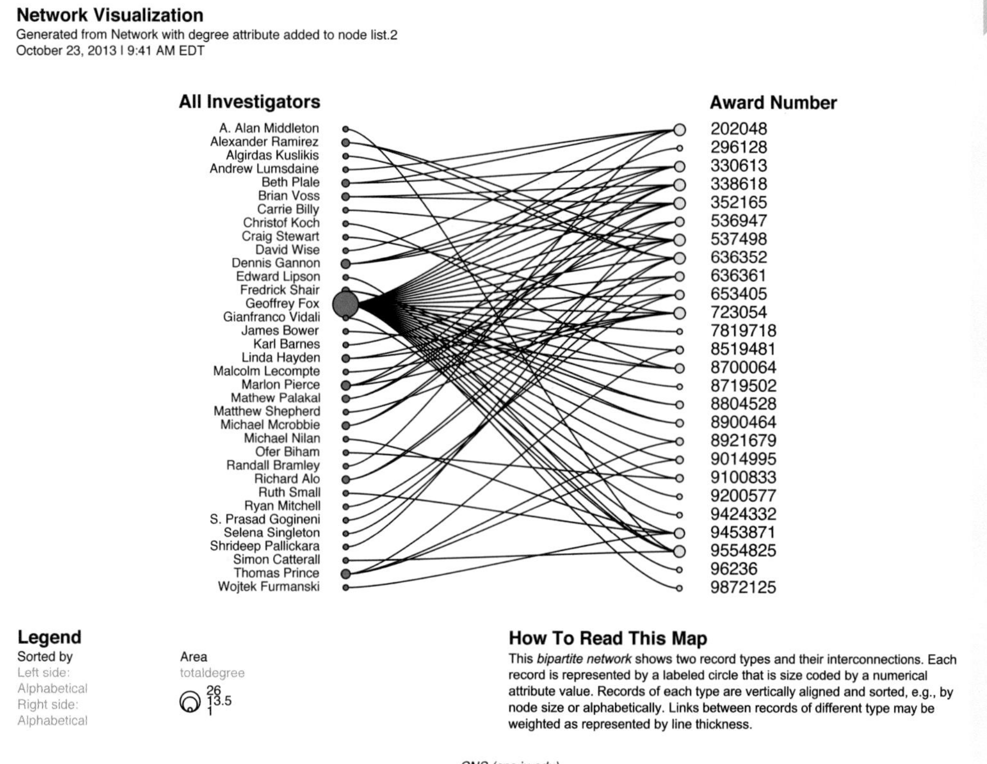

Figure 6.46 Bipartite network graph from 'All Investigators' in Geoffrey Fox's NSF funding profile to the 'Award Numbers' (http://cns.iu.edu/ivmoocbook14/6.46.pdf)

Homework

Download data of your choosing from the Scholarly Database (http://sdb.cns.iu.edu) and create a co-author network. For example, search for a specific investigator in the NSF database, and then create a network with his or her co-investigators.

THE HISTORY OF SCIENCE FICTION
FEAR AND WONDER
ART + SOCIAL CRITICISM
OBSERVATION
EXPLORATION
THE ENLIGHTENMENT
COUNTER-ENLIGHTENMENT:
ANTI-RATIONAL
STURM + DRANG
ROMANTIC MOVEMENT
THE GOTHIC NOVEL
EDGAR ALLAN POE
FRANKENSTEIN
SCIENCE ADVENTURE
FANTASY ADVENTURE
UTOPIAS
SUPERNATURAL
FOLK CULTURES
DETECTIVE STORY
WESTERNS
SIR WALTER SCOTT - HISTORICAL ROMANCE
"IVANHOE"
CASTLE OF ORANTO
JULES VERNE
FILM

Chapter Seven

Dynamic Visualizations and Deployment

Chapter 7: Theory Section

Some visualizations are too large or too complex to comprehend easily. In these cases, a dynamic deployment that supports interactive search, filtering, clustering, zoom and pan, or details on demand is beneficial. Tools like Tableau,[1] Gephi,[2] but also GUESS,[3] and Cytoscape[4] available as Sci2 Tool plugins, support interactive visualizations for data exploration and communication. In this chapter, we discuss the design of dynamic visualizations and the deployment of interactive visualizations via desktop programs, interactive online visualizations, and large touchscreens. Online visualization services such as Microscoft's Zoom.it[5] or Gigapan[6] that support sharing of very high-resolution images such as large-scale visualizations are discussed in the Hands-On Section of this chapter.

We divide the theory part into two sections: dynamic visualizations and deployment of visualizations. In the first part we discuss different means to communicate change over time. In the second section we introduce different means to DEPLOY visualizations (see final, or purple, step in the needs-driven workflow design in Figure 1.12).

7.1 DYNAMIC VISUALIZATIONS

There are different types of dynamics that we might like to explore or communicate: (1) Data attributes might change over time and temporal graphs might be used to show changing properties or derivative statistics over time (see Chapter 2 for examples). (2) The number of data records, their attributes, and the attribute values change over time. Here, a static base map/reference system (e.g., a chart, graph, geospatial map, or network graph) might be used together with a dynamically changing data overlay. (3) Data and reference system change. An example is changing political boundaries or evolving networks with data overlays indicating, for example, migration trajectories or evolving collaboration networks. In this case, the reference system and the data overlay might have to be updated for each time step.

There are different ways to show dynamics, or change over time. We might need only **one static image** to say it all. An example is Charles Joseph Minard's *Napoleon's March to Moscow* (Figure 2.3). We can show **multiple static images**, typically using the very

1 http://www.tableausoftware.com
2 http://gephi.org
3 http://graphexploration.cond.org
4 http://www.cytoscape.org
5 http://zoom.it
6 http://gigapan.com

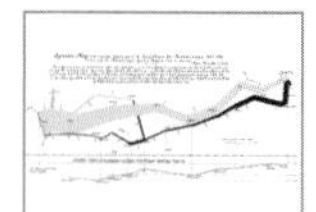

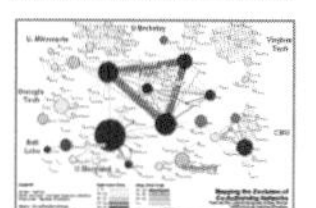

same reference system, side by side or as an animation. As time passes, the data overlays change. An example of multiple static images was discussed in Chapter 3: Minard's *Europe Raw Cotton Imports in 1858, 1864, and 1865* (Figure 3.1). An animation using a static network layout is the *Evolving Co-authorship Network of Information Visualization Researchers for 1986 to 2004* (Figure 1.7) discussed in Chapter 1. Some animations can be started, stopped, and rewound. Alternatively, **interactive visualizations** can be implemented to visualize dynamics. Examples are given in Section 7.2.

When presenting data, visualizations, and insights to others, it is important to ensure that our audience understands (and later remembers) the entire story. Ben Shneiderman[7] coined the phrase "overview first, zoom and filter, and then details on demand," and it has guided the presentation of static visualizations as well as the design of interactive systems since then.

Ideally, when presenting our visualizations, we tell stories in a sequential manner as a narrative. The stories should be as simple as possible. They should be informative. They should be true. They should be contextualized in the past, present, and future. They should be familiar. They should be very concrete and actionable (i.e., if people really understand and are taken by the story, they have a way to act). Hans Rosling's Gapminder presentation on the wealth and health of nations entitled *200 Countries, 200 Years, 4 Minutes*[8] or Al Gore's *Inconvenient Truth*[9] are excellent examples of how to tell great stories that inspire many to take action.

7.2 INTERACTIVE VISUALIZATIONS

In this section we present five different deployment types for interactive visualizations. The first uses a combination of high-resolution printout on paper and low-resolution illumination via projection screens. The second one uses a large-scale touch panel display. The third is an online service that supports researcher networking. The fourth is a web service that provides a unifying visual query interface to different data silos. The final example shows how Sci2 Tool algorithms can be used in an online web service.

---

7 Shneiderman, Ben. 1996. "The Eyes Have It: A Task by Data Type Taxonomy for Information Visualizations." In *Proceedings of the 1996 IEEE Symposium on Visual Languages*. Washington, DC: IEEE Computer Society.

8 http://www.youtube.com/watch?v=jbkSRLYSojo

9 http://www.imdb.com/video/imdb/vi2897608985

The **Illuminated Diagram Display** (Figure 7.1) combines the high-data density of a print with the flexibility of an interactive program. This technique is generally useful when there is too much pertinent data to be displayed on a screen but the data is relatively stable. The computer can direct the eye to what is important by using projectors as smart spotlights, for example, to give an overview of major activity in science, to highlight query results, or to animate the spread of an idea's influence over time.

Figure 7.1 Illuminated Diagram setup

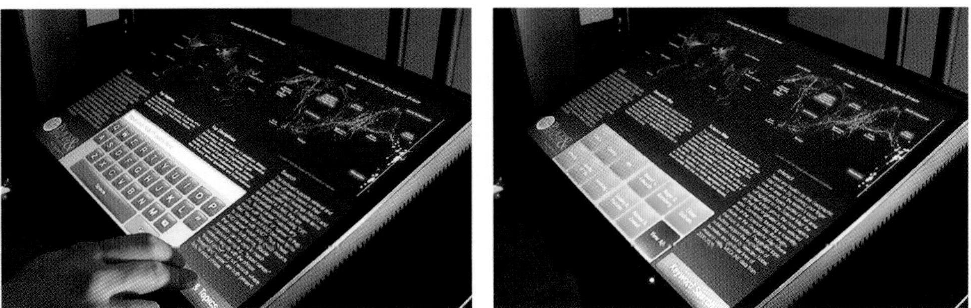

Figure 7.2 Illuminated Diagram touch panel display

An exemplary setup that travels with the Mapping Science exhibit[10] is shown in Figure 7.1. It features two large displays with transparent overlays of a map of the world (left) and the UCSD Map of Science (right) (see Section 4.4 for details on the design and usage of the map). Additionally, there is a touch panel display that can be used to select any area on the map of the world, on the map of science, or to enter search terms (see interface in Figure 7.2).

10 http://scimaps.org/exhibit_info/#ID

Using the touch panel display, we can select any area on the map of the world (by brushing our finger over an area on the touchscreen). This highlights all scholarly institutions in this area on the map of the world and in the map of science, and all publications by these institutions are highlighted. That is, we get to see what expertise (in terms of publication results) exists in the selected geographic location. Analogously, a topic area in the map of science can be selected (e.g., the social sciences), which highlights all institutions on the map of the world that perform research in that area. In addition, we can use the search interface (see Figure 7.2, left) to enter a name (e.g., your name). If we happen to have publications in the MEDLINE database,[11] which provides the data for this particular display, then we can see our intellectual footprint on the map of the world and on the map of science.

In addition, there are buttons for interdisciplinary research areas and buttons for different Nobel laureates (Figure 7.2, right). Pushing any of these buttons highlights all works in a particular area or by which Nobel laureate in both maps. Exemplarily shown is the data overlay for the late Elinor Ostrom of Indiana University. She was the first woman to win the Nobel Prize in Economics.

The **AcademyScope** uses a 55-inch, high-definition, multi-touch display to support the exploration of publications by the National Academy of Sciences, National Academy of Engineering, Institute of Medicine, and National Research Council, from twenty years ago

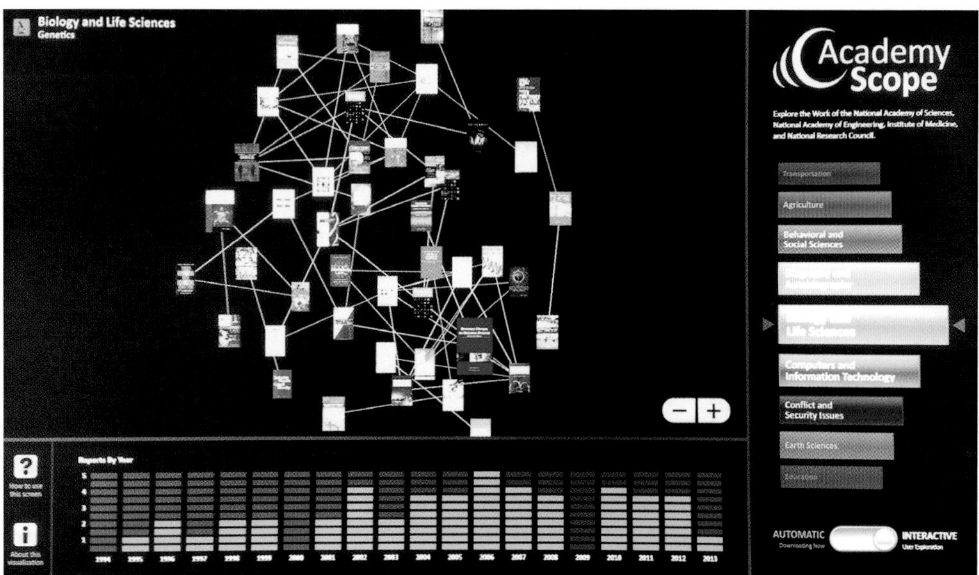

Figure 7.3 AcademyScope in interactive mode

[11] http://www.nlm.nih.gov/bsd/pmresources.html

to today.[12] It was created by the Cyberinfrastructure for Network Science Center at Indiana University in partnership with the U.S. National Academy of Sciences.[13]

The *Automatic Mode* of the visualization uses a real-time data feed of online user activity to show the 100 most frequently downloaded reports of the previous seven days as well as newly released reports. Displayed downloads, including download totals, are current within the minute.

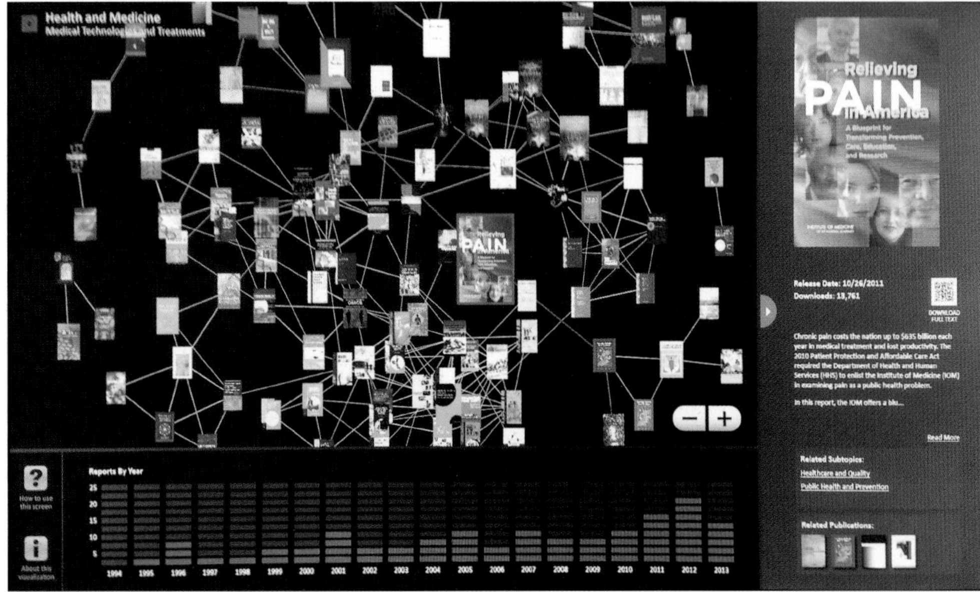

Figure 7.4 AcademyScope in interactive mode for a specific report with detailed information

The *Interactive Mode* supports browsing and exploration by topic, subtopic, and accessing individual reports (Figure 7.3). Users can select a topic on the right to reveal all of its subtopics, and touch one of the subtopics to display all reports in that area and their relatedness to each other. Links between reports are automatically generated based on the incidence of shared key terms and phrases. Touching any report brings up detailed information on the right side of the display (Figure 7.4). There's also a QR code that allows users to download a PDF of the report to their smart device.

---

12 http://www.youtube.com/watch?feature=player_embedded&v=pdqKBna1Fos

13 Börner, Katy, Chin Hua Kong, Samuel T. Mills, Adam H. Simpson, Bhumi Patel, and Rohit Alekar. 2013. *AcademyScope* [Interactive Display]. Bloomington, IN: Cyberinfrastructure for Network Science Center.

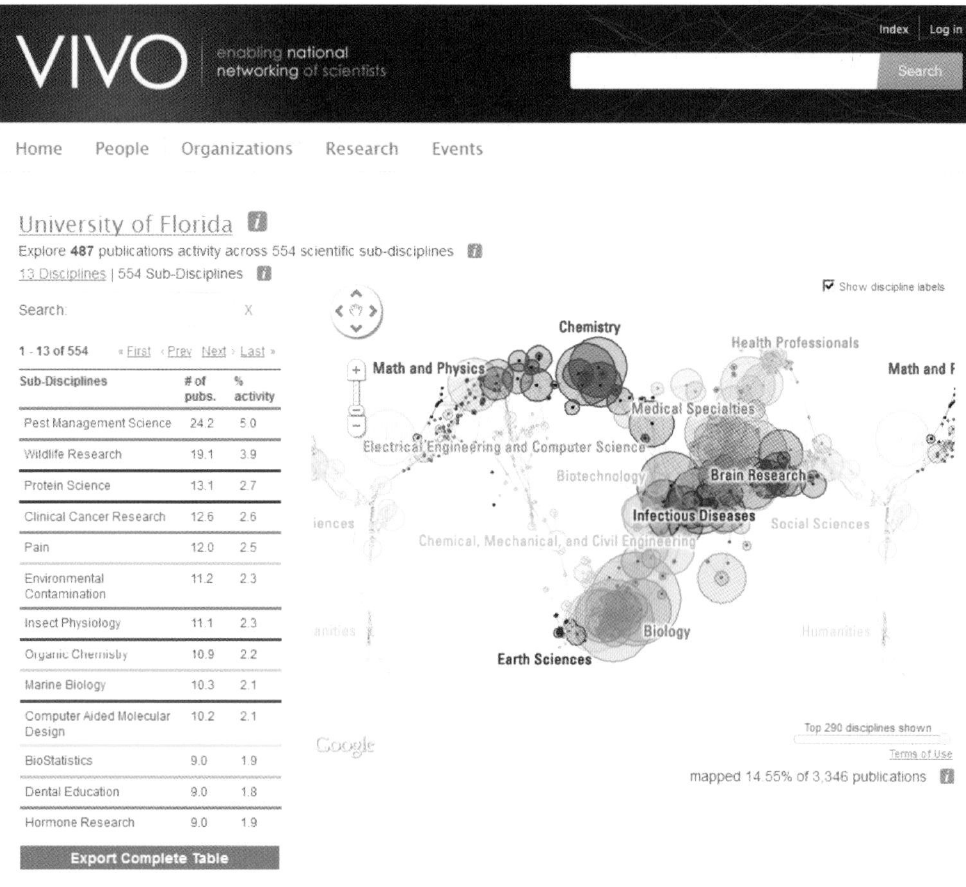

Figure 7.5 VIVO interface showing the UCSD "Map of Science" with data overlays of the topical expertise of researchers at the University of Florida

The **VIVO International Researcher Networking Service**[14] supports scholarly networking and collaboration using high-quality instructional data—for example, human resources data to uniquely identify scholars, their affiliation, and geolocation; scholarly data on publications; course credit data on teaching; and sponsored research data on funded projects. It differs from Facebook or LinkedIn in that it offers services such as printing curriculum vitae in government agency-specific formats. Plus, VIVO is open source.[15] Anyone can download and install it for use by a university, publishing house, agency, or scientific society; connect it to existing databases, and use it to serve data in XML format; or to render high-quality content web pages and visualizations that show temporal trends, topical coverage of expertise, and evolving collaboration networks.

---

14 Börner, Katy, Mike Conlon, Jon Corson-Rikert, and Ying Ding, eds. 2012. *VIVO: A Semantic Approach to Scholarly Networking and Discovery*. San Francisco, CA: Morgan & Claypool Publishers LLC. http://cns.slis.indiana.edu/docs/publications/2012-borner-vivobook.pdf

15 http://vivoweb.org

Figure 7.5 exemplarily shows the topical expertise of researchers at the University of Florida (UF) by overlaying publications by all UF faculty members on the UCSD Map of Science (see Section 4.4). The interface supports navigation through the organizational hierarchy (e.g., zooming into specific schools or departments to find out what kind of expertise different units have). It also supports the comparison of different departments or schools as well as data downloads.

Interested in understanding what VIVO instances exist and which datasets they contain? Simply use the International Researcher Network[16] service to find out (Figure 7.6). The online service shows a zoomable map of the world with data overlays indicating what institutions have adopted VIVO (in blue), Elsevier's SciVal Expert System (orange), Harvard's Catalyst Profiles (red), etc. Different data types can be selected: circles represent people, squares publications, diamonds patents, triangles funding records, and pentagons courses. We can click on any of them to see a listing of detailed data below the map and explore the coverage and quality of the different datasets available via the different instances.

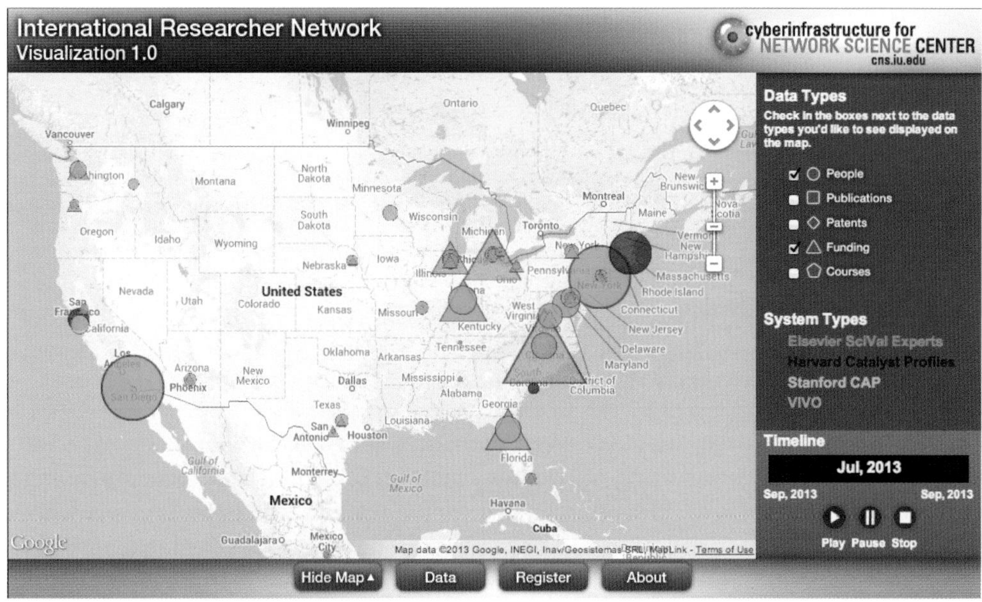

Figure 7.6 U.S. map showing the type and data coverage of different researcher networking services

The **Mapping Sustainability Research**[17] (Figure 7.7) service was created to help sustainability researchers and practitioners understand what papers, patents, and grants exist on biomass and biofuel research. The online service uses a U.S. map and the UCSD Map of Science map as an interactive interface to seven different datasets: three types of publications, three types

16 http://nrn.cns.iu.edu

17 http://mapsustain.cns.iu.edu

of funding, and U.S. patents. We can select any dataset, as well as a range or years, and a keyword. For publications or patents, we can request citations or counts. Results are displayed as data overlays: publications are indicated by squares, funding is indicated by triangles, and patents are indicated by diamonds. The Google Maps JavaScript API is used to provide a geographic map at the state level and at the city level. The same API also renders the map of science—at the 13 disciplines level and the 554 subdisciplines level. In both maps, we can click on any symbols to get more information on the records it represents. In the map, search results for "corn" are shown (Figure 7.7). Clicking on the funding triangle symbol for California brought up relevant funding by the U.S. Department of Agriculture (USDA) and the National Science Foundation (NSF) in the right hand panel. We can click on the NSF links to read the full funding record. Alternatively, if we search for "Miscanthus," a special energy biomass crop for second-generation biofuel, we get a very different search result.

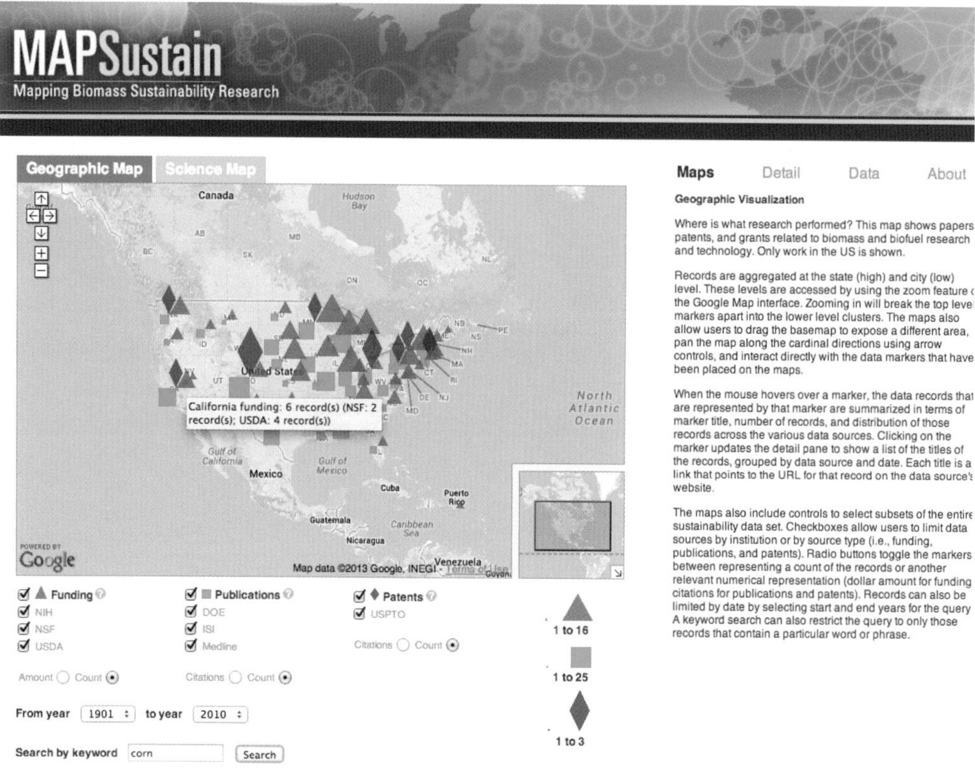

Figure 7.7 MAPSustain interface with search results for "corn"

Sci2 Web Services will soon become available on the National Institutes of Health (NIH) Expenditures and Results site, also called RePORTER. This is a unique collaboration between NETE AV and CNS. Using the new services, we will be able to request temporal analysis, geospatial analysis, topical analysis, or network analysis of data provided by the NIH (i.e., funding data and linked publications and patents) using a simple 4-step process (Figure 7.8). First, we select a type of analysis (e.g., a temporal analysis answering a WHEN question). Second, we select a dataset (e.g., principal investigators by name or by organization). Third, we have to choose the type of analysis. Fourth, we visualize the data (e.g., using a temporal bar graph) (see Section 2.6). Other visualization types such as the proportional symbol map, the UCSD Map of Science, and the bipartite network graph are available as well.

Figure 7.8 Sci2 Web Services serving analyses and visualizations of NIH RePORTER data

Other examples of interactive visualizations that we might like to explore are the Max Planck Research Network[18] and the National Oceanic and Atmospheric Administration's Science On a Sphere.[19]

18 http://max-planck-research-networks.net

19 http://www.sos.noaa.gov

Self-Assessment

Identify other visualizations that use one static image, multiple static images, or animation to communicate data dynamics.

Chapter 7: Hands-On Section

7.4 Exporting Dynamic Visualizations from Gephi with Seadragon

Data Types & Coverage	
Time Frame:	1955-2007
Region:	Miscellaneous
Topical Area:	Network Science
Network Type:	Co-Author Network

Analysis Types/Levels	● (small)	● (medium)	● (large)
Temporal			
Geospatial			
Topical			
Network		X	

In this workflow you will create a co-authorship network from the same ISI data we used in Section 6.6 and make it available via Microsoft's Seadragon service, recently renamed Zoom.it. This is one of the easiest ways to create an interactive visualization and is especially useful for sharing and exploring very large visualizations online.

Exemplarily, we will load the raw ISI data into Sci2, extract the co-authorship network, visualize the network using Gephi, and export it using the Seadragon plugin, which will create a zoomable interface that can be mounted directly to the Web.

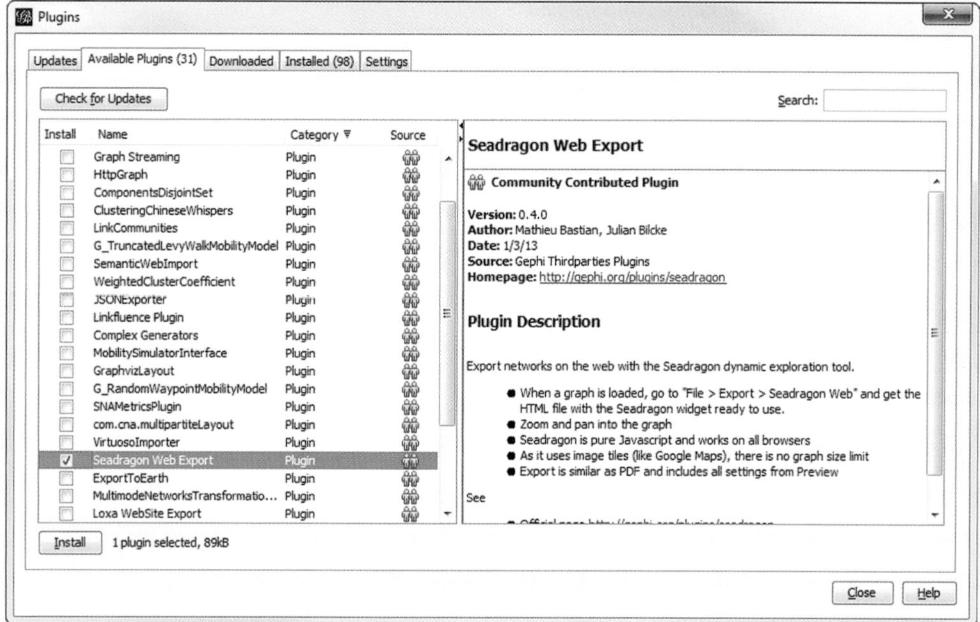

Figure 7.9 Adding the Seadragon Web Export plugin to Gephi

The workflow requires the use of Gephi, an open-source network visualization tool.[20] Once Gephi has been installed, you will need to add the Seadragon plugin to the tool. Adding plugins to Gephi is very simple. With the tool launched, click on *Tools* > *Plugins* and this will launch the plugin interface. You will need to select the 'Available Plugins' tab and choose the Seadragon Web Export plugin (Figure 7.9) and click 'Install'. After it has been successfully installed, you will be prompted to restart Gephi. You can check to see if the plugin has been installed by selecting *File* > *Export* and look for the Seadragon plugin available. Note, you will have to have a Gephi project started or network loaded in order to access the menu.

Now, we will create the co-authorship network that we will ultimately deploy using Seadragon. Open Sci2 and load the *FourNetSciResearchers.isi* file.[21] Once the dataset has been loaded, two files will appear in the 'Data Manager'. Select the table labeled '361 Unique ISI Records' and then select *Data Preparation* > *Extract Co-Author Network* (Figure 7.10).

When you choose to extract a co-author network, you will be prompted to indicate the type of data with which you are working; in this case select ISI data and click 'OK' (Figure 7.11).

The result of the network extraction will be two files in the 'Data Manager'. The first file is the 'Extracted Co-Authorship Network'. These networks connect authors based on whether they have co-authored a paper. Two attributes were added to these nodes: the number of times a person has authored (number of times they appear in the dataset) and number of times an author is cited. One attribute was added to the edges: number of times two authors have co-authored (the weight of the edges that connect the authors). These attributes will allow us to visually enhance the network and convey more information about our data. The other file that appears in the 'Data Manager' after extraction is the author information table, which allows users to merge identical authors; see Section 6.6 for details. Now, load the network in Gephi by selecting the file and running *Visualization* > *Networks* > *Gephi* (Figure 7.12).

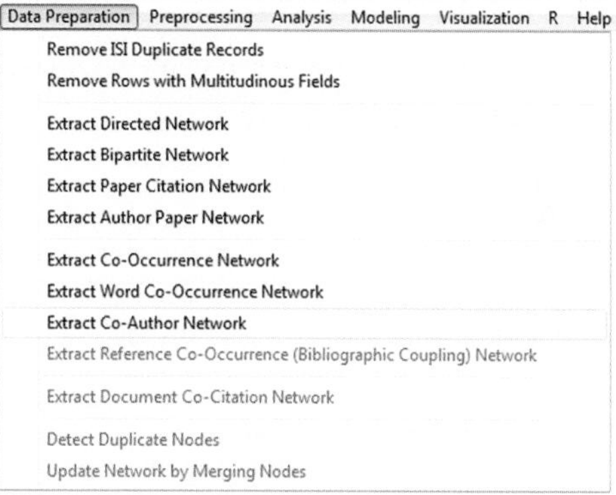

Figure 7.10 Extracting a co-author network

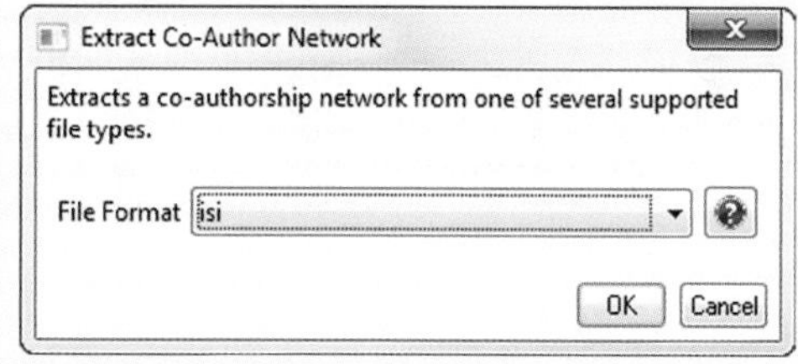

Figure 7.11 Select that you are working with ISI data

[20] http://gephi.org

[21] *yoursci2directory*/sampledata/scientometrics/isi

When the network loads in Gephi you will be shown an import report, which will give you information on how many nodes and edges are in the network and will prompt you to load the network as an undirected graph; click 'OK'. Co-authorship networks are a type of co-occurrence network, which are undirected. When the network loads in Gephi it will be laid out randomly, but you will notice that the program automatically detects edge weights, which in this case corresponds to the number of times two authors have collaborated (Figure 7.13).

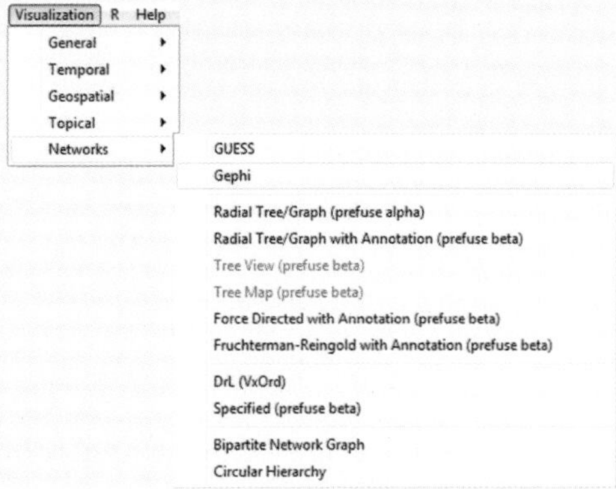

Figure 7.12 Visualization of co-author network in Gephi

The first step is to apply a different layout that will allow you to see the structure of the network more clearly. To apply a different layout in Gephi you must be in the 'Overview' window (Figure 7.14).

Choose a layout from the list in the layout pane on the left side of the screen. Apply the 'Force Atlas' with the 'Gravity' set to 50.0 and the 'Attraction Strength' set to 1.0 (Figure 7.15). This allows you to see four distinct clusters that correspond to the four authors in this dataset. Feel free to play around with the parameter values for the layout; changing these will affect how the network is displayed. Information about what each parameter does will be given at the bottom of the 'Layout' pane.

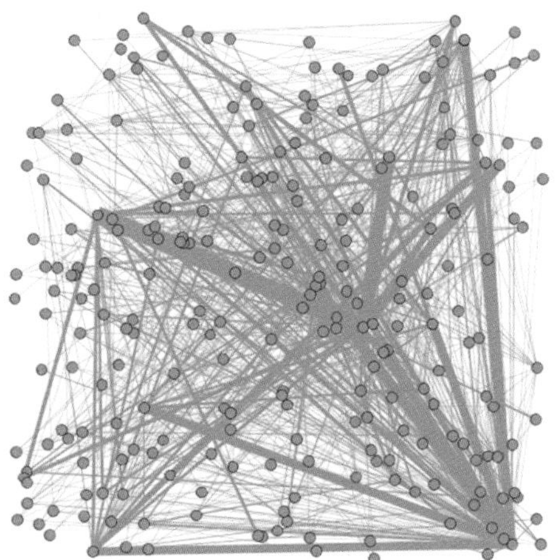

Figure 7.13 Co-authorship laid out randomly in Gephi with edge with edges weights automatically displayed

Next, resize the nodes based on the number of times the author appears in the dataset. This gives you a sense of the impact of the authors in our dataset. In the top-left corner of the 'Overview' window, select the 'Ranking' tab, choose 'Nodes', select the 'Size/Weight' button with the

Figure 7.14 'Overview', 'Data Laboratory', and 'Preview' window tabs shown under the menu in Gephi.

red diamond icon, set the 'rank parameter' to 'number_of_authored_works', and click 'Apply' (Figure 7.16). Enter your desired size range, in this example you are sizing the nodes from 10 to 50. Gephi displays the values below the size range. In the case of this particular dataset, the minimum number of times an author appears is once and the maximum number of times an author appears is 127 times.

Next, recolor the nodes on a gradient based on the number of times the authors have been cited. This mapping of data variables to graphic variable type color value will start to tell us the importance of certain authors in this dataset. Still in the 'Ranking' pane, select the 'Color' button with the color wheel icon immediately to the left of the Size/Weight button. Set the 'rank parameter' to 'times_cited', and click 'Apply' (Figure 7.17). You can change the color scheme by selecting the small square color palette to the right of the color gradient.

To label nodes in the network select the 'Show Node Labels' button with the dark grey T icon at the bottom of the 'Graph' window (Figure 7.18). Once you have applied the node labels, you may want to run the 'Label Adjust' layout, which simply moves the labels around so they are no longer overlapping.

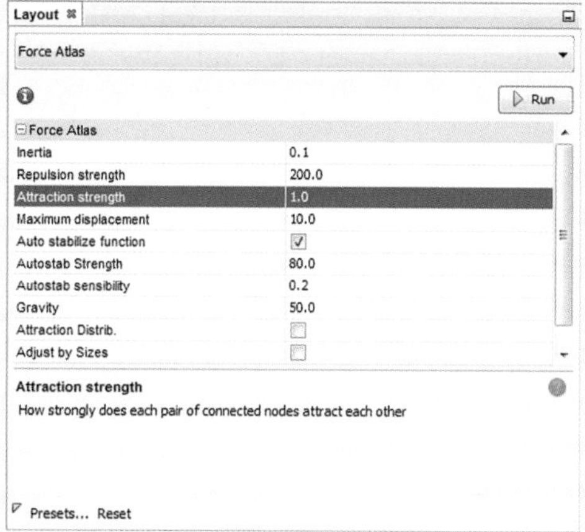

Figure 7.15 'Layout' pane in Gephi with 'Force Atlas' layout applied and information on the 'Attraction Strength' parameter shown

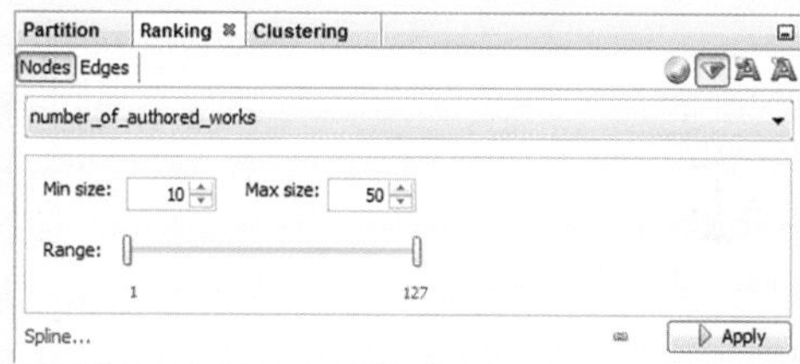

Figure 7.16 Resizing nodes from 10 to 50 based on number of authored works

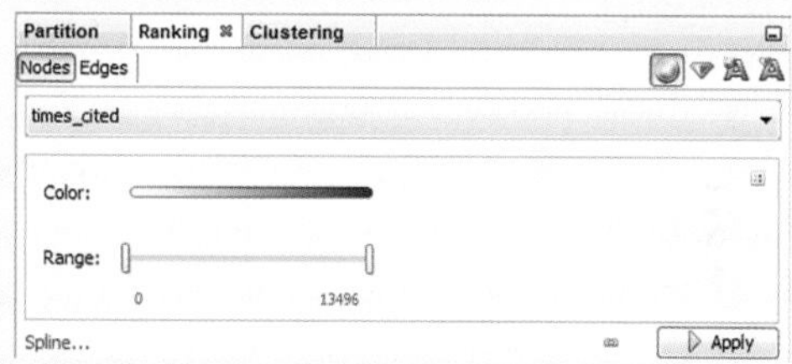

Figure 7.17 Coloring nodes based on the number of times cited

Figure 7.18 The 'Show Node Labels' button selected to display the author names associated with each node

Before you export your network using Seadragon, you can select or edit different visual attributes of the network using the 'Preview Settings' pane on the left side of the tool in the 'Preview' window (Figure 7.19). In this example we have left the network view set to 'Default Curved', and selected 'Show Labels' with 'Proportional Size' unchecked. To see your changes you will need to click the 'Refresh' button at the bottom of the 'Preview Settings' pane.

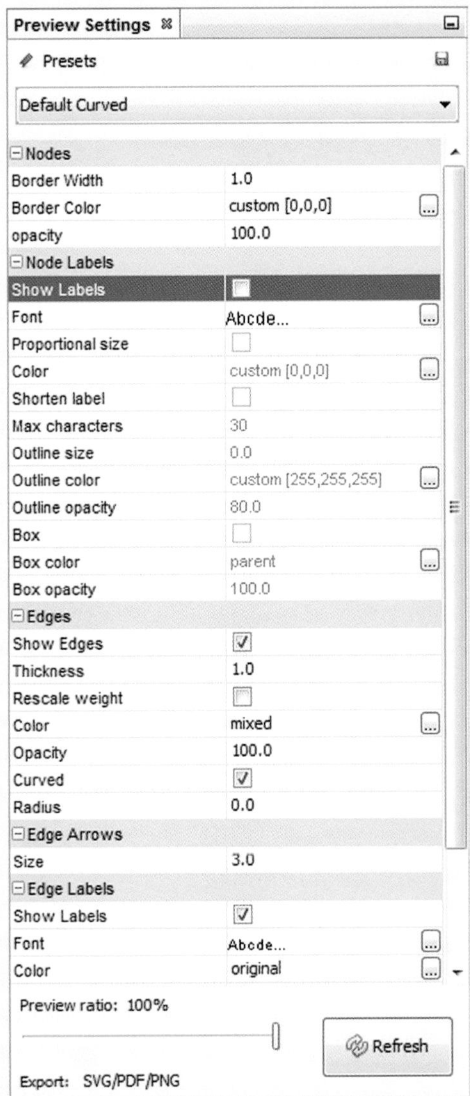

Figure 7.19 'Preview Settings' pane in Gephi

In the resulting co-authorship network (Figure 7.20) the nodes are sized proportional to the number of times the author appears in this dataset, and colored based on the number of times that author has been cited; yellow is fewer citations and red is more citations. This gives you a sense of the relative importance of authors in this dataset and could potentially guide your research in this topic (i.e., you may want to read articles written by highly prolific and highly cited authors). Furthermore, you can see the connections between different authors and the strength of these connections based on how frequently they co-author, giving you a better understanding of the research field.

Now, suppose you want to create an interactive interface for this visualization. As you can see, it is not easy to read every label on every node. However, if you were able to zoom in to certain areas, all the node labels would become legible. You can easily create a zoomable interface for this network by using the Seadragon Web Export plugin we installed in Gephi at the beginning of this workflow. To export the network, switch back to the 'Overview' window in Gephi and select *File* > *Export* > *Seadragon Web...* (Figure 7.21).

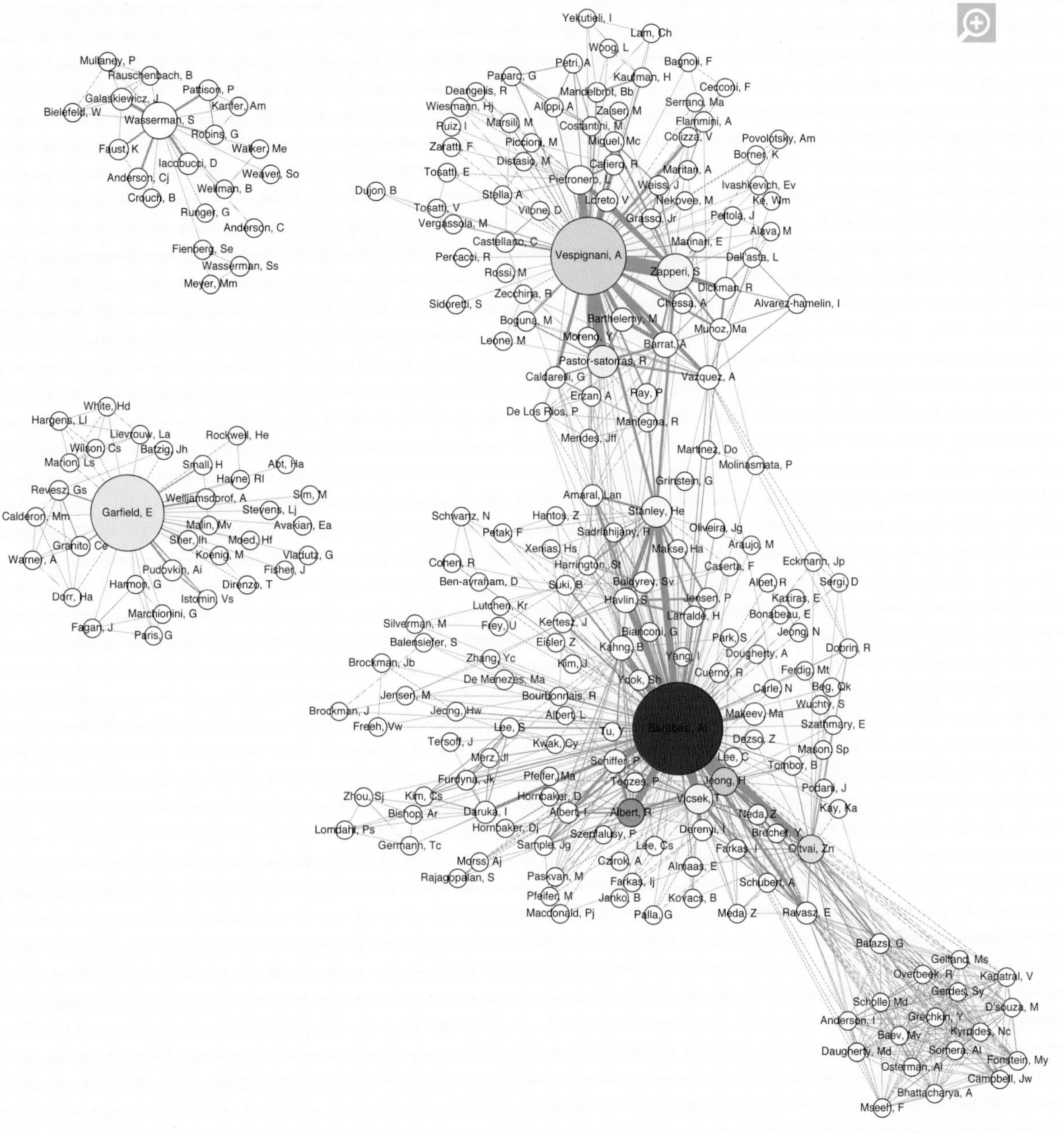

Figure 7.20 Interactive online visualization of the co-author network (http://cns.iu.edu/ivmoocbook14/7.20.pdf

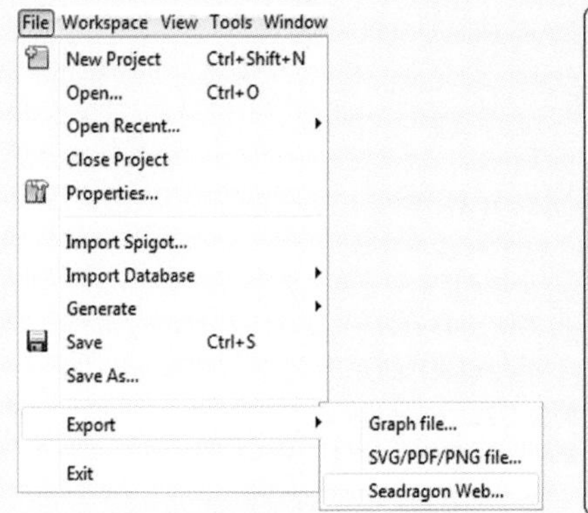

Figure 7.21 Exporting networks with the Seadragon Web Export plugin

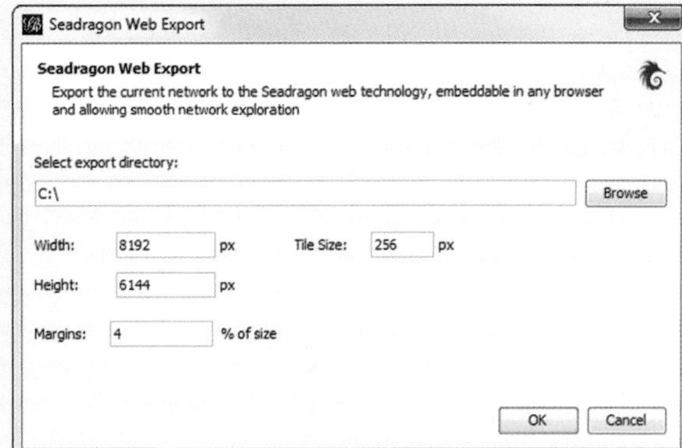

Figure 7.22 Seadragon Web Export parameter window

The Seadragon Web Export window will appear and ask you to specify where you would like to export the visualization and the associated files for mounting it to the Web. Provide a size in pixels (Figure 7.22). The larger the size, the more users will be able to zoom in, but the longer it will take to export.

The result can be viewed directly in a web browser of your choice from your local hard drive. An exception is Chrome, which will only display if permissions are set to "-allow-file-access-from-files." Open the HTML file in the browser of your choice. The buttons in the lower right of the visualization allow users to zoom in and pan across the network (Figure 7.23). Below the visualization are listed the instructions for mounting the visualization on a web site.

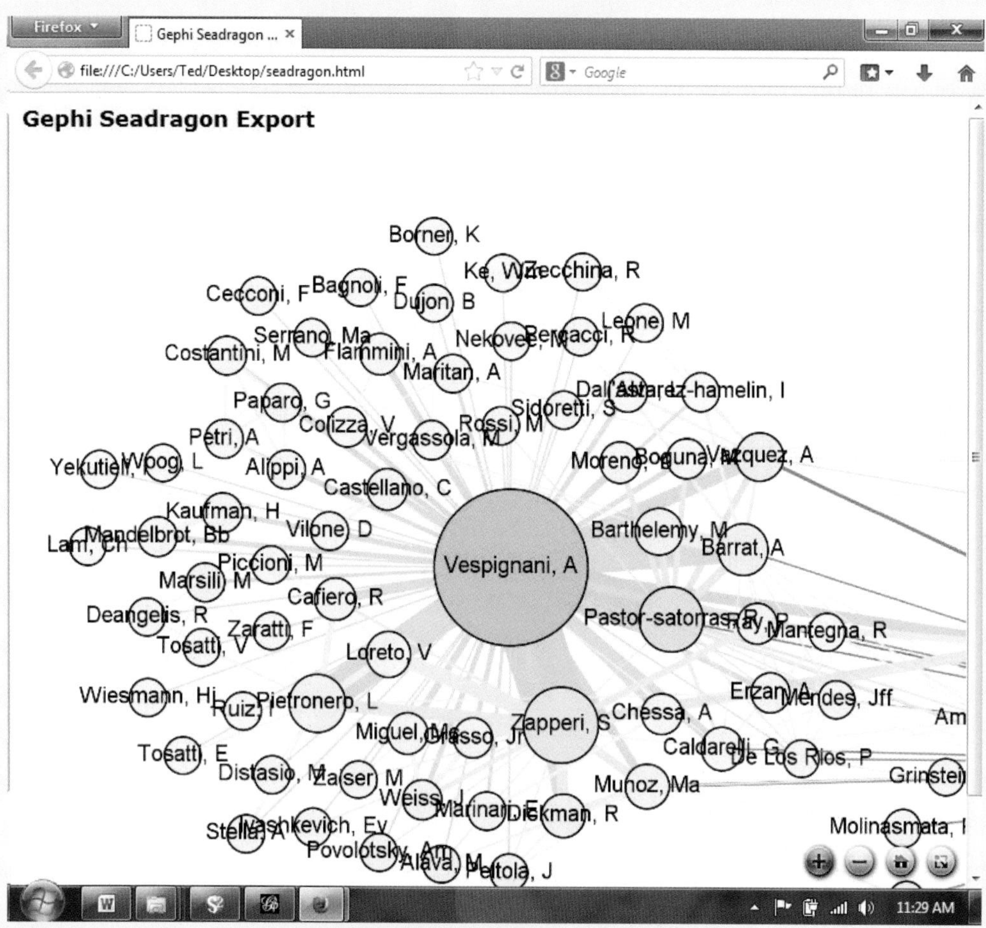

Figure 7.23 Interactive online visualization of the co-author network

Chapter Eight

Case Studies

These case studies are the results of the Information Visualization MOOC 2013 client projects. The students were asked to form groups of four to five and select a real-world project from a list of potential client projects. The clients made their data available to the students, who worked to conduct a requirement analysis, develop an early sketch, conduct a literature review, preprocess and clean the data, and finally perform analysis and visualization. The students then submitted their visualizations to the client for validation. The following chapter highlights six of these projects, including feedback and insights from the clients.

Case Study #1

Understanding the Diffusion of Non-Emergency Call Systems

CLIENT:
John C. O'Byrne [jobyrne4@gmail.com]
Virginia Tech

TEAM MEMBERS:
Bonnie L. Layton [bllayton@indiana.edu]
Steve C. Layton [stlayton@indiana.edu]
James S. True [jitrue@iu.edu]
Indiana University

PROJECT DETAILS

Local governments throughout the United States began adopting non-emergency call systems in the late 1990s. Known commonly as "311 systems," they free 911 emergency systems from being overloaded, provide citizens with a single number to call for requests, increase bureaucratic efficiency, and give citizens the opportunity to participate in local government. Virginia Tech Center for Public Administration and Policy doctoral candidate John O'Byrne's dissertation studied the factors influencing the adoption of 311 systems. His data included the years 1996 to 2012 when large U.S. cities implemented 311. He examined various factors that encouraged adoption: the size of the cities' populations, their forms of government, and their crime rates. A team of Indiana University (IU) informatics graduate students designed four versions of geospatial visualizations showing the 311 diffusion across the United States. They created the versions to explore differences between the level of user engagement, sense making, and retention with touchscreen interactivity to that of print and online visualizations.

REQUIREMENTS ANALYSIS

O'Byrne, the project client, requested a visualization that would indicate when the rate of 311 adoption reached a "critical mass" large enough to encourage other cities to follow suit. He wanted to show how closely the 311 data compared with Everett Rogers's Diffusion of Innovation curve, which was modeled on hundreds of innovation-focused studies.[1] These

1 Rogers, E.M. 2003. *Diffusion of Innovations*, 34, 344–347. New York: Free Press.

studies have tracked acceptance of innovations in many disciplines, including science, medicine, technology, and sociology. The team proposed combining two datasets in a year-by-year bar graph indicating the cumulative adoption of cities with proportional symbols (circles) below each bar to represent how many had adopted that year.

O'Byrne had created an extensive database of cities' populations, crime rates, and forms of government. The team proposed three maps that would visualize the researcher's hypotheses that

1. cities with larger populations would adopt 311 faster,
2. cities with higher crime rates would adopt it faster, and that
3. cities with mayor-council governments would adopt it faster.

The team created static, animated, and interactive versions of the maps to compare their effectiveness.

RELATED WORK

The visualization team incorporated visual-processing principles and theories postulated by Stuart Card, Jock Mackinlay, and Ben Shneiderman. Card and Mackinlay define visualization attributes as being constructed from (1) marks, such as points, lines, surface, area, and volume; (2) their graphical properties; and (3) elements requiring human-controlled processing, such as text.[2] They delineate two kinds of human visual processing as "automatic," in which users identify properties such as color and position using highly parallel processing but are limited in power, in contrast with "controlled processing" in tasks such as reading that have powerful operations but are limited in capacity. These classifications were useful in breaking down the task of visualizing the geospatial and temporal data of the U.S. map and bar chart (automatic) in combination with the trend data consisting of text explaining each of the adoption factors. Shneiderman's basic-principles mantra of "overview first, zoom and filter, then details on demand" guided the team in creating an adoption overview first (the S-curve and proportional-symbol map) and allowing users to click (filter) to isolate each adoption factor.[3]

---

2 Card, S.K., and J. Mackinlay. 1997. "The Structure of the Information Visualization Design Space." In *Proceedings of the IEEE Symposium on Information Visualization*, 92–99. Washington, DC: IEEE Computer Society.

3 Shneiderman, B. 1996. "The Eyes Have It: A Task by Data Type Taxonomy for Information Visualizations." In *Proceedings of the IEEE Symposium on Visual Languages*, 336–343. Washington, DC: IEEE Computer Society.

THE DIFFUSION OF 311

In 1996, U.S. cities began adopting 311 call systems to lower the number of non-emergency calls being made to 911. Local governments also wanted to provide a more efficient way for citizens to contact various city departments to handle simple complaints like potholes.

Researchers studied the adoption process of cities through the "diffusion of innovation" theory. "Diffusion" is a process by which an invention or a new way of doing things is communicated and then adopted.

The years they examined began with the first year 311 systems were introduced until the "critical mass point" of 311 adoptions. Based on the diffusion of innovation theory, the critical mass point — when enough city governments adopted systems so that the further rate of adoption became self-sustaining — occurred in 2003.

The following graphics explain what researchers gleaned through the process:

BY POPULATION

Researchers accurately predicted that larger cities would adopt 311 systems earlier. They assumed they would want to reduce the burden of 911 calls they were receiving. For example, after adopting 311, Baltimore reduced 911 calls by almost 5,000 a week.

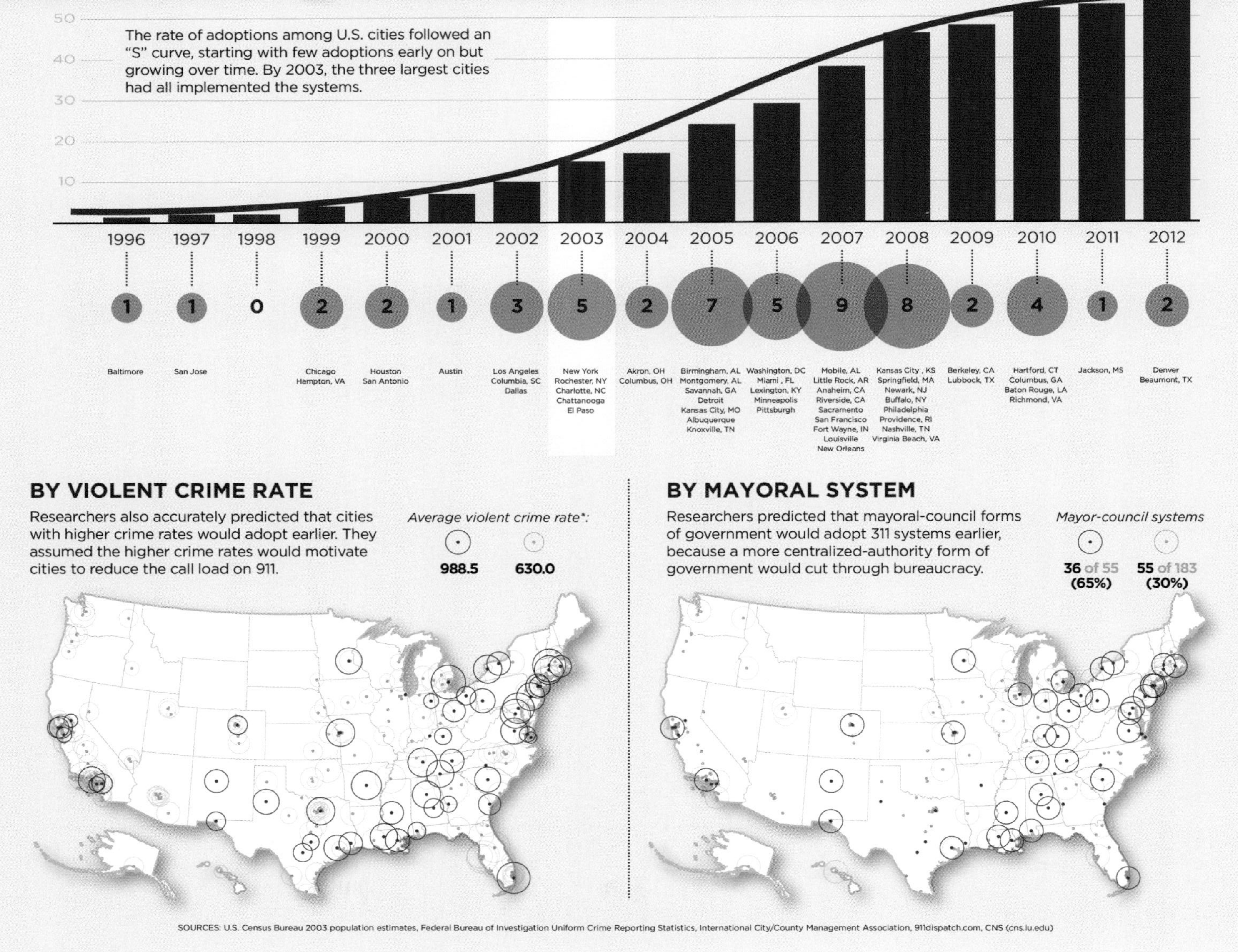

Figure 8.1 The Diffusion of 311 (http://cns.iu.edu/ivmoocbook14/8.1.jpg)

DATA COLLECTION AND PREPARATION

The visualization team used O'Byrne's database of cities as the basis for maps and adoption curve visualization. The team generated latitude and longitude data to plot the cities, incorporated census figures, and generated vector files of the municipal data from the proportion symbol map tool in the Sci2 visualization software.[4] The files were brought into Adobe Illustrator to customize the colors and lines and exported into Adobe InDesign. By using InDesign's Digital Publishing Suite overlays, the team produced animations showing each city as they adopted 311 systems. The interactive online visualization that incorporated buttons was created using HTML and the JQuery JavaScript framework. For the touchscreen visualization, the team created an iPad version using InDesign.

ANALYSIS AND VISUALIZATION

The team recognized the complexity of the data and determined it would be useful to compare a static visualization with animated versions using the same data. They separated each factor (population, crime rate, government form) into discrete temporal visualizations. Furthermore, the team recognized that understanding the visualization would require both "automatic" and "controlled" processing, which they assumed would be more efficiently processed through a self-paced, interactive experience. The four visualizations consisted of the mouse-controlled, self-paced version, the non-interactive animated version, the touchscreen-controlled, self-paced version, and the static version (Figure 8.1).

Although team members sent all four versions to O'Byrne, they concentrated their questions on the print version, since he planned to insert it into his dissertation.

O'Byrne's feedback overall was extremely positive. He said the organization and hierarchy of the visuals reflected their relative importance and encouraged proper eyeflow from the center to the right column leading down and below to the left. When asked whether he would have preferred using the city population bar chart at bottom right as the dominant element instead of the map, he said he thought New York's extremely tall bar would create awkward trapped space, so he thought it should stay as a secondary element.

In regard to the color palette, the client preferred the three-color version, although he said he would be receptive to using a map in which the blue "non-adopters" were shown in green, the complement of red.

The client recognized the diffusion of innovation adoption rate bar chart in the lower left would require deeper reading concentration (Shneiderman's "controlled processing") because of its multivariate nature. But he said pairing the proportion symbols below the bars and labeling the cities would not complicate the information too much.

---

4 Sci2 Team. 2009. "Science of Science (Sci2) Tool." Indiana University and SciTech Strategies. http://sci2.cns.iu.edu.

Since the client's main objective is to use the visualization in his dissertation, he said that he would prefer the maps and charts broken into separate figures for inclusion, but would use the design intact for use at a conference poster session. The dissertation version will have to be in black and white, so the team agreed to send him each map separately.

DISCUSSION

The maps in conjunction with the proportion symbol comparison clarify and support the client's three hypotheses. In the first map, especially, it's clear at a glance that the larger populations are colored red (adopters). If readers study the proportion symbol comparison labels, they see that the average city population of adopters is 685,160 compared to a much smaller average population average of 215,173 for non-adopters. The actual adoption rate of cities aligns closely with Rogers's Diffusion of Innovation curve, which the client also hypothesized. The bar chart at bottom right supports visually the hypothesis that the largest cities adopted earlier.

The team was pleased with the client's reaction. The complexity of the data presents a large challenge in creating a static visualization. In order to create a readable, aesthetically pleasing print version, the team needed to use at minimum a tabloid size, although a poster version of 2′ × 3′ (.609 × .914 meters) allowed viewers to see details with more clarity. The print version also lacks the opportunity to layer information through rollovers and taps the way the online/touchscreen versions do. The team feels the scalability of the interactive model would not be constrained by geography (e.g., creating a world map of diffusions versus limiting it to the United States). However, it's still necessary to assess the processing demands on users. After evaluating client feedback during the initial prototyping process, the team realized the complexity of some information and attempted to simplify further. In a future iteration, the team would like to layer more data on the interactive version to encourage more interactivity (e.g., a graphic that could allow users to zoom into any municipality and see a choropleth map of population breakdown with rollover information about the city's adoption). Shneiderman's principles underline the importance of providing an overview while allowing users to drill down. In trying to visualize geospatial/temporal/quantitative 311 data most efficiently, the interactive versions seemed better suited.

ACKNOWLEDGMENTS

The authors would like to recognize the help and assistance of Dr. Katy Börner, director of the Cyberinfrastructure for Network Science Center at Indiana University, School of Informatics and Computing, Department of Information and Library Science doctoral student Scott E. Weingart, and CNS research and editorial assistant David E. Polley.

Case Study #2

Examining the Success of *World of Warcraft* Game Player Activity

TEAM MEMBER:
Arul Jeyaseelan [ajeyasee@indiana.edu]
Indiana University

TEAM MEMBER/CLIENT:
Isaac Knowles [iknowles@indiana.edu]
Indiana University

PROJECT DETAILS

In the video game development and publication industries, analytics and visualization are increasingly used to drive design and marketing decisions. Especially for games that are based in large virtual worlds, a game's "virtual geography" is a matter of significant importance. The costs and benefits of moving to one place or another bear enormously on player decisions. Specialized tools are needed to help analysts and developers understand how players respond to their virtual surroundings, and how well those surroundings engage players.

Case in point: Activision Blizzard's *World of Warcraft* (WoW). WoW is a massively multiplayer online role-playing game based in an immense virtual world. In the game, players may traverse four continents, each with its own unique geographical features, challenges, transit routes, and economic centers. Some parts of the virtual world are visited more than others, but every place must meet strict quality standards. Underused areas represent losses on investments, while overcrowded regions can cause server or client crashes. Thus geospatial analyses are vital to identifying and generating solutions to these and other issues.

To that end, we built a tool that helps users understand the movements of players through the World of Warcraft. Using a map of that world, we created a geographical information system for the game, which allows users to explore the travel behavior of players in an underlying dataset. The user can pull up and compare player trends across many geographical locations in the game. The tool helps answer questions like:

1. What are the major travel hubs?
2. How do travel habits change over time?
3. How do location and travel habits vary with server population and in-game zone population density?

The clients for this project were Isaac Knowles (also a participant) and Edward Castronova, two economists at Indiana University whose research focuses on the economies of virtual worlds. In an effort to better understand how people work together in groups, our clients had collected many thousands of "snapshots" of player activities inside WoW. These players were all members of competitive raiding guilds. In WoW, guilds are formally recognized player groups. Some of these groups take part in "raids," which are comprised of a series of battles against computer-controlled monsters, and which require the coordination of a large number of players to complete successfully. The world's highest ranked raiding guilds were chosen by Knowles and Castronova for their study.

REQUIREMENTS ANALYSIS

The initial client requirement was very broad, emphasizing only that our end visualization should help discern patterns and trends in the data. Consequently, our idea of building a customized visualization tool, rather than a single visualization, was met with the clients' considerable interest and approval. During the design phase, we were fortunate in that the client-participant was able to react to the group's ideas and suggest amplifications or changes on the fly. He also had a great deal of first-hand knowledge about the data we were using, which he had already cleaned and analyzed prior to beginning the project. This was a significant advantage and time saver.

RELATED WORK

The bulk of our work consisted of designing and deploying a new and unique tool for data exploration. In doing this, we created several visualizations to help users understand some of the basic geospatial and demographic patterns that are in the data. These visualizations are similar to those found in several previous works on *World of Warcraft*.

Christian Thurau and Christian Bauckhage investigated 1.4 million teams in *World of Warcraft*, spanning over four years.[1] They identified some of the social behaviors that distinguished guilds and analyzed how different behaviors affected how quickly guild members leveled up. They used histograms and bar charts to indicate the development of guilds both in the United States and European Union. In addition, they used network analysis to demonstrate how U.S. and EU guilds evolved over time.

---

1 Thurau, C., and C. Bauckhage. 2010. "Analyzing the Evolution of Social Groups in World of Warcraft." Paper presented at the *IEEE Conference on Computational Intelligence and Games*, IT University of Copenhagen.

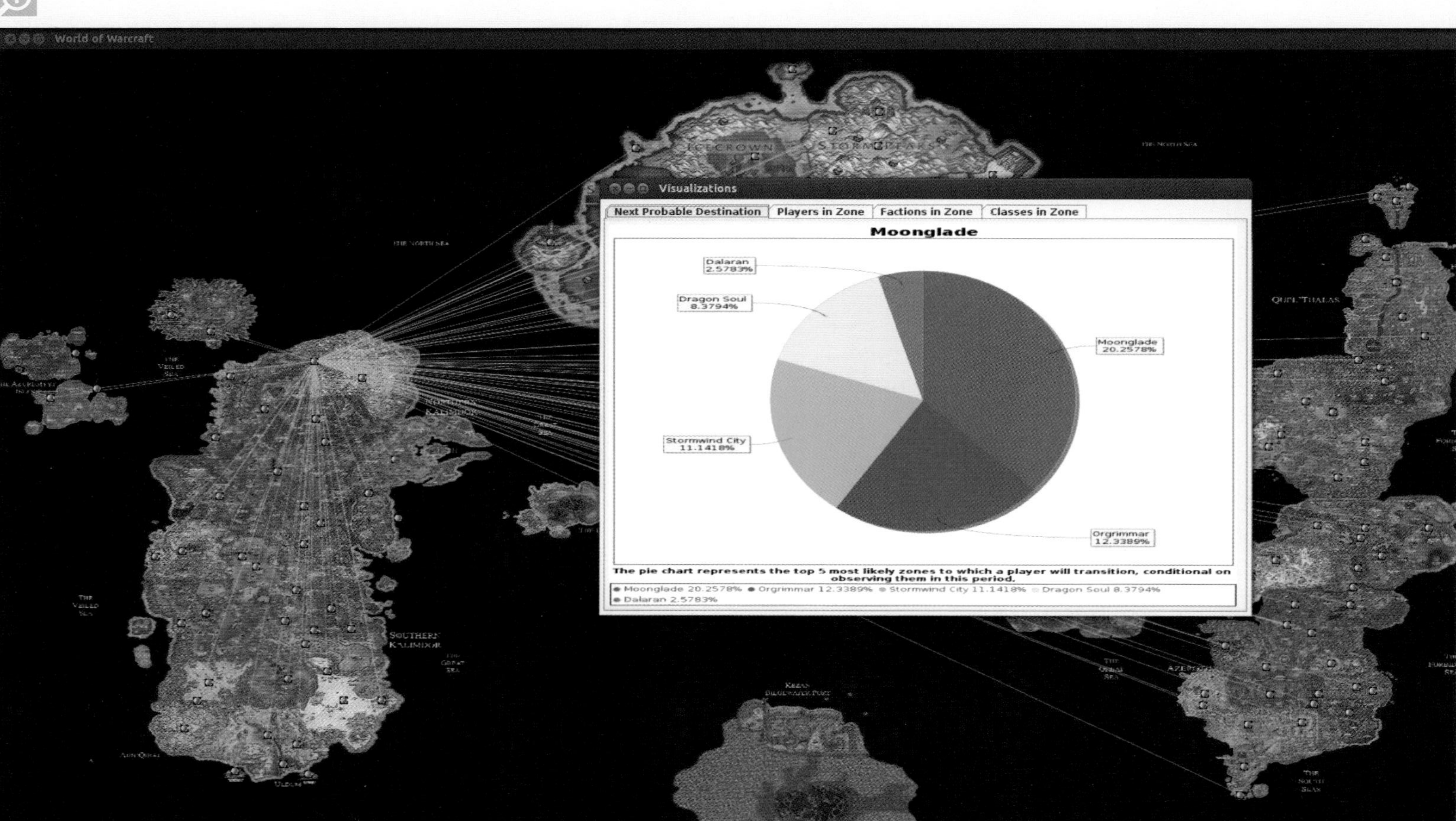

Figure 8.2 Final visualization showing lines of transit and next-location probabilities displayed for the Moonglade region of WoW (http://cns.iu.edu/ivmoocbook14/8.2.jpg)

Nicolas Ducheneaut et al discuss the relationship between online social networks and the real-world behavior in organizations in more depth.[2] They use histograms, bar charts, and line charts to do this. Besides the network analysis, they also use statistics to show the extent and nature of players' behavior in the virtual world. In another article, Ducheneaut et al analyze many of the broader trends of class, faction, and race choice; zone choice; and transit using data very similar to the one used here.[3] While their goal was to "reverse engineer" design patterns in WoW, our project aims to reveal patterns of behavior in WoW players.

DATA COLLECTION AND PREPARATION

The data were comprised of periodic snapshots of players' characters, including information about their in-game location, real-world location, guild membership, class, race, and language spoken. Players' chosen faction—which can be Horde or Alliance, and which limits player communication to that faction—was also recorded. Approximately 48,155 *characters* appear in the data; the number of *players* represented by those characters could be considerably smaller (30,000 to 40,000), as one player may take on multiple characters. Only players that were online at the time of a snapshot can appear in that snapshot. Snapshots were taken at roughly half-hour intervals, from December 2011 to May 2012, with some gaps due to game server outages or scraping program bugs. Table 8.1 contains basic information about the data, which required very little cleaning prior to loading into our server.

Table 8.1 Basic Data Facts

Region	Servers	Players	Guilds	Total Records
US	58	31,995	382	2,966,757
EU	59	18,520	107	2,272,390

VISUALIZATION

The final visualization consisted of an interactive, high-resolution map of the world. Owing to the size of the high-resolution map image file (9000 × 6710, 13MB) and the short duration of time available to produce a prototype, a web application format was abandoned in favor of a desktop client model that would have all resources prepackaged. The desktop client was developed as a Java application with the data on a MySQL server as the backend.

2 Ducheneaut, N., N. Yee, E. Nickell, and R.J. Moore. 2006. "'Alone Together?': Exploring the Social Dynamics of Massively Multiplayer Online Games." In *Proceedings of the SIGCHI Conference on Human Factors in Computing Systems*, 406–417. New York: ACM.

3 Ducheneaut, N., N. Yee, E. Nickell, and R.J. Moore. 2006. "Building an MMO with Mass Appeal: A Look at Gameplay in World of Warcraft." *Games and Culture* 1, 4: 281–317.

For the user, clicking on a location button resulted in two major events. First, it caused lines to be drawn from the chosen flag to every other flag on the map at which players were next seen in the data. Second, a new window popped up containing several tabs, which provided different visual breakdowns of the player-base that was found at a particular location. We used pie charts to display probabilistic information, line graphs for temporal population data, and bar graphs for comparing static player information.

The positions of all the zones with respect to the original full-scale image were maintained in a CSV file that the application would access at startup. For example, the city Orgrimmar can be found at pixel (2205, 3679) of the map. With this information, the map could be scaled to fit various monitor resolutions and still have each zone's position updated correctly. As we were dealing with more than 5 million records (see Table 8.1), performance was a major concern. Though optimized when possible, the application did face slowdowns when fetching information for locations that had heavy player traffic. Once fetched, the data from the various queries were used to generate the transit lines, and charts were generated using JFreeChart.[4]

DISCUSSION

Work continues on making a more user-friendly version of the tool. A web equivalent of the desktop application is currently being developed using Javascript with D3 for the front end and PHP with MySQL for the backend. The new version of the application will try to address some of the issues mentioned by our classmates and validators. Among these are the non-interactivity of links between zones, the difficulty of comparing information between zones, and the quality of the visualizations themselves; for example, the use of a pie chart to display information on where players travel. The primary challenge remains: finding an efficient way to serve the map image to the client.

Though our team was fortunate to have several skilled programmers, the interface was difficult to produce and complete. We thus faced limitations on the functionality of the interface at the time it was presented to our classmates and our clients. There are a few improvements to the tool that we continue to work on.

First, the information that is served by the tool is currently static; it provides no way to look at or compare data from different time periods. It is also not possible to look at smaller cross-sections of the data. For example, we could not separately visualize the data for particular servers, guilds, factions, players, or other groups within the data. To correct

---

4 http://www.jfree.org/jfreechart

this, we will add interface elements to the visualization, as well as the capacity to generate suitable queries to get the information from the server.

Second, and more important, although making the tool more dynamic is a relatively minor technical task, making it easy to work with will require considerably more work. In its current form, for example, the only way to compare information at two locations or more is to call up their information windows and compare them side by side. While this is better than having no tool at all, small differences will be difficult to detect without visuals that more effectively afford comparison.

Third, though we do not specifically deal with the fact that our data are comprised of competitive guild members, in the future our interface could be modified to analyze guild success. For example, zone choice and transit speed may bear on the efficiency of a guild, and therefore its final place in the competition.

ACKNOWLEDGMENTS

The authors wish to thank their other team members (in alphabetical order): Shreyasee Chand, Zhichao Huo, Sameer Ravi, and Gabriel Zhou. Thanks also to Edward Castronova for his comments and for his support in producing the data we used. We also appreciate the advice and encouragement we received from Katy Börner, Scott E. Weingart, David E. Polley, and all of our Information Visualization classmates.

Case Study #3

Using Point of View Cameras to Study Student-Teacher Interactions

CLIENTS:
Adam V. Maltese [amalteste@indiana.edu]
Joshua Danish [jdanish@indiana.edu]
Indiana University

TEAM MEMBERS:
Michael P. Ginda [mginda@indiana.edu]
Tassie Gniady [ctgniady@indiana.edu]
Michael J. Boyles [mjboyles@iu.edu]
Indiana University

Laura E. Ridenour [ridenour@uwm.edu]
University of Wisconsin-Milwaukee

PROJECT DETAILS

The goal of this project and the resulting visualizations and analysis is to help researchers identify how they might understand student engagement within science, technology, engineering, and mathematics (STEM) classes in the future. More specifically, this project aims to see if there is a correlation between the activity of the instructor in large science lectures and the corresponding activities of the students by using cameras that record student actions from Point of View (POV) cameras instead of self-report or external observation in real time. The educational research clients did not provide a concrete research hypothesis but were interested to see and understand their data in new ways by means of data visualizations.

The team consisted of four individuals affiliated at the time with Indiana University. Michael Ginda, Tassie Gniady, and Laura Ridenour were graduate students within the School of Library and Information Science. Michael Boyles was also an Informatics graduate student and manager of the Advanced Visualization Lab at Indiana University. Our client was Dr. Adam Maltese from Indiana University's School of Education and his colleague, Dr. Joshua Danish.

REQUIREMENTS ANALYSIS

The researchers had used three methods to collect the data: video of the instructor teaching the class, POV cameras mounted on baseball caps and worn by students, and Livescribe Pens with audio.[1] Our group set out to determine what data is most useful and what should be collected and preprocessed, along with which methods of visual analysis are best suited for this problem. The clients wanted a sustainable workflow leading to visualizations their team could recreate, as well as a way to highlight student actions as they corresponded with instructor actions.

RELATED WORK

Student attrition within STEM programs is greatest within the first academic year of study. High attrition rates within lecture formats have been linked to a lack of student engagement with materials, instructors, and other students.[2,3] Large lecture settings can create impediments to involvement by limiting student conceptualization through active engagement. Conversely, lectures that utilize a conversational tone and a self-critical method that explain thought processes behind ideas and that examine mistakes have been shown to positively impact student engagement.[4,5]

Efforts to visualize student engagement with instructional materials have utilized student activity data derived from online courses using course management software and social networks.[6] Data visualizations derived from course management software have allowed instructors to temporally track student engagement with course materials, discussions, and performance, which can help instructors improve course materials and track student behavior and learning outcomes.[7]

---

1. Livescribe. 2007. Livescribe Echo Pen. http://www.livescribe.com/en-us/.
2. Gasiewski, J.A., M.K. Eagan, G.A. Garcia, S. Hurtado, and M.J. Chang. 2011. "From Gatekeeping to Engagement: A Multicontextual, Mixed Method Study of Student Academic Engagement in Introductory STEM Courses." *Research in Higher Education* 53, 2: 229–261. doi:10.1007/s11162-011-9247-y.
3. Gill, R. 2011. "Effective Strategies for Engaging Students in Large-Lecture, Nonmajors Science Courses." *Journal of College Science Teaching* 41, 2: 14–21.
4. Long, H.E., and J.T. Coldren,. 2006. "Interpersonal Influences in Large Lecture-Based Classes: A Socioinstructional Perspective." *College Teaching* 54, 2: 237–243
5. Milne, I. 2010. "A Sense of Wonder, Arising from Aesthetic Experiences, Should Be the Starting Point for Inquiry in Primary Science." *Science Education International* 21, 2: 102–115.
6. Badge, J.L., N.F.W. Saunders, and A.J. Cann. 2012. "Beyond Marks: New Tools to Visualise Student Engagement via Social Networks." *Research in Learning Technology* 20, 16283). doi:10.3402/rlt.v20i0/16283.
7. Mazza, R., and V. Dimitrova. 2004. "Visualising Student Tracking Data to Support Instructors in Web-Based Distance Education." *Proceedings of the 13th International World Wide Web Conference on Alternate Track Papers & Posters*, 154. New York: ACM Press. doi:10.1145/1013367.1013393.

In the area of semantic web research, semantic browsers have offered various fields robust tools to organize and visualize temporal categorical data. Semantic browsing visualizations have been applied to video conference recordings, such as distance learning lectures, through the indexing of participant activities to help user information retrieval needs.[8] Implementing this approach in a dynamic visualization environment, such as that provided by the Tableau Dashboard,[9] allows for both efficient and effective visualization.

DATA COLLECTION AND PREPARATION

In an effort to examine introductory science students' (overt) cognitive actions and how they adjust their attention in response to classroom activities, POV video data and pen recordings were collected from about 50 students over multiple class sessions in an organic chemistry course and an introductory biology course. The data we discuss in this paper come from a subset of data including videos from six students, pen data from seven students, and classroom video recordings from a single organic chemistry lecture. The screen captures below demonstrate the type of POV data collected from the participants. Student POV video and pen data were coded using a grounded, iterative approach to identify emerging trends. Instruction was coded with specific behaviors defined in the revised Teacher Dimensions Observation Protocol (TDOP).[10] Several deviations from the revised TDOP were used to more closely capture instructor behavior–student response dynamics.

In this study, we coded each instructor action independently and without regard to time durations. This is a deviation from the prescribed method for the use of TDOP codes, which recommends coding behaviors concurrently within two-minute time segments. We felt that in order to flesh out how the individual actions of the instructor induced a student response, it was important to monitor the class as a continuum. In this manner, we can more easily pinpoint the results of specific actions, as opposed to observing a grouped generalized course of behavior. It is important to note that this method of coding only allows for the use of one type of behavior code at a given instance. This results in small segments of action that if viewed as raw data may appear as if the instructor spent the majority of the class period randomly jumping from topic to topic. However, when a full timeline of the codes are compiled and presented as a continuum it becomes clearer that the instructor may be frequently switching between pedagogical techniques

8 Martins, D.S., and M. da G.C. Pimentel. 2012. "Browsing Interaction Events in Recordings of Small Group Activities via Multimedia Operators." *Proceedings of the 18th Brazilian Symposium on Multimedia and the Web*, 245. New York: ACM Press. doi:10.1145/2382636.2382689.

9 Tableau Software. 2013. Tableau Public. http://www.tableausoftware.com/public.

10 Hora, M., and J. Ferrare. 2010. "The Teaching Dimensions Observation Protocol (TDOP)." Madison: University of Wisconsin-Madison, Wisconsin Center for Education Research.

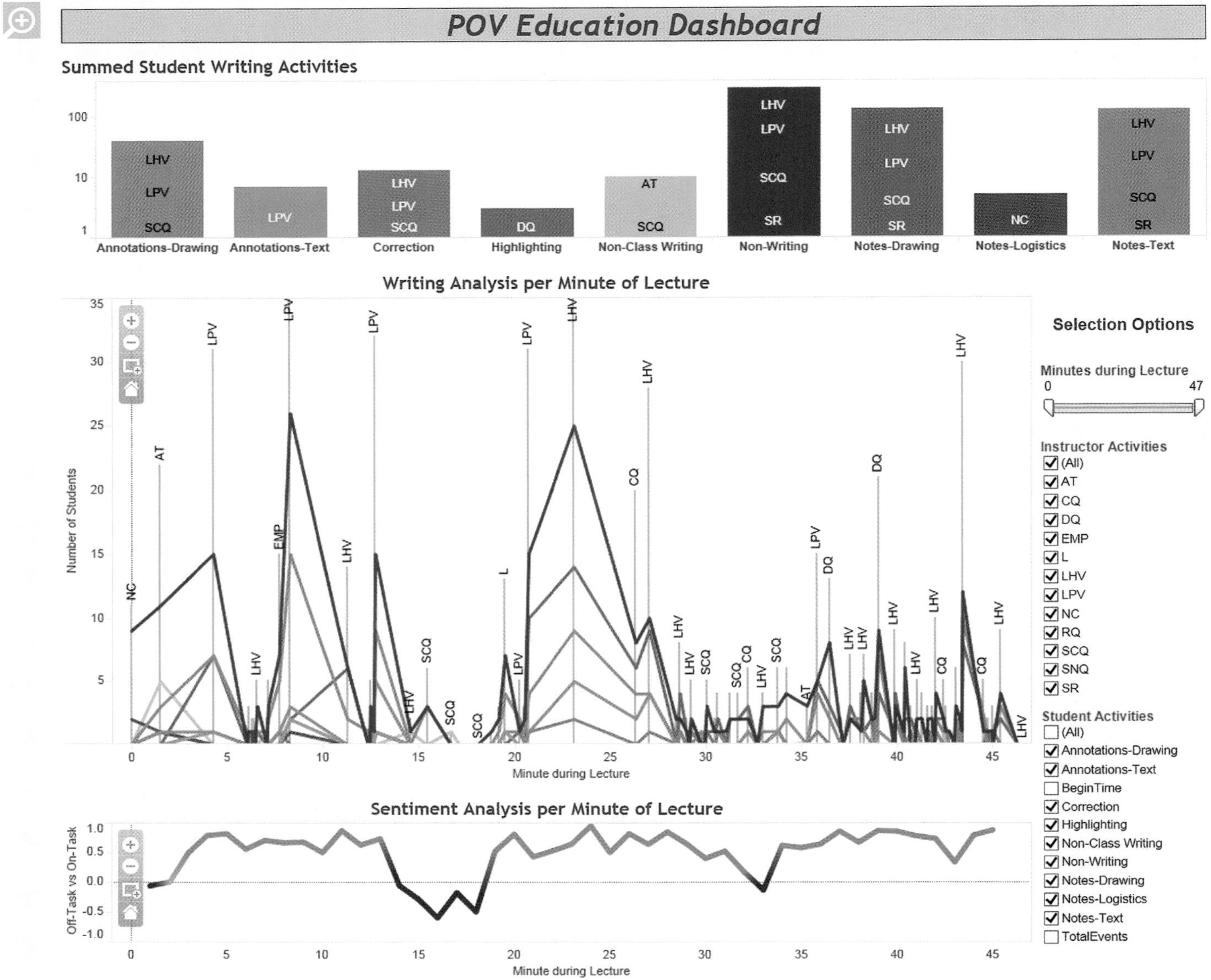

Figure 8.3 POV Education Dashboard created with Tableau Public (http://cns.iu.edu/ivmoocbook14/8.3.jpg)

that symbiotically flow together. Data coding was conducted using the ELAN qualitative software package.[11] Each different stream of data had the common element of an audio track. We were able to use the audio tracks to sync up all the video and pen recordings so that comparison across students and across data sources was reasonable.

Table 8.2 Instructor and Student-Writing Codes

Teacher Code	Meaning	Student Code	Meaning
AT	Administrative Task	1	Non-writing
CQ	Instructor Comprehension Question	2	Notes-Text
DQ	Instructor Display Question	3	Notes-Drawing
EMP	Emphasis	4	Notes-Logistics
L	Lecture	5	Annotations-Text
LHV	Lecture with Handwritten Visuals	6	Annotations-Drawing
LPV	Lecture with Pre-made Visuals	7	Correction
NC	No Code		
RQ	Instructor Rhetorical Question		
SCQ	Student Comprehension Question		
SNQ	Student Novel Question		
SR	Student Response		

All data were time stamped and coded using a coding system for student and instructor activities (see Table 8.2). The original coding scheme included 46 possible instructor actions of which 10 were used. Student codes were numerical, from 1 to 9, each with its own assigned meaning.

A variety of data preprocessing and reorganization was performed using Python and Excel. Instructor actions and individual student actions were programmatically combined into a single event timeline. Sentiment analysis for the six POV cameras was aggregated by minute of instruction and averaged to give an overall sentiment for each minute. Each of these are appropriate for analysis using the same 45-minute timeline.

ANALYSIS/VISUALIZATION

Using Tableau Public[12] an interactive aggregation of the POV data was created. Summed Student Writing Activities, Writing Analysis per Minute of Lecture, and Sentiment Analysis

[11] Brugman, H. and A. Russel. 2004. "Annotating Multimedia/Multi-modal resources with ELAN." *Proceedings of LREC 2004*, 2065–2068. Fourth International Conference on Language Resources and Evaluation.

[12] http://bit.ly/YC7eY0

per Minute of Lecture are all displayed and may be manipulated to focus on any of the "Selection Options" on the right-hand side of the visualization via a list of checkboxes (Figure 8.3). The core of the dashboard facilitates both a collective overall view of student-writing activities as well as a time-based view of student writing and sentiments in relation to instructor activities.

Using the POV Education Dashboard, a researcher can see the interactions between student and instructor data by hovering the mouse over the different times in the Writing Analysis graph. More detailed exploration is enabled using the zoom-and-pan feature available in all three views. Instructor codes are linked between the student-writing overview and time-based views. Summarily, since select instructor and student-writing activities can be filtered out, the dashboard provides an extremely flexible environment for the quick exploration of a number of scenarios.

DISCUSSION

The project team identified and preprocessed both the instructor activities and student-writing codes into the following three categories: (1) no interactions between the instructor and students, (2) student-led interactions, and (3) instructor-led interactions. Coded student actions were aggregated for the duration of each set of instructor actions. The client can easily adjust these groupings as their needs and research ideas evolve while utilizing similar visualization techniques by choosing other criteria to group interactions.

Student engagement measured through PEN actions is shown to be higher when instructors pose questions broadly to students during the lecture. Conversely, student engagement is shown to be lower when their peers pose questions to the instructor during the lecture.

Further work with this data should explore the capabilities of Tableau for overlaying and comparing different types of STEM lectures and different instructor approaches. For example, a logical follow-up to our work would extend the existing dashboard to include tabs that link to the same data but provide many different views.

ACKNOWLEDGMENTS

The project team would like to thank Scott E. Weingart and David E. Polley for their technical assistance and expertise and Drs. Adam Maltese and Joshua Danish for the initial project idea and their willingness to review and work through many iterations as we converged on a final solution.

Case Study #4

Phylet: An Interactive Tree of Life Visualization

CLIENT:
Stephen Smith [blackrim@gmail.com]
University of Michigan

TEAM MEMBERS:
Gabriel Harp [gabrielharp@gmail.com]
Genocarta, San Francisco, CA

Mariano Cecowski [marianocecowski@gmail.com]
Ljubljana, Slovenia

Stephanie Poppe [spoppe@umail.iu.edu]
Shruthi Jeganathan [sjeganathan@indiana.edu]
Indiana University

Cid Freitag [cjfreitag@gmail.com]
University of Wisconsin

PROJECT DETAILS

Phylet visualizes a subset of Open Tree of Life (OToL[1]) data using a graph network visualization (spring forced directed acyclic graph using D3 Javascript library[2]). The Phylet web application employs an incremental graph API (HTTP JSON requests), a client-server data implementation (Neo4j, Python, py2neo, web cache), database and local searches (JavaScript, Python), a Smart Undo/Session interface (Javascript), and a browser-based UI (HTML5, Bootstrap.js).

Phylet was developed in six weeks—synchronously and asynchronously—by a global team. The project is an open-source project under the Apache 2.0 license hosted at the Phylet code repository[3] and continues in affiliation with the Smith Lab at the University of Michigan, the National Center for Evolutionary Synthesis (NESCent), and a growing network of at-large contributors.[4]

---

1 http://blog.opentreeoflife.org

2 http://d3js.org

3 Phylet code repository: http://bitbucket.org/phylet/phylet

4 http://www.onezoom.org and http://tolweb.org/tree

REQUIREMENTS ANALYSIS

The Open Tree of Life is a large-scale cyberinfrastructure project aimed at assembling, analyzing, visualizing, and extending the use of all available phylogenetic data about global extant (living) species. We found that variation in the collection and analysis of phylogenetic data results in evolutionary tree visualizations that obscure the extent of (1) social disagreement among scientists about species lineages and classifications, (2) sources and ubiquity of the evidence used to support relationships, and (3) the biological and genetic messiness that exists within diverse species assemblages.

After exploring zoomable trees for informal public educational purposes (OneZoom and Tree of Life Web Project),[5] our focus evolved into creating a visualization to assist researchers and specialists in the areas of phylogenetics, biology, evolutionary biology, and others in identifying unresolved regions of conflict among OToL data. This tool is to encourage research exploration, hypothesis generation, and data conflict resolution. The resulting visualization of these conflicts can illuminate the as-yet-unresolved areas of important biological and methodological questions.

During the initial phase of the project, we studied and implemented several visualization methods, including dynamically loaded trees, circular trees, and circle packing within D3, as well as complete networks within Gephi. Our final product uses a forced-based dynamically loaded graph using D3.

The representation of evolutionary histories using tree-like graphs began long before Charles Darwin wrote *The Origin of Species*, and since Darwin, visual explanations of phylogenetic relationships have diversified.[6] Despite these advances, the visual grammar and notational precision of evolutionary biology and phylogenetics remains fairly fuzzy.

This is important because psychologist Mihaly Csikszentmihalyi described how more precise notational systems make it easier to detect change and evaluate whether or not individuals or groups have made original, creative contributions to a particular domain.[7] In music, for example, there are a variety of different use contexts and each of these different use contexts is supported by the precision of music's notational system, which includes different semantic marks. When a domain like evolutionary biology and phylogenetics employs an increasingly precise notational system, it means that creative contributions can be detected, shared, and rewarded more easily, making the domain more flexible, responsive, and innovative. This can potentially open a field up to insights from other domains using at least two distinct leverage

---

5 Phylet is migrating to http://phylet.herokuapp.com or http://phylet.com. At the time of this writing the Phylet development site can be reached at http://mariano.gmajna.net/gol/index.html.

6 Pietsch, T. W. 2012. *Trees of Life: A Visual History of Evolution*. Baltimore: Johns Hopkins University Press.

7 Csikszentmihalyi, M. 1988. "Society, Culture, and Person: A Systems View of Creativity." In *The Nature of Creativity: Contemporary Psychological Perspectives*, edited by R.J. Sternberg, 429–440. Cambridge: Cambridge University Press.

points for signaling to other communities, public engagement, and broader impact: the level of *social agreement* within the field and the *threshold for meaningful contributions* to that field.

Our project then consisted of two distinct efforts: a *visual grammar* for the dataset and a *web application* for browsing and navigating the dataset. This fit well with our client's goal of using the visualization as a preliminary map of the massive OToL dataset.

RELATED WORK

Given the task of representing loosely hierarchical data, we investigated several visualizations of phylogenetic data, as well as hierarchical and network information in general.

We evaluated several web applications available to visualize small phylogenies (a few hundred species), which included basic bifurcating trees in either a traditional or circular dendrogram format, including PhyloBox, Archaeopteryx, OneZoom, DeepTree, and Dendroscope, all freely available online. Nevertheless, some are dynamic in nature, but all are focused in a strictly tree-like taxonomy structure, and in the best cases, such as Mesquite, it allowed for comparison of two different and conflicting taxonomy trees.

Other non-strictly hierarchical visualizations such as the network-based GNOME suffer from scalability problems, relying on the complete dataset to form a visualization, and can only handle small sets or predefined subsets.

In terms of workflows and task analysis, requirements around the Encyclopedia of Life provided some articulation for specific requirements to engaging their communities of practice.[8]

DATA COLLECTION AND PREPARATION

The original OToL data comprised approximately 1.9 million species and included 2,159,861 nodes, 9,037,190 properties, and 6,505,797 relationships. Phylet visualization data were drawn from a subset and included 120,461 nodes, 504,866 properties, and 367,334 relationships. OToL investigator Stephen Smith supplied the data in the Neo4j database format, which we used to build the visualization along with the visualization libraries and the Python-based API.

For the visualization, we were unable to make use of all the data features and chose to simplify the fields to include child-parent relationships, data source, and the presence or absence of any conflicts in child-parent relationships. We also created additional properties: the number of children and the number of parents. This allowed sizing of collapsed nodes according to number of children, providing an additional navigational cue. We were primarily interested in a visual grammar that would orient the viewer towards regions of conflict, while providing secondary visual cues around species diversity.

---

8 http://wiki.eol.org/display/public

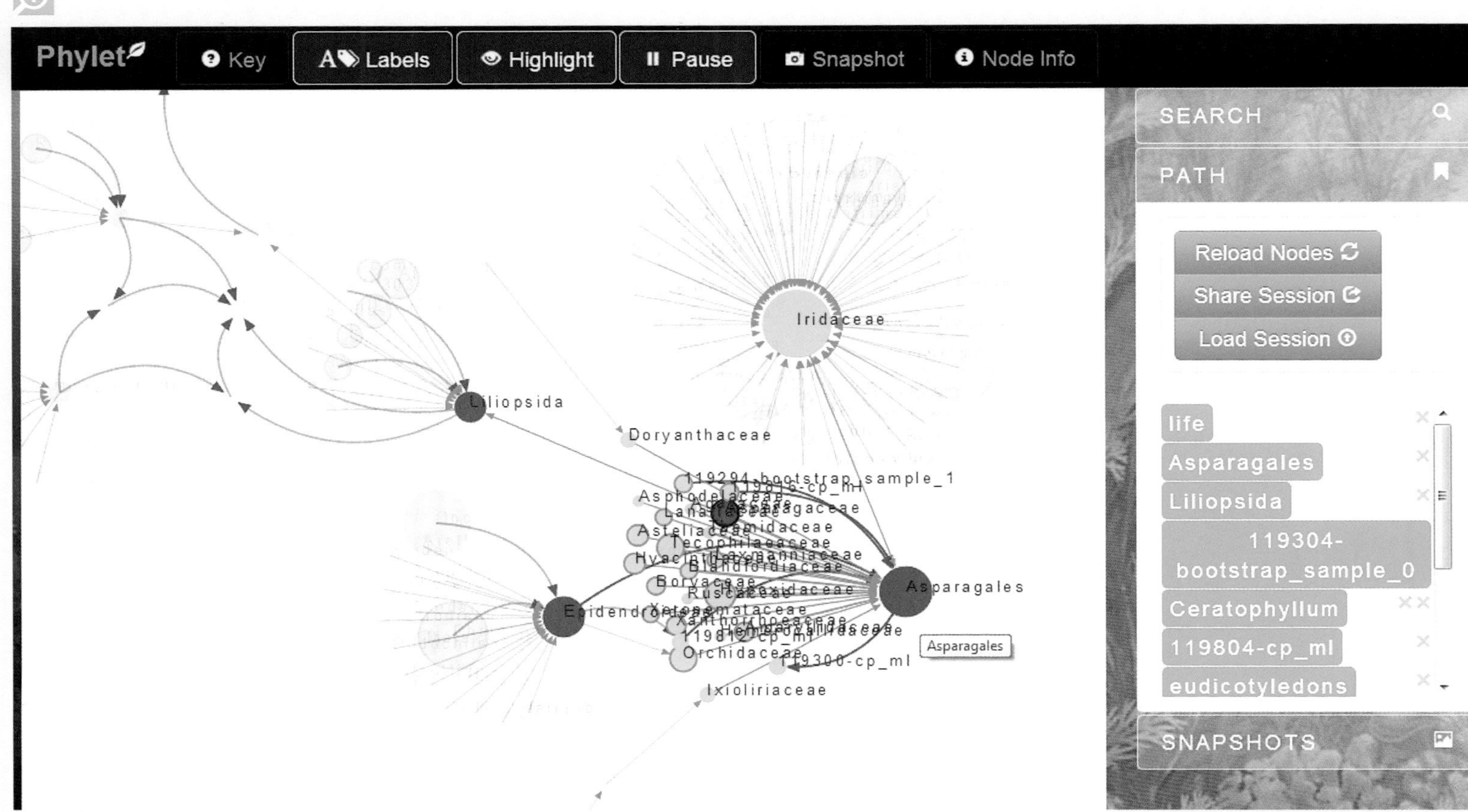

Figure 8.4 Phylet web application view with visualization network graph (left), session tools (right), and information toggles (top navigation) (http://cns.iu.edu/ivmoocbook14/8.4.jpg)

ANALYSIS AND VISUALIZATION

Based on the observation that evolutionary trees and similar representations often function as *boundary objects* that connect the technical and meaning-making practices of different communities—from the scientific to the non-scientific,[9] we considered tasks a user might want to do: share a relationship, their working session, or specific images or information.

We also aimed for a visual grammar that would scale well. The properties of our data visualization can be seen in Figure 8.4 and are summarized as follows:

- Children and parent nodes: colored green for resolved if there is only one parent node or red for unresolved if there are two or more parent nodes
- Nodes sized according to number of children nodes
- Presence of black, stroked node indicates more relationships to be explored
- Blue edges for resolved nodes
- Red curved edges for unresolved nodes using "cp_ml," "bootstrap," and other identification methods

We rapidly prototyped a variety of sketches, workflow tasks, and visualizations to include a handful of interaction tasks:

- Drag-pan-zoom the visualization
- Toggle on/off node labels
- Display the node info and metadata about parents, children, etc.
- Highlight node path on hover to highlight the node's parents and children
- Search for a node in displayed nodes/remote data including wildcard entries
- Path info track the clicks made to reach a node
- Remove actions from path
- Share, save, and load work sessions
- Snapshots of current graph saved as an SVG
- Gravity toggle to stop the movement of nodes

User research and prototyping revealed several important insights, including the need for clear narration, definitions, and storytelling around the goals of the visualization, supported tasks, workflows, and opportunities for creative appropriation of Phylet's functionality.

---

9 Star, S.L., and J.R. Griesemer. 1989. "Institutional Ecology, Translations' and Boundary Objects: Amateurs and Professionals in Berkeley's Museum of Vertebrate Zoology, 1907–39." *Social Studies of Science* 19, 3: 387–420.

Users did not enjoy switching tasks (e.g., switching between the visualization and the legend). This suggests that the interface should contain all relevant information, while resources for learning about use (e.g., node-click interactions) should be embedded into the visualization itself. Additionally, users wanted to selectively disclose waypoints during work sessions to assist dataset navigation.

Additional work remains to be done on the UI, interaction, and graphics, but these will develop as our skill with the software and data improves. Improvements to the backend data processing and visualization architecture will support better frontend usability, real-time dynamic views, improved usability, and shareability. In our next steps, we plan to add a tree-view visualization option that will fit many users' prior expectations for this context.

DISCUSSION

Although our technological fluency limited the rate at which we could work, our biggest challenges were social. Distributed collaboration is still a relatively new experience for any team. Computer and network-supported collaborative tools like Skype, Google+ Hangouts, instant messaging, email, large file transfer services, project management dashboards, and others lower the barriers to cooperative effort, but replicable strategies are needed for teams to formulate goals, uncover best practices, provide feedback, resolve conflicts, identify complementary skills, and coordinate roles. We know of no toolset or resource for collaboratively carrying out many of the specialized tasks associated with data and information visualizations. This would be a fantastic area for future research.

Our team benefitted from multiple and frequent face-to-face conferences, and in general, we made quick, provisional decisions. Our big leaps came with each prototype, demonstration, write-up, or contribution submitted by team members. In this sense, the project was built largely from the initiative and iterative contributions of each member. Using a version control system (e.g., Mercurial/Git) to host and track changes during software code and documentation development helped the team progress. However, our choices of technology significantly excluded some members of the team from participating in the technical implementation—although they remained influential in design, strategy, and research.

Ultimately, the collaboration and mutual reinforcement helped team members develop new skill sets and capabilities. The work is not complete, but the important lesson is that we have created a visualization that asks as many more questions than it answers. This generative characteristic is critical for the designer and the user and will be instrumental in guiding the Phylet project forward.

ACKNOWLEDGMENTS

The authors wish to acknowledge and thank Katy Börner, David E. Polley, Scott E. Weingart, Karen Cranston, and Chanda Phelan for their cooperation, guidance, and contributions.

Case Study #5

Isis: Mapping the Geospatial and Topical Distribution of a History of Science Journal

CLIENT:
Dr. Robert J. Malone [jay@hssonline.org]
History of Science Society

TEAM MEMBERS:
David E. Hubbard [hubbardd@library.tamu.edu]
Texas A&M University

Anouk Lang [anouk@cantab.net]
University of Strathclyde

Kathleen Reed [reed.kathleen@gmail.com]
Vancouver Island University

Anelise Hanson Shrout [anshrout@davidson.edu]
Davidson College

Lyndsay D. Troyer [ld.Troyer@gmail.com]
Colorado State University

PROJECT DETAILS

This project explores the history of science through the geospatial distribution of authors and trending topics in the journal *Isis* from 1913 to 2012. The project was requested by Dr. Robert J. Malone, Executive Director of the History of Science Society, and the analysis was completed by a project team comprised of a chemist, two academic librarians, and two digital humanists. Major insights include shifts in author contributions from Europe to the United States, as well as more geographically dispersed authorship within the United States over the last century. In addition to changes in authorship, contributed articles shifted from the study of individuals to collective endeavors with greater social context.

REQUIREMENTS ANALYSIS

Isis, an official publication of the History of Science Society, was launched by Belgian mathematician George Sarton in 1913. Dr. Malone sought a visual representation of *Isis* contributors and their locales over the past 100 years—one that would provide a dynamic picture of how scholarship in the history of science has shifted over the last century. The client also expressed interest in displaying the visualization as a poster, so the visualization needed to be static and possess sufficient resolution for a large display. The challenge for the project team was to represent temporal changes in the geospatial distribution of authors within a static visualization. While not specifically requested by the client, the project team also conducted a topical analysis of the journal article titles to explore major publication themes over the last 100 years.

RELATED WORK

Most studies visualizing the geospatial aspects of authorship utilize proportional symbols,[1,2,3] though choropleth maps can and have been used.[4] In the studies cited, the absolute number of publications is encoded onto a geographic map for a specified date range. The present study extends this approach by mapping the difference in publication activity between two historical periods. Another aspect of the current study employs Kleinberg's burst detection algorithm to explore topical trends.[5] The approach is similar to Mane and Börner's exploration of topic bursts and word co-occurrence in the *Proceedings of the National Academy of Sciences,*[6] though the current study is limited to article titles. To date, there are no known studies of *Isis*, or any other history of science publication, using these types of visualizations.

DATA COLLECTION AND PREPARATION

The spreadsheet obtained from the client contained 2,133 entries for articles published in *Isis* from 1913 to 2012. The main attributes used for the analysis were publication year, article title, and geographic location of the first author for each entry. The article titles were cleaned up, foreign language article titles were translated, and the geographic location and date formats normalized. The topical analysis (i.e., burst detection) was then

---

1 Batty, M. 2003. "The Geography of Scientific Citation." *Environment and Planning A* 35, 5: 761–765.

2 LaRowe, G., Ambre, S., Burgoon, J., Ke, W., Börner, K. 2009. "The Scholarly Database and Its Utility for Scientometrics Research." *Scientometrics* 79, 2: 219–234.

3 Lin, J.M. , Bohland, J.W., Andrews, P., Burns, G.A.P.C., Allen, C.B., Mitra, P.P. 2008. "An Analysis of the Abstracts Presented at the Annual Meetings of the Society for Neuroscience from 2001 to 2006." *PLoS ONE* 3, 4: 2052.

4 Mothe, J., Chrisment, C., Dkaki, T., Dousset, B., Karouach, S. 2006. "Combining Mining and Visualization Tools to Discover the Geographic Structure of a Domain." *Computers, Environment and Urban Systems* 30, 4: 460–484.

5 Kleinberg, J. 2002. "Bursty and Hierarchical Structure in Streams." *Proceedings of the Eighth ACM SIGKDD International Conference on Knowledge Discovery and Data Mining*, 91–101. New York: ACM.

6 Mane, K.K., Börner, K. 2004. "Mapping Topics and Topic Bursts in PNAS." *Proceedings of the National Academy of Sciences of the United States of America* 101, Suppl. no.1: 5287–5290.

One Hundred Years of *Isis*

David E. Hubbard (Texas A&M University), Anouk Lang (University of Strathclyde), Kathleen Reed (Vancouver Island University), Anelise Hanson Shrout (Davidson College) and Lyndsay D. Troyer (Colorado State University)

Changes in *Isis* Authorship: 1913-1937 to 1988-2012.

This map and chart show geographic shifts in *Isis* authors' locations across two time periods of 25 years each: 1913-1937 and 1988-2012.

Countries and states tinted brown had a greater number of articles published in the 1913-1937 period, while those tinted green had a greater number published in the 1988-2012 period.

Germany and the United States experienced the most extreme shifts in authorship. Authors located in Germany published 37 fewer articles between 1988-2012 than they did in 1913-1937. Authors located in the United States published 31 more articles between 1988-2012 than they did in 1913-1937.

Countries and states in gray had the same number of of published articles in both periods, while those with no color (i.e., white) had no publications in either period.

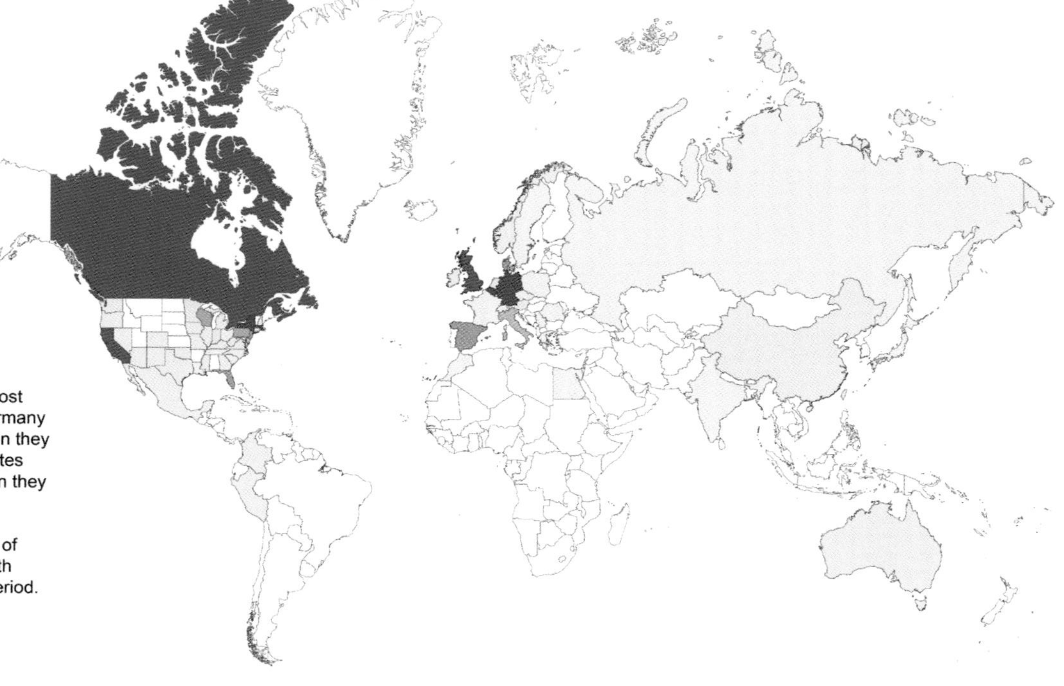

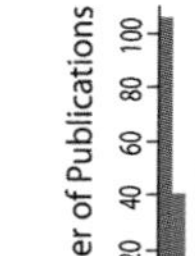

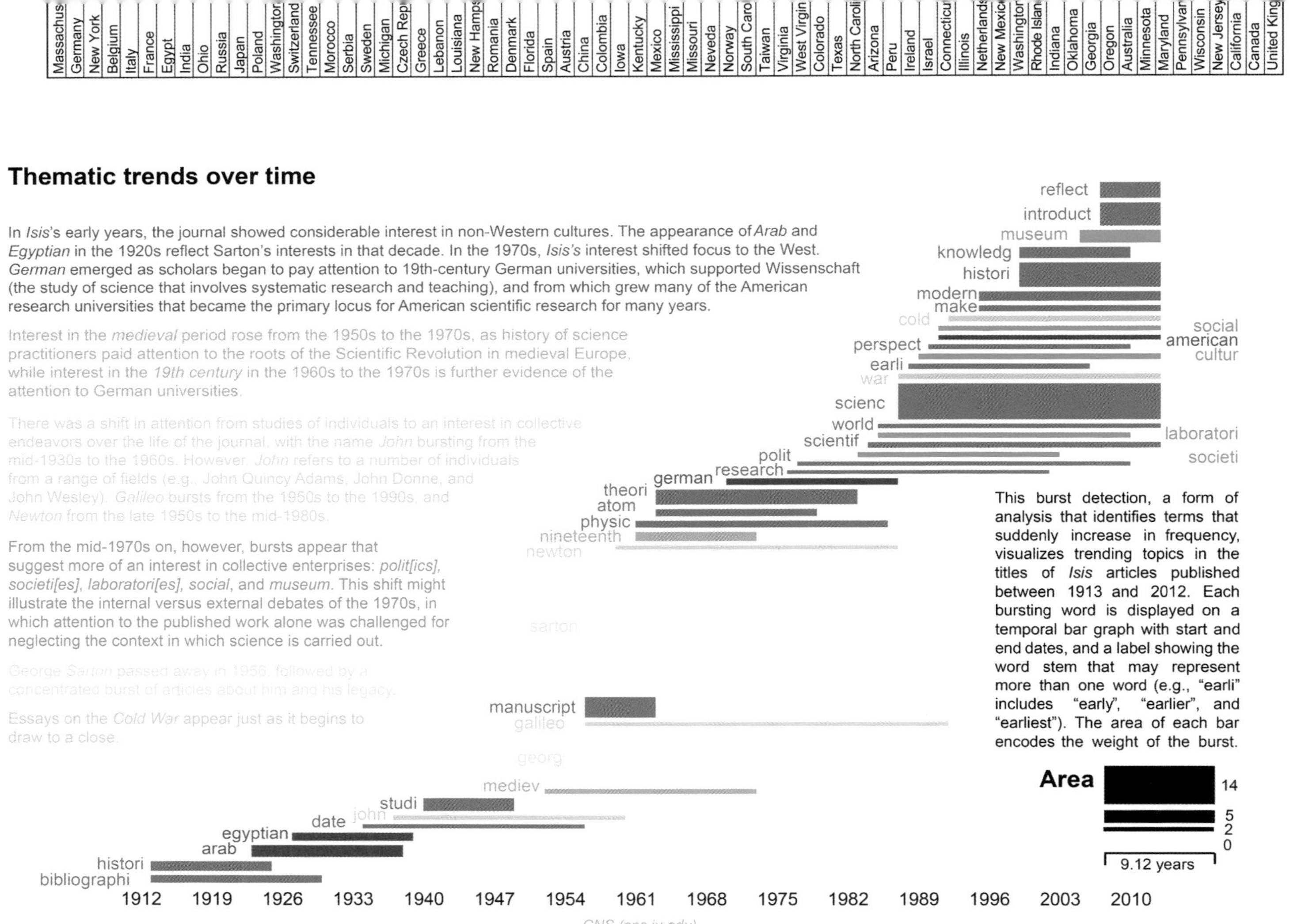

Figure 8.5 Final visualization: geospatial and topical analysis of *Isis* (http://cns.iu.edu/ivmoocbook14/8.5.jpg)

performed on all 2,133 article titles using burst detection in Sci2.[7] Due to absence of many geographic locations for the authors in the client data, the project team decided to compare the first 25 years (1913–1937) to the most recent 25 years (1988–2012) for the geospatial analysis. Once limited to the two 25-year periods, the spreadsheet contained 438 entries for 1913 to 1937 and 430 entries for 1988 to 2012.

ANALYSIS AND VISUALIZATION

A number of approaches were explored to visualize the data prior to the final visualization. The initial topical analyses brought to light a number of functional words (e.g., *volume*, *index*, and *preface*) in the article titles whose inclusion was distorting the dataset and potentially crowding out other more interesting terms. The visualization was improved by removing additional common terms, identified with the help of AntConc,[8] and categorizing words that experienced a sudden increase in their usage frequency as identified in the burst detection. The topical bursts, displayed as weighted horizontal bars, were color-coded to match accompanying explanatory text in the final visualization.

The initial geospatial visualizations utilized proportional symbols to encode the number of authored articles onto geographic maps for the two historical periods, but there was considerable crowding of the proportional symbols in some geographic locations. Using a choropleth map rather than proportional symbols offered an alternative. By calculating the difference between the number of articles published for each country in the 1913–1937 range and the number published in the 1988–2012 range, the difference in the number of articles authored between the historical periods could be encoded onto a single choropleth map. Since a large number of authors from the United States dominated both historical periods, each U.S. state was encoded in the same manner as a country. The geospatial visualization used a divergent brown-green color scheme to indicate decreases and increases in publication activity. The final visualization combined the geospatial and topical visualizations, as well as a bar graph to display the absolute number of publications for each country (Figure 8.5).

DISCUSSION

Sarton moved from Belgium to Cambridge, Massachusetts, after the outbreak of World War I and re-launched *Isis*.[9] This may explain the concentration of contributors from the Northeast

---

7 Sci2 Team. 2009. "Science of Science (Sci2) Tool." Indiana University and SciTech Strategies. http://sci2.cns.iu.edu.

8 Anthony, L. "AntConc." http://www.antlab.sci.waseda.ac.jp/software.html (accessed February 27, 2013).

9 McClellan, J.E., III. 1999. "Sarton, George Alfred Léon." In *American National Biography*, vol. 19, edited by J.A. Garraty and M.C. Carnes, 295–297. New York: Oxford University Press.

during the early period (1913–1937), which after Sarton's death in the 1950s became more dispersed throughout the United States in 1988 to 2012. In terms of changes in author locales, Germany and the United States experienced the most extreme shifts in authorship.

In relation to the burst detection analysis, there appears to be an editorial shift in the 1950s because the burst patterns that precede this decade, and those that follow it, are markedly different. This shift coincided with the death of Sarton in 1956. After the 1950s, attention shifted to different geographic regions and time periods and from studies of individuals to those of larger groups. For example, interest in the medieval period rises from the 1950s to the 1970s as history of science practitioners paid attention to the roots of the Scientific Revolution in medieval Europe. There was also a shift in attention from studies of individuals to an interest in collective endeavors. The name John, for example, bursts from the mid-1930s to the 1960s, representing figures such as John Quincy Adams, John Donne, and John Wesley. Galileo bursts from the 1950s to the 1990s, and Newton from the late 1950s to the mid-1980s. From the mid-1970s on, however, the bursty words that appear suggest more of an interest in collective enterprises: *polit*[*ics*], *societi*[*es*], *laboratori*[*es*], *social*, and *museum*. This shift might illustrate the internal versus external debates of the 1970s within the history of science field, in which attention to the published work alone was challenged for neglecting the context in which science is carried out. The project team put their hypotheses about the significance of these patterns to the client during the validation process, and he and a colleague in the discipline provided contextual information that fleshed out these hypotheses.

Using all 100 years might provide a fuller picture and the opportunity to study changes decade-by-decade, as would using other standard bibliometric approaches (e.g., co-citation analysis). The client asked about Charles Darwin, but Darwin did not appear as one of the "bursty words." Further refining of the burst detection could also be performed on the named persons from the titles of articles (e.g., Charles Darwin). The dataset only contained 2,133 articles and three main attributes (year, article title, and location), but contained sufficient complexity to justify and benefit from geospatial and topical visualizations. The approaches utilized in this study could be used for other publications and scaled to larger projects.

ACKNOWLEDGMENTS

We would like to thank Dr. Robert J. Malone for the opportunity to work on this project, assistance securing the data, and feedback. We also extend our appreciation to the anonymous History of Science Society member who answered our questions and provided insights into the history of science.

Case Study #6

Visualizing the Impact of the Hive NYC Learning Network

CLIENT:
Rafi Santo
Indiana University

TEAM MEMBERS:
Simon Duff [simon.duff@gmail.com]
John Patterson [jono.patterson@googlemail.com]
Camaal Moten [camaal@gmail.com]
Sarah Webber [sarahwebber@gmail.com]

PROJECT DETAILS

Hive NYC Learning Network, an out-of-school education network made up of 56 organizations, aims to develop a range of techniques, programs, and initiatives to create connected learning opportunities for youth, building on twenty-first-century learning approaches.[1] The network is being studied and supported by a group of researchers from Indiana University and New York University called Hive Research Lab.

Learning networks like Hive NYC have great potential to act as an infrastructure for improving the skills and abilities of local populations, the young in particular. They can also open up opportunities for greater collaboration and innovation amongst educators and learning organizations. Understanding how individual learning networks operate and grow may provide valuable insight into opportunities for development and improvement of other learning networks.

REQUIREMENTS ANALYSIS

The client in this instance was Rafi Santo, project lead of Hive Research Lab and a doctoral candidate at Indiana University. The dataset obtained by the client provided information on organizations who received funding, the project name, year and date of award, type and amount of grant funding, and the number of youth the project reached.

The brief given by our client was very broad and summarized as "[provide] substantive insight into various patterns within the network, most importantly the patterns of collaborations between organizations over time and the numbers of youth reached for the amount of resources used in a project."

1 Hive NYC Mission Statement: http://explorecreateshare.org/about/ (accessed August 2013).

Our team sought to answer three questions with the visualization. First, who had received most funding and who had worked with whom and when? Second, what was the return on investment in terms of project funding versus amount of youth reached? Third, what does the urban geography of Hive NYC look like and how might this have influenced the project? To answer these questions, three different visualizations were designed:

1. A network diagram showing patterns of collaboration over time.
2. A graph depicting the funding awards and number of youth reached.
3. A map supporting understanding of the geography of the Hive.

RELATED WORK

For visualizing information sharing and collaboration over time, a display static visualization such as the history flow interface, used to show the evolution of Wikipedia entries over time,[2] can be used. However, Reda et al. suggest that for temporal visualization of the emergence, evolution, and fading of communities or dynamic social networks, graph-based representations are not ideal and they argue for employing interactive visualizations. Animation of network graphs were implemented by Leydesdorff et al. to communicate the evolution of scholarly communities.[3,4] Harrer et al. argued for a three-dimensional visualization that places the network structure within the first two dimensions, and representing change over time on the third axis—moving through "time slices" enables viewers to explore the dynamics of the network.[5] Falkowsi and Bartelheimer propose two approaches to displaying social network dynamics: one is aimed at visualizing stable subgroups, the other more transient communities where members join in and out. Both use temporal displays to show the communities at each point in time.[6] Finally, Börner presents a suitable workflow for the production of network "with whom" analysis which was used in the project.[7]

---

2 Viégas, F. B., M. Wattenberg, and K. Dave. 2004. "Studying Cooperation and Conflict between Authors with History Flow Visualizations." *Proceedings of the SIGCHI Conference on Human Factors in Computing Systems*, 575–582. New York: ACM.

3 Reda, K., C. Tantipathananandh, A. Johnson, J. Leigh, and T. Berger Wolf. 2011. "Visualizing the Evolution of Community Structures in Dynamic Social Networks" *Computer Graphics Forum* 30, 3: 1061–1070.

4 Leydesdorff, L., Schank, T. 2008. Dynamic Animations of Journal Maps: Indicators of Structural Change and Interdisciplinary Developments, *Journal of the American Society for Information Science and Technology* 59.

5 Harrer, A., S. Zeini, S. Ziebarth, and D. Münter. 2007. "Visualisation of the Dynamics of Computer-Mediated Community Networks."

6 Falkowski, T., and J. Bartelheimer. 2006. "Mining and Visualizing the Evolution of Subgroups in Social Networks." *Proceedings of the 2006 IEEE/WIC/ACM International Conference on Web Intelligence*, 52–58. New York: ACM.

7 See Figure 6.10 in this book.

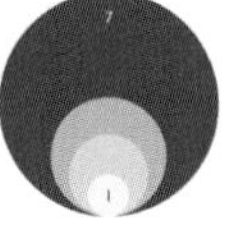

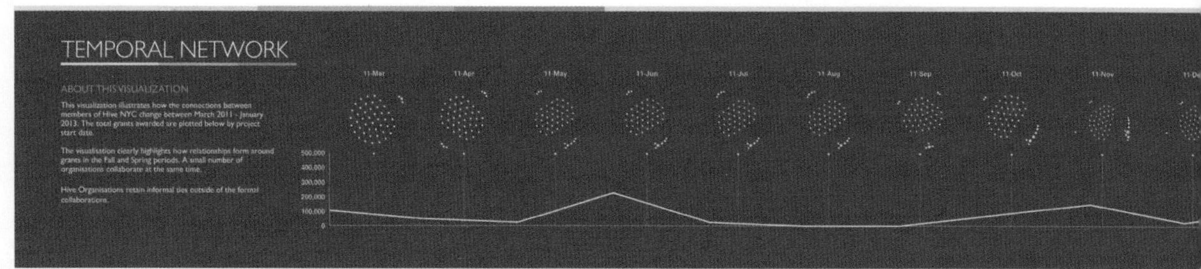

Figure 8.6 Hive NYC geospatial map (top), collaboration network (top right), bipartite network (middle), ROI Bubble Plot (middle right), and temporal network evolution (bottom) (http://cns.iu.edu/ivmoocbook14/8.6.jpg)

tions map the connections between Hive NYC members and community projects using various perspectives.
ned from the Hive Fund Projects Database, which consisted of 54 projects and 47 members from 2011-2013.

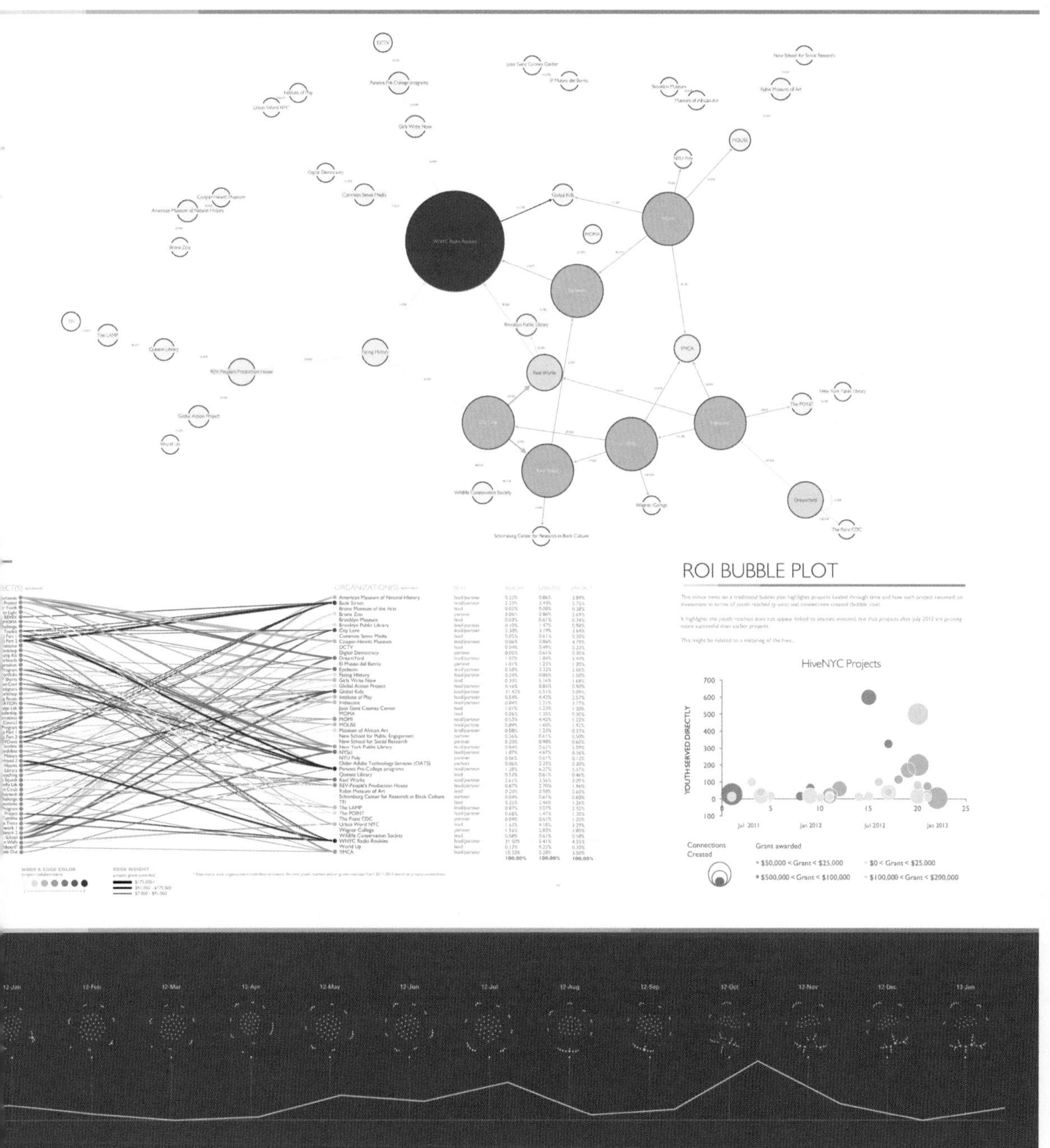

DATA COLLECTION AND PREPARATION

The dataset provided by Hive Research Lab consisted of 54 projects that 47 member organizations engaged in between 2011 and 2013. Data preprocessing involved correcting typos in organization names, looking for duplicate records and filling in missing values, and normalizing data to the same formats (e.g., dates in U.S. calendar notation). We enriched the data by appending any new data we needed to create our proposed visualizations—for example, geocoding organization addresses to append the latitude and longitude coordinates to the dataset. We also gathered a range of contextual background information on Hive NYC. Next, range summary statistics were calculated (see Table 8.3).

Table 8.3 Basic Statistics

Total # of Projects	54
Total # of Organizations	47
Average $ per Award	$60,200
Total Awarded (all projects)	$3,300,000
Average Youth Reached per Project	76
Total Youth Reached	3,449
Average Partners per Project	2.3
Average Cost per Youth Engaged	$1,697

ANALYSIS AND VISUALIZATION

The outputs generated from the analysis were five distinct visualizations that were combined with narrative to form the final visualization:

1. A geospatial network visualization to show Hive NYC member organizations, project links, and encode funding, youth reached, and funding type as points on the map. This provided a sense of the geographical distribution and collaborative links of partner organizations. Generally, organizations are tightly geographically clustered, but there are clearly strong links being forged between more distant partners, such as Bronx Zoo and NYSci.
2. A network showing 47 Hive NYC partner organizations as nodes, and the collaborative relationships between them as edges, directed from project leads towards secondary project participants. Nodes are labeled with organization names, while the link between any two nodes is labeled with the cumulative grant amount of the projects.
3. A bipartite network analysis was conducted to illustrate the participation of organizations (listed on the right) according to projects (listed on the left). Each record was represented using a labeled circle encoding project connections and edges weighted by grant amount. The goal was to illustrate each organization's contribution to the overall impact of the Hive NYC learning network. At a glance, one can identify organizations that helped secure the most participation, grant awards, or shared the workload.
4. The team also created a ROI Bubble Plot, using a traditional bubble plot that highlights projects funded through time and how each project returned on investment in terms of youth reached (*y*-axis) and connections created (bubble size). It demonstrates that the number of youth reached does not appear to be correlated with amount invested, but that projects after July 2012 are proving more successful than earlier projects. This might indicate a maturing of Hive NYC.

5. A temporal network visualization, presented as a small multiples graph, shows collaboration during a specific timeframe. It illustrates how the connections between Hive NYC members change from March 2011 to January 2013. The total grants awarded are plotted below each project start date. The visualization clearly highlights how relationships form around grants in fall and spring periods. A small number of organizations collaborate at the same time.

Finally, a large-format visualization was created by combining all of these visualizations (see Figure 8.6).

DISCUSSION

A number of insights can be gained from the visualizations:

- The Hive NYC learning network has grown rapidly, and funding has been key to this growth. The use of a three- to four-stage funding cycle by the learning network helps retain partners over the long-term.
- There was no correlation between funding amount and youth reached, where one might otherwise expect that more funding results in more youth reached. This is unsurprising given that the network sees itself as innovation oriented and thus takes higher risks.
- The bulk of Hive NYC organizations are clustered in the central boroughs of NYC with some organizations further out where there is a strategic link (e.g., zoos, universities, and other more unique institution types).

Initially, Hive NYC was viewed as a constantly evolving and growing network with more and more "live" relationships developing and being sustained. The temporal network suggests an alternative view: formal relationships are created around projects funding and then disband into informal relationships afterward; successful projects might then lead to future collaborations fueling a positive feedback cycle that is propelled by projects that make a difference.

Throughout the project, a number of challenges, including poor comparability between grants and projects data and limited documentation for the dataset. The six week time frame also posed a significant challenge.

ACKNOWLEDGMENTS

We would like to thank our client Rafi Santo, the Hive Research Lab, and Indiana University professors and staff for feedback, information, and encouragement; the Hive NYC Learning Network member organizations and the Mozilla Foundation for performing and supporting all the projects that we visualized; and Stamen Design for making awesome map tiles.

Chapter Nine

Discussion and Outlook

Chapter 9: Discussion and Outlook

This chapter reviews lessons learned in the IVMOOC as delivered in Spring 2013. We briefly review feedback provided by students, present results of an in-depth analysis of IVMOOC data, and conclude with a discussion of planned activities related to the further development of MOOC content and delivery.

9.1 IVMOOC EVALUATION

Co-authored with Miguel Lara

The IVMOOC at Indiana University attracted 1,901 students from more than 90 countries. However, few of the IVMOOC 2013 students completed the course—a feature it shares with most other MOOCs. As a graduate-level course, the midterm and final were particularly demanding, and many students could not complete the client work due to prior commitments.

A majority of the 98 students who provided detailed feedback in the course evaluation form graded the quality of the overall course, the instruction, and the video materials (as good or excellent). Asked what they liked most about IVMOOC they responded with the following:

1. *Hands-on session*. Videos were helpful and well developed. The hands-on exercises reinforced the lectures (26%).
2. *Content*. The subject matter, material, and resources provided were interesting and relevant (25%).
3. *Video lectures*. The videos were engaging and promoted critical thinking by analyzing different visualizations (17%).
4. *Client projects*. Providing the opportunity to work in a real-world problem was motivating and interesting (12%).
5. *Ability to create artifacts*. Students felt motivated by having the ability to create their own visualizations through the tools covered in the course (11%).
6. *Course structure*. The course was well organized, highlighting the progression of the data visualization activities. The course structure made it easy to follow it (8%).

Students disliked the following:

1. *Course pace*. In general, the workload in the course was heavy, covering a lot of content and exercises in the time period given (22%).
2. *Online forum*. The online forum was difficult to use, and it took too long to set it up. Students had already started using a Google+ hangout, and there was confusion about what communication tool to use (22%).

3. *Technical support*. There were several technical and content-related issues in which participants needed support, but their questions were not answered in a timely manner. This could have been partly due to the various avenues that participants had to post questions (Twitter, online forum, and Google+) (16%).
4. *Client project timing*. The client project was introduced too late in the course. There was not enough time for coordinating with all team members and completing the client project effectively (14%).
5. *Final assessment*. Compared to the midterm, the final assessment took significantly longer and was more difficult. Mentioning in advance the time estimate required for the final is desired (7%).
6. *Sci2 issues*. There were some issues installing and using Sci2 on specific platforms. Solving these issues required participants to invest more time than expected to cover the course content (5%).
7. *Team-based client project*. Some students were unable to join existing teams to work on client projects whereas others who did join a team experienced lack of commitment from their teammates to complete the project (5%).

Students also provided reasons for completing the course:

1. Interest in the topic (57%).
2. Experience of client project (22%).
3. Letter of accomplishment and/or digital badge (21%).

as well as reasons for not completing the course:

1. *Lack of time*. Multiple personal and professional activities and commitments prevented participants to keep up with the pace of the course (70%).
2. *Inability to work on client project*. Some students chose not to participate in client projects. It was time consuming and difficult for them to join, participate, and communicate with others within a project (10%).
3. *Workload in client project*. Not enough time for completing the client project (6%).
4. *Software issues*. Technical difficulties using the tools required in the course or lack of technical support (6%).
5. *Online forum issues*. Unable to register to use online forums. Not able to add profile picture. Lack of technical support (4%).
6. *Forgetting deadlines*. Not keeping track of key deadlines (4%).

Even though the course is not actively taught right now (September 2013), around five students register for the course every single day. The information students provide when they register (e.g., what they want to learn and why, and the questions they submit when they attempt to use tools for novel analyses) is invaluable for optimizing information visualization research, teaching, and tool development.

9.2 IVMOOC DATA ANALYSIS

Co-authored with Robert P. Light

We extensively logged teacher and student activities in the 2013 IVMOOC to ultimately support four user groups that have very different needs and questions:

- Empower teachers: How to make sense of the activities of thousands of students? How to guide them?
- Support students: How to navigate learning materials and develop successful learning collaborations across disciplines and time zones?
- Inform MOOC platform designers: What technology helps and what hurts?
- Conduct research: What teaching and learning works in a MOOC?

Specifically, we harvested data from Google Course Builder (GCB) v 1.0 used to deliver course content and to run assessments; CNS web servers that hosted the course home page, client project instructions, FAQ, and Drupal forum; YouTube and the TinCan API to log MOOC-related video downloads; Twitter and Flickr to count the number of comments and visualizations shared using the #IVMOOC tag. We collected student logins, course activities, and scores on the midterm and final in the IVMOOC Database to calculate final grades but also to help teachers understand and respond to the demographics (e.g., level of expertise) and the continuous progress (Twitter, Flickr activity or exam submissions) of several thousand students.

For example, in the pre-course questionnaire, we asked students in which portions of the course they planned to participate. Among the 1,901 students (as of May 2013), there was an 85% response rate to this question with 98% of students indicating they planned to watch videos, 67% indicating they planned to take the exams, and 32% indicating they planned to work with clients. When registering for the course, students were asked to identify their job category from the list. The IVMOOC participants consisted of faculty (21%), people working in government (4%), industry professionals (15%), non-profit professionals (5%), students (10%), and people working in an area other than these (8%). A significant number of participants did not identify their job category (35%). In addition to identifying their job category, we asked participants to identify relevant subjects with which they have some experience, and 925 participants provided feedback, rendered as a word cloud in Figure 9.1.

Figure 9.1 IVMOOC students' areas of experience

We included a question on the pre-course questionnaire asking students to rank current knowledge of information visualization on a five-point Likert scale from *very low* to *very high*. There was a 76% response rate to this question with 1% of students reporting their current knowledge of information visualization as *very high*, 5% *high*, 36% *medium*, 37% *low*, and 21% *very low*. In addition, we performed a number of temporal, geospatial, topical, and network analyses, the initial results of which we report here.

WHEN: Teacher-Student Activity over Time

The IVMOOC opened for registration on January 22, 2013. By May 11, 2013, 1,901 students had registered. Figure 9.2 shows registrations sorted vertically by time of registration over time (x-axis). Red squares indicate when a student registered, green squares show when a student watched videos on YouTube, purple triangles indicate taking the midterm or final exam, and orange diamonds indicate Twitter activity.

WHERE: Students' Country of Origin

A proportional symbol map with circles size-coded by the number of students per country of origin is shown in Figure 9.3. Students from the United States account for the majority (33%), followed by India (6%), the United Kingdom (5%), Canada (4%), and the Netherlands (3%); 253 students did not provide this information.

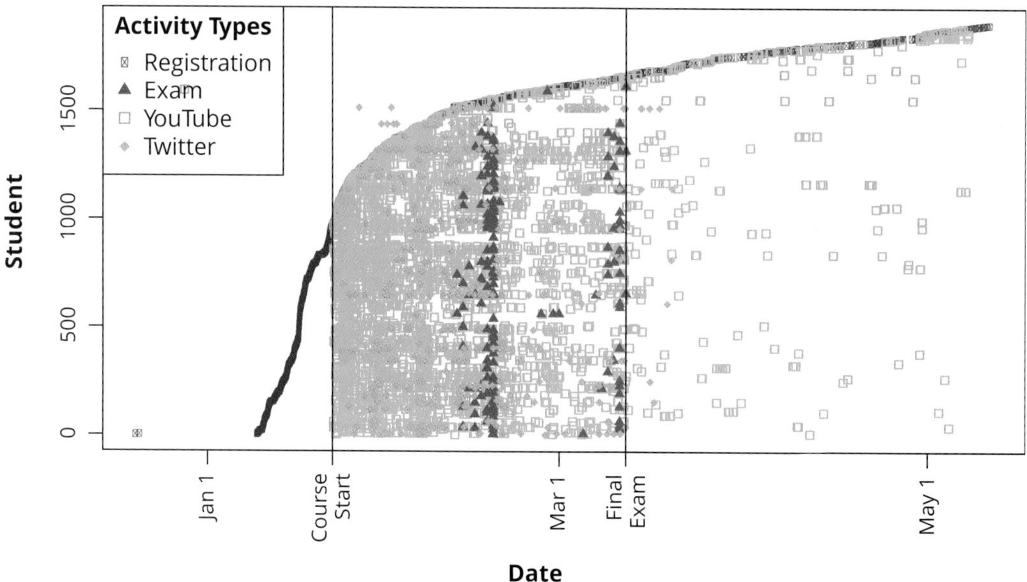

Figure 9.2 Student registration, exam taking, YouTube and Twitter activity over time

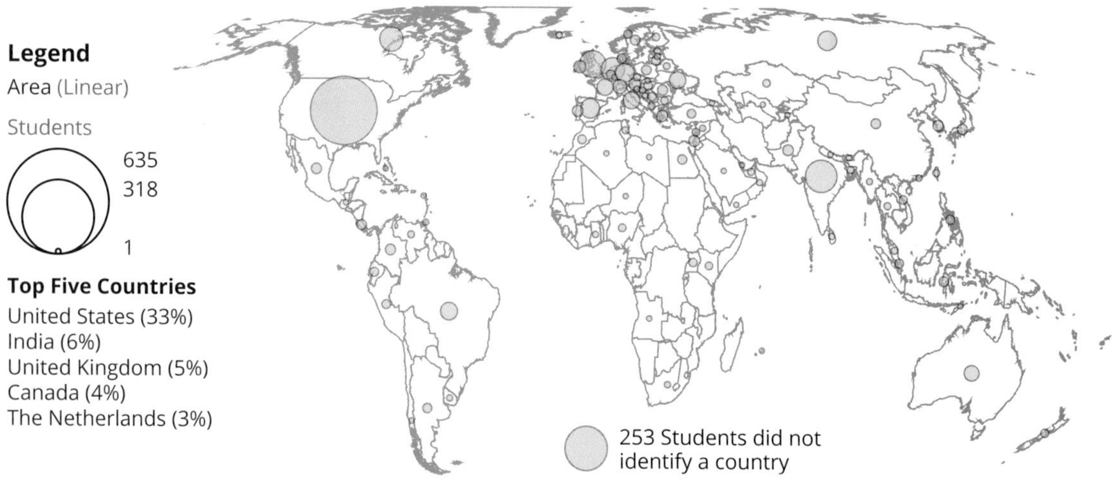

Figure 9.3 World map showing the origin of IVMOOC students by country (http://cns.iu.edu/ivmoocbook14/9.3.pdf)

WHAT: What Materials Were Used How Often?

Figure 9.4 shows how often the class videos for the seven weeks were accessed. Vertically, videos are sorted by week and then by presentation order. The bars are color-coded based on whether they correspond with a theoretical lecture or a hands-on instructional video. The graph shows the expected decline over time, with video views largely stabilizing by Week 5, after the midterm.

WITH WHOM: Student Interaction Networks

As part of the course, we required students to form groups of four or five to work on client projects. In total, 15 groups with a total of 77 students participated in these groups. Group formation and communication was facilitated by the Drupal course forum. In addition, students interacted via Twitter. Of the 193 students using Twitter, only 28 created Drupal forum profiles that made it possible to link their Google ID on the forum to their Twitter ID.

Student interaction networks are shown in Figure 9.5. The networks contain two different types of interaction: group membership and direct communication between students on Twitter (one student tweeting another).

To generate the network, we extracted from the IVMOOC database a CSV file with all students who had Twitter or client collaboration activity. We also extracted a co-occurrence network of all student interaction. Then we visualized the network in GUESS using the Fruchterman-Reingold layout, and saved the node positions. Next, we extracted a network from just the student group membership data, visualized in GUESS, and performed the layout using the node positions from the total interaction network node positions. Then, we extracted a directed network from the Twitter communication data, visualized in GUESS, and again performed the layout using the total interaction network node positions. We then overlaid the Twitter communication network and the student group membership data on top of each other. Finally, we assigned different colors to nodes based on "level of experience with information visualization" and "area of expertise." We exported the image, saved it as a PDF, and post-processed it in Adobe Illustrator. Note that the Twitter network is directed—showing the directionality of communication (i.e., a tweet from one user [source] to another [destination]). Figure 9.6 shows the student interaction network with the same layout but the nodes are colored based on the student's area of expertise.

Knowledge Gained

Taking an online course provides a world of new experiences, connections to students and experts, and stimulating discussions. Here, we are interested to understand if students gained knowledge in the topic area of the course.

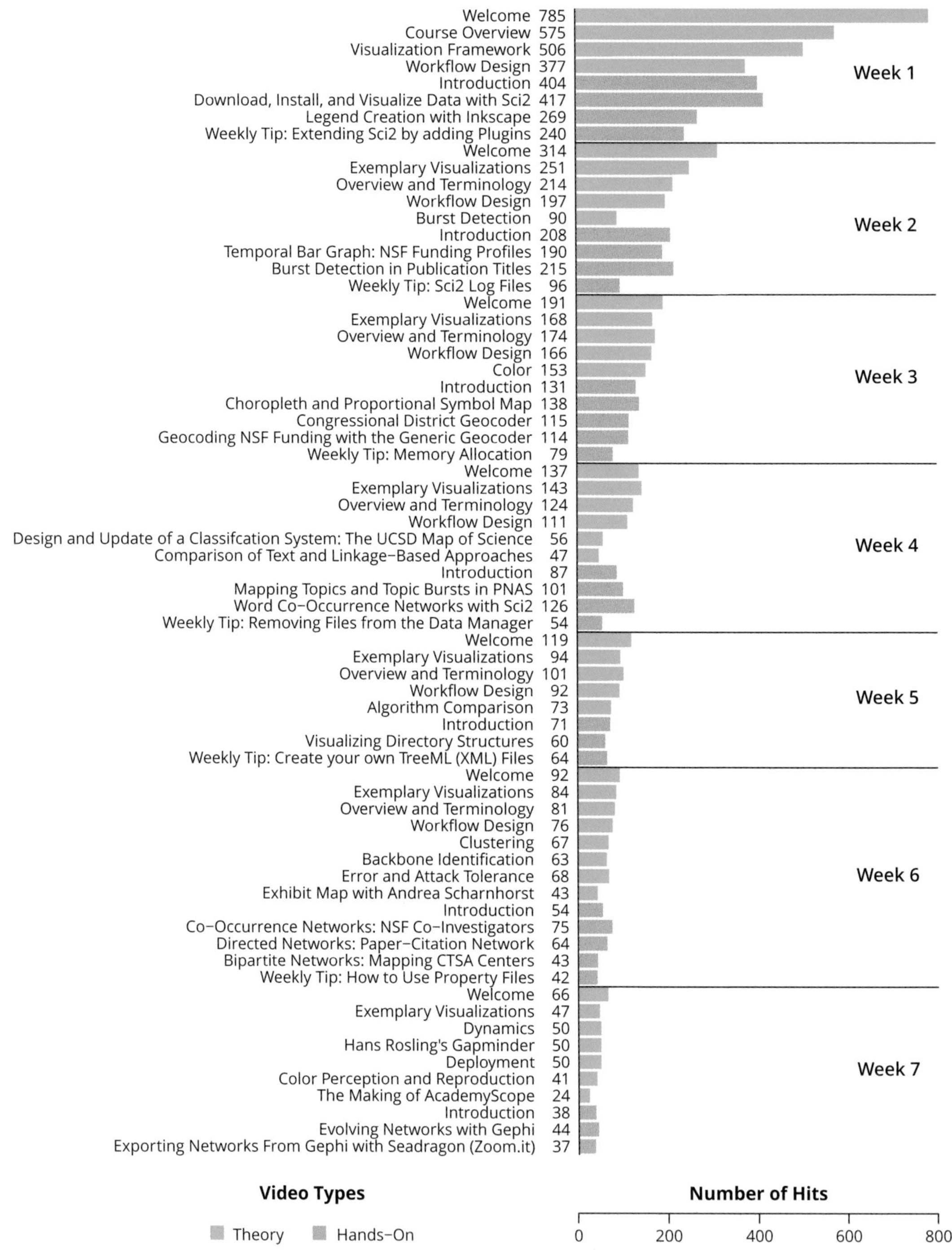

Figure 9.4 Number of video views over seven weeks

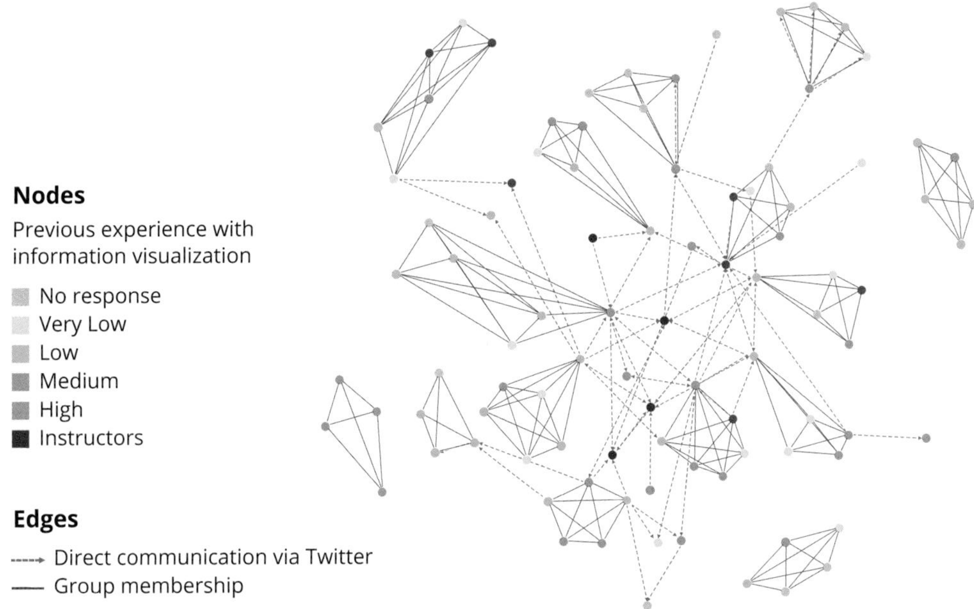

Figure 9.5 Student interaction networks with nodes colored based on previous experience with information visualization

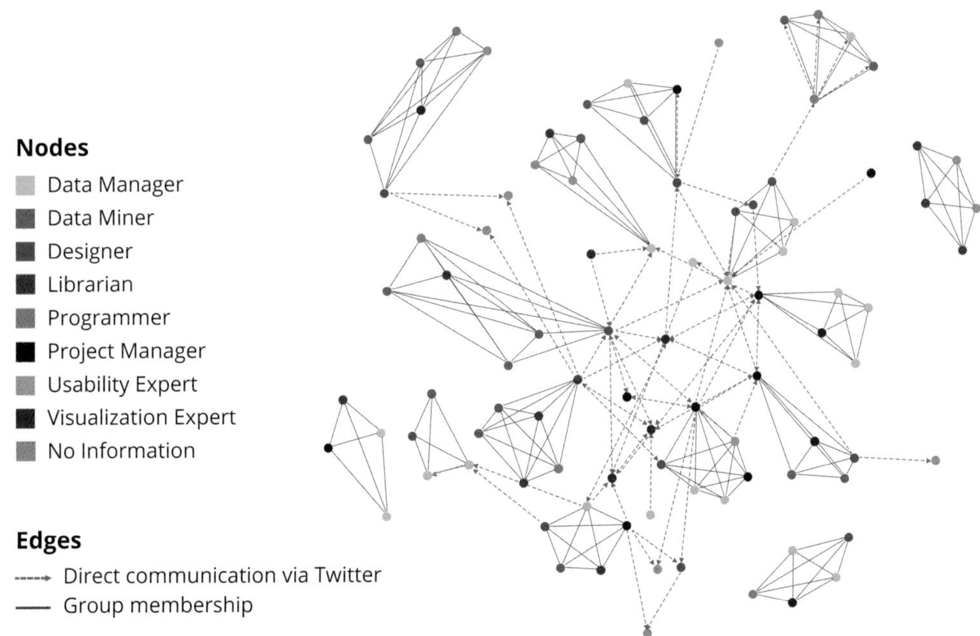

Figure 9.6 Student interaction networks with nodes colored based on areas of expertise

The IVMOOC registration form asked students to provide information on their expertise in information visualization. We correlated this self-reported expertise with performance on the three graded elements: midterm, final, and client project (see Figure 9.7).

While there was a noticeable correlation between initial expertise and client project score (Spearman rho=0.44, p = 0.007), the same effect for the midterm was not significant. This could imply that the midterm was less challenging, or that the knowledge students self-identified as relevant to the course was not covered until the latter half, and thus was not covered on the midterm. The number of students per expertise level is rather small; not all students reported their level of expertise, and few students took the midterm and/or final exam and participated in client project work.

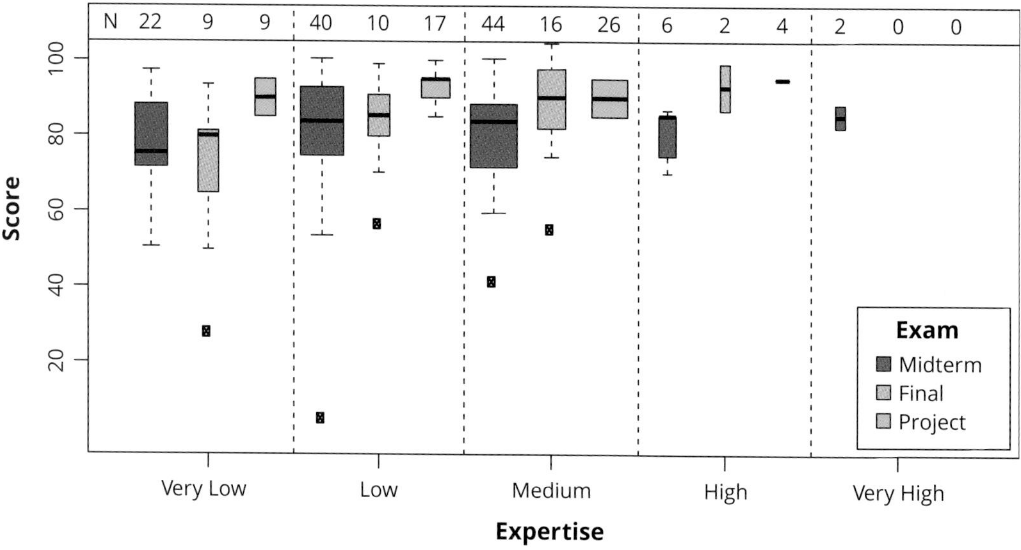

Figure 9.7 Exam scores by self-reported expertise

9.3 PLANNED IVMOOC EXTENSIONS

Co-authored with Scott B. Weingart

For IVMOOC 2014, we will bolster the areas that appealed to students the most—content and hands-on sessions—while improving the issues that prevented some participants from completing the course. IVMOOC 2014 will feature improved documentation for working with the forum and the site in general, and an easier way to retrieve course updates and test courses through RSS and email integration. Students will also enjoy more continuous interaction with instructors through the forums, and will benefit from examples of the previous year's students (e.g., the case studies included in Chapter 8 of this book).

In order to allow students more time to dedicate to their client work, we have decided to add four weeks of course time to working with clients and their teams, beyond the original seven-week plus finals week course. The original schedule will remain largely unaltered, but we will replace client work with homework specifically suited to the topic of the week. As with IVMOOC 2013, students will form their teams early, and will be encouraged to collaborate on their homework in their team sub-forums. They will pick their team project by Week 4, and by the end of the first eight weeks will have a draft that instructors and other teams can review. The final four weeks will be dedicated to validating, redesigning, and polishing.

In addition to the extended time, we will introduce new content and hands-on sessions to appeal to the diverse interests of the participants, as well as two new badges: in order for participants to have a fuller handle on the workflow from data to insight, we are adding a statistics module and badge, which will include sessions on diverse statistical subjects such as basic textual analyses, specifically latent semantic indexing (LSI), and multidimensional scaling (MDS) by noted statistician Michael W. Trosset at Indiana University. The statistics module will include both lectures and hands-on sessions, and be available either for a badge or as optional lectures for other students interested in learning the material. The second new badge and module we will introduce in IVMOOC 2014 is for digital arts and humanities, to provide instruction for a wider population of scholars than are usually targeted in information visualization courses. We will add new lectures and hands-on sessions throughout the course, on topics including initial data preparation from humanities sources, data cleaning, interpretations of visualizations, and specialized humanities tools. Lectures will be given by both the course instructor for IVMOOC 2014, Scott B. Weingart, and various leaders in the area of digital humanities research.

Students of IVMOOC 2014 can sign up for either or both of the additional modules, which will require added self-assessments and additional material on the midterm and final exam. We believe the additional content, the restructuring of the course, and additional support for navigation and the completion of coursework will improve the experience of participants and provide them with an even greater breadth of education.

Appendix

CREATING LEGENDS FOR VISUALIZATIONS

The mapping of **data variables** to **graphic symbol types** (e.g., color hue or size) is captured in a legend. Without a legend, it is often impossible to interpret a visualization, and the visualization reverts to eye candy.

Here, we provide suggestions for how to edit the vector files in Adobe Illustrator or open-source alternatives, such as Inkscape. See the next section for information on how to save visualizations in vector format. We will demonstrate legend design for the Florentine family network (see Figure 6.33 in Chapter 6). In this network, data variables are mapped to graphic symbol types as follows: Nodes are area-size coded based on wealth and color-value coded based on the number of seats held in the civic council. Edges are color-hue coded based on the type of relationship that connects the families, either business, marriage, or both. All three mappings, plus data value ranges, are shown in the legend (Figure A.1). Note, the legend size is increased to make it easier to read. In its original presentation, the node symbol size in the legend corresponds directly to the node size in the graph.

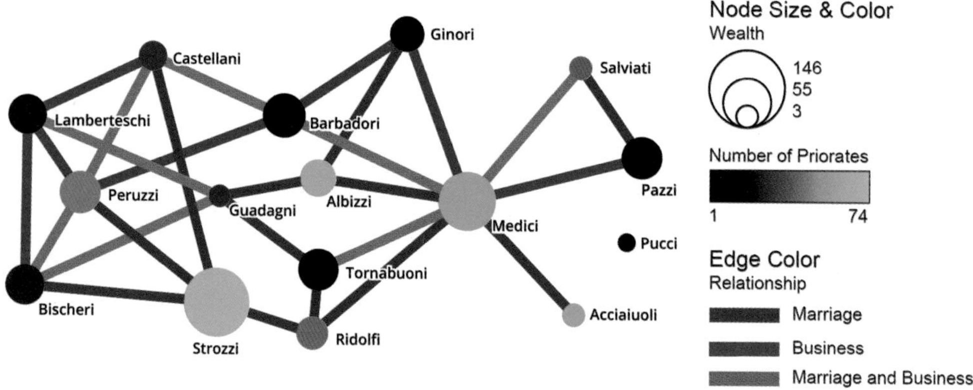

Figure A.1 Florentine families network visualization with enlarged legend

To render the **Wealth** legend, identify the smallest, medium size, and the largest node as well as the values they represent. In the case of the Florentine network, the largest node corresponds to the Strozzi family with a wealth of 146 thousand lira. The wealth value can be obtained as follows: In GUESS there is an 'Information Window' that provides metadata about the network, and if a user hovers their cursor over a specific node, all the node attributes will be displayed in this window. In Gephi there is a 'Data Laboratory', which allows users to view the data behind the network in table format. Finally, it is possible to extract this information from the raw NET data, assuming all the attributes we want to visualize are present. Opening network files in Notepad++ and searching for specific nodes or edges, using 'Ctrl + F' is one more way to obtain attribute values. With the vector file open in Adobe Illustrator or Inkscape you can identify the node of interest and copy its border to use as a symbol in the legend.

As for the **Number of Priorates** legend, identify the smallest and largest values in a similar fashion as well as the colors used for each. Most image editing programs provide an "eyedropper" to make color sampling and reuse easier. Adobe Illustrator[1] and Inkscape[2] both provide a way to create a gradient between two or more colors; see online links in footnotes.

Relationship type is a qualitative variable. An edge might represent marriage, business, or both. Consequently, three color hues are needed. The color that represents both types of relationships might best be rendered as a mixture of the two single relation colors. In Adobe Illustrator or Inkscape, simply draw three rectangles and fill them with the three colors of your choice and add the correct data value next to it.

In addition to the legend, provide descriptive text that highlights key insights, describes the data and its provenance, and information on how the visualization was generated, including the tools used. Add the names of the creator(s), contact information, and affiliation(s) so that others can share comments and suggestions.

SAVING VISUALIZATIONS IN VECTOR FORMAT

Sci2, GUESS, and Gephi visualizations can be saved in vector format (e.g., as PDF or SVG files). **Sci2** also provides the option to save PostScript files directly from the 'Data Manager'. These files can be converted into PDFs for viewing/editing with another program. See the next section for information on how to convert PostScript files to PDF files. In **GUESS,** use *File > Export Image* to save the visualization as a PDF or SVG. **Gephi** allows visualizations to be exported in vector format from the 'Preview' window. In the lower left-hand corner there is a button labeled 'Export: SVG/PDF/PNG' that allows users to export their images for viewing and editing with another program.

1 http://helpx.adobe.com/illustrator/using/apply-or-edit-gradient.html

2 http://inkscape.org/doc/basic/tutorial-basic.html

CONVERTING POSTSCRIPT FILES TO PDFS

Some Sci2 visualizations, such as the Temporal Bar Graph, the Bipartite Network Graph, the Map of Science, and the Choropleth and Proportional Symbol Maps output as a PostScript file in the 'Data Manager'. To view these visualizations, save the PostScript file to some location on your computer using right-click and selecting 'Save'.

Adobe PostScript files can be converted to PDF files using Adobe Distiller and viewed in Adobe Acrobat. There are several free alternatives such as using Ghostscript[3] or Zamzar[4] to convert to PDF. GSview[5] is a free PostScript and PDF viewer. An addition, there is an online version of Ghostscript, called the PS to PDF Converter.[6]

SCI2 TOOL TIPS

In this section we provide additional tips for using Sci2 such as how to increase the memory used by Sci2 to handle larger datasets, how to use log file and property files effectively, and how to extend Sci2 functionality by adding new plugins.

Memory Allocation

The amount of memory (RAM) available to Sci2 must be determined before the application starts. The current default allotment of 350 megabytes (MB) is a balance between providing sufficient memory for most uses of the tool, while not causing Sci2 to crash on machines with too little memory. For larger datasets, memory should be increased to make full use of the system's available memory. To do so, open the Sci2 configuration settings file (Figure A.2, left) in a text editor.

The file contains three commands (Figure A.2, right). The second line states that 15 MB will be allocated to Sci2 when the tool first starts. Do not change this number. The third line states that 350 MB is the maximum amount of memory that can be allocated to Sci2. This number can be increased to roughly 75% of the total available memory on your machine, but should not be set any higher or Sci2 will fail to start. Make sure that the formatting is displayed exactly as shown in Figure A.2, as the file can be sensitive to extra spaces or multiple arguments on a single line. After making any changes, save the file and the new settings will be applied the next time Sci2 is launched.

---

3 http://pages.cs.wisc.edu/~ghost/doc/GPL/gpl901.htm

4 http://www.zamzar.com/convert/ps-to-pdf/

5 http://pages.cs.wisc.edu/~ghost/gsview/get49.htm

6 http://ps2pdf.com

sampledata	9/18/2013 2:37 PM
scripts	9/18/2013 2:37 PM
workspace	9/18/2013 2:37 PM
artifacts.xml	9/18/2013 2:36 PM
eclipsec.exe	9/18/2013 2:36 PM
sci2.exe	9/18/2013 2:36 PM
sci2.ini	9/18/2013 2:36 PM

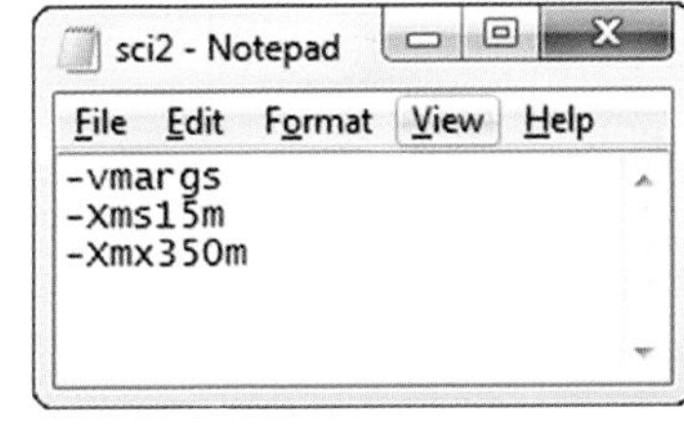

Figure A.2 The Sci2 configuration settings file

Log Files

All information about operations performed during a Sci2 run is saved in log files. Each time a user starts, the tool creates a new log file in the logs folder in the Sci2 directory. Log files provide users with more information on the algorithms, including who the implementer(s) and integrator(s) of the algorithms are, time and date information for algorithm execution, and algorithm input parameters. Log files also give information about any errors that may occur during Sci2 operation. To examine Sci2 log files, open the logs folder in the Sci2 directory (Figure A.3). Each log file has a file name that includes the day and time of creation, and most are rather small. Open a log file in any text editor, such as Notepad, to view (Figure A.4).

cishell-user-06-19-2013-09-10-AM.0.0.log	6/19/2013 9:11 AM	Text Document	2 KB
cishell-user-06-26-2013-02-30-PM.0.0.log	6/27/2013 12:29 AM	Text Document	2 KB
cishell-user-06-27-2013-09-17-AM.0.0.log	6/27/2013 10:03 AM	Text Document	26 KB
cishell-user-06-27-2013-10-02-AM.0.0.log	6/28/2013 2:03 PM	Text Document	82 KB
cishell-user-07-15-2013-03-47-AM.0.0.log	7/15/2013 7:44 AM	Text Document	61 KB
cishell-user-08-16-2013-03-09-PM.0.0.log	8/16/2013 3:15 PM	Text Document	3 KB
cishell-user-09-20-2013-09-00-AM.0.0.log	9/22/2013 10:08 AM	Text Document	8 KB
cishell-user-09-22-2013-10-24-AM.0.0.log	9/22/2013 3:21 PM	Text Document	28 KB

Figure A.3 Log files for eight different Sci2 sessions

Log files are essential to ensure replication of results. Many workflows involve ten or more algorithms with diverse parameter settings. Log files make it easy to keep track of parameter settings. Users may also need to know what paper should be cited if a specific algorithm was used—the log files provide the complete citation information and associated URLs for all algorithms executed during a Sci2 session. Figure A.4 shows a complete workflow from loading the data, extracting a directed network, and visualizing that network with Gephi. Note, we have removed some of the information specific to algorithm processing captured by the log file to make it easier to read.

In addition, log files provide detailed error messages. Figure A.5 shows a parsing error message. This particular error occurs when a user tries to visualize a co-author network (co-occurrence network) with the Bipartite Network Graph. The algorithm expects to see a bipartite type attribute associated with each node and without these is unable to parse the network for display in the Bipartite Network Graph visualization.

Future releases of Sci2 will offer the possibility to re-run workflows, for example, to replicate existing workflows with new data, to analyze old data using workflows with minor modifications, or to run parameter sweeps, (i.e., to adjust the value of a parameter through a user defined range).

```
Oct 17, 2013 11:36:29 AM org.cishell.reference.gui.
log.LogToFile logged
INFO: Loaded: D:\Users\dapolley\Desktop\
sci2-N-1.0.0.201206130117NGT-win32.win32.
x86(2)\sci2\sampledata\scientometrics\isi\
FourNetSciResearchers.isi
Oct 17, 2013 11:36:46 AM org.cishell.reference.gui.
log.LogToFile logged
INFO: .........
Extract Directed Network was selected.
Author(s): Timothy Kelley
Implementer(s): Timothy Kelley
Integrator(s): Timothy Kelley
Documentation: [url]http://wiki.cns.iu.edu/display/
CISHELL/Extract+Directed+Network[/url]
Oct 17, 2013 11:36:54 AM org.cishell.reference.gui.
log.LogToFile logged
INFO:
Input Parameters:
Source Column: Authors
Text Delimiter: |
Target Column: Journal Title (Full)
Oct 17, 2013 11:37:07 AM org.cishell.reference.gui.
log.LogToFile logged
INFO: .........
Gephi was selected.
Author(s): The Gephi Consortium
Integrator(s): David M. Coe
Documentation: [url]http://wiki.cns.iu.edu/display/
CISHELL/Gephi[/url]
```

Figure A.4 A complete workflow from loading the file, extracting a directed network, to visualizing with Gephi

```
Oct 17, 2013 11:48:34 AM org.cishell.reference.gui.
log.LogToFile logged
SEVERE: An error occurred when creating the
algorithm "Bipartite Network Graph" with the data
you provided.  (Reason: edu.iu.nwb.util.nwbfile.
ParsingException: org.cishell.framework.algorithm.
AlgorithmCreationFailedException: Bipartite Graph
algorithm requires the 'bipartitetype' node
attribute.)
Exception:
org.cishell.framework.algorithm.
AlgorithmCreationFailedException: edu.iu.nwb.util.
nwbfile.ParsingException: org.cishell.framework.
algorithm.AlgorithmCreationFailedException:
Bipartite Graph algorithm requires the
'bipartitetype' node attribute.
```

Figure A.5 Error message displayed in a log file

Property Files

Property files, referred to as Aggregate Function Files in the Sci2 interface, allow additional attributes of a dataset to be appended to either nodes or edges. For example, suppose we want to create a directed network that points from National Science Foundation grants back to the researchers they fund and sizes the nodes based on the amount of money researchers received. The best way to add this type of information to a network is to use a property file during network extraction.

All property files follow the same pattern:

```
{node|edge}.new_attribute = table_column_name.[{target|source}].function
```

The first part specifies whether an action will be performed on a node or an edge. The next part, *new_attribute*, is a name selected by the user, which indicates the name of the attribute. The *table_column_name* is the name of the column in the data table that will be used to generate the attribute values for the final nodes or edges. It is important that the new attribute name not be the same as the column name in the data or the new attributes will not be created. The next part indicates whether or not the function is to be performed on the target node or the source node, which applies only to directed networks. Finally, *function* determines how the data are aggregated. Sci2 has several functions available:

- **Arithmetic mean** – finds the average of an independent node attribute
- **Geometric mean** – finds the average of a dependent node attribute
- **Count** – counts the instances of a node attribute
- **Sum** – the sum of each node's attribute values
- **Max** – the maximum value of each node's attribute values
- **Min** – the minimum value of each node's attribute values
- **Mode** – reports the most common value for an attribute

Figure A.6 shows a property file next to the data to illustrate the property file's interaction with the data. This particular property file is counting the number of authors, the number of co-occurrences between authors, and adding up the total times cited for each author. The result is a network with two additional node attributes: 'numberOfWorks', and 'timesCited', and one additional edge attribute: 'numberOfCoAuthoredWorks'.

```
node.numberOfWorks = Authors.count
edge.numberOfCoAuthoredWorks = Authors.count
node.timesCited = Times Cited.sum
```

Abstract	Authors	Authors (F	Beginning	Book Seri	Book Seri	Times Cited	Cited Pate	Cited Refe	Cited Refe
Backgrour	Wuchty, S|Barabasi, AL|Ferdig, MT					7		42	ALBERT R,
	Balazsi, G|Barabasi, AL|Oltvai, :		103			0		0	
	Barabasi, AL		433			0		0	
	Barabasi, AL		68			2		22	*NAT RES
A complet	Macdonald, PJ|Almaas, E|Barak		308			14		35	ABDELWA
	Oliveira, JG|Barabasi, AL		1251			15		10	1984, COR
Recent ev	Balazsi, G|Barabasi, AL|Oltvai, :		7841			29		37	ALLEN TE,
The dynar	Barabasi, AL		207			32		28	ANDERSO
	Barabasi, AL		639			7		14	ALBERT R,
Subgraph:	Vazquez, A|Oliveira, JG|Barabasi, AL					5		21	ALBERT R,
Conventic	Makeev, MA|Derenyi, I|Barabasi, AL					2		24	AJDARI A,
For many	Eisler, Z|Kertesz, J|Yook, SH|Ba		664			10		22	2003, TRAI
Recent ev	Vazquez, A|Dobrin, R|Sergi, D|		17940			44		38	ALBERT R,
We provic	Palla, G|Farkas, I|Derenyi, I|Barabasi, AL|Vicsek, T					0		26	ALBERT R,
The obser	de Menezes, MA|Barabasi, AL					19		25	ABARBAN
As extens	Makeev, MA|Barabasi, AL		316			3		77	ALANISSIL
Off-norm:	Makeev, MA|Barabasi, AL		335			4		47	BARBER D.
Most com	Barabasi, AL|de Menezes, MA|		169			3		48	ALBERT R,
The elucic	Yook, SH|Oltvai, ZN|Barabasi, A		928			94		45	ALBERT R,
Backgrour	Dobrin, R|Beg, QK|Barabasi, AL|Oltvai, ZN					41		26	ALBERT R,

Figure A.6 Property file that counts the number of authors, their co-occurrences, and sums the 'Times Cited' value for each author

Adding Plugins

We can extend the functionality of Sci2 by downloading additional plugins. These plugins are too large to be distributed with the official release, such as the Cytoscape plugin, or they are newly implemented algorithms that are made available between releases of Sci2. They can be downloaded from the Sci2 documentation wiki in Section 3.2.[7] Some plugins are provided as JAR files. Others are zipped up into a folder, and we have to extract the JAR files. To use the plugins, download them, unzip as needed, and then copy the JAR files (not the folders in which they are contained) into the plugins folder in the Sci2 directory. Figure A.7 shows the plugins folder with the Cytoscape plugin added. Cytoscape[8] is an open-source software platform for visualizing networks and integrating these with any type of attribute data.[9]

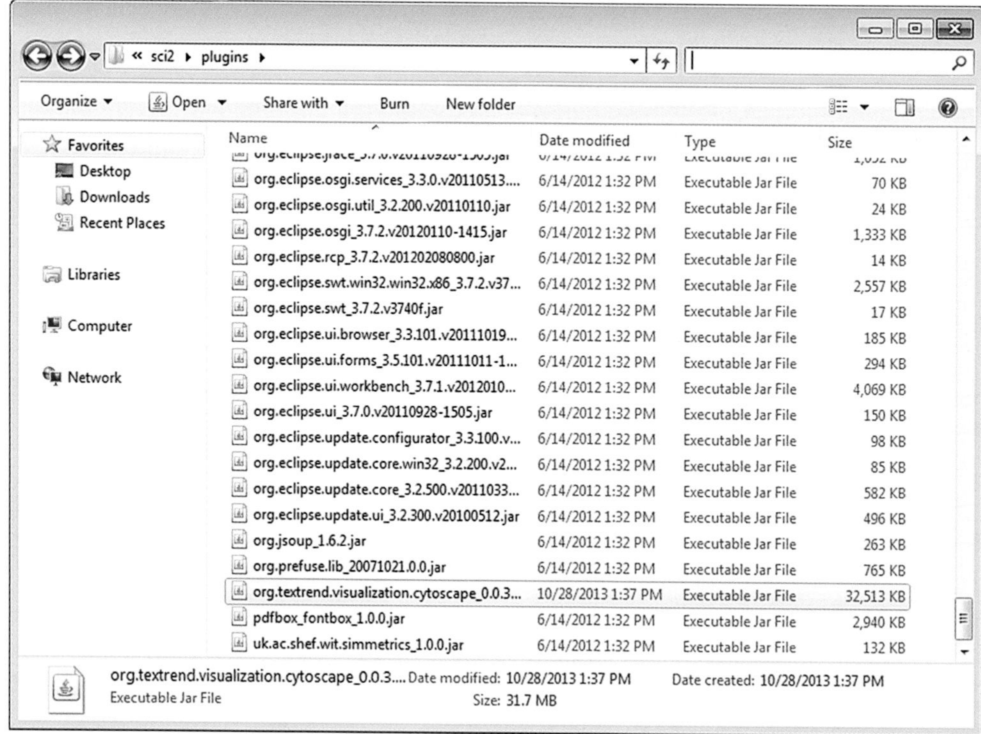

Figure A.7 Cytoscape plugin in Sci2 plugins directory

Looking at the size for the Cytoscape plugin, we can clearly see how large it is relative to the other plugins. Cytoscape's size is the main reason it is provided as an additional plugin and not bundled with the tool.

7 http://wiki.cns.iu.edu/display/SCI2TUTORIAL/3.2+Additional+Plugins

8 http://www.cytoscape.org

9 Saito, Rintaro, Michael E. Smoot, Keiichiro Ono, Johannes Ruscheinski, Peng-Liang Wang, Samad Lotia, Alexander R. Pico, Gary D. Bader, and Trey Ideker. 2012. "A Travel Guide to Cytoscape Plugins." *Nature Methods* 9, 11: 1069–1076.

SELF-ASSESSMENT SOLUTIONS

Chapter 1: Theory Section
1a; 2b; 3b, c, d

Chapter 1: Hands-On Section
"NetWorkBench: A Large-Scale Network Analysis, Modeling, and Visualization Toolkit for Biomedical, Social Science, and Physics Research" funded at $1,120,926.

Chapter 2: Theory Section
1a; 2d; 3a; 4a

Chapter 3 Theory Section
1a; 2b; 3b; 4a

Chapter 4 Theory Section
1a; 2c; 3d; 4d

Chapter 5 Theory Section
1c; 2a; 3c; 4a: 1, 2, 1; 4b: 6, 2, yes, yes, no

Chapter 6 Theory Section
1a: 4, 3; 1b: l; 2a: 9, 8, 2; 2b: no, no, no, yes, no; 3a: 9/8(8-1)/2 = 9/28 = 0.32, 4

Image Credits

Chapter 1—Opening spread image courtesy of Wikimedia Commons, http://commons.wikimedia.org/wiki/File:Lorimerlite_framework.jpg; Figure 1.1 (left): Purchased from istockphoto.com; Figure 1.2: Courtesy of *Places & Spaces: Mapping Science*; individual maps credited elsewhere; Figure 1.10: Courtesy of Angela Zoss; Figure 1.14: Courtesy of Worldmapper; Figure 1.15: Courtesy of World Bank; Figure 1.16: Courtesy of Eric Fischer, using data from the Twitter streaming API; Figure 1.17: Courtesy of Olivier H. Beauchesne, www.olihb.com

Chapter 2—Opening spread image courtesy of Wikimedia Commons, http://commons.wikimedia.org/wiki/File:Sundial_2r.jpg; Figure 2.1: Courtesy of xkcd.com; Figure 2.3: Courtesy of Edward Tufte, Graphics Press, Cheshire, Connecticut; Figure 2.4: All HistFlow maps courtesy of Fernanda Viégas and Martin Wattenberg, IBM; Figure 2.5 and CCR Logo: Copyright © Council for Chemical Research, www.ccrhq.org; Figure 2.8: Courtesy of BabyNameWizard.com; Figure 2.11: Courtesy of World Bank; Figure 2.12-13: Courtesy of the Max Planck Institute for Demographic Research, Germany; Figures 2.16-17: Courtesy of Time Series Data Online, Datamarket.com

Chapter 3—Opening spread image courtesy of NASA/JPL-Caltech, downloaded from Wikimedia Commons, http://commons.wikimedia.org/wiki/File:North_America_from_low_orbiting_satellite_Suomi_NPP.jpg; Figure 3.1: Courtesy of the David Rumsey Map Collection, www.davidrumsey.com; Figure 3.2: Courtesy of the Library of Congress, Geography and Maps Division; Figure 3.3: The Jules Verne Voyager tool was developed by Dr. Louis Estey (UNAVCO). The background cloudless composite satellite image of the earth is from ARC Science simulations (www.arcscience.com); Figure 3.5: Courtesy of Vittoria Colizza, Alessandro Vespignani, and Elisha Allgood; Figure 3.6: Courtesy of Ben Fry; Figure 3.8: Design by John Yunker, www.bytelevel.com; Figure 3.9: Courtesy of Mark E. J. Newman; Figure 3.14, 16 Courtesy of Cynthia A. Brewer, Penn State Geography

Chapter 4—Opening spread image courtesy of Wikimedia Commons, http://commons.wikimedia.org/wiki/File:Austrian_National_Library_-_State_Hall_-_Bookcase_LXV_-_July_2009.jpg; Figure 4.1: Courtesy of Keith Nesbitt; Figure 4.2: Courtesy of Steven A. Morris; Figure 4.3: TextArc visual layout by W. Bradford Paley, source material by Henry Smith Williams; Figure 4.4: "In Terms of Geography" © 2005, André Skupin, data processing and coding by Shujing Shu; Figure 4.9-10: Image from the Visual Thesaurus. Copyright © 1998-2013 Thinkmap, Inc. All rights reserved

Chapter 5—Opening spread image courtesy of Wikimedia Commons, http://commons.wikimedia.org/wiki/File:Bare_Oak_Tree.jpg; Figure 5.1: Courtesy of Moritz Stefaner; Figure 5.3: Treemap setup, visualization, and Netscan graphics courtesy of Marc A. Smith, Microsoft Research

Chapter 6—Opening spread image courtesy of Wikimedia Commons, http://commons.wikimedia.org/wiki/File:ToileBruine2.jpg; Figure 6.1: Hagman et al. 2008. *PLOS Biology* 6, e159; Figure 6.2: Courtesy of Bruce W. Herr II, Todd Holloway, Elisha Allgood, Kevin W. Boyack, and Katy Börner; Figure 6.3: "Maps of Science: Forecasting Large Trends in Science," © 2007, The Regents of the University of California, all rights reserved, UCSD Map of Science and Mercator projection, Visualization of the ISI and Scopus Databases, and legend courtesy of Richard Klavans and Kevin W. Boyack, SciTech Strategies, Inc., www.mapofscience.com; Figure 6.4: Copyright © Maximilian Schich, 2010 (maximilian@schich.info); Figure 6.5: Courtesy of César Hidalgo; Figure 6.23: Courtesy of Ben Fry

Chapter 7—Opening spread photo of Ward Shelley's *History of Science Fiction* courtesy of David E. Polley; Figure 7.3-4: Reprinted with permission from the National Academy of Sciences, courtesy of the National Academies Press, Washington, D.C.

Chapter 8—Opening spread image courtesy of Wikimedia Commons, http://commons.wikimedia.org/wiki/File:NAB_Convention_Floor_Las_Vegas_2010.jpg; Figure 8.1: Courtesy of Bonnie Layton; Figure 8.2: Courtesy of Isaac Knowles; Figure 8.3: Created with Tableau Public by Michael J. Boyles; Figure 8.4: Courtesy of Stephanie Poppe; Figure 8.5: Courtesy of David E. Hubbard, Anouk Lang, Kathleen Reed, Anelise H. Shrout, and Lindsay D. Troyer; Figure 8.6: Courtesy of John Patterson

Chapter 9—Opening spread image courtesy of Wikimedia Commons, http://commons.wikimedia.org/wiki/File:Freighters_on_horizon.jpg

Concept by Katy Börner, design by Samuel T. Mills: Tables 1.1-3, Figures 1.1, 1.12-13, 1.18-20, 2.7, 2.14-15, 3.11, 4.7-8, 5.5-10, 6.6-8, 6.10-15, 6.20, 7.5-9

Screenshots by Joe Shankweiler: Figures 1.21-22, 2.25-2.38, 3:18-36, 4:15-17, 5:11-17, 5:19-21

Screenshots by David E. Polley: Figures 3.37, 4.5, 5.18, 6.24-25, 6.26-46, 7.9-23, 9.1, 9.3, 9.5-6, A.1-7

Screenshots by Katy Börner: Figures 1.3-8, 1.11, 2.18-22, 3.10, 3.17, 3.27, 4.6, 4.11-12, 6.16-19, 6.21-22, 6.26

Screenshots by Robert P. Light: Figures 9.2, 9.4, 9.7

Index